Yorelyn Villalta

Ben Blackwell and Randy Hatchett have put together an eminently readable introduction to Christian theology for students. It contains a good balance of Bible, church history, and theological description, is ever mindful of contemporary application, and explains strange topics with simplicity and clarity. A valuable resource for anyone beginning theological studies.

Rev. Dr. Michael F. Bird, academic dean and lecturer in theology, Ridley College, Melbourne, Australia

This is the theology textbook that I wish I had been reading during my undergraduate and seminary theological education. It engages the Bible but is not simply the homogenized biblical-theological approach that I encountered. This work understands hermeneutics and presents theological method, yet it is practical. It points to the boundaries of orthodoxy and to questions that may be open. It understands that theology develops through history (and without quoting J. H. Newman). It opens the student up to dialogue with a variety of Christian perspectives and with other major religions, yet there is a firm core commitment. It is clearly Protestant, even Evangelical, but it is open to Roman Catholic, Orthodox, and other perspectives as well. I heartily recommend its use as a teaching text or as a work to learn how to present Christian theology clearly and how to dialogue without slipping into a relativistic approach.

Rev. Peter H. Davids, New Testament editor, Word Biblical Commentary

Professors Blackwell and Hatchett have provided us with a thoughtful volume to introduce students to many of the wide-ranging topics, themes, and issues in the field of systematic theology. In these pages, readers will find helpful biographical portraits of significant Christian thinkers, interaction with various religious traditions, and insightful applications focused on spiritual formation and the life of the church. Though some readers will ponder the inclusion or exclusion of some topics or some of the authors' conclusions, they will nevertheless be encouraged and helped by the authors' commitments to Trinitarian orthodoxy, to the importance of key aspects of the Christian tradition, and to genuine theological engagement.

David S. Dockery, chancellor and professor of Christianity and culture, Trinity International University

Engaging Theology is an excellent resource for the classroom. Blackwell and Hatchett ably summarize the fundamentals of the Christian faith, demonstrating the biblical warrant, historical development, dogmatic location, and cultural implications each of the major doctrines. While readers will inevitably quibble with certain modes of argument or specific theological conclusions, the authors' judicious approach, ecumenical awareness, and charitable spirit are just as important for the classroom as the clarity of their doctrinal summaries.

Matthew Y. Emerson, Dickinson Associate Professor of Religion, Oklahoma Baptist University

Engaging Theology brings together Christian history, biography, spirituality, and the development of doctrine in a narrative at once coherent and comprehensive. It is inviting, accessible, irenic. I welcome this new book and recommend it highly!

Timothy George, research professor of divinity at Beeson
Divinity School, Samford University, and general editor of
the Reformation Commentary on Scripture series

Introductory theology textbooks are a dime a dozen. What separates *Engaging Theology* from the rest of the pack is that it is genuinely engaging in multiple ways: it engages the reader with lively prose and common-sense language, engages the Christian tradition in faithful and informed ways, engages the contemporary world beyond theology, and engages practice as it speaks into ministry, vocation, and praxis. Theology is on the move, and Blackwell and Hatchet realize this and help readers navigate the terrain in responsible and informative ways. This is the sort of introductory text students are now looking for and need.

Myk Habets, head of school of theology, Laidlaw College,
Auckland, New Zealand, and professor of theology

The Christian pilgrimage involves pursuing knowledge of Christian theology—either intentionally or unintentionally. R. L. Hatchett and Ben Blackwell in *Engaging Theology* have provided a rich reading resource for beginning that part of the journey, either in the university or in a local church. *Engaging Theology* is an excellent primer for communities that need a theology book that is Trinitarian in structure; comprehensive, ecumenical, and nondogmatic in spirit; emphasizes the narrative nature of theological development; and interacts with the broader church and other religious traditions.

Berten A. Waggoner, former national director of Vineyard USA

With historical breadth, doctrinal clarity, and pastoral acumen, Blackwell and Hatchett invite students into the study of Christian theology with a text that is comprehensive without being daunting. Written with the student in mind, their book provides a confessional and welcoming approach to the study of theology. This is a book for those who love Jesus but might be skeptical as to why we need clarity about who God is and what God has done.

Myles Werntz, associate professor of Christian ethics and practical theology,
T. B. Maston Chair of Christian Ethics, Logsdon School of Theology

Engaging
Theology

Engaging
Theology

A Biblical, Historical, and
Practical Introduction

Ben C. Blackwell and
R. L. Hatchett

ZONDERVAN
ACADEMIC

ZONDERVAN ACADEMIC

Engaging Theology
Copyright © 2019 by Ben C. Blackwell and R. L. Hatchett

Requests for information should be addressed to:
Zondervan, *3900 Sparks Dr. SE, Grand Rapids, Michigan 49546*

CIP Library of Congress Cataloging-in-Publication Data

Names: Blackwell, Ben C., 1974- author. | Hatchett, Randy Lynn, author.
Title: Engaging theology : a biblical, historical, and practical introduction / Ben C. Blackwell, R. L. Hatchett.
Description: Grand Rapids : Zondervan, 2019. | Includes index.
Identifiers: LCCN 2019034337 (print) | LCCN 2019034338 (ebook) | ISBN 9780310092766 (hardcover) | ISBN 9780310092773 (ebook)
Subjects: LCSH: Theology, Doctrinal—Introductions. | Christianity--Essence, genius, nature.
Classification: LCC BT65 .B53 2019 (print) | LCC BT65 (ebook) | DDC 230--dc23
LC record available at https://lccn.loc.gov/2019034337 LC ebook record available at https://lccn.loc.gov/2019034338

Cover design: Micah Kandros
Cover images: ibusca, duncan1890, GeorgiosArt / iStockphoto
Interior design: Kait Lamphere
Interior images: Marc Hinds

Printed in the United States of America

22 23 24 25 26 27 28 29 30 31 /LSC/ 21 20 19 18 17 16 15 14 13 12 11 10 9 8 7 6 5 4 3

Contents

Acknowledgments

At the heart of Christian theology is an interaction with the great tradition. As we participate in this wider conversation, we are especially mindful and grateful for gifted teachers and learners who have enriched our study and guided us within this wider conversation. I (RLH) am indebted to friends and faculty at Dallas Baptist University and Southwestern Baptist Theological Seminary. At Southwestern, James Leo Garrett, David Kirkpatrick, and Bert Dominy taught me theology through course work and friendship. I (BCB) have had a wonderful collection of mentors and friends from Ouachita Baptist University, Dallas Theological Seminary, and Durham University. In particular, Scott Duvall, Danny Hays, and Terry Carter at Ouachita, Kent Burghuis, Jeff Bingham, and Scott Horrell at DTS, and John Barclay and Tom Wright at Durham.

We are grateful for our fellow faculty members, past and present, in the Department of Theology and the School of Christian Thought at Houston Baptist University and now Houston Theological Seminary. Our circle here shares an encouraging fellowship and concern for one another. We are grateful for their steady friendship and interest in the project.

This book primarily emerges from our teaching a required undergraduate course titled Christian Theology and Tradition, as well as classes for our majors in systematic and historical theology. The remarkable and wonderful diversity of our students influenced almost every discussion we had about this book, and we are thankful for our students from these courses. The challenge and privilege to teach them has been stimulating; their kindnesses and conversations are greatly appreciated.

Other students, faculty members, and friends deserve thanks for reading portions of the text and sharing substantial feedback. The list includes Jason Maston, Adam Harger, Paul Sloan, Jeremy Greer, Calvin Williams, Nathan Cook, Mike Skelton, Mike Skinner, Cullen Ware, Adam Chaney, Joel Burdeaux, Foye Stanley, Philip Tallon, Derek Hickle, Spencer Jones, and Jade Myers. Additionally, Brian Hébert, Derick Hatch, and Joshua Salas gave special feedback concerning our treatment of world religions. Taylor Choate, our student and research assistant, read numerous sections and offered valuable editing and review.

The project as a whole was supported in various ways from my (BCB) church, Sugar Land Vineyard. We are especially indebted to several from my home group who read the entire manuscript: Pat Dorsey, Beth Wilhelm, and Heather Blackwell. The personal encouragement and support from the group has been life-giving for many years. Another life-giving relationship is that of Bert Waggoner. He not only inspired me to read Charles Taylor in the first place, but he is a model of a pastor-theologian. Bert and his wife, Evelyn, welcomed us into their home as Bert gave feedback from his careful reading. Though he didn't respond directly to the chapters, my pastor Reagan Waggoner has significantly influenced my theology regarding the kingdom of God.

Our sons, Elam Blackwell and Austin Hatchett respectively, read the entire manuscript and rendered brutally honest observations as well as valuable insights. They substantially improved the project. Additionally, Debbie Hatchett, Amy Hatchett Sims, Ashley Ashcraft, and Amber Reynolds also reviewed portions of the text. Every writing project requires a big sacrifice of time. I (BCB) am grateful and humbled by the support of Heather, Silas, and Elam.

We are also appreciative of Katya Covrett, executive editor for Zondervan Academic, for her enthusiasm for and interest in the project. She and Matthew Estel thoroughly read the manuscript and contributed valuable insight and patience. Joshua Kessler of Zondervan Academic ably provided help in production, support, and publicity for the project. Special thanks goes to Marc Hinds, who worked to make our diagrams ready for print. Our student and assistant Phillip Morrow helped with numerous tasks, most especially creating the index.

Preface for Teachers

After teaching theology for many years, we have learned that those sitting in the classroom and sanctuary alike are disengaged from the doctrines of the church. This disconnection arises for a variety of reasons. Some people come from church movements that are loyal to the Bible but suspicious of tradition and efforts at systematizing ideas. As a result, they see theology as speculative, more like philosophy than an exposition of biblical truth. A more common problem, unfortunately, is that people have not engaged the Bible or the church deeply in the first place. Many are fed a steady diet of sermons about the practicalities of life but see theology as ivory-tower thinking for academics. Many more are nominally tied to the church and see the whole enterprise of Bible and theology as cultural nostalgia better suited for history books. In our diverse context in Houston, those who practice other faith traditions like Hinduism, Islam, and Buddhism comprise a growing part of our community, and they often know little of Christian theology beyond stereotypes. One thing is common among all these diverse groups—Christian theology is disconnected from life to the extent of being irrelevant. Our goal with this book is to address this by giving our readers an approach to theology that is relevant and engaging.

Over the years, we have used a number of fine textbooks from within our evangelical community to help foster theological discussions. These textbooks often assume that their readers are insiders to theological conversations and that they have already bought into the idea that theology matters. To help those who are disconnected to engage theology, we propose beginning and ending in a different way, by showing how theological reflection is embedded deeply in the biblical narrative and in contemporary life, in addition to narrating the traditional content of theology. Drawing from our respective academic disciplines, we bridge the biblical (BCB) and historical (RLH) contexts out of which ecumenical consensus has arisen.

Within this wider ecumenical discussion, we have unique perspectives. That is, we represent Baptist and charismatic evangelical traditions, but we have distinct interests in wider ecumenical concerns. For example, our doctoral studies were generated out of engagement with Roman Catholic biblical interpreters (RLH) and Eastern Orthodox theology (BCB). This ecumenical interest is also spurred by the many theological traditions represented among our students at Houston Baptist University. To engage a theologically diverse population, we follow a "mere Christian" approach, where the central aspects of the Trinitarian faith expressed in the Nicene Creed guide the book's progression.[1]

We find the contemporary engagement with global theology to be invaluable, but due to the space constraints of the volume, we primarily converse with historical theologies. In areas of traditional orthodoxy, our approach is *prescriptive*, but at many other points we are more *descriptive* of the diversity represented in the church. With our desire to foster understanding and discussion between the various Christian traditions today, we attempt to describe the different views impartially in order to allow those who are teaching or learning to focus on your own theological conclusions. This is especially evident in the chapter sections concerning contemporary relevance. Moving beyond one-sentence discussion questions, we give a paragraph or so for key topics. We offer these as kindling for your more expansive treatment.

Of course, we not only have Christian diversity but wider religious diversity in our postmodern world. Based on *US News & World Report*, our institution, Houston Baptist University, has been the most ethnically diverse Protestant campus in the United States for several years.[2] That means that we have an equally diverse range of doctrinal, denominational, and faith perspectives among our student body, and that diversity has helped strengthen the preparation of this volume. Accordingly, our primary goal is to cultivate a conversation between these diverse traditions, though obviously our own views will be clear as well. As a result, in addition to traditional Christian perspectives, we also engage the perspectives of divergent Christian groups (such as the Latter-day Saints and Jehovah's Witnesses) and major world religions (Judaism, Islam, Hinduism, and Buddhism) in each chapter. Again, the scope of the volume limits our treatment of each tradition, and so we intend these sections to be conversation starters.

Perhaps the most unique aspect of the book is the engagement with applied theology. Most theology textbooks are written within and for an academic context. While we surely employ the insights from this context, theology is most at home in the church and in the lives of the believing community. By offering ideas for the practical embodiment of theology, we hope to provide a more holistic approach and to help restore the balance between the head (with the heart) and the hands.

With this kaleidoscopic approach to theology (biblical, historical, and practical), our goal is to help readers learn how relevant and engaging theology is. We hope this volume serves as a valuable tool for your classes that helps move theology beyond abstract ideas to a lived-out reality as students in community engage our living and active God.

---

1. See the introduction ("How the Conversation Will Take Place") for fuller details on the specific progression of each chapter.

2. "Campus Ethnic Diversity," *US News & World Report*, www.usnews.com/best-colleges/rankings/regional -universities/campus-ethnic-diversity (accessed April 15, 2019).

CHAPTER 1

Introduction

ENGAGING A CONVERSATION

As you start a book on **theology**, you might have a spark of interest. You might also come with a bit of hesitancy. Theology might feel a bit foreign because it seems so disengaged from the rest of life. Maybe theology should be reserved for other people, like pastors and seminary professors, not people like you. If you come from a tradition where the Bible is taken seriously, theology may seem too speculative, closer to philosophy than biblical truth. Many more of you do not come from traditions that engaged the Bible deeply, so engaging theology feels even more foreign and a bit daunting. You might stand outside of the Christian tradition altogether, either as a nonreligious person or as a faithful member of another religious tradition. You might only be reading this book as part of a required course. Wherever you are coming from, our goal is to bring theology down from the ivory tower. Our goal is to provide a relevant and engaging introduction to Christian theology.

While obvious to some, others will be unclear about what *theology* even means. The word derives from the Greek term for God (*theos*). Medieval theologian Thomas Aquinas captures the heart of the task well: "Theology is taught by God, teaches of God, and leads to God."[1] God's centrality is clear, and for Christians God is not simply a generic god up in the sky but a specific, personal God, who exists as **Trinity**: Father, Son, and Holy Spirit.[2] Similarly, we do not approach theology in a generic manner. Everyone does theology from a particular vantage point within various religious and historical traditions. For instance, the authors of this book are evangelicals who come out of Baptist and charismatic traditions. These vantage points shape us, but our goal is to provide an **ecumenical** look into the world of Christian thought and practice.

As part of this ecumenical approach, we will focus on things that unite Christians across traditions, but we will also explore the differences between these traditions. In other words, there will be parts where we are more *prescriptive* (explaining what the

---

1. Kelly M. Kapic, *A Little Book for New Theologians: Why and How to Study Theology* (Downers Grove, IL: InterVarsity Press, 2012), 36.
2. Bolded terms show up in the glossary in the back of the book.

church has historically argued you should believe) and parts where we are more *descriptive* (explaining the diversity we find in the church without giving preference to one or the other). In the descriptive sections, some of you will just want to know the right answer, but we purposefully do not provide one. Our goal is to give you a starting point for further study and conversation. We follow the model of an early Protestant theologian Rupertus Meldenius: "In essentials unity, in non-essentials liberty, and in all things charity."[3]

When it comes to the essentials of Christian theology, there is no better place to start than the Nicene Creed. This **creed** is a statement of faith that was agreed upon at the Council of Nicaea in AD 325.[4] It soon began to serve as the ecumenical confession of faith that unites Christians of all major traditions.[5] As the SparkNotes of the Bible, this creed summarizes the scope of the biblical narrative from beginning to end, from Genesis to Revelation. It has three articles, or sections, which respectively focus on God as Trinity (Father, Son, and Holy Spirit), and it emphasizes God's triune act of creation, reconciliation, and transformation—God over us, God for us, and God in us.[6]

NICENE CREED (AD 325/381)

We believe in one God,
the Father, the Almighty,
maker of heaven and earth,
of all that is, seen and unseen.

We believe in one Lord, Jesus Christ,
the only Son of God,
eternally begotten of the Father,
God from God, Light from Light,
true God from true God,
begotten, not made,
of one Being with the Father;
through him all things were made.
For us and for our salvation
he came down from heaven,
was incarnate from the Holy Spirit and the Virgin Mary
and became truly human.
For our sake he was crucified under Pontius Pilate;

---

3. Phillip Schaff, *History of the Christian Church*, 8 vols. (Grand Rapids: Eerdmans, 1910), 7:487.
4. The creed came to final form in AD 381 at the Council of Constantinople.
5. The term *creed* comes from the Latin *credo* ("I believe").
6. Daniel L. Migliore, *Faith Seeking Understanding: An Introduction to Christian Theology*, 3rd ed. (Grand Rapids: Eerdmans, 2014), 70.

he suffered death and was buried.
On the third day he rose again
in accordance with the Scriptures;
he ascended into heaven
and is seated at the right hand of the Father.
He will come again in glory to judge the living and the dead, and his kingdom
    will have no end.

We believe in the Holy Spirit, the Lord, the giver of life,
who proceeds from the Father [and the Son],
who with the Father and the Son is worshiped and glorified,
who has spoken through the prophets.
We believe in one holy catholic and apostolic Church.
We acknowledge one baptism for the forgiveness of sins.
We look for the resurrection of the dead,
and the life of the world to come. Amen.[7]

The creed shows God's action in the narrative of history. That means that **eschatology** is at the heart of theology. With eschatology, most people just think in terms of end times, but a holistic eschatology speaks of God's act to bring salvation to the world through Christ and the Spirit. Through the activity of the Holy Spirit, the **kingdom of God** is here now, not just when Christ returns. In other words, Christianity is a rescue religion, and that rescue (or salvation) is understood in Trinitarian and **eschatological** terms. Don't worry if these concepts are hard to understand; the rest of the book will explore what these ideas mean. Our intent here is to frame theology as a wider narrative with God the Father, Son, and Holy Spirit as the main character.

(Im)Practical Theology

By asserting that the Trinity, eschatology, and the creed are the heart of theology, we face the challenge of disconnection again. Most of you reading this (Christian or not) probably had not read the Nicene Creed before, and you have done all right without it. Perhaps your theology is shaped by a different narrative. (Everyone has a functional theology—a narrative they live by—even if they would not call it a "theology.") Maybe talking about God as Trinity seems as important as determining the number of angels that can dance on the head of a pin. While the Trinity is central to creedal theology,

---

7. This translation is drawn from the ecumenical texts project at English Language Liturgical Consultation, "Praying Together," English Language Liturgical Consultation, 1998, www.englishtexts.org/.

numerous cultural factors influence readers to reject the creed's centrality and key ideas. One major factor is our culture's rejection of external authorities (like "tradition") in favor of personal experience. For instance, many today would describe themselves as "spiritual but not religious." For most, that means that they have rejected traditional forms of worship and practice, but they still seek spiritual experiences. Without the boundaries of traditional forms, these spiritual experiences can come in various (often nontraditional) ways. Many now see more ancient worship practices (i.e., **liturgy**), such as using the Nicene Creed or taking weekly communion, as not helping but hindering worship because the goal of worship has become having a personal and authentic feeling of connection with God. Religion and its cousin theology, then, are seen as a roadblock to being spiritual. But can you truly be spiritual without a connection to the Trinity and the ideas expressed in the Creed?

The question of what makes an experience authentically spiritual is not new. One of the longest letters in the New Testament, 1 Corinthians, is an extended attempt by the apostle Paul to refine the Corinthians' understanding of spirituality. Paul's perspective undergirds the thrust of the whole book: the most authentically Christian experiences of God are Trinitarian, and these Trinitarian experiences fundamentally shape the way we engage one another and the world around us.

In 1 Corinthians 1–4, for example, Paul addresses the division and infighting that had taken over the church. Surely, you might say, the doctrine of the Trinity cannot apply to the problems they were having. However, when we consider the clear action of the Father, Jesus, and the Holy Spirit, we see how Trinitarian theology is at the heart of Paul's response. After detailing the issue of division (1 Cor 1:10–17), Paul's first point is a distinctly theological one: God's wisdom is most fully revealed in the "foolishness" of the cross of Christ (1:18–31). If you want to know the Father's heart, you must look at Jesus, particularly his willingness to suffer for others. You cannot truly have God without a suffering Jesus. This is not ivory-tower theology for Paul. If Jesus reveals what God is like, then we too should live for others rather than dominating them (2:1–5).[8] According to Paul, if the Corinthians truly understood Trinitarian theology, they would not treat each other this way. Not stopping at the Father and Son, Paul then makes an extended appeal to the Spirit: those who are led by the Spirit will follow the wisdom of God displayed by the crucified Christ (2:6–3:4). Spirit people will be cross people, sacrificing themselves for one another rather than trying to control and best one another.

The theology of the Trinity is inherently practical for Paul: if you understand who God is and how he works, then the link between theology, obedience, and flourishing becomes clearer. Do you see the difference between Paul's theology and being "spiritual but not religious"? Paul's spirituality is distinctly bound by the nature of the God we are engaging. They cannot be spiritual without the Spirit, nor can they be Christians without

---

8. The theological term for this is **cruciformity**, following Christ in his path of crucifixion for the sake of others, even your enemies.

Christ. The Corinthians are reminded that they cannot be Christian without committing daily to the crucified and resurrected Christ. Paul also reminds them that they cannot be spiritual without being connected to the Spirit, who leads them on the path of Christ. Our goal for this book is to explore the intersection of all sides of theology—the biblical narrative that communicates the story of God, the systematic exploration of theology via the triune lens of the Nicene Creed, and the challenge of practicing faith.

Practicing the Faith

In speaking of the creed, we are drawing on the distinct emphasis on right belief within Christianity. Accordingly, **orthodox** perspectives are distinguished from ones that are heterodox.[9] The term *orthodox* derives from the combination of two terms: *ortho* (right) and *doxa* (glory/worship). Thus orthodoxy is built on a relationship with God in which we rightly approach him in worship. Right beliefs do not merely give us cognitive information; they orient us to God in a manner of worship because worship, like all relationships, is based on a personal encounter.

While worship is the formative and normative context for doing theology, theology often is taught and studied in academic settings. This distinct setting has disconnected theology from the practical realities of life. Almost no theology textbooks mention how to practice the ideas presented there, besides perhaps noting a prayer or hymn at the end of a chapter. Our book works from the idea that humans are loving creatures, not just knowing or believing creatures.[10] Accordingly, when we equate doctrines only with ideas, it does not cohere with how God made us. Rather, the interconnection between doctrine and its practice shapes, forms, and motivates us.[11]

For this reason, proper belief about Jesus leads to, even entails, a life of obedience to God through Jesus by the Spirit. In short, orthodoxy cannot be separated from orthopraxy, or right action.[12] If someone struggles with obedience to Christ, this demonstrates not only a weak will but a deficient theology about who God is and how he acts. People can say they believe all sorts of things, but their actions more clearly demonstrate their belief system. Heteropraxy reveals heterodoxy. Given this manner of interaction between faith and action, this book explicitly unites the discussion of orthodoxy with orthopraxy.[13]

The Nicene Creed may seem like a stale and dated list of theological facts, but it speaks to a living faith. It arose out of ancient baptismal practices and the various expressions

---

9. However, this little-o orthodox should not be confused with the big-O Eastern Orthodox confession, which includes Russian Orthodox, Greek Orthodox, and other communions.

10. Cf. James K. A. Smith, *Desiring the Kingdom* (Grand Rapids: Baker, 2009), 39–63. See also Smith, *You Are What You Love: The Spiritual Power of Habit* (Grand Rapids: Brazos, 2016).

11. Smith, *Desiring the Kingdom*, 68–70.

12. *Orthopraxy* comes from *ortho* and *praxis* (action).

13. There are several good resources that describe the life of faith, though these resources do not always frame their discussions using (systematic) theology. See, for example, Nathan Foster, *The Making of an Ordinary Saint: My Journey from Frustration to Joy with the Spiritual Disciplines* (Grand Rapids: Baker, 2014); and Mark Scandrette, *Practicing the Way of Jesus: Life Together in the Kingdom of Love* (Downers Grove, IL: InterVarsity Press, 2011).

of the early church's **rule of faith**, which narrates the story of God. The resulting creed was not just a statement of faith ("We believe . . .") but a baptismal confession. It is a statement of commitment to obedience to the God represented in the creedal narrative. That is, "We believe in . . ." not just "We believe that . . ." Just as baptism is not merely an individualistic event but one that engages the whole community, so too we engage theology as a part of a historical community that has been holding this conversation for the past two thousand years. As a result, we will regularly introduce you to "members of the family" who have important stories to tell or perspectives to add to the discussion.

HOW THE CONVERSATION WILL TAKE PLACE

Our journey to engage theology will take place through conversations with different partners. As an introductory textbook for Christian theology, we ground topics in the biblical narrative and substantially engage debates and practices relevant to the life of the church. Accordingly, each chapter follows the pattern of story, doctrinal exposition, theological relevance, and spiritual practices.

Story. Each chapter begins with a brief and engaging account of a key figure in church history whose personal story highlights a key aspect of the doctrine at hand. Their stories help show why theology matters, and over the course of the book you will be introduced to many of the key theologians in the history of the church.

Doctrinal Exposition. The heart of each chapter is an exposition of key elements of the doctrine, with particular attention to its Trinitarian basis. Focusing on areas of ecumenical agreement, we highlight core and debated elements while clarifying heterodox perspectives. We ground each area in the narrative of Scripture (not just biblical references) and then address historical and contemporary developments.

Contemporary Theological Relevance. While theology's relevance is clear throughout each chapter, this section highlights its relevance to modern concerns, including interaction with heterodox and non-Christian faiths. It identifies current theological problems besetting the church and shows how a proper understanding and integration of orthodox theology begins to address these problems.

Practicing the Faith. Since orthodox theology should have a direct influence on one's spiritual formation and practice, each chapter concludes with practical encouragement and discussion about how each doctrine can be integrated into one's personal and communal life.

INTRODUCING OUR CONVERSATION PARTNERS

Christians from the History of the Church

While today almost all orthodox Christians fit into one of three confessions (Protestant, Roman Catholic, or Eastern Orthodox), these traditions are built upon centuries of debates about how best to pursue the faith handed down from Jesus. Accordingly, we will not just read the Bible or debate with present-day Christians, but we will engage in a conversation about theology across the spectrum of church history. See figure 1.1 for a basic map of the interconnections between the different groups, which attempts to show that geographic as well as doctrinal influences have shaped the development of Christianity. (Figure 1.2 adds more key events and people that helped shape this map.)

FIGURE 1.1: SIMPLE MAP OF CHURCH HISTORY

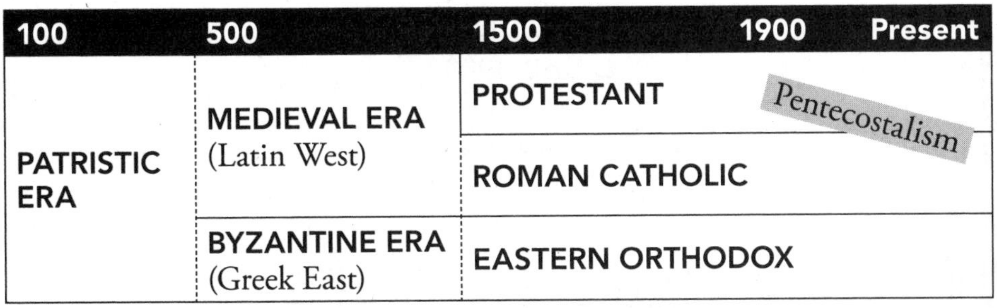

100	500	1500	1900	Present
PATRISTIC ERA	MEDIEVAL ERA (Latin West)	PROTESTANT	*Pentecostalism*	
		ROMAN CATHOLIC		
	BYZANTINE ERA (Greek East)	EASTERN ORTHODOX		

Patristic Era. This time period runs roughly from AD 100 to 500, and geographically it covers both the Latin West and the Greek East. The term *patristic* derives from the Greek and Latin words for "father" (*pater*), so this period describes the time of the fathers and mothers of the church. During this period the central message and doctrines of Christianity, such as the **Trinity, Christology**, and **pneumatology**, were refined through debates and councils. The end of the **patristic era** is marked by the fall of Rome in the West in AD 476 and the rise in dominance of the (Eastern Roman) **Byzantine** Empire with its capital in Constantinople (now Istanbul). Even though many key leaders and theologians of this age are considered saints by the Eastern Orthodox and Roman Catholic confessions, it is anachronistic to say patristic theologians were Eastern Orthodox or Roman Catholic since those distinctions did not exist during this time.

The Eastern Church

Byzantine Era. This period runs roughly from AD 500 to 1500, and geographically it pertains to the area of eastern Europe under the influence of the Byzantine Empire. While the Greek-speaking church was the cultural and theological center of the era, a plurality of languages and traditions flourished, as with the Slavic countries (central/eastern Europe and Russia). The Greek church began to have political and theological disputes with the Latin-speaking church after the patristic era, leading to disparate identities within the church. Eventually the two sides suffered an official break (excommunication) in 1054, known as the Great Schism. The end of the Byzantine era is often marked by the fall of Constantinople in 1453 to the Ottoman Turks.

FIGURE 1.2: DETAILED MAP OF CHURCH HISTORY

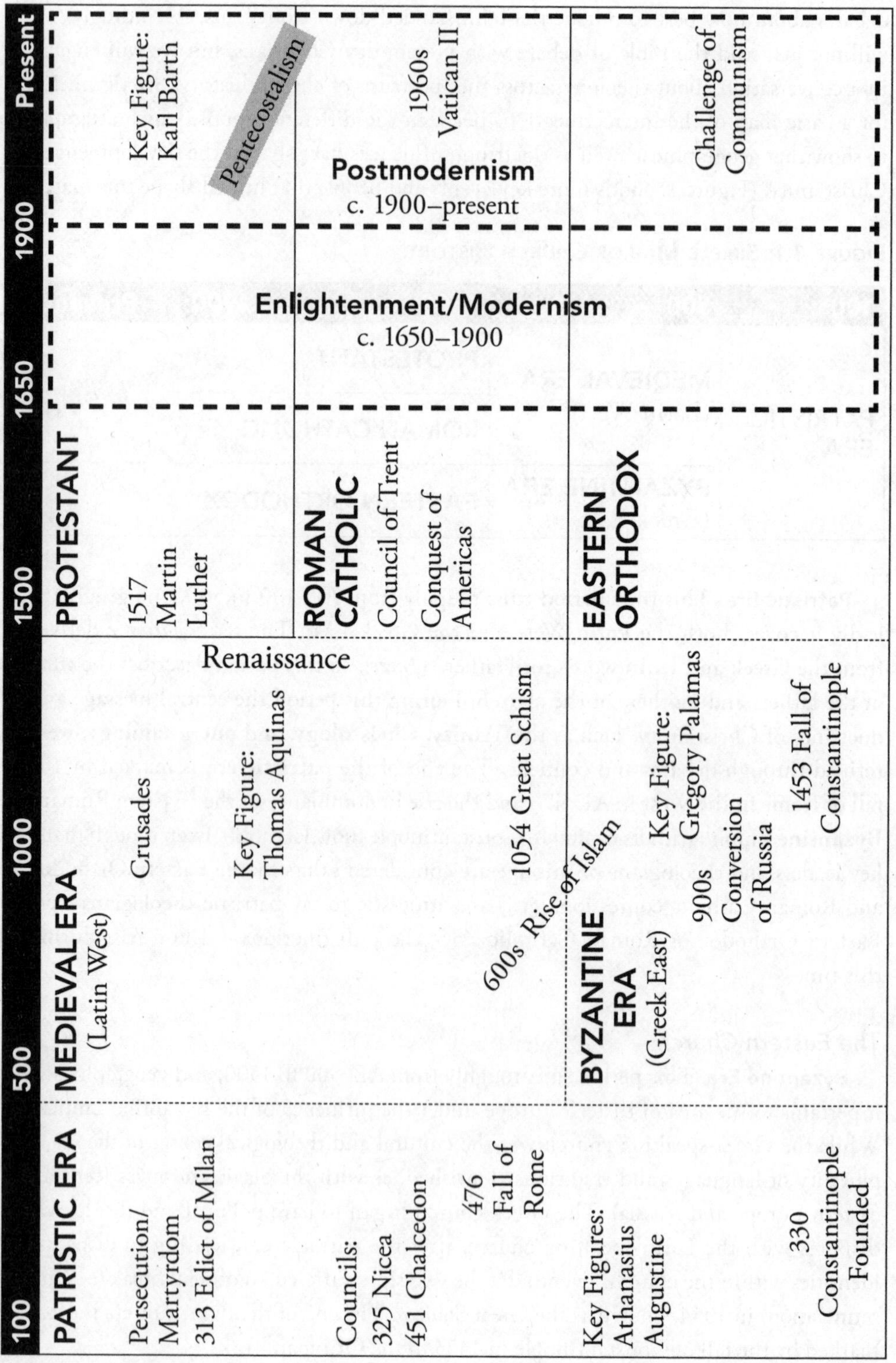

Timeline axis: 100 | 500 | 1000 | 1500 | 1650 | 1900 | Present

PATRISTIC ERA (Latin West) → **MEDIEVAL ERA** → **PROTESTANT**

- Persecution/Martyrdom
- 313 Edict of Milan
- Crusades
- Key Figure: Karl Barth
- Pentecostalism
- 1517 Martin Luther

Councils:
- 325 Nicea
- 451 Chalcedon
- 476 Fall of Rome
- Key Figure: Thomas Aquinas
- Renaissance

ROMAN CATHOLIC
- Council of Trent
- Conquest of Americas
- 1054 Great Schism
- 1960s Vatican II

Postmodernism c. 1900–present

Enlightenment/Modernism c. 1650–1900

BYZANTINE ERA (Greek East) → **EASTERN ORTHODOX**

- 600s Rise of Islam
- Key Figures: Athanasius, Augustine
- 330 Constantinople Founded
- Key Figure: Gregory Palamas
- 900s Conversion of Russia
- 1453 Fall of Constantinople
- Challenge of Communism

Eastern Orthodox. The Byzantine church (with its link to Greek patristic theology) serves as the formative influence for the Eastern Orthodox tradition. As Orthodox theology spread over central/eastern Europe and Russia, the church maintained its influence by encouraging cultural and linguistic diversity. Many years later, Orthodox influence was directly challenged by the radically antireligious pressures of communist ideology in the twentieth century. The ecumenical patriarch of Constantinople is a central figure in the Orthodox church but does not have central authority like the pope; rather, the Orthodox communion is represented today by autonomous but cooperating ecclesial groups, which are often but not always demarcated by national boundaries. Central examples of this confession are the Greek Orthodox, Russian Orthodox, and Antiochian Orthodox communions.

The Western Church

Medieval Era (i.e., Middle Ages). This period runs roughly from AD 500 to 1500, and geographically it pertains primarily to western Europe and the Latin-speaking church under the authority of the pope. In distinction to the diversity of leaders and languages represented in the Byzantine churches, the medieval church focused on one language (Latin) and one leader (the pope). Thus after the Great Schism the medieval church came to be identified as the *Roman* Catholic Church.[14] This period featured regular shifts in the balance of power between European royalty and the popes. The crusades are an example of the blended nature of political and spiritual goals at this time. Monastic movements regularly arose to bring reform and renewal to the church. The rough end point for the **Middle Ages** is 1500, which coincides with the effects of the Renaissance and of the Protestant Reformation which began in 1517.

Roman Catholic. The Roman Catholic Church (RCC) is a fluid continuation of the medieval church, although the influences of the Renaissance, the Protestant Reformation, and the Counter-Reformation (expressed through the Council of Trent, 1545–63) shaped the direction of the church. Although there are many movements within Roman Catholicism (e.g., the Dominican, Franciscan, Jesuit, and Carmelite monastic orders), they share a common confessional and ecclesiastical tradition. While predominant in southern Europe, the RCC continues to be shaped by the European colonization of the Americas since the majority of Catholics now reside there. There have been many important councils, but the Second Vatican Council (Vatican II, 1962–65) was especially significant. It allowed, and even encouraged, the Mass and Bible reading in the language of local worshipers rather than Latin, which had been previously required. Other changes include the provision of both wine and bread for communion to the laity and greater ecumenical engagement with the Orthodox and Protestant traditions.

---

14. The term *catholic* comes from the Greek word for "universal," so this was seen as the Latin or Roman part of the universal church.

Protestant. In response to disagreements over theology and practice within the RCC, a reform movement arose in 1517—now called the Protestant Reformation. The original movement was led by people like Martin Luther, John Calvin, and Ulrich Zwingli. After meeting resistance from the RCC, these leaders helped form autonomous church movements that eventually formed into separate national churches, denominations, and independent (nondenominational) churches. While having differences of opinion over theology and practice, these denominations and churches generally agree on their protest against the RCC, hence the name Protestant. The Protestant church consists of a *huge* variety of groups and subgroups. The main groups include Baptist, Methodist, Pentecostal, Presbyterian, Anglican/Episcopalian, and nondenominational traditions. Perhaps the fastest growing religious movement in history is the global adoption of Pentecostal and charismatic theology, which arose around 1900 and crosses denominational lines, even influencing Catholicism.

We have entered an era of the global church, and the values of major theological traditions (Eastern Orthodox, Roman Catholic, and Protestant) are constantly interacting in new and diverse cultural expressions. Our volume is focused on historical discussions, but as a next step we highly encourage you to explore the wonderful depth of Christian faith and practice in Africa, Asia, and South America.[15]

Cultural and Philosophical Influences

In addition to these church-focused categories, two major cultural and philosophical movements have influenced Europe and North America: **modernism** (epitomized by the Enlightenment; c. 1650–1900) and **postmodernism** (1900–present).

Enlightenment/Modernism. The Enlightenment dates more specifically to 1650–1800, but its influence runs strongly until the postmodernism of the early to mid-1900s. Modernism is characterized by an eminent trust in objective reason, individual autonomy, and the scientific method, with a resulting extreme distrust of external authorities, whether monarchs or religious tradition. Ultimately, this led to the increasing influence of **secularism**.

Postmodernism. As a response to the (unfounded) optimism of the Enlightenment, postmodernism rejected the ideas that reason could both escape human limitations and rule in every human endeavor. Rather than focusing on universal truths, postmodernism values the perspective of individuals and particular communities. Thus **pluralism**, tolerance, and **relativism** are key values.

Modernism and postmodernism have had an enormous influence on the West, which is the primary context for our study of theology and that of our students, so we regularly attend to issues raised by these movements.

---

15. For an exploration of church history from a global perspective, see Dale T. Irvin and Scott W. Sunquist, *History of the World Christian Movement*, 3 vols. (Maryknoll, NY: Orbis, 2001–). See also additional material related to these volumes at http://hwcmweb.org/.

Other Christian-Adjacent Traditions and World Religions

Most discussions of Christian theology are set as in-house debates like those between Protestants and Catholics, Baptists and Presbyterians, or **Arminians** and Calvinists. We too will examine these debates, but when you narrow your focus to certain disputes, the importance of issues can be distorted. I (BCB) remember having several debates in high school and college about whether you could lose your salvation, as if that was *the* central aspect of Christian theology and therefore a reason for division. Having developed a wider perspective, I now realize that this (still important but internally focused) argument missed the huge amount of common ground that I shared with my dialogue partners.

Given the growth of religious pluralism in our contemporary setting, Christians must discover not only their own faith but others' as well. This has the dual benefit of building bridges for new friendships, while also revealing to Christians where their commonalities lie in distinction to other perspectives. There are many good resources to help foster understanding of other faith traditions, and we realize that our brief treatment is inadequate. Nevertheless, we would like to foster further conversation by placing these initial discussions side by side.

In each chapter we will discuss Christian traditions that stand outside of historic orthodoxy (Mormonism, Jehovah's Witnesses, and **deism**) and the major world religions (Judaism, Islam, Hinduism, and Buddhism) according to the topic at hand. While the offshoots from Christianity often follow traditional theological structures, other religions do not necessarily arrange their religious perspectives according to the categories provided by Christian doctrine. We attempt to do our best to note this and facilitate your understanding of these traditions in conversation with our approach to Christianity. A number of other significant religions are worthy of study beyond these we approach. With our space constraints we limited ourselves to those that are widely dispersed.

Before we address these various traditions, it is important to note the distinction between the official tenets of a faith tradition and the lived-out experience of its adherents. Every religion has centralizing tendencies, whether from an agreed upon institutional leadership or an informal confluence of traditions. These centralizing tendencies often result in defined beliefs, sanctioned practices, official pronouncements, and so on. Importantly, the average adherent to a particular religious tradition may or may not know of these boundary-marking statements or even follow them if they know of them. Religions are often based around religious texts, so adherents often have greater affiliation with the texts (or the leaders behind the texts) than the contemporary institutional claims to authoritatively interpret and hand down the texts. Thus, when we encounter a religion, we encounter it at two levels: at the professional level (of scholar or priest) and at the level of common experience and practice. In our short summaries, we are giving the standard version of the religion as generally held and promoted by professionals within their respective orthodoxies. At the same time, every religion has cultural and regional distinctives that are then engaged in various ways by laypersons, who are the vast majority of adherents. This everyday experience by nonprofessionals is called *folk religion*.

Many people leave high religion to the professionals (priests, pastors, imams, monks, etc.) and engage religion as much as a cultural phenomenon as it is something that relates to transcendent realities. Accordingly, folk religion is often shaped by the practical realities of life. For instance, someone following Buddhism might have a shrine at home but only irregular engagements with a temple, such as during festivals, whereas someone else might have frequent engagement with temple practice. At the same time, consistent practice does not entail specific beliefs or orthodoxy according to the main standards of a religion. In expressions of folk religion, people are often quite syncretistic, engaging in practices and beliefs deemed explicitly unorthodox. Think of the number of Christians, for example, who also read horoscopes. What we briefly summarize or what you study in a religion's scriptures may or may not reflect someone's experience of that religion. *The best thing you can do is have coffee or a meal with someone who practices the tradition to see how their experience matches the treatment here.* Just as the Christian doctrines we discuss are not represented in each church, so also the same, if not greater, diversity appears in other religious traditions. With this in mind, we will now introduce our conversation partners.

Christianity and Other Christian Traditions. For the Christian traditions outside of traditional orthodoxy, we focus on the largest two denominations, namely Mormonism and Jehovah's Witnesses, as well as (functional) deism. These traditions accept the Protestant Bible and use many of the same terms and concepts as historical Christianity, though they have differences that we will explore along the way. Mormonism, or the Church of Jesus Christ of the Latter-day Saints (LDS), arose in the early to mid-1800s through the ministry of Joseph Smith. The easiest way to engage Mormon theology is through the website of the Latter-day Saints, and the text *Gospel Principles* gives an accessible summary of the key tenets of their theology.[16] Jehovah's Witnesses arose in the late 1800s through the ministry of Charles Taze Russell. Their official website contains a variety of information, among which the page "What Do Jehovah's Witnesses Believe?" in the FAQs gives a good though brief primer.[17] Unlike Mormonism and Jehovah's Witnesses, deism does not represent an organized religious group, but its theology has been hugely influential. Arising from the time of the Enlightenment (c. seventeenth and eighteenth centuries), deism is a view of God that emphasizes his (and other spiritual beings') disengagement from the world. While this view of God was initially tied to liberal Protestantism, the influence of deism has been widely documented among traditional Christian churches; hence we treat *functional* deism. In this view, God's distance results in a mechanized view of the universe and a greater emphasis on personal effort.

---

16. *Gospel Principles* (Salt Lake City: Church of Jesus Christ of Latter-day Saints, 2011), https://www.lds.org/manual/gospel-principles.

17. "What Do Jehovah's Witnesses Believe?," JW.org, May 25, 2018, *https://www.jw.org/en/jehovahs-witnesses/faq/jehovah-witness-beliefs/*.

We turn now to the major world religions. As we discuss some orienting perspectives within the other world religions, you always need to keep two key caveats in mind: (1) every religion has many interpretations and subtraditions, and (2) many world religions prioritize orthopraxy over orthodoxy. Therefore, as we focus on the ideas and doctrines of these religions, *we are only capturing a partial aspect of their religious tradition*.

Judaism. Judaism is considered the first Abrahamic faith because the Jewish nation came from Abraham (c. 1800 BC) and his descendants through Jacob (i.e., Israel). The story of the Jewish people is long and varied. After events such as the Babylonian exile (586 BC) and later the Roman destruction of the temple in AD 70, Jews spread out over the Middle East and Europe. This plurality of experience makes Jewish theology difficult to categorize. In the United States today, for example, there are three main branches of Judaism: Orthodox, Conservative, and Reformed. As we summarize Jewish theology, we have tried to balance between Orthodox and Conservative perspectives when we can, but it is always important to remember the wide diversity in perspectives. As one window into Jewish faith, we list here the thirteen principles of faith proposed by Maimonides (a medieval Jewish theologian), which is now included in Jewish liturgy through "Yigdal" and *Ani Ma'amin* ("I believe") prayers.

1. God is creator.
2. God is one.
3. God is incorporeal.
4. God is eternal.
5. God is worthy of being served.
6. The words of the prophets are true.
7. The prophecy through Moses is especially true.
8. Torah is from heaven [God].
9. The written and oral Torah is complete.
10. God sees all human deeds.
11. God rewards obedience and punishes disobedience.
12. The Messiah is coming.
13. There will be a resurrection of the dead.[18]

Though generally confessed, the interpretation of these ideas is quite varied.

Islam. The Muslim faith sees Muhammad (c. AD 570–632) as the seal of the series of prophets, such as Adam, Noah, Abraham, Moses, David, and Jesus. Each of the earlier prophets brought truth from Allah (God), but these truths have been corrupted.

---

18. Maimonides "13 Foundations of Judaism," trans. Marc Mermelstein, Mesora.org, http://www.mesora.org/13principles.html. For Conservative Judaism, see "Emet Ve'Emunah: Statement of Principles of Conservative Judaism" Masorti Olami (World Council of Conservative Synagogues), https://masortiolami.org/wp-content/uploads/2014/03/Emet-VEmunah-Statement-of-Principles-of-Conservative-Judaism.pdf.

Now infallible truth has been communicated through Muhammad, the final prophet, in the Qur'an. Sunni and Shia are two main branches of Islam, and the large majority are Sunni. Though many associate Islam with Arabic culture, the majority of Muslims live outside of the Arab world today.[19] The "five pillars" of Islam are key practices that guide the faithful (faith, prayer, charity, fasting, and pilgrimage), and the first is the most basic confession of faith (the *shahada*): "There is no god but Allah (God). Muhammad is the prophet of God."[20] Beyond this central confession, it is common to note these six articles of Islamic faith:

1. Belief in the Oneness of God
2. Belief in the Angels of God
3. Belief in the Books of God
4. Belief in the Prophets or Messengers of God
5. Belief in the Day of Judgment
6. Belief in the Divine Decree (God's providence)

Hinduism. Hinduism is one of the oldest of the religions that we discuss, and it arose on the Indian subcontinent. Since Hinduism does not have a founder or one set of texts that unite the religion, there are a diversity of ways of approaching its common themes. At times, Hinduism is described as a "way of life" (*dharma*) rather than a creedal religion. There are three progressive but interconnected movements within Hinduism, each with their unique texts and paths (*yogas* or *margas*): Vedic (*karma yoga*), philosophical (*jnana yoga*), and devotional (*bhakti yoga*) Hinduism. The vast majority of Hindus follow the last of the three, which focuses on the incarnations (*avatars*) of the gods (Vishnu, Shiva, etc.), which are variously understood as reflecting Brahman, the ultimate reality. The ideas of *karma*, *samsara* (the cycle of rebirth), and *moksha* (liberation) undergird Hindu thought.

Buddhism. Buddhism arose from the teaching of Siddhartha Gautama (or Shakyamuni) around the sixth century BC. Coming from India, Buddhism maintains some continuity with the cyclical nature of experience through *karma* and *samsara* like Hinduism. In distinction, the Buddha (the "awakened one") realized that the goal of life is *nirvana* ("blowing out" like a candle). This path to *nirvana* is captured by the famous Four Noble Truths:

1. To live is to suffer.
2. Suffering (*dukkha*) is caused by attachment.

---

19. The largest Muslim nation by population is Indonesia. Stephen Prothero, *God Is Not One: The Eight Rival Religions That Run the World* (New York: HarperOne, 2010), 28.

20. Carl Medearis, *Muslims, Christians, and Jesus: Gaining Understanding and Building Relationships* (Minneapolis: Bethany House, 2008), 58.

3. To eliminate suffering one must eliminate attachment.

4. One can eliminate attachment by following the noble eightfold path.

The eightfold path includes: the right view, the right intention, the right speech, the right action, the right livelihood, the right effort, the right mindfulness, and the right concentration.[21] Within the three major schools of Buddhism (Theravada, Mahayana, and Vajrayana [or Tibetan]), there is a wide array of texts, interpretations, and applications.

As we go forward, remember that we will only scratch the surface as we engage these other religions. Each one has much regional diversity. The depth and breadth of the Christian tradition that we explore in this book is easily matched by rows and rows of books about Christianity in any library. That same depth and breadth exists in each of the religions we discuss here, so do not confuse our partial and broad outlines for a comprehensive treatment. Also, almost no one follows the "textbook" version of their religion, which is why we encourage personal conversation to see how your friends and neighbors actually practice their faith. With that in mind, let's engage theology together.

---

21. Winfried Corduan, *Neighboring Faiths: A Christian Introduction to World Religions*, 2nd ed. (Downers Grove, InterVarsity Press, 2012), 320–21.

CHAPTER 2

Theological Method

How to Do Theology

Big Idea:
God's acts in the world
(through Christ and the
Holy Spirit) shape the
way we know him and
how we think about him
through the four sources
of theology.

Key Terms:
- Scripture
- Revelation
- Sources of Theology
- Analogy

Key Passages:
Exod 34:6–7;
Deut 6:4–5;
Rom 5:12–21;
1 Cor 8:6; 15:1–4;
Phil 2:6–11;
1 Tim 2:5–6; 3:16

INTRODUCTION

When I (BCB) lived in England, people often asked why I was living there, since I obviously did not sound local. Knowing that people did not want the twenty-minute summary of my dissertation on **patristic hermeneutics**, I would say I came to study **theology**. I was amazed at the number of people who said, "theology, what's that?" Deriving from the Greek word for "God" (*theos*), theology is the study of God and his activity in the world. The general lack of knowledge about basic terms told me that a lot of people do not know what theology is or how to do it. Just like in other areas of study, the subject of theology determines the approaches and methods that help make sense of the topics. Most of our book will be about the *content* of theology and its basis in **Scripture**. However, to help communicate how we are making sense of God and his activity in the world, this chapter addresses the topic of *method*— that is, how to do theology. Rather than starting with concepts, each chapter will begin with an account of how particular Christians before us have made sense of the topic at hand, and this chapter explores two of the most revered teachers in the church.

FAITH SEEKING UNDERSTANDING: THE TWO GREATEST DOCTORS OF THE CHURCH

Thomas Aquinas

Two New Trends

Thomas was born in 1225 to a wealthy noble family from Aquino in Italy. He was sent to school at the nearby Benedictine monastery in

Monte Cassino and at age fifteen moved to the university at Naples to finish his general education. At Naples, Thomas encountered two life-changing realities.

(1) He accepted the recently popular and controversial philosophy of Aristotle. Aristotle's vision employed the idea of conceptual realities from Plato (i.e., the Forms) but saw them as encoded into the material things of the earthly world rather than as a sharp **dualism** between the changeless conceptual world and the changing material world like in Plato. The shift was important. Platonic dualism (God's ideas versus the corrupt world) gave way to Aristotle's more purposeful integration (God's ideas ordering, informing, and integrating the material world). Though Aristotle's ideas had ancient roots, they led to a new and controversial theological vision of God and world that Thomas embraced.

(2) Thomas's embrace of the new, radical Dominican order was equally controversial. It must have seemed like a cult to his affluent family, who respected older forms of monasticism. They knew a monasticism devoted to silence, prayer, and contemplation. These older monastic orders often administered great wealth and land. Thus Thomas's nobility was well suited for one of these orders. But Thomas chose to join the Dominicans, a newly formed order of "mendicants," or beggar preachers, who renounced holding wealth. Their spiritual strength centered not on silence but on speaking, teaching, and engaging the new urban environments and universities, and the calling of poverty gave potency and clarity to their preaching.

Dominican and Doctor

The Dominicans sent Thomas to Paris and Cologne where he studied with the famous Albert the Great. Albert recognized Thomas's genius and was instrumental in seeing him return to Paris to finish his degree and begin teaching. His routine was the simple life of the schoolman; he would study and teach and write—with the entire venture undertaken as an act of prayerful devotion. In time, he had secretaries to help him write eleven million words. Though he is known today primarily as a philosopher and a theologian, he wrote more biblical commentaries than anything else.

One of his most consistent themes was this: what God had revealed about himself in Scripture fit with the best human thinking about God and the world. He challenged the false impression that God's **revelation** and human understanding led to different sets of answers. His famous phrase, "grace completes nature,"[1] captures the unity of all truth that Thomas championed: theology integrates with what you may learn elsewhere and will not contradict it. If your study of theology comes to one conclusion and your study of physics comes to a contradictory conclusion, you have made a mistake; your theology is wrong, or your physics is wrong (or maybe both).

---

1. These sentiments derive from Thomas's *Summa Theologiae* 1.1.8, ad. 2. See Frederick Christian Bauerschmidt, *Holy Teaching: Introducing the Summa Theologiae of St. Thomas Aquinas* (Grand Rapids: Brazos, 2005), 38.

Straightlaced or Radical? Rationalist or Mystic?

Thomas was a contradiction. On the one hand, this heavyset man was steady, substantial, slow to speak, well born, and meticulously orthodox. On the other hand, he was a pioneer for truly radical theological and social innovation. Thomas was no mere egghead; he was profound in wisdom and matters of the Spirit. Students are surprised to learn he reported having visions throughout his life. The exact circumstances escape us, but it seems that a series of visions near the end of his life profoundly touched Thomas. He set aside his writing and reported that his work seemed like straw after his encounter with God. Can it be that this rigorously rational theologian had been a mystic all along? This chapter argues that his magnificent integration of reason and faith was designed not to conquer the truths of God but to protect God's mystery. God is truly infinite and mysterious. He is not bound by nature, but neither is he absent from it, working in and through nature. Before exploring this further, let us turn to another pillar in the history of theology.

Karl Barth

If Thomas is known for integrating reason and revelation, Karl Barth (pronounced "Bart" without the *h*) is the voice crying for the return to revelation in rejection of deistic rationalism. Born in 1886, Barth came from a family of **Reformed** ministers in Switzerland. Becoming a professor when Karl was young, his father was conservative and worried over the influence of liberalism upon ministers. As a boy Barth is remembered as both a bright student and somewhat of a ruffian. Though he had an academic setting for his upbringing, it was his confirmation class that sparked his interest in theology.

University and Liberalism

Even though it worried his conservative father, Barth studied with the most recognized scholars of his day. He thought his teachers were brave pioneers. They uncovered the true history behind many of the distorting traditions that had grown up around Christianity. These "classical liberals" usually went one of two directions. Some like the famous Adolf von Harnack (1851–1930) saw Jesus as a simple preacher of morality and not someone who ever intended to be worshiped as a God. Harnack sought to restore Jesus's vision of God's universal fatherhood and the transforming moral vision called the **kingdom of God**. Others, like Barth's favorite Wilhelm Hermann (1846–1922), believed that theology could be grounded in inner religious experience.

Pastor and Preacher

Barth completed his studies with distinction and took up the task of preaching. Eventually he landed in a small Swiss village of largely blue-collar workers (1911–21). His studies had given him little to say or proclaim, so he invested in social activism. Barth and his pastor friend, Eduard Thurneysen, complained about the theological bankruptcy arising from their training, and they hungered for a way forward. When their distinguished professors signed a document supporting the German war policy in 1914, they became disillusioned. Barth believed the statement placed loyalty to German culture above the Christian faith: they had replaced the God of the Bible with a god subservient to German culture. Now it seemed his professors were not brave pioneers but humble captives to culture. Still looking for a way forward, Barth finally determined to return to Scripture. This time he would not employ methods designed to reconstruct historical origins; instead, he would return to the text sharing the church's trust that God awakens faith and addresses the reader.

Professor and Protestor

In 1919 Barth published a theologically oriented commentary on Paul's letter to the Romans that caused a great stir. Claiming that Christ was a challenge to all human reasoning, the work undercut the culture's confidence. He argued that culturally sophisticated persons were blind to God's ways apart from the disruptive Word from God (that is, the **incarnation** of the Son of God). The book led to teaching posts in Germany: Göttingen (1921–25), Münster (1925–30), and Bonn (1930–35). In 1934, he contributed to the *Barmen Declaration*, a statement of believers condemning Nazism. In 1935, he was forced to leave Germany when he refused to give unqualified allegiance to Hitler. Welcomed to Switzerland, he taught thereafter at Basel.

After several starts, Barth finally made progress with his *Church Dogmatics*, the most influential work of systematic theology in the last century. Still unfinished at his death, it spans over nine thousand pages. His theology included (1) a rejection of human efforts to find God. This human effort is inherent in a natural theology with a deistic, distant God. Even further, the Nazi reinvention of God was idolatry—man making God in the image of man. He taught that (2) the Son's revelation of God vindicated the teaching of the church. The doctrines of the Trinity and **Christology** were the essential to orient Christian speech about God. His work also required (3) a return to the Bible as an act of faith. God is the subject of theology, a person we encounter through faith and not an object of study. As progress on the *Church Dogmatics* slowed, Barth joked that the angels in heaven laughed at him pushing all his books around in a wheelbarrow.

Aquinas and Barth: Frenemies?

These two greats, perhaps the two greatest theological voices of the church, share several things. They were both radical in their defense of Christian tradition (Trinity and Christology); they left massive bodies of work; they both left their greatest work unfinished; near the end of their lives they spoke humbly of their work in the face of encountering God—Thomas's straw and Barth's wheelbarrow of books. However, scholars commonly consider them to be opposing voices: Thomas builds upon the foundation provided by reason, whereas Barth sees such efforts as dangerous and insists upon relying on God's revelation. The reality is more nuanced.

While some may put these two theologians as two contrasting poles in the history of theology—one for seeing the coherence of grace and nature (Aquinas) and the other rejecting this very thing (Barth)—they both attend to the active role of our infinite God in the world. God is not just a better version of ourselves, like a superhero; rather, God is outside the system and at the same time intimately and consistently involved in it. This activity is climactically revealed in the death and **resurrection** of Jesus and through the work of the Holy Spirit. God's activity is why theology is so relevant to the pressing issues of the day, such as wealth and poverty for Aquinas and the rise of Nazism for Barth. How you understand God has great impact on your current social engagement. Their particular approaches to the task of theology are helpful as well, and we will return to them after laying the groundwork with particular terms and ideas.

How Do We Do Theology?

The Nature of Theology and Its Practice

As we begin our journey into the discussion of theology, we will first set out some general principles that set the context for our study. Then with these items in mind, we can come back to some of the questions and issues that shape our approach to the practice of theology.

Doctrine and Doctrines

First, there is "Doctrine," and there are "doctrines." Doctrine (or teaching) is the simplest summary of the Christian story, and doctrines are the smaller component parts of the story.[2] We will use "Doctrine" to designate the overall message or teaching of Christianity. Theology is often focused on doctrines, but Doctrine is the big picture that gives us our orientation and frame of reference.

Early Christians employed a narrative summary of the Christian faith (often called the **rule of faith**) to communicate the basic ideas of its Doctrine. We seek to capture the same idea by focusing upon the narrative sweep of Scripture. Here is our paraphrase of this basic narrative:[3]

> God created people in a good creation; he generously wished to have communion and dwell in fellowship. Humans turned away, breaking faith with God, and creation fell into corruption. Through his elect people Israel and in fulfillment of his covenants with them, God sent his divine Son from his uncorrupted experience into our corrupted world to teach us that God is our Father. He bears the gone-wrong-ness of the world with us and finally for us by dying on the cross. The Son breaks the bonds of

---

2. Donald Fairbairn develops this theme in *Life in the Trinity: An Introduction to Theology with the Help of the Church Fathers* (Downers Grove, IL: IVP Academic, 2009).

3. See Phillip Schaff, *History of the Christian Church*, 8 vols. (Grand Rapids: Eerdmans, 1910).

corruption, of evil and death, through being resurrected. Then the Son is exalted to his place with the Father. God's Spirit works on us and in us to join us to the Son and the Father, with the goal that we share in God's incorrupt life.

Note two things about Doctrine—the big picture—expressed here. (1) Doctrine is explained in irreducibly Trinitarian terms: the Father sends the Son and the Spirit to address and engage the world. (2) Also Doctrine or Christian teaching calls for our transformation through engagement with this triune God. As we progress through this book, we will use the Doctrine expressed in the **Nicene Creed** to guide our discussion because of its attention to this personal and transformative engagement with the triune God.

Our attention to Doctrine gives us orientation to the doctrines (subcategories), such as **anthropology** (who people are), Christology (who the Son is and what he does), **soteriology** (what salvation is and how we are delivered), and **ecclesiology** (who and what the church is). Our chapters will explore these areas in much more detail. As we do, we will continually return to the larger story so that doctrinal talk remains connected to the life-giving source of Doctrine.

Unity and Diversity

In theology the main elements of Doctrine are often called the "essentials." Responding to a theological dispute, an early Protestant theologian (Rupertus Meldenius) argued for the following: "In essentials unity, in non-essentials liberty, and in all things charity."[4] We will pursue the noble goal of affirming the essentials and allowing diversity in the nonessentials. But this is no simple task because theologians cannot agree on what is dogma (or Doctrine, an essential teaching) and what is nonessential. We will humbly proceed by bearing witness to what we think is the core of Christian belief and by stubbornly seeking unity with other followers of Christ. We will love and honor dogma without being dogmatic. We desire to be *catholic* (addressing the entire church), *evangelical* (reflecting our gospel-centered Protestantism), and *missional* (being attentive to the circumstance of culture). In spite of the divisions among the church, we are confident that there is much that holds Christians together.

Belief and Practice

Rather than focusing on a set of ideas, theology speaks to the holistic relationship between God and his creation. As we noted in the introduction, the creeds arose from baptismal confessions of faith in which new Christians did not just believe that God exists but believed in God. They committed themselves to him. We talk about this holistic approach to theology on an individual level using the language of head, heart, and hands—knowing, trusting, and doing. Thus theology is not only about ideas (head)

---

4. Schaff, *History of the Christian Church*, 7:487.

but also about faith (heart) and practice (hands). We are shaped by the customs, routines, and habits of the church—caring for the poor, taking the Lord's Supper, attending worship. The practices possess an interior, unspoken code, an embodied knowledge that influences and informs our cerebral efforts. As a result, we explore practices related to the doctrines at the end of each chapter.

How Did Theology Get Separated from Practice?

Originally the great theologians were also pastors and bishops in the church, but with the rise of universities, the people who practiced theology in the church and those who theorized about theology in the universities developed separate identities. With the dawn of the Enlightenment, different fields and disciplines were treated as isolated silos rather than integrated wholes. With an emphasis on belief (over against practice), doctrines came to be emphasized without the coherence of Doctrine in the narrative of Scripture and the life of the church.

Community and Conversation

We intentionally invite onlookers and outsiders to share in the conversation and exploration that is Christian theology. Nevertheless, the natural environment for theology is among the people who are learning to follow Jesus. Theology arises from and flourishes in the community of faith. Paul compares church life with a body (1 Cor 12–14). Members (body parts) are assigned special services and tasks; members serve but also benefit from the service provided by other members. Like discipleship, thinking about God is not a solo affair. Reading in community produces a stereo effect. The rich history of our community's conversation shapes our reflection. Great family members like Thomas and Barth frequently enter the conversation. As a way to explain the particular aspects of this conversation, we now discuss the **sources of theology**.

Sources of Theology

We depend upon various sources in our reflection on God and the world. Some argue that Scripture (the Bible) should be the only source of theology, but almost all concede that the Bible does not address every theological issue (certainly not every contemporary ethical issue), so we need other sources as well. The four primary sources commonly used are: *Scripture, tradition, reason,* and *experience.* (These are colloquially known as the Wesleyan Quadrilateral, but they are not limited to Wesleyans/Methodists.) Among these we affirm the centrality of Scripture, as the only infallible and inspired source, but Christians also appropriately draw from the other three. Since we are learning about God through these sources of theology, we recognize that we depend on the Spirit as we engage each.

Scripture

Many events in the story of God reveal him, his purpose, and plan. Through the Spirit we have the Bible, which captures the narrative of God's acts for us in Christ. Although the Bible is our central authority, biblical interpretation is not straightforward. To help us avoid reading the Bible unchristianly, we need the entire church (with its gifts and discernment from the Spirit) to rightly interpret the entire Bible (with Christ as its center).

Our attention will be on the great narrative of Scripture, though time and space will require that we often only cite Bible references as confirmation for our verdicts. This practice could leave the wrong impression—that the Bible is a cluster of free-floating factoids. Two time-honored strategies for Christ-centered readings will demonstrate how trusting and employing the Bible actually serves as a source for theology. (1) The Bible's teaching is grasped in the unfolding Story of the Bible. (2) The Bible is read **typologically**—that is, the stories have a shared shape or pattern (type, *tupos*) that illuminates their meaning in the larger Story. (The Story/stories relationship is akin to the Doctrine/doctrines relationship.)

A Free-Floating Factoid Bible

As a modern person, I (RLH) confess the Bible seems messy. Too many genres and authors scattered over too long a time. Left to my own vain imagination, I would think the book from God would be a series of numbered statements or propositions. These would be catalogued by topic and have a great index, along with a FAQ section. Each piece would stand alone and in about sixty pages give you every vital piece of information you need. It would be a factoid Bible, free-floating from all the interconnected and ambiguous narratives.

In contrast, the Bible (and therefore theology!) does not tell the story of God and history in a pristine lab setting. This God seems messy; he enters the gone-wrong world; he takes his time to move his story along. This type of theology requires virtue and patience (not just intelligence) from his readers as we engage the narrative and not just free-floating factoids.

Tradition

Tradition is the collective conversation that results from Christian thinking, teaching, and worshiping throughout history. In conversation, we engage a living tradition, not a dead orthodoxy. The tradition's authority derives from the more foundational authority of Scripture and the illuminating work of the Spirit. We are grateful for this great tradition, but we are not bound to it in the same way we are bound to the Bible. We readily disagree with some great teachers (you must because they do not all agree), yet we believe the Spirit who guides us has guided teachers before us. When the family speaks with a common voice, we pay attention with the greatest respect. The Nicene Creed is the central example of **ecumenical** tradition which binds virtually all Christians, and we trust the common voice as rightly having reflected and reasoned upon the Scriptures.

Some Catholic theologians viewed tradition as a body of teaching that was specifically entrusted to the followers of Jesus as a supplement to the teaching of Scripture. More nuanced Catholic voices recognize the priority of Scripture as the earliest and most authoritative part of tradition. Many mistakenly claim that the Reformers rejected tradition in their break from the Catholic church. The Reformation did not reject tradition; they simply asserted that Scripture stands over tradition. Luther and Calvin both insisted that whoever reads the Bible and disregards the traditional theological statements of Nicaea and Chalcedon is not reading as a Christian.[5] It was the later (**secularizing**) cultural and philosophical movement of the Enlightenment that pushed some Protestants to reject tradition altogether.

Reason

Reason is rooted in creation's order and goodness, coming from God himself, the Creator. Early Christians even identified a strong connection between Jesus as the *Logos* (the "Word" or "Principle [of Reality]") and creation as *logikos* ("rational") because it comes from him. In a broad sense the use of and appeal to reason relates to rational argumentation, such that Christian theology rejects logical contradictions, such as where an idea and its opposite are equally affirmed.[6] Beyond this more general level, the methods of rational inquiry that impact theology most often come through appeals to science and historical investigation. For instance, a common goal for biblical interpretation is an objective and historical investigation, unbiased by the stance of the interpreter.[7] This approach to interpretation, distinctly influenced by **modernism**, is undergirded by rationalism. The conflicting ideas of Thomas and Barth relate to questions about the inadequacy of human reason (natural theology) in distinction to divine revelation (revealed theology). So questions of priority regarding reason and Scripture are often in play.

Experience

Appeals to reason often focus on objectivity, but discussions of experience often focus on subjectivity. By subjectivity, we mean the aspects of life and perception that are

---

5. Like the council that met in Nicaea (AD 325), a later council met in Chalcedon (AD 451) to discuss the relationship of Christ's divine and human natures in his one person. See D. H. Williams, *Retrieving the Tradition and Renewing Evangelicalism: A Primer for Suspicious Protestants* (Grand Rapids: Eerdmans,1999), 69.

6. We will return to the idea of paradoxes below, but we should note here that a paradox is not a contradiction. For instance, the oneness and threeness of God as Trinity is a paradox not a contradiction since one and three are not opposites.

7. Two common methods using this approach are the historical-critical method and (its evangelical cousin) the historical-grammatical method.

unique to individuals and interpretive communities. On a personal level, past experience is highly informative to one's view and engagement with the world. The shared cultural context of local and regional communities crucially influences the way we engage the world. Since God is a person (an acting subject and not merely an object of study), theology relates to a personal and subjective encounter. At the same time, God is not only what we make him to be; theology is not just about our desires and wants but about situating our experience in submission to God as the primary subject and initiator in the process.

FAITH NOT MERELY COGNITIVE

Søren Kierkegaard (1813–55), an influential theologian and early **existentialist**, is misunderstood as a **relativist** in part because selections from his work entitled "Truth as Subjectivity" are reprinted in introductory textbooks on philosophy. But he is not saying that some truths are subjective (true for you but not me) and others are objective (always true). In these terms Kierkegaard is firm; for example, the statement "Jesus is Lord" is firmly and absolutely true. Kierkegaard does, however, claim that some truth requires a different sort of response. Affirming a simple math fact may be done with some emotional distance on the part of the knower. "Jesus is Lord" requires an embrace by the knowing subject. It is not sufficient to respond, "Well, I guess Jesus is indeed Lord." This claim requires a response rooted in love, service, and worship. Other responses are actually rebellious rejections to the claim.

Putting the Sources Together

We affirm these four sources, though they are not all equal. Our primary source for engaging God is Scripture, so it is in the center of the figure below (see figure 2.1). The arrows show the influence and perspective provided by the sources. As the dark, outward arrows show, interpretive priority is given to Scripture as it shapes the way we view the other sources. In other words, tradition, reason, and experience should submit to the truth of Scripture, even when the Bible seems odd, countercultural, or unappealing. However, Scripture does not exist in a vacuum, so the other sources also shape how we read Scripture (hence the inward arrows). These other sources serve as checks and balances on each other (the perimeter arrows).[8]

In church history the question is not *whether* Christians read the Bible—but *how*. There are many differences over the past two thousand years, but a quick and helpful description of the differences indicates which of the other three sources is given priority.

---

8. The influence of tradition, reason, and experience on the interpretation of the Bible is explored through discussions of hermeneutics, the practice of interpretation.

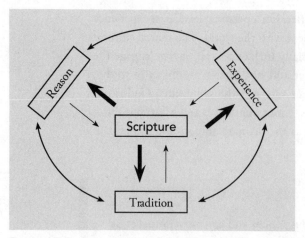

FIGURE 2.1
Picturing the Sources of Theology

The other sources are not excluded, but we see one of the sources given priority in each of these timeframes:[9]

Patristic/Medieval/Byzantine	Tradition
Modernism/Enlightenment	Reason
Postmodernism	Experience

In earlier eras, the temptation was to overemphasize tradition (a communal thing), but there has been a distinct shift toward the individual in the last several hundred years. As a result, today we are much more likely tempted to make the message of Scripture submit to reason or experience. That is, if the ideas from the Bible seem unreasonable or uncomfortable, we are tempted to trust our own views rather than the Bible or tradition. The real challenge comes when people do this unconsciously, especially in a religious setting. They take bits of Scripture and so think they are being biblical, but in reality they have allowed reason or experience to filter out the parts of the Bible that they did not like because they are not attending to the larger Story. This is why we constantly need to listen to all of the sources as we engage the Bible.

By discussing the sources of theology, we have laid out the *tools* that we use for doing theology. Now we will address the telos, or goal, of theological inquiry: knowing and speaking about God. As we do, we will pick up the issues Aquinas and Barth raised since they relate to how we order the sources.

Speaking about God

If we have these sources and tools, do they give us the ability to find certainty in theology, or a precision in all our theological decisions? If theology is a search for truth, then all things that are true are equally true, right? Does that mean truth that is ascertained from one source is equal to truth from another source? These are all questions about the topic of **epistemology** (from the Greek word *episteme*, "knowledge"), concerning what one can know and how one can know it. To make sense of these questions, we return to Aquinas and Barth who help us clarify what we are doing when we use human words to speak of God.

Literally Speaking: Three Ways

To speak more precisely about God, Thomas appeals to the more cautious literal sense. He believed there were logically three ways we could use our words to speak

9. For further detail, see the discussion of the history of biblical interpretation in ch. 4.

literally about God. First, consider the different ways people may use the same word to describe two different realities.

Approach 1: The exact same meaning for each reality. I might say that my dog has a bark and that your dog has a bark. I have described two different dogs using the word *bark*. But the word *bark* means exactly the same thing in each claim. Thomas labeled this approach "univocal."

Approach 2: Completely different meanings for each reality. I can also claim that my dog has a bark and that the tree outside my window has bark. Again, I have used the word *bark* to describe two different environments or realities. But notice here the word carries a completely different meaning. Thomas labeled this approach "equivocal."[10]

Thomas believes neither of these approaches works for Christian descriptions of God. Let's consider the claims that my human father is wise and that God is wise. While my dad is a wonderfully wise man, his wisdom is not on par with God. Dad's wisdom is less profound than God's wisdom and is not as pure or perfect as God's. My dad's judgment may be compromised by his bias or a deficiency in virtue. Thomas thinks I speak dangerously and even idolatrously if I speak univocally—that is using the word *wise* to mean exactly the same thing. If I speak univocally of God, I assume I can know God exhaustively. Yet since God is infinite I cannot say all there is to say about God with finite language. Thomas (with almost the entire Christian tradition) thinks God has wisdom maximally: he possesses all wisdom; he is the very source of all wisdom. Any wisdom that my father has derives from God's own wisdom. Speaking univocally won't work; there is more to God than I can say.

Neither will it do to speak equivocally about God. If God's wisdom and my human father's wisdom are unrelated, then we likely do not know what we mean when we speak about God being wise. God is beyond our finite categories, but Thomas thought that our language is meaningless and useless in helping us understand God if we only speak about God equivocally.

Since neither one of these two ways of speaking (the univocal and the equivocal) was the appropriate way for Christians to speak about God, Thomas offered a third approach:

Approach 3: The analogical approach. Thomas believed that creation bears a genuine resemblance to God even if it is incomplete and imperfect. When we speak of God in this fashion we recognize that an analogue, such as the wisdom of my father, is both like and unlike God's wisdom.

---

10. Frederick Christian Bauerschmidt, *Holy Teaching: Introducing the Summa Theologiae of St. Thomas Aquinas* (Grand Rapids: Brazos, 2005), 68.

It is important to affirm that our language about God genuinely and truly means something, but our speech about God does not capture everything about God or his wisdom. I'm constantly aware that our great and infinite God is wiser than I can comprehend. The middle way of **analogy** means, we can speak meaningfully but not exhaustively. Analogical language recognizes similarities and dissimilarities. My most cautious language still has an asterisk that reminds me God is like my father in a profoundly greater way than I can even say.

In our skeptical age, nonbelievers often think that God is a projection; the concept of God is rooted in something we know from the concrete world written big in our imaginations. We are anxious to be reminded that we can really know God and say something meaningful about him. Thomas was more anxious to protect God's mystery and majesty. Even if God's imprint rests on the world, we cannot just measure my dad's wisdom against God's wisdom. It would not make sense to score my dad's wisdom a six and rate God's wisdom at sixty or six thousand. To put God on a scale is wrong, and to put God and my dad on the same scale is wrong. To contemporary eyes, it looks like Thomas is projecting an image of God from below, but he was doing the inverse, explaining the infinite God from above.

Analogy in the Christian Conversation

Analogy plays an important role in the history of theology. Thomas created a grand vision that pictured the revelation of God and the best human reasoning as fitting together snugly. This vision despite its grandeur did not win the day in the new universities. John Duns Scotus (c. 1266–1308) and others like him proved more popular. Scotus felt that theology had become intertwined in tedious and technical qualifications. Seeking a precision and clarity, he countered Thomas. He claimed our speech about God was univocal (an exact fit) and not analogical (like and unlike).

A crucial issue will illustrate what is at stake: the word (or network of words) "to-be." It seemed to some Thomas had it all figured out. God was the very source of "be-ing." Everything that has being derives it from God. God has being in a complete and absolute way; we share in being in an incomplete yet genuine way (analogy). Thomas's PowerPoint might have looked like this:

First, there is God who uniquely is.*

Then there is the class of all things who share in God's being.
Created beings like you, me, rocks, and possibly Martians

*Indeed, Thomas and those before him often say God is beyond being, since he does not fit our categories.

Scotus protested that the words *to be* apply to God and everything else in exactly the same way. His power point might appear like this:

> First, there is the category of existing things.
>
> Then there are all the existing things (things exhibiting be-ing), God, you, me, rocks, and maybe Martians

Theologians in Thomas's camp think that Scotus's view changes things radically in a few ways—and not for the better. God is now envisioned as one more actor or force among other forces. Even if he is mega powerful, he still belongs in the category of existing things. This was exactly what Thomas sought to avoid: he saw this as idolatry because it put God and creation on the same scale. Thomas thought God was like the architect whose touch left an imprint of the rational order on his creation. Thomas believed that God's reason was coded into the world's fabric and character. But for Scotus things were the way they were just because that's the way God had chosen them to be. The world was simply what God had chosen to do at that moment, not the creation that reflected the rational character of God. People following Scotus's approach tended to distinguish the various agents and spell out their unique contribution.[11] Are God and I both 50 percent responsible for my behavior?

Barth and Analogy

Some theologians inspired by Thomas, but not Thomas himself, developed analogy as a lens for viewing and speculating about the relationship between God and the world from below rather than from above. A thought experiment may help illustrate this (see figure 2.2). God is the very source of all beauty, making it and possessing it maximally. Humans may share in beauty-making in varying degrees. Regarding music, for example, we may picture Mozart sharing more of this with God than Eric Clapton (I, RLH, am the product of my age). Clapton would possess a greater quotient than Buddy Holly. Buddy Holly would share more of God's beauty-making quality than an amateur mandolin player. There is an alluring romantic quality to this mindset. Even the simple

---

11. In ch. 5 (see figure 5.1), we explain how God being part of the system leads to a competitive view of **agency** rather than a noncompetitive view, which better fits Christian theology.

musician can share in this God-given quality. The richness of God can be sensed in the world that he infuses and fashions.

A problem arises when we attempt to reverse the process and work from the world back to God. For example, we admire some feature of the world and then conclude that this quality belongs perfectly to God. This makes for *natural theology*, where we move from our observation in nature to draw a conclusion about God (a theology from below). Karl Barth adamantly rejected this approach. Such reasoning was not just executed poorly, it was fundamentally wrongheaded. Though seemingly an overstatement for effect, Barth maintained his absolute "no" to natural theology. Barth claimed that natural theology was idolatry—perhaps in slow motion. We end in fashioning a God in our own image. We see what we like in creation and propose that God is like what we like. It follows that God likes us for likening what he likes. Before it is all done, we are sure that we are like God and he is like us.

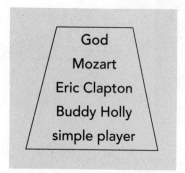

FIGURE 2.2
Hierarchy of Musical Creativity

This was Barth's theological explanation for the Christian affiliation with Nazism. The Nazis created a God who was like them. When we remember that Barth lived among the brown shirts of the Nazis, we can be a little more patient with him. He first protested that his liberal professors surrendered to national interest before World War I and then witnessed a demonic religion displace Christianity afterward. He sought to expose the wicked racism and cultural elitism upon which Nazi theology rested. Stripped of his Jewishness, Jesus was recast in the imagery of folkloric Germanic ancestors. They believed the Jews had to be dealt with because they could pass for white and weaken the race. Other races, deviants, and "the retarded" would also be exterminated or subjugated in due time. Barth showed us that a common Christian conviction can take on a sinister tone—we become like what we worship. This is the high price of treasonous idolatry.

An ironic contrast emerges between these two theologians on analogy:

- Thomas insisted upon analogy to prevent overly ambitious theologians from idolatrously describing God in human terms.
- Barth vigorously rejected analogy because he saw it as the tool for idolatrous theologizing toward a demonic idol-making and self-worship.

Barth later proposed a proper analogy in theology. He believed we cannot start with nature and then approach God; we must begin with God's revelation and then reason analogously toward insights about creation (a theology from above). For example, we cannot start with a human definition of human personhood and then question whether Jesus is a person. We should begin with the revelation that Jesus is a person and ask if we are genuinely human persons.

Analogy and Metaphor

We not only speak by analogy but also employ **metaphor**. Both protect the mystery of God. Metaphor is commonly understood as a poetic yet somewhat careless (or overstated) way of speaking, secondary to straightforward literal speech. This understanding shows up when pastors and theologians give preference to the "real theology" found in the logical argumentation of the New Testament letters, leaving the narratives in the Gospels or the Old Testament for children in Sunday school. Of course, both are part of God's revelation, so we need to do more work to recover the role of narrative in theology. As a result, we will pay attention to the orienting Story of the Bible (Doctrine) as we explore the various doctrines (or topics of theology).

Analogy and metaphor speak even more directly to our understanding of God. We can speak confidently about God while we maintain a necessary and healthy sense of mystery. We should never think our description of God's character is so complete that we could predict what God would do in every circumstance. An illustration from marriage may help. I (RLH) have studied my wife. Jokingly we call it Debbie-ology. I know her better than anyone else. Sometimes I know what she wants for dinner before she does. Yet there are moments when she spectacularly surprises me. I am not claiming that God is merely human or capricious. Knowing God, however, is like knowing a person, a reality that is more vibrant and alive than a set of ideas. Wonderfully, the God of Jesus Christ is known and knows with the dynamic qualities of personhood. The living, vibrant God is trustworthy and dependable but not predictable. Sending his Son to reclaim the world is consistent with his character but not required by some external logic. It is right to think of knowing him and trusting him.

Both Story and God's identity, which are shaped by analogy, bring us to a pair of theological terms: *economia* and *theologia*. *Economia* is the story of God's act, and *theologia* is our contemplation of God's divine identity. God's being and God's act are distinctly bound together, and our engagement of the two is reciprocal (see figure 2.3).[12] We will unavoidably theologize (think cogently about who God is) about the basic story and history of what God is doing (*economia*). *Theologia* depends and reflects on *economia*. We fail if theologizing strays too far from the God-given narrative, or if we do not think carefully about the narrative God has given us.

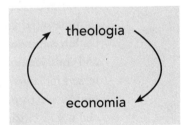

FIGURE 2.3
Theologia and *Economia*

Accordingly, we affirm that we can have true and reliable knowledge about God, but his infinite nature and our finite perspective mean that we must approach the whole task with humility. This theological humility goes hand in hand with an **apophatic** approach to theology that considers how God's infinite realities cannot be fully grasped by our finite

---

12. In the next chapter we will discuss the Trinity, and we will see how *economia* and *theologia* map directly to ideas of the economic Trinity (God as we know him through his acts in history) and the immanent Trinity (God as we know him outside of time).

understanding. In this way, we can sometimes more easily describe what God does not do or is not than to describe these things positively. That said, we are not left without resources to have a **cataphatic** approach to theology, making direct and substantive claims about God. We focus on developing theology using the narrative of the Bible, not just individual facts accumulated from the Bible. So we know some things with more certainty than we know other things. The idea of "orthodox" theology includes both the essentials (the things we are sure of) and the nonessentials (things that Christians debate). To speak of orthodoxy is to focus on things that are true, but it also relates to things that are false, "heterodox" theology. (Sometimes this latter category is termed "heresy.")

The word *orthodoxy* often leads our minds to the idea of certainty, but this is where central place of metaphor, analogy, and narrative come into play through another *-dox* word: paradox. Christian theology and practice are often situated in paradox. Among several key theological ideas, paradox is central: God is three persons with each sharing one nature; Christ is one person but with two natures; Scripture is both fully God's Word and fully human words; the kingdom of God is both here and not here. Mystery and paradox stand at the center of each. Thus our exploration of orthodoxy is fundamentally an exploration of the mysteries, paradoxes, and God (who is beyond being) engaging this world.

CONTEMPORARY THEOLOGICAL RELEVANCE

We have set out an approach to theology that attempts to balance the concerns of great theologians like Aquinas and Barth. We are not just talking about ideas but encountering the infinite God. Weighing the sources of Scripture, tradition, reason, and experience to understand God's activity is not a simple mathematical process or algorithm. The church continues to grapple with these issues. So now we turn to raise questions, debates, and considerations that impact the practice of theology. These brief discussions are only teasers for larger, more complex debates. As you consider your responses by engaging the sources and through discussion, you are embodying the reality that theology is practiced and not just inculcated.

All Truth Is God's Truth

Though theology seems to be a narrow topic, historically Christians have viewed theology from a more universal perspective. Since God created the whole world and all knowledge, theology is in some way related to everything concerning knowledge of the world. In fact, this is why theology was called the "queen of the sciences" and why Christians continue to propagate universities. All truth about the world is God's truth and therefore open for Christian investigation. Many agree when considering this macro-level perspective, but complications arise when some propose (potentially) competing models of truth. What if the different sources of theology appear to reach different conclusions?

How does the corruption from evil in the world influence the idea of coherence between all forms of truth? Is there knowledge we should not pursue?

All Things Equally True?

There is a dilemma related to the idea that "all truth is God's truth." Namely, are all true things equally true? For instance, we have used the language of *essentials* and *nonessentials* to distinguish between the central and peripheral aspects of Christian theology. Are the essentials more true than the nonessentials? Some people confuse the topic of truth with the idea of certainty. If something is true, they argue, we should be able to be certain about it. However, given our focus on analogy and mystery in our approach to theology, we have to recognize that while truth exists, we cannot have absolute mastery of knowledge because we are finite beings speaking about an infinite God. The confusion of truth and certainty can lead in two directions: (1) everything in theology is essential, or (2) nothing in theology is essential. We tend to associate the former with fundamentalism, and the latter with **postmodernism**. How should we understand the relationship of truth and certainty, of essential and nonessential? How can we know, for example, if one religion is more true than another?

Can Theology Change?

In addition to questions about the association of truth and certainty, some talk about "timeless truth." If theology is associated with a pursuit of truth, does that mean theology has an unchanging or timeless quality? Does theology always lead to dead orthodoxy rather than a living tradition? Should theology change? Should different settings produce different theologies? Appeals to timeless truth are often based in modernist rationalism in which the universal was always preferred over the particular, the objective over the subjective. But if experience is a part of developing and shaping theology, then theology must take on an embodied character. Theology should have differences because of human experience. How much should the different sources of theology shape theology? How does one include experience without letting it dominate?

Doing Theology in a Secular Age

The central tenets of Christian theology were developed in the patristic and medieval/Byzantine eras. People in those timeframes held an "enchanted," or supernatural, worldview. In contrast, most today, at least those in the modern West, think of the world in mechanistic terms, running unaided according to the laws of nature. The modern Western "disenchanted" worldview has expunged the active role of God and other spiritual agents, such as angels and demons. This move toward disenchantment, along with a pluralistic environment, has led to what is called a secular age.[13]

---

13. For a good but brief introduction on these issues, see James K. A. Smith, *How (Not) to Be Secular: Reading*

How do **secularism** and **pluralism** influence the context and practice of theology? Is it possible to do authentic Christian theology when even Christians do not hold an enchanted and mysterious worldview like that of the biblical authors and early Christian theologians? How can one embrace nonsecular approaches to theology?

Further Issues

- **Faith, Mystery, and Doubt.** What place should doubt and mystery have in Christian theology? Does your view on whether theology should change influence your position?

- **Theology from Above and Below.** The perceived dispute between Aquinas and Barth relates to the possibility of a theology from below (natural theology) or the exclusivity of theology from above (revealed theology). How should these theologies relate to one another? For natural theology, how do we avoid creating God in our image? For revealed theology, how do we balance God's acts in creation with his acts of new creation?

- **The Theology of Narrative.** Why did God give us such a challenging book like the Bible? We might imagine that God would have given us a small handbook with clear propositions and an exhaustive index. What does this strange book say about God or how we might know him?

PRACTICING THE FAITH

The previous section expressed the ongoing debates and discussions related to the practice of theology. This section suggests how theology may be relevant to your personal and communal faith journey. Accordingly, we address the heart and hands here, not only the head. We encourage you to practice theology in this holistic manner since the goal of Christianity is a lived-out faith.

Believing That versus Believing In

The first step in one's engagement with theology is also one that characterizes the whole path, and that first step, as in the Nicene Creed, is faith: "We believe." Faith distinguishes theology from other academic pursuits. Other disciplines include the first aspect of faith—"We believe *that*." We believe that water is composed of two hydrogen atoms and one oxygen atom, or we believe that the purpose of a business is to maximize shareholder wealth. Likewise, a basic premise of Christian theology is we believe that God exists. However, Karl Barth called out the fundamental problem with limiting theology to the traditional standards of academic practice. This makes God an object of study, someone we stand over and control using certain methods. Theology, he argued,

---

Charles Taylor (Grand Rapids: Eerdmans, 2014). For the more detailed engagement, see Charles Taylor, *A Secular Age* (Cambridge: Belknap, 2007).

is an engagement with a person. God is the subject of theology, the person who calls and encounters us. We are called not only to believe *that* God exists but also to believe *in* God, to enter into a posture and disposition of trust and surrender. You might believe (as knowledge) that eating vegetables makes you healthy, but it is not until you actually eat them regularly that you commit yourself to that reality. The latter is real faith. Therefore, the best context to study theology is not a classroom but a community of faith and worship.

Theology and Practice

When you study theology, the discussion seems to devolve into abstract terms like *Trinity* and *begottenness*. It's easy to have your brain shut off, like when you see an algebraic equation like this: $(a + b)^3 = a^3 + b^3 + 3a^2b + 3ab^2$. Perhaps, however, theology is closer at hand than we think. My (BCB) son attended a Montessori school for several years, and one of the key principles there is to take children from the concrete to the abstract. One of the manipulatives (objects for the students to use and put together) is a binomial cube: it is a collection of multicolored and multishaped blocks that, when put together properly, forms a cube. Children from early preschool ages are just getting the colored blocks to fit together to form the cube. They don't know it, but the cube illustrates physically the outcomes of $(a + b)^2 = a^2 + b^2 + 2ab$ and $(a + b)^3 = a^3 + b^3 + 3a^2b + 3ab^2$. At a young age, children figure out how it works with physical materials, and they are introduced to the algebraic theory many years later. This is the way Christianity works. We're like children playing with blocks. We do not begin by learning the depths of who God is, but our lives are shaped by God's act and revelation as Father, Son, and Spirit. Look deeply at the language and practice of the church, and you will likely be surprised at how much the Trinity infuses prayer, worship, and preaching. We do not just develop theology and then practice it; our practices teach us theology.

Abiding in Scripture

If Scripture is the central source of theology, then there is no substitute to immersing yourself in the Bible, not just to accumulate facts but to understand the Story. There are numerous practices for engaging the Bible (reading, memory, prayer, etc.) through a variety of means (using apps, books, devotionals, etc.). The accessibility of the Bible on our phones tricks us into thinking we can always get to it when we need it. But hearing the voice of God through Scripture is more like retirement savings, you have to make regular deposits over a long period of time to get the great payoff.

Embracing Tradition

With modern and postmodern influences, the idea of giving place to the community and to tradition is seen as the worst possible way to be "authentic." If we agree that the Spirit can speak through teachers today, then we should affirm that he has been speaking throughout history as well, and tradition is the cumulative witness to Spirit's voice in history. We miss the riches of God's work by ignoring the cumulative voice of ecumenical tradition, especially the Nicene Creed. New Testament scholar Luke Timothy Johnson writes regarding the use of the creed:

> In a world that celebrates individuality, they [Christians] are actually doing something together. In an age that avoids commitment, they pledge themselves to a set of convictions and thereby to each other. In a culture that rewards novelty and creativity, they use words written long ago. In a society where accepted wisdom changes by the minute, they claim that some truths are so critical that they must be repeated over and over again. In a throwaway, consumerist world, they accept, preserve, and continue tradition. Reciting the creed at worship is thus a countercultural act.[14]

One of the best ways to engage theology is to learn the creed and what it means.

Further Issues

- **Embracing the Story.** Given that narrative and poetry are by far the largest portion of the Old and New Testaments, how might you better appropriate narrative to develop and shape your understanding of Christian theology? What do you learn of God and his ways through these (often messy) narratives? How might you explore **typology** more fully in your reading of the Bible?
- **Signs and Symbols of the Kingdom.** Theology is embodied in signs and symbols, analogies and metaphors. What space do you make for signs of God's reality? The ancient temple was full of imagery to aid in worship. How do you pursue beauty in worship and in life? Might you consider other signs and imagery that point to his role in your life, such as a tattoo? Is a tattoo with a Christian theme an appropriate sign or image for today?
- **Sacraments and Mystery.** The term *sacrament* originates from the Greek word for "mystery." The Eastern Orthodox Church continues to refer to the sacraments as "divine mysteries." As embodied metaphors of theology, communicating different layers of reality simultaneously, these practices provide an opportunity for living out theology.

As we conclude, we remember that the practice of theology is not simply about mastering ideas, but about engaging God and understanding his ways in the world. With Barth and Aquinas we are doing theology from above rather than a theology from below. Accordingly, as we consider the different sources of theology, we cannot mechanistically combine them to achieve certainty. Rather, in order to know God, we patiently explore

---

14. Luke Timothy Johnson, *The Creed: What Christians Believe and Why It Matters* (New York: Image, 2005), 40–41.

each source in community so that we can be confident about the essentials of faith while allowing for diversity with regard to the nonessentials.

CLOSING PRAYER

Eternal God, who enriched your Church with the learning and holiness of your servant Thomas Aquinas: give to all who seek you a humble mind and a pure heart that they may know your Son Jesus Christ as the way, the truth, and the life; who is alive and reigns with you, in the unity of the Holy Spirit, one God, now and for ever.[15]

---

15. *Common Worship: Daily Prayer* (London: Church House Publishing, 2005), 452.

CHAPTER 3

Trinity
Father, Son, and Holy Spirit

INTRODUCTION

When people find out I (RLH) teach theology, they often ask if it is hard because so many people don't believe in God. The challenge is not so much the atheists (or polytheists) but those who believe in a generic or hybrid god of Western culture. It is difficult to teach people who think they already know god that the Christian God is different. Since theology is ultimately telling a story about God, this chapter, and the whole book really, asks: Who is this God? Is there a god, the god, many gods, or no god? At the core of the Christian understanding of God is the teaching that there is one God who is Father, Son, and Spirit. This is captured in the core structure of the Nicene Creed, a statement of faith that unites all the major Christian traditions:

> We believe in one God, the Father, the Almighty . . .
> We believe in one Lord, Jesus Christ, the only Son of God . . .
> We believe in the Holy Spirit, the Lord, the giver of life . . .

Exploring the identity of the biblical God pertains to all of Christian history, but it came to a head in the fourth century with the monk (and later bishop) Athanasius of Alexandria and his defense of the theology expressed in the creed from Nicaea (a city in Asia Minor, modern Turkey).

ATHANASIUS AND THE STORY OF NICAEA

The city of Alexandria in Egypt was spectacular. It was a commercial center with two ports which facilitated export of the Egyptian grain on which the Roman Empire depended. It was also one of the anchors of Christianity in the ancient world. Christians engaged a spirited and culturally diverse city, an intellectual center that boasted a library of 500,000 scrolls (a collection that Christians have been falsely and fraudulently accused of burning). A venerable bishop in Alexandria named Alexander took notice of a young boy for his devotion and intelligence. The old bishop helped raise and educate the boy who later became his secretary and eventually followed him as bishop. The boy's name was Athanasius. His enemies called him the "black dwarf." Talk of his dark skin and his speaking the Coptic language lead us to think he was a Copt, an ancient North African ethnic group.

In the first decade of the fourth century, the Roman Empire subjected Christians to a cruel persecution. But when the Roman leader Constantine gained power over part of the empire, he worked to ease the legal burden of Christians, and he pushed for the religious toleration granted in the Edict of Milan in AD 313. Inspired by some sort of Christian vision, his army secured his rule over the entire Roman Empire. Apparently, the emperor embraced Christianity. Early in his reign (AD 325), he gathered the bishops of the church to address an in-house feud that began in Alexandria.

The Clash and Nicaea

The feud likely began when Arius, a young pastor under the bishop Alexander, was troubled by the bishop speaking of Jesus in such exalted terms. For Arius, speaking so highly of the Son's deity compromised the deity of God the Father. His instincts prompted him to protect the Father's divine status. According to Arius, the Father alone was eternal, beyond suffering, changeless, and unoriginated, not the Son. Arius created chants or songs to counter the teaching of his bishop. The dispute gripped the city. Riots broke out. Shoppers complained they could not buy fish without a theological argument. The bishop Alexander called a conference that ruled in his favor, but Arius found refuge under the protection of another bishop. Soon the whole empire was roused—the dispute had "gone viral."

In response, Emperor Constantine welcomed more than two hundred bishops from churches across the empire to Nicaea in AD 325 to settle this dispute. The bishops presenting Arius's side could have taken a defensive posture. Instead they declared Arius's teaching with unapologetic boldness, and their strategy backfired. The other bishops booed and would not let them proceed. An interesting story, or legend, may fit here: a bishop you have heard about your whole life supposedly punched Arius in the face—ole Saint Nicholas. In a way it was over as soon as it began because the assembly quickly recognized Arius's teaching as deprecating Jesus and demoting his identity as Son of God.

It is important to note that everyone in the conversation was devoted to Scripture. They read and employed it differently, but all appealed to passages that strengthened their conclusion. Arius pointed to passages where Jesus served and showed deference to the Father, arguing that the lesser serves the greater. The pro-Nicaeans appealed to passages that declared the Son's divine status. The decision to use nonbiblical terms like **homoousion** (as we describe below) to nail down biblical interpretations was bold and controversial. But if the Bible's terms were being disputed, then another set of terms were necessary for clarification.

For the next two months the bishops negotiated this matter and numerous others that demanded attention. The challenge was to fashion a statement most bishops could embrace but that excluded Arius's depreciation of Jesus's status and bond with the Father. At the risk of oversimplification, Arius used God's timelessness and immutability to view his fatherhood, whereas Nicaea used the Son's **revelation** of God to view his father-hood—an inherently Trinitarian idea.

Picturing Jesus with a lesser rank was not uncommon, but Arius went too far when he declared the Son had a completely *different nature* than the Father. The council responded with a knockout term: *homoousion*. This Greek term, used in construction and philosophy, means "of the same nature, out of the same stuff." The term has a good deal of flexibility. "Build a porch for my house out of the same stuff" could mean several things: use the same kind of brick, use identical brick, take brick from the back and use it for the new porch (use the exact same brick). What *homoousion* cannot mean is the Son has a different make up or nature than the Father. The Nicene Creed was signed by all but two bishops. Nicaea's statement corrects Arius at every turn, but most of the bishops were somewhere between the camps of Arius and Athanasius. Ultimately, the creed argues that the Son is 100 percent God; whatever God is, the Son has 100 percent of that.

What Does Begotten (or Generated) Mean?

The theological debate between Arius and Athanasius is really about how to interpret the Bible. One of the key biblical affirmations about Jesus is that he is the "only begotten Son" of the Father (John 3:16). ("Begotten" is a King James Bible word, so many theologians use the more modern term "generated.") "To beget" means to father a child, and thus it describes here a Father-Son relationship. When this biblical language is used, two elements might be emphasized: (1) a son shares the same nature as his father, and (2) a son has a beginning when he was born. The term can mean either or both. With *homoousion* the orthodox position emphasizes the first (same nature) since the **Trinity** has eternally existed, whereas **subordinationists** like Arius emphasize the second (has a beginning).

Drama after Nicaea

Sadly, the Council of Nicaea did not settle things. The controversy raged for more than four decades. Folks loyal to Arius were theologically and politically shrewd. A string of emperors just wanted a workable resolution. The fortunes of the debate between the Arians and the Nicaeans went back and forth—usually due to the emperor's disposition. Several times it seemed like the Arians had won.

In AD 328 Alexander died, and Athanasius was selected to take his place. In 336 Arius died, and others took up his cause. In time a compromise term, *homoiousion* (instead of *homoousion*), was proposed. Emperors and many others wanted Athanasius to give his blessing to this new term, meaning "of similar nature." Now Athanasius was on the hot seat, but he would not compromise. He was exiled five times, being forced to leave his post and city for a third of his years as bishop. He spent time in hiding, time among the monks. Once he even went west toward Rome. These exiles worked to his favor as he made strong alliances with monks and powerful friends in the West.

Monk or Punk?

Athanasius fought for the Nicaean cause. Like almost everyone in his day, his tactics were suspicious: people used violence on his behalf; he likely manipulated grain shipments going to the empire; he disciplined people severely. Drama and mischief aside, he was a person of great devotion. His most famous book, *Life of Anthony*, opened the life of this champion of spiritual warfare, Anthony the Great, for the larger world to see. Athanasius spent one of his exiles among the monks in the desert wilderness. He admired the monks, and they admired him because he lived a remarkable life of discipline in the midst of the city.

Despite banishments and hardships, Athanasius held out for Nicaea's verdict. Look closely—there is only one (Greek) letter distinguishing the disputed terms: *homoousion* (Nicaea) vs. *homoiousion* (compromise term). His tenacity is popularly thought to inspire the old expression, "There is not one iota's difference between . . ." Some see Athanasius as a stubborn man who refused to unite the church under a reasonable compromise. Others see him as discerning and wise. He sought to protect not only the status of the Son but the unity of God. If the Son was one kind of God, and the Father was another kind, he feared Christianity would be recast as another Mediterranean (polytheistic) religion.

True Worship and Salvation at Stake

Athanasius's position, with its biblical foundation, was rooted in the language of the church's worship and theology of salvation. In worship, the language of the Trinity was pervasive, and Christians had authentic experiences of God by worshiping Jesus. This worship of Jesus that unites us with God reflects the church's understanding of salvation. For Athanasius, God the Father was beyond the created world, and God's act of creation was a sign of his love and desire to share his being. Though the world suffered a gone-wrong-ness, God once again acted in love: the Father sent the Son into creation to restore it. God created the world, so it had to be God who re-created it. The Son had entered the corrupted world and established a solidarity with us so that we can enter into communion with God. Someone other than God cannot unite us with God. We are united with God the Father through the Son by the Spirit; our salvation and worship rest on the mystery of God's unity as Trinity. After a lifetime of struggle, Athanasius's instincts were eventually received as the theological legacy of the church.

THE TRINITY: WHAT DOES IT MEAN?

The Basics

In light of God revealing himself to us, we come to the term *Trinity*, which is derived from the term "threeness." With the Trinity we think in terms of the threeness of the one God and have to acknowledge that God is beyond our categories. There is mystery to this God. Mystery is not a riddle; riddles are solved when an apparent problem is resolved by an alert insight. Neither is mystery irrational nonsense. We are not saying three is the same value as one, or one is three. Mystery seeks to protect what is unveiled. Accordingly, when Christians are asked *what* God is, we answer, "God is one, he has a unity about him." But, when asked *who* God is, we answer, "God is three; he is Father, Son, and Holy Spirit."[1] In short, we define the Trinity in this way:

> God eternally exists as three persons—Father, Son, and Holy Spirit—who each equally share one divine nature.

Christians cannot tell their story without recourse to Father, Son, and Spirit. A creating Father God sends his Son among his Jewish people to reclaim his gone-wrong world. The Son (full of the Spirit) lives among us and bears this gone-wrong-ness with us and for us. Ultimately, he is crucified, raised from the dead, and ascends to heaven. The Spirit descends in power to encourage and empower the church in the ongoing work of the Father's mission. Christianity is unavoidably Trinitarian. In short, *the Father is Creator, the Son is Savior, and the Spirit is Completer.* Or from another angle, life is *from the Father, through the Son, and by the Spirit.* Father, Son, and Holy Spirit are equally God working together. This confession grows out of a careful and close reading of the Bible and is found in the DNA of the early church.

Trinity Is Rooted in the Bible

The idea of the Trinity was refined and developed through the centuries, but the concept was not invented by fourth century theologians. Trinity talk (though not the word "Trinity") pervades the Bible. So Trinity is not a foreign idea we read into the Bible but an interpretive outlook we embrace from the Bible itself. We arrive at this perspective by trusting the earliest believers whose voices in the Bible give witness to God's progressive self-revelation through his acts in the world. Theologians call this perspective, which focuses on God's act in history, the economic view of the Trinity, or the **economic Trinity** (for short).[2]

From the very start of the Bible, God is the main character: "In the beginning God

---

1. Roger E. Olson, *The Mosaic of Christian Belief: Twenty Centuries of Unity & Diversity* (Downers Grove, IL: IVP Academic, 2002), 227.

2. The term *economic* comes from the Greek term for the "world," so this is a focus on God's engagement with the world.

created the heavens and the earth" (Gen 1:1).[3] At the same time, the inclusion of humanity is central to creation, and the rest of the biblical story is an account of human beings and God interacting. This interaction climaxes through God's work in Jesus and the Holy Spirit, and this threefold act and self-revelation of God as Father, Son, and Holy Spirit in the biblical narrative will be our focus here.

Old Testament

Though God's story climaxes in the New Testament, it begins in the Old Testament. There we see how the creator God **covenanted** with the Jewish people in order to bless them and the whole world in accordance with his creational intentions to bless and give life. A key example of this is when God appears to Moses and the Jewish people as he redeems them from Egypt. The nature and identity of the Jewish God is unique within the ancient Mediterranean context. He is "Yahweh" (the LORD).[4] This name is associated with the Hebrew word "to be"—reflecting his personal pronouncement "I AM WHO I AM" (Exod 3:14)—but is not limited by that term. This redeeming God is not merely one regional God among many; he is the only God. At the same time, the focus is that he is a personal God, not just a distant figure.

IS "GOD" HIS NAME?

"God" is just a generic term for the divine. Much like the term "human," it doesn't signify much by itself. For instance if I said, "I'm married to Human, and we have two children named Human and Human," that doesn't tell you much. It matters that we have the specific revelation of God's identity as Yahweh, whom we later more fully understand as Father, Son, and Holy Spirit.

Yahweh covenants with his people, and we find a summary of the key aspects of the covenant in the Ten Commandments. These first two commandments reinforce a **monotheistic** faith in light of the **polytheism** that surrounded the Jews:

I am the LORD [Yahweh] your God, who brought you out of Egypt, out of the land of slavery.

You shall have no other gods before me.
You shall not make for yourself an image [idol]. (Exod 20:2–4)

---

3. This active God is no Aristotelean "unmoved mover."
4. This name Yahweh is not pronounced among Jews, in order to follow the third commandment (Exod 20:7), so in the Old Testament where the Hebrew has written "Yahweh," Hebrew readers say "Adonai" (Lord), and English Bibles use "the LORD" (in small caps) to distinguish it from the more generic term *lord*, or master.

Faith in Yahweh was not merely an ascent to a set of ideas but a commitment of allegiance, a way of life. Faith (commandment 1) and practice (commandment 2) go hand in hand. This intersection between a monotheistic faith and loving obedience is reiterated in the Shema, a confession of faith Jewish people recite to this day: "Hear [*shema*], O Israel: Yahweh [the LORD] is our God, Yahweh alone. You shall love Yahweh your God with all your heart, and with all your soul, and with all your might" (Deut 6:4–5 NRSV; cf. Mark 12:28–34). This combination of faith and practice—orthodoxy and orthopraxy—is what undergirds our whole book.

Yahweh is the focus of the Old Testament, but we see glimpses beyond his singular identity. Christian writers have highlighted the following in light of the New Testament:

- Plural pronouns for God (Gen 1:26; 3:22; 11:5–8).
- An elevated, semidivine king or lord (Ps 110:1; Isa 9:6; Dan 7:9–13).
- Personified divine figures—the Spirit (Gen 1:2; Isa 48:16; 63:10; Ezek 36–37) and Wisdom (Prov 1:20–33; 8:1–9:6).

However, without the perspective of the New Testament, one is hard-pressed to see multiple persons as part of God's identity in the Old Testament. Though New Testament writers find more complexity in the identity of God, they always affirm that the God of the New Testament is identical to the God of the Old Testament. Yahweh is just progressively revealing more of himself.

New Testament

Like the Old Testament, the New Testament emphasizes the creating, covenanting, and saving work of God. Since there is only one God, the God acting in and through Jesus and the Spirit is none other than Yahweh, the Lord. For example, Jesus names the Shema, which affirms God's unique identity and the need to love him alone, as the interpretive key for the whole Bible (Mark 12:28–34). The apostle Paul also utilizes the **monotheism** of the Shema to argue against the idolatry and polytheism of the Greeks (1 Cor 8). However, Paul's interpretive move reveals the Trinitarian thrust of the New Testament: God alone is not mentioned; now Jesus is also incorporated into the description of God's work using the language of the Shema: "There is but *one God*, the Father, from whom are all things and for whom we live, and *one Lord*, Jesus Christ, through whom are all things and through whom we live" (1 Cor 8:6; cf. 1 Tim 2:5–6). This inclusion of Jesus within the divine identity provides initiative for a Trinitarian interpretation of the whole New Testament (cf. Phil 2:5–11; Col 1:15–20). Of course, once a sense of plurality is considered within God's identity, the continual distinction of the Spirit along with the Father and Son creates space for seeing the Spirit as a coequal person rather than a metaphor of God's action.

The early Christian community had a direct and distinct experience with Jesus Christ and with the Holy Spirit. The direct encounter of the person of Jesus is without question.

The question is whether this person was God **incarnate**. When we think of the church's encounter with the Holy Spirit, the question reverses. They knew their encounter with the Holy Spirit was an encounter with God, but was the Spirit a distinct person? The book of Acts points to the direct and doctrinally formative experience of the Spirit. At Pentecost, which was the first Jewish festival after Jesus's resurrection, the disciples had a profound (and public) experience of the divine Spirit (Acts 2). Later, when a group of gentiles experienced the Spirit (Acts 10), this helped the early Jewish Christians realize that the experience of God was not limited to those who were Jewish and those who followed **Torah**.

> ### KEY BIBLICAL PASSAGES
> Passages throughout the New Testament show the triune nature of the Christian experience. Read these and see how formative God's interaction as Father, Son, and Holy Spirit serves to shape early Christian faith and practice:
>
> - Matt 28:19–20
> - Mark 1:9–11
> - 1 Cor 2:1–4
> - 1 Cor 6:11
> - 1 Cor 12:3–6
> - 2 Cor 1:21–22
> - 2 Cor 13:14
> - Gal 4:4–7
> - Eph 1:1–14
> - 1 Pet 1:2
> - 1 John 4:2–3
> - 1 John 4:13–15

The early church's theology of the Trinity and their practice of worship mutually reinforce one another. This is evident in baptism, both Jesus's baptism (Matt 3:13–17) and that of believers (Matt 28:19–20). In Matthew 28 Jesus gives commands to the church to make disciples and "baptize them in the name [notice the singular noun] of the Father, and of the Son, and of the Holy Spirit" (v. 19). Of course, this experience of God as Father, Son, and Spirit had room for further exploration and description. The next few centuries were especially formative in this development.

Historical Development
Second to Fourth Centuries
Arising from the church's experience with and worship of God, the language of the Trinity is imprinted upon the hymns, creeds, and rituals of the early church. Notice the Trinitarian prayer of Polycarp, a bishop in what is now Turkey and a "rock star" of the early church. Taught by the apostle John, the eighty-six-year-old Polycarp faced death rather than deny Christ. Before he was killed he said, "I glorify you, through the eternal and heavenly high priest, Jesus Christ, your beloved Son, through whom be glory to you, with him and the Holy Spirit, both now and for the ages to come."[5]

---

5. The Martyrdom of Polycarp 14.3 (c. AD 167), in *The Apostolic Fathers*, ed. Michael W. Holmes, 3rd ed. (Grand Rapids: Baker, 2007).

The Trinitarian foundation is evident in the **rule of faith**, a narrative summary of Christian belief. Representing a common perspective, versions circulated in the second and early third centuries by Irenaeus (from modern-day Turkey and later France), Tertullian (North Africa), and Origen (Egypt). These three fathers hold distinct perspectives and come from different regions, yet they each teach this summary of doctrine with very little variation. Each version is Trinitarian, showing the widespread and early Trinitarian orientation of the early church. Read Irenaeus's version:

> This then is the order of our faith, and the foundation of the building, and the edifice and the support of our conduct: God, the Father, uncreated, uncontainable, invisible; one God, the Creator of all: this is the first article of our faith. And the second article: The Word of God, Son of God, Christ Jesus our Lord, who was revealed by the prophets according to the character of their prophecy and according to the nature of the economies of the Father, by whom all things were made, and who, in the last times, to recapitulate all things, became a man amongst men, visible and palpable, in order to abolish death, to demonstrate life, and to effect communion between God and humanity. And the third article: The Holy Spirit, through whom the prophets prophesied and the patriarchs learnt the things of God and the righteous were led in the path of righteousness, and who, in the last times, was poured out in a new fashion upon the human race renewing humanity, throughout the world, to God.[6]

Around this core tradition there was much diversity in terminology and perspective. In the fourth century greater precision would come, as we will now see.

Two Councils and the Creed: Nicaea (AD 325) and Constantinople (AD 381)

The Council of Nicaea (AD 325) clarified the relationship between the Father and the Son and ruled that the Father and Son have the same nature (they are *homoousion*).[7] The unity between the Father and the Son was central to the unfolding logic of the Trinity and, therefore, the Bible. The Council of Constantinople (AD 381), strongly influenced by the Cappadocians, further refined our doctrinal understanding. The term *Cappadocians* refers to three men from Cappadocia, in modern-day Turkey: Basil the Great, Gregory of Nazianzus, and Gregory of Nyssa. These friends were recognized as great scholars and people of profound devotion. Basil and Gregory of Nyssa were indebted to the spiritual influence of their sister, Macrina.

---

6. St. Irenaeus of Lyons, *On the Apostolic Preaching*, trans. John Behr (Crestwood, NY: St. Vladimir's Seminary Press, 1997), 143.

7. There have been a variety of local, regional, and ecumenical councils in the history of the church. At these councils, bishops gathered to discuss items and help settle theological disputes. In a retrospective manner, Nicaea was proclaimed the first ecumenical council.

The Cappadocians' influence was felt in the Council of Constantinople in several ways. First, they championed the central verdict of Nicaea: the Son was of the same nature as the Father. Second, they clarified the language that Constantinople employed. They stipulated that terms like ***ousia*** referred to God's substance or nature (answering the "what" question) and that the term ***hypostasis*** referred to the identity of the Father, Son, and Spirit or persons (answering the "who" question). This clarity was a great step forward for later interpretations and discussions concerning the Trinity. Third, the Cappadocians extended the logic about the Son to the Spirit. Constantinople revised the statement issued at the Council of Nicaea, exploring further the Spirit's work on earth. In fact, the creed that many recite each Sunday in worship is actually the Nicene statement as reworked by the Council of Constantinople. The Trinitarian structure of the Nicene Creed[8] is unmistakable:

> We believe in one God, the Father, the Almighty,
> maker of heaven and earth, of all that is, seen and unseen.
>
> We believe in one Lord, Jesus Christ, the only Son of God,
> eternally begotten of the Father,
> God from God, Light from Light,
> true God from true God,
> begotten, not made, of one Being [*homoousios*, "consubtantial"] with the Father;
> through him all things were made.
> For us and for our salvation
> he came down from heaven,
> was incarnate from the Holy Spirit and the Virgin Mary
> and became truly human.
> For our sake he was crucified under Pontius Pilate;
> he suffered death and was buried.
> On the third day he rose again
> in accordance with the Scriptures;
> he ascended into heaven
> and is seated at the right hand of the Father.
> He will come again in glory to judge the living and the dead, and his kingdom
>   will have no end.
>
> We believe in the Holy Spirit, the Lord, the giver of life,
> who proceeds from the Father [and the Son],

8. Technically, this is the Niceno-Constantinopolitan Creed. See also the *Apostles' Creed* and the so-called *Athanasian Creed*. This translation is drawn from the ecumenical texts project at English Language Liturgical Consultation, "Praying Together," 1998. *English Language Liturgical Consultation*. www.englishtexts.org/ (August 10, 2013).

who with the Father and the Son is worshiped and glorified,
who has spoken through the prophets.
We believe in one holy catholic and apostolic Church.
We acknowledge one baptism for the forgiveness of sins.
We look for the resurrection of the dead,
and the life of the world to come. Amen

Note how 90 percent of the creed addresses the acts of God and only about 10 percent covers philosophical statements about unity. The creed is much more interested in the Story of the Bible and only incorporates philosophy in order to clarify how to read the Story rightly. Nature (*ousia*) speaks to oneness, and person/subsistence (*hypostasis*) speaks to threeness. We are not able to discern fundamental distinctions between the three persons since they share one activity and one will. The creed focuses on their relationships drawn from biblical language without attempting to clarify the nuances: the Son is *begotten* of (or generated by) the Father eternally, and the Spirit *proceeds* from the Father.

TRINITARIAN TERMS

English	Greek	Latin
essence / substance / nature (the what)	*ousia*	*essentia / substantia*
person / subsistence (the who)	*hypostasis / prosopon*	*persona*
of the same stuff	*homoousion*	*consubstantia*
mutual indwelling / interpenetration	*perichoresis*	*circuminsessio*

What Did the Fathers Determine?

The debates and refinements by these church fathers helped shape our understanding and interpretation of the Bible. Just as the church has affirmed some things about God, they have rejected other explanations. They wisely (we think they were guided by the Spirit) avoided some misunderstandings and misappropriations of key ideas.

Trinity Is Not Tritheism

From the beginning the church rejected any notion of tritheism (three distinct gods). We can hardly find an actual believer advocating the three gods named Father, Son, and Spirit because the church was decisively rooted in the monotheistic Hebrew (Old Testament) tradition that saw God as one.

Trinity Is Not Modalism

Similarly, the church rejected the approach called **modalism** or *Sabellianism (see figure 3.1)*. Sabellius, an early third-century theologian, proposed that God is not three distinct persons; the Father, Son, and Spirit were merely modes, or roles, that the one real God as *one person* took on during the drama of salvation. For modalism, think of a single ancient actor playing three different parts in three successive acts of a play. A mask would allow God to appear as different roles (or modes): as Father for the first part of the drama, later as Son, and finally as Spirit. This teaching sought to guard against polytheism by emphasizing Christianity's monotheistic roots: a supreme God is the one, true, ruling God or monarch (a version theologians call *modalistic monarchianism*). Since modalists did not adequately distinguish Father, Son, and Spirit, critics thought they insulted the Father by implying he could suffer just like the Son (patripassionism). In addition, modalism does not do justice to the Scriptures, which show the interaction and relationship between Father, Son, and Spirit at the same time (e.g., Jesus's baptism and Gethsemane). Perhaps more important is the recognition that modalism's God remains unknown and unrevealed because he only appears in modes or behind masks. The church, however, believed God truly exists as three distinct (though not separate) persons who truly engage believers.

Trinity Is Not Subordinationism

The church also rejected **subordinationism** (see figure 3.2), but it was even more challenging. This approach to the Trinity, sometimes called a *dynamic monarchianism*, pictures the Father as the "full octane God"—the monarch—and the Son as a lesser and different god (a semidivine being) who serves his Father.[9] And the Spirit is an even lesser god. *Arianism* is the most well-known form of subordinationism. This protected the one supreme God, the Father, from suffering (leaving that to the Son). According to this view, the Bible pictured the Son as a dutiful servant to the Father in a world where the weak or lesser served the strong or greater. Recall Athanasius's story, which reveals how the church came to see that Arius's approach was insufficient. A different god (the Son, according to Arius) could not fully unite us with the real God (the Father). Additionally, the church's experience of God in the worship of Jesus was too authentic to overlook. By ruling out subordinationism the church avoided the ancient religious idea of a lineup of gods possessing varying levels of purity and potency.

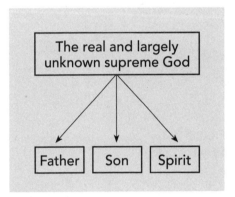

FIGURE 3.1
Modalism

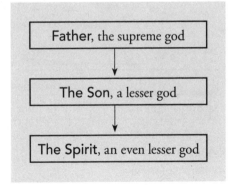

FIGURE 3.2
Subordinationism

---

9. A more radical version of subordinationism is an "adoptionist" view of Jesus, which holds that he was merely a good man who was later considered to be called (or become) divine.

One of the key questions revealed by these debates is this: How much does God's action in the world (**economic Trinity**) reveal the eternal nature of God (**immanent**, or ontological, **Trinity**)?[10] Modalism affirms that God's actions are disconnected from his (eternal) identity by placing the immanent over the economic, whereas subordinationism affirms that the actions of the three persons are essentially connected to their three distinct identities by placing the economic over the immanent. Trinitarianism, as we noted earlier, affirms a mystery. It holds a balance between God's eternal identity (the immanent Trinity) and his action as Father, Son, and Spirit (the economic Trinity) rather than placing them in competition. God acting in the world does not limit God to the created and temporal sphere. This tension between the economic and immanent perspectives is captured in the image commonly called the Shield of Faith (see figure 3.3).

Since the three persons share one nature, they are inseparable, but the church looked to biblical language to help describe what distinguishes the three: the Father generates, the Son is generated (or begotten) from the Father, and the Spirit proceeds from the Father.[11] Though affirming this distinction, theologians have consistently asserted that we cannot achieve a more fundamental explanation than the distinctions offer. We are left with mystery. The Bible does not focus on the static image of figure 3.3 (representing the immanent Trinity), as helpful as that image is, but rather the Bible narrates the Story of God acting in the world (the economic Trinity). Thus, in figure 3.4, we see how the timeless God engages the world, and we come to know God best through the missions of the Son in his **incarnation** and of the Spirit as in Pentecost.[12]

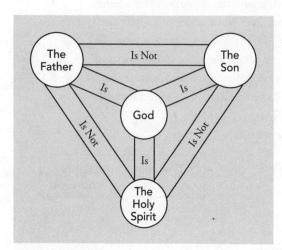

FIGURE 3.3
Shield of Faith

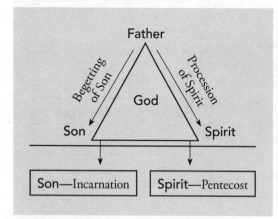

FIGURE 3.4
Trinitarian Missions

---

10. By distinguishing between the immanent Trinity and the economic Trinity, we are not saying there are two trinities, but rather two perspectives on understanding the Trinity.

11. See chs. 6 and 7 for more discussion on these issues.

12. Figure 3.4 is drawn and adapted from Fred Sanders, *The Deep Things of God: How the Trinity Changes Everything*, 2nd ed. (Wheaton, IL: Crossway, 2017), 65–66.

Key Contemporary Moves

The basic agreement reached by the patristic church has held throughout the centuries. Of course, ideas about God were not static over this time, as we can see from the shift in emphasis from the divine nature to the divine will in the late **Middle Ages**. Contemporary views of God have been highly influenced by the seventeenth-century "Enlightenment." The title captures the movement's attempt to break away from what they considered crude religions and social institutions that inhibit the free and independent thinking of individuals. The light of reason would lead to progress and prosperity. Religion was seen as a dangerous threat to the way forward because people cling to religious traditions with irrational zeal and will believe crude or wildly speculative ideas like the Trinity. They argued that traditional notions of god needed to be abandoned or revised to allow a peaceful and moral future.

The great truncation of the Christian God arising out of the Enlightenment was called "**deism**." Deism pictures God like an old clockmaker who keeps his distance from his handiwork after he sets it in motion. Deism served as a halfway house to atheism; one could hold to the idea of a self-sufficient and self-operational world and still hold on to the idea of a God who rewards genuine morality after the world runs its course.

In this climate the Trinity was stifled. An evolutionary model of religion dominated in the West: Crude understandings of many gods (**polytheism**) gave way to peoples showing loyalty to their own God (henotheism), and this gave way to the superior idea of a single God (**monotheism**). Lower forms of monotheism then evolved when crude distinctive teachings of Judaism, Christianity, and Islam gave way to a few ideas that formed a common generic God—a sort of God of the least common denominator. This generic God served as a civically acceptable God for the modern nation-state. The nation-state was a big enough umbrella to allow many different religions to coexist under a single flag. The Trinity, if affirmed at all, had been relegated to a private religious matter, subservient to the generic notion of one "God" under which the nation stands.

The voices in the debates about God in the contemporary period are too numerous to detail, so we note two key figures that serve as a window to wider perspectives: Friedrich Schleiermacher and Karl Barth.

Friedrich Schleiermacher (1768–1834) is commonly known as the father of modern liberal theology. His book *The Christian Faith* is one of the most influential in modern Christianity. He thought that the doctrines of theology were a secondary expression of the genuine heart of religion. Real piety rests in the experience, feeling, or the awareness we have before God—the consciousness of our absolute dependence before God. He argued that many doctrines were important as outward expressions of this essential experience, even if they were untrue. Traditionally, interpreters believed Schleiermacher did little to incorporate the Trinity. He did not treat the Trinity until the conclusion of his book, reinforcing the idea that the Trinity is a speculative thought experiment that has little to do with real life. Whether Schleiermacher intended this or not, many readers thought he had neglected the teaching. Overemphasizing personal experience, liberals and conservatives alike often minimize the Trinity.

Karl Barth (1886–1968) was the most important theologian of the last century. He broke from his liberal training which had been influenced by the work of Schleiermacher and others. He wrote six million words dedicated to leading the church back to the triune God, whom he believed was revealed in Jesus, the Word. Although he explores a variety of perspectives on Trinitarian themes, the Trinity is everywhere present in Barth's work. He notably places the doctrine at the very beginning rather than the end. Rather than starting with the human experience of (a deistic) God, Barth begins with God's action in the world as seen in Christ and the Holy Spirit. His influence, along with the rediscovery of some Roman Catholic and Orthodox theologians, has led to a resounding rediscovery of the Trinity in our own day. Our book celebrates this approach.

SIMPLE RULES FOR RIGHT THINKING

The "Athanasian Creed," a mislabeled statement from the fifth or sixth century, offers two rules for avoiding Trinitarian heresy: (1) do not "confuse the persons" or (2) "divide the essence." As with (1), confusing the distinctive persons may lead to modalism (one real God posing as more). As with (2), abandoning the unity of God may lead to subordinationism (several gods ranked beneath a supreme God).[13] A variety of Trinitarian approaches seek to abide by these two rules.

Main Approaches to Trinitarianism

As the shift between Schleiermacher and Barth shows, views about God are not static. We provide here a taxonomy of three main approaches to the Trinity:[14]

FIGURE 3.5: MAIN APPROACHES TO TRINITARIANISM

Title	Advocates	Summary
Traditional Trinitarian approach	Augustine, Thomas Aquinas	One God is also three persons
Approaches avoiding "persons"	Barth, Rahner	The one personal God existent as Father, Son, and Spirit
The social (or relational) Trinity	Moltmann, Gunton	Three persons who are one God

13. Richard J. Plantinga, Thomas R. Thompson, and Matthew D. Lundberg, *An Introduction to Christian Theology* (New York: Cambridge University Press, 2010), 131.

14. Amended from Plantinga, Thompson, and Lundberg, *An Introduction to Christian Theology*, 130–40.

Traditional Trinitarian Approach

Augustine and Thomas represent classical Western Trinitarian theory. They rely upon the tradition that God is simple. God is not a composite thing to be taken apart; instead, he is one character all the way through. Thinking of God as essentially simple presents a challenge in affirming the three persons. Thomas follows Augustine in offering a restricted and abstract understanding of person. The persons are not centers of consciousness. The Son is not a separate God who is generated; the Spirit is not a separate God who is breathed out. Father, Son, and Spirit are called relations (not relationships) seeking to avoid misspeaking of three beings instead of one.[15]

Approaches Avoiding Persons

Karl Barth and Karl Rahner are pioneers in the Trinitarian revival. The Father, Son, and Spirit are at the heart of all they say about God. Trinity is not just the way God reveals himself; it is his nature. They avoid the word *person* because modern people unavoidably think of persons as independent self-directed agents (more like tritheism). Though they adamantly reject modalism, they recommend the language of *modes* and *manners* of being (following some patristic use) instead of *persons*, and they struggle not to be seen as modalists by some who consider them "neomodal."

The Social Trinity

Social Trinitarians like Jürgen Moltmann affirm that the Father, Son, and Spirit are persons who are capable of relationships pictured in the New Testament. They struggle to maintain the unity of the Trinity, appealing more often to *perichoresis* (the mutual indwelling or interpenetration of the members of the Trinity) rather than an abstract shared nature. Each person is present and shares the work of the other persons. The unity of God is protected in the shared identity, work, and love of the persons.

These debates show that affirming orthodox boundaries does not stamp out ongoing debates about theology!

Simplifying the Trinity?

Numerous theologians, the great Augustine for example, have offered analogies for the Trinity. The following analogies are common:

- Woman that is a daughter, a mother, and a sister
- *H2O* as water, ice, and steam
- Three people sitting around a table
- An egg with yoke, egg white, and shell
- Fire, light, and heat

---

15. Denys Turner, *Thomas Aquinas: A Portrait* (New Haven, CT: Yale University Press, 2014), 126.

- Mind as remembering, understanding, and loving
- Three notes in a chord
- Three leaf clover

Each analogy has strengths and weaknesses. If you push any one of these analogies to their logical ends, they actually end up supporting one of the heretical positions! Analogies may help, but they can never capture the mystery of our infinite God. There is no created being analogous to God.[16] In addition to analogies, many have found the pictorial representation of Andrei Rublev's icon of the Trinity helpful for capturing elements of the nature and identity of God.

A. H. Strong captures the key ideas in a simple acrostic:[17]

TRIUNE

T Three recognized as God
R Regarded as three distinct persons
I Immanent and eternal, not merely economical or temporal
U United in essence
N No inequality
E Explains all other doctrines yet itself inscrutable (i.e., mysterious)

Where Do We Get in the End?

We began with mystery, and it is important to return there. As the saying goes, "Truth is often stranger than fiction." God is more complex and interesting than we ever imagined, and this is just the first chapter in our exploration of his interaction with us and the world! As a short summary of the Trinitarian doctrine, we return to this:

God eternally exists as three persons—Father, Son, and Holy Spirit—who each equally share one divine nature.

In this we affirm both unity and distinction: God is one in nature, three in persons (or we might say, "one what, three whos"). Each person is fully and truly God. We spoke before of how the Father generates, the Son is generated (or begotten), and the Spirit proceeds. These important distinctions related to the immanent Trinity (how God exists timelessly outside creation) arise from biblical passages (e.g., John 3:16; 15:26), but it is important to note that the Bible predominantly presents the economic Trinity (how God engages the world and thus reveals himself through his actions). In the Story of the Bible,

---

16. Google "St. Patrick's Bad Analogies." You won't be sorry.
17. Augustus Hopkins Strong, *Systematic Theology: A Compendium* (Valley Forge, PA: Judson, 1907), 304–52, as cited in Roger E. Olson, *The Mosaic of Christian Belief: Twenty Centuries of Unity and Diversity*, 2nd ed. (Downers Grove, IL: InterVarsity Press, 2016), 141.

the Father creates and covenants, the Son saves and redeems, and the Spirit sanctifies and completes.[18] It is not that each person acts independently; rather, the Father acts through the Son by the Holy Spirit.

ECONOMIC TRINITY:
> The Father is Creator
>> The Son is Savior
>>> The Spirit is Completer

If you get lost in the technical details, return to the biblical story and attend to the way God reveals himself as he engages the world. We will explore his character and nature throughout this book, but it is in the biblical story that we see his love, his holiness, his power, and ultimately his willingness to suffer death to bring restoration to a broken world. This is the God we worship and obey.

CONTEMPORARY THEOLOGICAL RELEVANCE

Having explored key ideas related to the doctrine of the Trinity, now we will explore a limited number of areas where this doctrine relates to wider issues in the contemporary world and church.

The Trinity and Christian Identity

As we noted before, theology is ultimately telling a story about God (Greek: *theos*), so the question before us is this: Who is God? Is there a god, the god, many gods, or no god? By affirming faith in God, Christians are distinct from agnostic and atheist belief systems. However, one of the dangers in theology is assuming that we all share an understanding of God. When you hear the word "God," what comes to mind? For example, when the president says, "God bless America," who is this "God"? Do we all worship the same God?

Of course, when we talk about the Trinity, we are affirming something very specific and particular about the God of Christianity. This raises the question of what other religions might fit within that *Christian* understanding of God. That is, how big is our Trinitarian tent?

Protestant, Catholic, and Orthodox Agreement?

Do Protestant, Catholic, and Orthodox Christians believe in and worship the same God? The answer is yes! All three explicitly or implicitly affirm the doctrine of God expressed in the Nicene Creed. Not only do the Catholic and Orthodox traditions affirm

---

18. Stanley J. Grenz, *Created for Community: Connecting Christian Belief with Christian Living*, 2nd ed. (Grand Rapids: Baker, 1998), 46.

the Nicene Creed, but it forms an essential part of their **liturgy**. Some Protestants formally affirm the Creed whereas others affirm its doctrines without attributing special authority to it. What unites all these Christians is a common hope in the Father's act to save us through Jesus Christ by the Holy Spirit. Beyond this unity, other questions arise: Are there distinct views of God among Christian traditions? Should there be? How should a common view of the Trinity influence **ecumenical** discussions?

The Trinity and Other Christian Traditions

In the history of Christianity several movements have arisen that developed a separate identity from the traditional views found in Nicaea. Each of these groups explicitly affirm doctrinal positions at odds with a Nicene faith:

- **Unitarians**, generally influenced by the Enlightenment, are defined by their denial of the Trinity. They affirm that there is only one God with no distinctions.
- **Jehovah's Witnesses** affirm a subordinationist position very similar to Arianism. Jesus is not to be identified as Jehovah God in an ultimate sense but only in a limited or even metaphorical sense. The Son was created, they argue, and is also known as Michael the Archangel.
- **Mormonism** affirms the united Godhead consisting of three persons—Heavenly Father, the Son, and the Holy Ghost. This divine unity, however, is balanced by a belief that exalted humans will later achieve a similar form of deity as the Father and Jesus have, and thus divinity is not founded upon an absolute Creator-creature distinction. In distinction to Trinitarian theology, Mormons hold that the Father and Son have physical bodies, but the Holy Ghost exists immaterially.
- **United (or Oneness) Pentecostals**, a minority position within worldwide Pentecostalism,[19] affirm a position very similar to the modalist position we described, in that the Father is identical in nature *and person* with both the Son and the Spirit.

While there are other practices and beliefs that separate these groups from orthodox Christianity, it is ultimately their ascription of a different nature of God that makes them heterodox. While they use terms like *God* and *Jesus*, their understanding of what those terms mean deviates from historical Christianity and the biblical evidence.

Does this really matter? The identity of God is the most foundational aspect of a religion. Compare this to a wedding: the specific person you are marrying is important. I (BCB) am married to Heather, not Sarah or Jessica. Just because all three are *humans* doesn't mean I'm equally connected to them. Likewise, all those called "God" are not really the God who has revealed himself in the Bible. We should be charitable to all those who are members of these religions, while also understanding the differences that

---

19. Please note that the large majority of worldwide Pentecostals affirm the orthodoxy of Nicaea.

exist at this core level. How much should the doctrine of the Trinity influence Christian engagement with these other groups?

The Trinity and Other Religions

In an age of **pluralism**, differences between religions are often seen as irrelevant window dressing. Many follow a path of inclusivism, accepting all forms of religion as revealing something about the truth of the divine. Based on that idea, one might ask: Is the Trinity the same as Allah or Shivah or Zeus? So as not to repeat what we cover in the later chapters about the specific approaches to the divine in other religions,[20] we will focus here on the question of religious pluralism. Christianity (and Judaism) arose in an era of prevalent polytheism, and much in the Bible distinguishes its monotheism from other faiths. In fact, throughout the Old and New Testaments, idolatry (worship of other gods) is repeatedly condemned. As Paul critiques idolatry in Acts 17, he also presents a model of rapprochement between Christianity and other views by showing how Christianity, even though centered on Christ, relates to some of the same desires as other faiths. In that way, Paul modeled charitable engagement while holding to the exclusivity of God as revealed in Christ (and the Spirit).

The nature of Christian engagement will be different with explicitly monotheistic faiths like Islam and Judaism versus other Eastern religions like Hinduism or Buddhism.[21] In these discussions, the word *God* becomes even more vacuous in meaning since each of these religions means something radically different. We must not assume there is shared meaning because we are using a generic word for the divine; rather, we must explore the nature and identity of the god(s) being worshiped. While we will find many fundamental distinctions between Christianity and these other faiths, this should not preclude charitable engagement with others. We will explore those similarities and differences as we progress through this book.

How fundamental is the different view of God between different religions? How much does the doctrine of the Trinity separate Christianity from these other religions? Is the Trinity the same as Allah or Shivah or Zeus? Can we replace "God" with "Jesus" or "Allah" in the phrase "In God We Trust"?

Old Testament versus New Testament?

When we consider the Bible, how should we understand the seemingly diverse portrayal of God in the Old Testament and the New Testament? Some heterodox Christian groups (**Gnostics** and Marcionites in the second century) argued that there are literally two (or more) Gods—the creator God of the Old Testament, who judges in righteousness, and the (most high) God of the New Testament, who saves through mercy and forgiveness.

---

20. See especially ch. 5.
21. With regard to Hinduism, some propose a general correlation between the Trinity as Father, Son, and Holy Spirit and the Hindu Trimurti of Brahma, Vishnu, and Shiva, but the parallel is tenuous since deity in Hinduism is not constituted by oneness and threeness.

Of course, if Christians are monotheists, as we say we are, we believe that the one God reveals himself in both testaments. But even more importantly in light of the Trinity, the picture of Jesus we read about in the New Testament is not a separate identity from the God revealed in the Old Testament. In fact, the Trinitarian rule of faith that we find in Irenaeus (see above) is actually an introduction to how to read and understand the *Old* Testament. That is, he argues that you cannot read the Old Testament properly without having the Trinity as the key for understanding it, and so Jesus is not a separate picture of God.

As to the issue of judgment versus love that might distinguish the Old Testament from the New Testament, we see in places like Exodus 20:4–6 and 34:5–8 that the primary emphasis in the Old Testament is actually on God's loving nature rather than his judgment. We will explore this more directly in the eschatology chapter, but let us note here that we see love and judgment in the Old Testament and love and judgment in the New Testament. What changes is that the Old Testament is more communal and focused on the present, whereas the New Testament emphasizes the individual and focuses on the future (especially as it relates to judgment). Accordingly, the God revealed through Jesus is no different than the God we see as Yahweh in the Old Testament. How and why does God appear to reveal himself differently in the Old and New Testaments? How does this diversity relate to monotheism?

Further Issues

These issues about the nature of God in religious dialogue and the relevance of the Trinity only scratch the surface of how the Trinity relates to theology. In fact, our supposition is that all of Christian theology is founded on and influenced by God as Trinity, so the rest of the book will reflect this foundational doctrine. However, we list here topics that have specifically been debated with regard to the Trinity:

- **Love and Wrath.** When we consider the Son dying on the cross, to what extent is this a representation of the Father's love or an appeasement of the Father's wrath?
- **Gender.** To what extent should we understand God as gendered? For example, what should we think about the female representation of God in books like *The Shack*?
- **Faith and Revelation.** How much revelation about (or understanding of) God as Trinity is necessary to be Christian?
- **Image of God.** To what extent does the doctrine of the Trinity influence the idea that humans are in the "**image of God**" (Gen 1:26–28)?
- **Theosis.** In the Eastern Orthodox and Roman Catholic traditions, believers are so transformed in their experience of union with God that they are said to be "gods" (metaphorically), with the result that salvation can be described as **theosis** or deification. Why would they say that this does not impinge on the doctrine of the Trinity?[22]

---

22. We discuss this further in ch. 9.

PRACTICING THE FAITH

Dorothy Sayers, alluding to the Athanasian Creed, writes: "The Father is incomprehensible, the Son incomprehensible, and the whole thing incomprehensible. Something put in by theologians to make it more difficult—nothing to do with daily life or ethics."[23] While theological discussion of the Trinity can make the relevance of the doctrine seem speculative and irrelevant, the nature of the God we believe in is as important as the individual personality of the person we might marry. Though we might not often discuss the Trinity in our church settings in such direct ways, our experience of and faith in God as Father, Son, and Spirit is essential to each area of life and worship. For this reason, New Testament scholar Luke Timothy Johnson writes:

> The revelation of God through Jesus Christ and the Holy Spirit draws us into the mystery of God's own life. And since the goal of salvation and sanctification is to give humans a share in that life, the mystery of the trinity also reveals something of who we are and what we are called to reveal within creation.[24]

With this in mind, let's consider how the Trinity impacts our spiritual life.

Trinity and the God We Think We Know

The Trinity is foundational because it makes sense of everything else. The story of the Bible is that the triune God is approachable. Let's compare: If there are many gods, life is likely quite complicated. You struggle to appease these gods with their conflicting and arbitrary demands. Life is filled with ritual, superstitious coping. By contrast if god is an abstract principle like the philosopher Aristotle envisioned, then god has better things to do, such as pondering himself, than to be concerned with us. The Trinity makes sense of our faith experience; we do not meet a cacophony of competing voices nor an abstract disinterested god. The Trinity makes sense of a God who approaches us and welcomes us to approach him.

The Trinity, therefore, makes sense of the declaration that "God is love." A Trinitarian God has relationships in a way a modalist God cannot. At the heart of the triune God one finds love and mutual service. This God is capable of a relationship. This God cares and chooses to create for the sake of love. This Trinitarian God of love reaches out to us, particularly through Christ and the Holy Spirit, and we are called to respond to that embrace. Will you embrace the study of theology and practice of faith as an engagement with a person not just a set of ideas? How would that change your approach?

---

23. Dorothy L. Sayers, "The Dogma Is in the Drama," in *Whimsical Christian: 18 Essays by Dorothy L. Sayers* (New York: Collier, 1987), 25, as cited in Michael F. Bird, *Evangelical Theology: A Biblical and Systematic Introduction* (Grand Rapids: Zondervan, 2013), 94.
24. Luke Timothy Johnson, *The Creed: What Christians Believe and Why It Matters* (New York: Image, 2005), 134.

Destiny, Not Distraction: What Were We Made For?

A folksy story might help illustrate the influence of the Trinity. Imagine a young boy who spends his summer vacation on his grandparents' farm. His days are a strange mixture of routines and bigger-than-life adventures with farm equipment and animals. A long, late evening meal is a fixed part of the schedule. The meal features a lot of food and a lot of time for the boy to tell stories to appreciative listeners. At the close of the meal, everyone helps to clean up. Eventually Granddad takes his place on the front porch swing. Grandma soon joins him, and after a while they grow silent. Even the talkative boy senses that he should be silent as well. The silence is strangely satisfying, not in the least bit empty or wanting. This man and woman have lived full lives; they have made and kept promises, shared lives, raised children, and built the farm. The boy can sense how complete and beautiful the silence is. His grandparents are content just being with one another—enjoying presence, commemorating connection. This rich communion of love is palatable. The boy can sense it. Even as a child he decides that he would like to find this kind of communion. He wants to belong, to be united. Without a word he stands before them, backs up, and wedges himself between them. They happily make room. In this moment the boy feels more at home than ever before. Ancient Christians thought they would one day be admitted into the loving fellowship of the Holy Trinity (like the grandson being welcomed into the bond of love shared by his grandparents). Their destiny, their salvation was to experience the God who is love.[25] How should communion with God shape your practice of theology?

Christian Identity and Prayer

The Christian's loving relationship with God is the foundation of our identity as adopted sons and daughters of the *Father*, established by the *Son*, and through the presence of the *Spirit* (Rom 8:14–17; Gal 4:4–7; 1 John 3:1–3).[26] Jesus invites his followers to share in his status as Son, though he will always be the only unique Son. Prayer is an invitation here and now to share in the life of the Trinity. Jesus taught his followers to pray (Matt 6:9–13; Luke 11:1–4) and to relate to God as "our Father." We close our prayers with the phrase, "in Jesus's name." As we pray to the Father, we are participating in the Son's invitation to share in his status and relationship with the Father (John 17:21). And we pray with confidence that the Spirit assists our praying and even intercedes beyond what we understand (Rom 8:26–27). The work of the Son and Spirit allows us access to the Father (Eph 2:18). Yet we can also pray to the Son or the Spirit. The Jesus Prayer, for example, is an act of devotion and soul shaping, as many Christians across time and space have prayed, "Lord Jesus Christ, Son of God, have mercy upon me a

---

25. Adapted from Basil Pennington, *Call to the Center: The Gospel's Invitation to Deeper Prayer* (New York: New City, 2003), ch. 15. I reemploy his story which addressed contemplative prayer.

26. Keith L. Johnson, *Theology as Discipleship* (Downers Grove, IL: InterVarsity Press, 2015), 55–60.

sinner." Likewise, many pray, "Come, Holy Spirit," in hopeful expectation of his filling presence. Whether one recognizes it or not, the routines of Christian prayer require a working theory of the Trinity.

Christoformity as Theoformity

To be a follower of Jesus is to be his disciple. The heart of discipleship is really just being an apprentice, following the pattern of one who has mastered something. It is being transformed so that we live, act, and think like God as we are Jesus's apprentices. That is, we are being transformed into the image of God. If Jesus is the embodiment of God, then becoming like Jesus (christoformity) is becoming like God (theoformity). The New Testament frames discipleship as dying and rising with Christ. The Gospel of Mark, for example, on three occasions explains the nature of Jesus's role as the suffering **Messiah** and the way disciples should embody his suffering (8:27–9:1; 9:31–37; 10:32–45). Likewise, Paul encourages believers to live out Christ's narrative of death and life (e.g., Rom 6:1–4; 2 Cor 3–4; Phil 2:5–11). As we draw closer to God, we will look more like him. The New Testament consistently repeats the image that God, as embodied in Jesus, died and was raised for us and our salvation. We become like a sword put into a fire: it remains steel but it glows red and burns like the fire. As we are united with the triune God, we remain human but are transformed to be like him as we share in his life. In the West, this is often described as "union with Christ," whereas in the East they use the language of theosis (or deification).[27] How might you follow the divine pattern of Christ's obedient suffering?

Further Considerations

Since the identity of the persons of God is so important to the nature of our relationship with him, the spiritual formation implications are as wide and deep as God himself. We have only scratched the surface here. Let us suggest a few additional topics to consider as you continue to reflect:

- **Ten Commandments.** Luther, in his *Treatise on Good Works*, argues that all the commandments our founded on the first: "You shall have no other gods before me." The hope of virtue expressed in the commandments is only possible through faith in God.
- **Baptism.** In baptism we mark our union with God, the presence of the Spirit (Acts 2:38), and dying and rising with Christ (Rom 6:1–4).
- **Communion.** Through the Spirit, the bread and wine/juice embody the presence of Christ, and we experience the grace of God in unity with one another.

---

27. Since becoming like Christ is becoming like God, christosis is theosis.

- **Church Unity.** In 1 Corinthians 1–3, Paul founds the church unity that God desires on the people of the Spirit who are willing to embrace the cross of Christ (cf. 1 Cor 12:4–6).
- **Iconography.** Consider images like that of Andrei Rublev's *Trinity* or the Shield of Faith as a source of reflection about God's identity and work in the world.

The doctrine of the Trinity is not just philosophical speculation; rather, it is an affirmation that we encounter the one God in a threefold manner in the Bible. Since God is threefold, all of theology will be shaped by our encounter with the Father, Son, and Spirit, as the Nicene Creed encourages us to confess and practice. As Paul blessed the Corinthian community "May the grace of the Lord Jesus Christ, and the love of God, and the fellowship of the Holy Spirit be with you all" (2 Cor 13:14).

CLOSING PRAYER

Almighty and everlasting God, you have given to us your servants grace, by the confession of a true faith, to acknowledge the glory of the eternal Trinity, and in the power of your divine Majesty to worship the Unity: Keep us steadfast in this faith and worship, and bring us at last to see you in your one and eternal glory, O Father; who with the Son and the Holy Spirit live and reign, one God, for ever and ever. Amen.[28]

---

28. Prayer for the First Sunday after Pentecost: Trinity Sunday, in "Collects: Contemporary," *The (Online) Book of Common Prayer*, Episcopal Church (New York: Church Hymnal Corporation, 2007), www.bcponline.org/ Collects/seasonsc.html.

CHAPTER 4

Revelation

God Reveals Himself

INTRODUCTION

When we talk about **revelation**, we are talking about the act of God and not the book of the Bible titled Revelation. But the two terms are connected. The Greek term *apocalypse* means a "revelation" or "unveiling" of truth (like the visions John received in the book of Revelation). The doctrine of revelation considers how God has unveiled truth about himself and the world as it relates to him.

Since revelation is about God making himself known, it thus connects to the doctrine of the Trinity. However, we often first think of God making his will known to us as we consider important questions that arise from our personal experience and interests in flourishing: Whom should I marry? What job should I take? But when we think in terms of revelation, we need to think of God first, not ourselves. Revelation reveals God and his plan, not our personal destiny. As we learned in the previous chapter, God's identity as Father, Son, and Holy Spirit is greater and more mysterious than any of the categories and ideas that we create. Yet he wants to be known, so revelation (an unveiling) bridges the gap between the infinite God and our finite experience.

This chapter and the next serve as a pair because they delve into the ideas of how God interacts with the world. The present chapter talks about how God communicates with us (revelation), and the next chapter about how God interacts with us in other ways (God and the world). Christians do not always agree on how to make sense of the diverse biblical description of God's identity and action. Examining Irenaeus, an early Christian theologian, will give us a window into these issues.

Big Idea:
Revelation is the triune God making himself known through general acts in creation and special saving acts and writings.

Key Terms:
- General Revelation and Special Revelation
- Canon
- Inspiration
- Interpretation

Key Passages:
Exod 3:1–17; 34:1–7;
Pss 19:1–2; 105;
Acts 14:15–18; 17:22–34;
Rom 1:18–23;
1 Cor 15:1–42;
2 Tim 3:16–17;
Heb 1:1–4;
2 Pet 1:19–21

IRENAEUS: READING THE BIBLE LIKE A CHRISTIAN

Man of the Whole Church and the Whole Bible

Few particulars are known about Irenaeus (c. AD 140–202). He grew up in Smyrna (Asia Minor, modern-day Turkey). He studied theology in Rome and then ministered in Lyon (France). His life and theology span a great vista—from the East to the West, from creation to new creation. Since martyrdom was central to second-century Christian identity, he celebrated being taught by the famous Christian martyr Polycarp, who had been taught by the apostle John. The repression of the church also shaped his later life: brutal persecution erupted in Lyon (AD 177) when Irenaeus was in Rome appealing for unity and tolerance toward Eastern Christians who had distinct traditions. When he returned to Lyon, he learned that his bishop had been martyred. Irenaeus was called upon to take the bishop's office, which he occupied until AD 202 when it is likely that Irenaeus too was martyred.

Irenaeus's theology and ministry were oriented around story. Getting the story right meant getting salvation right. He believed God had revealed himself through the sweep of human history. His book *Demonstration of the Apostolic Teaching* (a long dormant text rediscovered last century in an Armenian translation) shows the Father overseeing his grand project. Irenaeus illustrates how the apostles demonstrated the truth of the Christian story through their interpretation of the Old Testament. A Christian reading of the Old Testament is guided by the outline of Christian teaching captured in the **rule of faith**:[1] the Father, Son, and Holy Spirit direct the Story from beginning to completion. Irenaeus held together the story of the Old and New Testaments, showing the continuity between God's work in creation and re-creation. God's **covenants** and promises to the Jewish patriarchs and prophets came together in Jesus and the work of the Spirit. Irenaeus recognized Jesus as the summation or recapitulation of Israel's story. Jesus faithfully recapped and relived the narratives of Adam and Israel.

Facing Disunity: Severed Bible and Church

Irenaeus's other surviving work is known by its famous shortened title, *Against Heresies*. In the work he argues against Gnostics and others (such as Marcion) across five books. **Gnosticism** dismissed and discounted the material world. In opposition to the orthodox conviction that the one true Father God created a good world, Gnostics believed that the evil world resulted from a weak or mean lower god. Gnostics thought that salvation required abandoning the concrete world. Their most high god had no desire for a concrete world. They pictured an otherworldly Jesus, who was a stranger to the Hebrew faith. Irenaeus countered Gnosticism by claiming that the Son and the Spirit were God's hands at work in the world; he believed that God was up to his elbows in the messy gone-wrong-ness of creation. For Irenaeus, the world was created good but

---

1. We quote a version of Irenaeus's rule of faith in ch. 3 and explore the idea more fully below.

was later corrupted by sin. The original good, though distorted, could still be seen, and creation was going to be fully made right. The Gnostic god cries, "It's a trick, get out of this evil mess—if you are one of the sophisticated elite." The orthodox God cries, "This is mine; trust me, I am making this right again."

COMMON ELEMENTS OF SECOND-CENTURY GNOSTIC SYSTEMS

The origin and history of Gnosticism is greatly disputed. Even the value of the term is challenged. J. N. D. Kelly wisely identified the common elements of the major Gnostic systems:

1. Gnostic schools embraced a moral and metaphysical **dualism** (a theory picturing two kinds of real things). Spiritual things that were regarded as inherently pure, while material things were seen as intrinsically evil.
2. The supreme reality or god is not the creator god. The material world resulted from the ignorance or mischievousness of a lower deity. Suggested culprits included a demiurge,[2] the Old Testament God, or Jesus (a lower-level god).
3. The true identity of persons resides in a spiritual or divine element. People are aliens in the evil material world and in their evil material bodies. Some Gnostics believed that only chosen ones had a spiritual element and were capable of escaping the evil material realm.
4. In successive aeons (or heavens), there have been a series of mediators who have helped people escape the evil material world.
5. Salvation involves liberating the authentic person or spiritual being from the evil material realm through knowledge.[3]

Putting the Pieces Back Together

In the ancient world, mosaics were created by an artist or workman and shipped to their destination with only a brief description of the image. The description would give the recipient a general sense of the mosaic's image—for example, the dark blue stones are the ocean water and belong in the bottom left. Even a recipient with little artistic flair could reassemble the stones and get the big picture right if they had the description as a guide. Today mosaics likely have numbered pieces and exact schematics to insure that the precise arrangement can be replicated when it is installed or reinstalled. Imagine the staggering variety of pictures you could create if you had no instructions at all. Irenaeus believed the rule of faith functioned like the ancient mosaic descriptions, giving interpreters the big picture of the Bible. Gnostics read the Bible with the intent to reconfigure

2. The "demiurge" is the creator or fashioner of the world.
3. J. N. D. Kelly, *Early Christian Doctrines* (New York: HarperCollins, 1978), 26.

the entire scope of the **Scriptures** and the identity of Jesus. Irenaeus compared them to crude workers who disassemble a mosaic of a noble king and reassemble the pieces to create a dog or a fox instead. Gnostic readers ignore the big picture and tediously twist, select, and supply images to recast the story. Reading the whole Bible in a Christian or Trinitarian fashion means reading by the rule of faith.

How did Irenaeus have such confidence that the rule of faith was the right picture? (1) Early church leaders had direct connections with the people Jesus had welcomed into his inner circle. Remember that Irenaeus's boyhood bishop knew the apostle John! The people following Jesus on earth for three years passed on his message and left written records of their encounter with him. It is a matter of publicly verifiable custody. Irenaeus's story makes more sense than later Gnostic claims that Jesus had a radically different identity and purpose that was only revealed secretly to others. (2) The rule of faith captures a summary of early Christian teaching from a broad and diverse group. (3) In the writings of the apostles, especially the letters of Paul and the four Gospels, we find the authentic revelation of God as Father, Son, and Spirit. Rather than using esoteric techniques to find hidden messages, Irenaeus encourages reading the Gospels as a continuation of the story from the Old Testament. The earliest leaders, informal doctrinal summaries, and writings all put the pieces together and come up with the same Jesus. In this case against the Gnostics, a memory device captures Irenaeus's three advantages with three Cs: (1) clergy, (2) creed, and (3) canon.

The temptation to separate creation from salvation or the Old Testament from the New Testament is still with us (as a latent Gnostic dualism). Have you heard someone ask why God seems so stern in the Old Testament and so kind in the New Testament? Irenaeus wisely instructs us to see salvation in terms of a restored creation because the big picture of the Bible is all the work of one God: the Father is Creator, the Son is Redeemer, and the Spirit is Completer. This correspondence of creation and salvation is what drives Christian thinking about revelation.

WHAT DOES *REVELATION* MEAN?

The church thinks in terms of two categories: **general revelation** with its focus on God's action in the created order and **special revelation** with its focus on God's saving acts. The categories are interrelated, as they come from the same God, but Christians have often treated special revelation as more foundational. Since general revelation is common to all, we will begin there.

General Revelation

General revelation is available to humanity in general. That is, the creational realities communicated are not limited to specific individuals (apostles and prophets) or to specific writings (holy Scriptures) but are available to all. Because God himself is the

Creator, we have, even if only partially, a revelation about God through nature (Ps 19:1–2; Rom 1:18–23; Acts 17:22–34), history (Ps 105; Acts 14:15–18), and reason (Prov 1:1–7). We might say that God's fingerprints are on his creation.

Theology derived from general revelation is called "natural theology," which we discussed as doing "theology from below" in chapter 2. Throughout church history, theologians have often recognized the harmony between natural theology and theology derived from special revelation, which is "theology from above." Yet some have seen them in opposition. In response to moves by Enlightenment thinkers to elevate the role of natural theology, special revelation has been emphasized over the last century.

Special Revelation

Special revelation concerns the ways that God makes himself known by specific action. As we consider the different forms of special revelation, we are indebted to a way of ordering things—the threefold Word of God. This order drawn from Martin Luther was redeployed by Karl Barth,[4] as he stood against overconfidence in natural theology. If our infinite God is greater, more mysterious, and different than us, then we need him to reveal himself to us. Our greatest thoughts about God are still finite. Apart from special revelation, they are just mental idols created in our image, which are no better than idols made of wood or stone.

Threefold Word of God

Revelation is ultimately about God's address to us: God unveils his identity, character, and nature. At the same time, this revelation is a call to respond to him. The term *Word* describes God's address. This Word spoken to us comes in different ways and in different levels of clarity. As explained below, we capture this diversity by envisioning three concentric circles—**incarnation**, **inspiration**, and **proclamation** (see figure 4.1). Each has its center in God's action; each is mediated by varied human means.

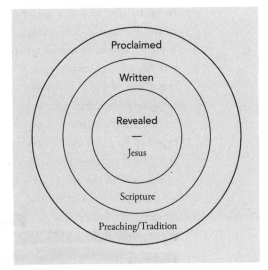

FIGURE 4.1
Threefold Word of God

Word of God Revealed: Jesus Christ

When considering the priority of revelation, the central location is not the Bible but Jesus Christ himself.[5] As we discussed in the chapter on the

---

4. See Karl Barth, *Church Dogmatics*, ed. G. W. Bromiley and T. F. Torrance, trans. G. W. Bromiley, 2nd ed. (Peabody, MA: Hendrickson, 2010 [1932]), I.1, §4.

5. Further consideration about God as revealed in Christ can be found in chs. 3 and 6, where we discuss the Trinity and Christology, respectively.

Trinity, Jesus is God, so whatever Jesus does is what God does. Jesus's action—of incarnation, ministry, death, and resurrection for us and for our salvation—reveals God most fully. It might seem a little odd to call a person "the Word" of God; however, this is just a way the Bible talks about how God has communicated himself to us. Hebrews 1:1–2 captures this sentiment: "In the past God spoke to our ancestors through the prophets at many times and in various ways, but in these last days he has spoken to us by his Son." Similarly, in the prologue to John's Gospel, John begins with the well-known affirmation about the Word, who is the Son of God: "In the beginning was the Word (*Logos*), and the Word was with God, and the Word was God" (John 1:1). Later he tells us, "The Word became flesh and made his dwelling among us" (John 1:14).

The revelation of God in Christ coheres with the written revelation in Scripture. But just as we would rather be with the person we are dating than just read a letter from them, the presence of God on earth demonstrates his heart for the world in a way writings could not. In other words, we could have Christianity without the Bible, but we could not have Christianity without Jesus. He is the center.

Word of God Written: The Bible

By affirming that the Bible is the written Word of God, we affirm that we hear God's voice in the texts of the Bible.[6] The theological term that captures this affirmation is **inspiration**. This term derives from 2 Timothy 3:16, which reads, "All Scripture is God-breathed [or "inspired"] and is useful for teaching, rebuking, correcting, and training in righteousness." Even though the letters, historical documents, poetry, and sermons found in the Bible are all written by human authors (using their language and personal writing style), these human words were inspired by God, so they can rightly be called the Word of God. Scripture is not just about God, it is a call from God to orient our lives in relationship with him.

We see the Trinity at play again but in a different way. Whereas God the Son is the primary focus of God's revelation in Jesus, God the Holy Spirit comes first when we consider Scripture. Throughout the Bible, the authors of Scripture attribute the writings to the work of the Spirit. For example, as the early disciples are praying in Acts 4:25, they introduce Psalm 2 by saying, "You spoke by the Holy Spirit through the mouth of your servant, our father David."[7] In fact, the term *inspiration* has a direct link to the Holy Spirit—notice the root of "in-*spirat*-ion."[8] Inspiration pictures the Spirit and the prophet not in competition but in cooperation.

---

6. The word *Bible* comes from the Greek word for book (*biblos*). To designate that this book is distinct from others, printers often add the term *Holy* as an adjective, making the title "Holy Bible."

7. Other passages that note the Holy Spirit's role are Acts 28:25; Heb 3:7; 10:15; 2 Pet 1:21.

8. This English linguistic connection is derived through the Latin. In Greek (the language of the New Testament), we can see the same connection. The term *pneuma* can mean wind, breath, or spirit depending on the context, and we find the connection in 2 Tim 3:16 where the term "God-breathed" is *theopneustos*.

THE BIBLE AND REVELATION

We drew the threefold perspective on the Word from Martin Luther, as mediated by the twentieth-century theologian Karl Barth. As we saw in chapter 3, the Trinity was central in Barth's thought, so it should not surprise us that he built his doctrine of revelation on the Trinity—Jesus reveals God because he is God. However, by elevating the Trinity in revelation, Barth also redefined the role of Scripture. Rather than calling Scripture "revelation" (as if it were on an equal level to Christ), he preferred to describe the Bible as a "witness to revelation." That is, Scripture tells the story of Jesus. While we affirm the relative priority that Barth gives to Christ and the Bible, we still use the direct language of "revelation" for Scripture.

Word of God Proclaimed: Preaching/Tradition

For the most part, Christians do not consider preaching and tradition to be special revelation because preachers and teachers are not "inspired" in the way the biblical writers were.[9] However, the Holy Spirit does continue to act through those who communicate the truth of Scripture. These preachers and teachers are fallible, but to the extent that they faithfully exposit the truth of Scripture through the Spirit, they are communicating the Word of God to the contemporary world. The meaning of Scripture is not always self-evident, so it must be interpreted. The relationship between Scripture and interpretation is complex, so we will return to it below.

There are at least three instances in which some Christians consider the Word of God proclaimed to be special revelation.

1. In response to the Protestant cry of *sola Scriptura* (Scripture alone), the Catholic Church officially confirmed in the Council of Trent (1545–63) that both Scripture and the (authoritative) tradition of the church can be considered as revelation because of the agency of the Holy Spirit. Three centuries later, the First Vatican Council (1869–70) affirmed that when the Pope speaks *ex cathedra* (in an official, authoritative statement) his pronouncement is infallible.
2. In charismatic churches, believers often receive a "word of knowledge" or a "prophecy" that is inspired by the Holy Spirit (see 1 Cor 12–14). These pronouncements are usually not treated as absolutely infallible, as Paul instructed Christians to evaluate prophecies and only hold on to what is good (1 Cor 14:29; 1 Thess 5:19–21).
3. The Bible regularly records people having divine dreams and visions that communicate God's will. Although certain theological traditions place more value on

---

9. In popular use, the term *inspired* means someone who has a bright idea. When we use it in a theological context, we mean that we can expect to hear God's words in these human words.

the role of dreams and visions, Christians from all the major confessions continue to affirm them. In many contemporary accounts, those who do not know Christ have dreams that prepare them for hearing the gospel.

In each case, the pronouncements and dreams do not hold the same authority as Scripture. They are more authoritative (in their contexts) than someone's opinion, but since they have to be tested in a way that Scripture need not be tested, their authority is clearly relative.

A CONTINUUM OF REVELATION

As we consider the topic of special revelation, it helps to think in terms of a continuum:

Manifestation. Christians believe God acts in history. He delivers the children of Israel from slavery, and he raises Jesus from the dead. Indeed, Jesus is God himself acting in the world.

Inspiration. Christians also believe God speaks. He does not speak mechanically, but he communicates through special spokespersons, sometimes called prophets. These prophets give us an authoritative interpretation of what God has done and what he seeks to accomplish. Their writings, the Scriptures, are the record of these prophetic words and are identified as revelation from God.

Canonization. Eventually these prophetic words are written, revered, and collected by the church. A **canon** is the list or collection of sacred writings. God oversees this process allowing the church in time to discern the sacred texts, though the church has never come to complete agreement about the boundaries of the Old Testament.

Illumination. God helps us make sense of the Bible. He guides readers by means of the Holy Spirit to understand and apply the Scriptures today.

Word of God Written: The Bible

Having only scratched the surface about the Bible, we will now explore a variety of aspects related to the Bible: what texts make up the Bible, the nature of inspiration, and the process of canonization.

The Canon: What Texts Make up the Bible?

It's been said that the Bible is not really a book but more like a library. This collection of texts is the canon. The term *canon* comes from Greek, and it relates to a "ruler," something you measure other things by. That is, the Bible is the measure and standard of truth, by which all other claims of knowledge are judged. This canon has a basic organization:

the (Protestant) Bible is a collection of sixty-six books, which are divided into two parts, the Old Testament and the New Testament.[10] The term *testament* comes from the Latin word for "covenant," so God's covenants are a key organizing principle for the Bible.

Old and New Testaments. The Bible has two primary sections: the Old and New Testaments. The Old Testament is a collection of thirty-nine books written by the Jewish people, primarily in the Hebrew language. The historical timeframe that they describe spans almost two thousand years (roughly 2000–150 BC). The Old Testament (in English) is organized into four broad groups: Pentateuch (the five books of Moses), History, Wisdom/Poetry, and Prophets. The New Testament is a collection of twenty-seven books (mostly letters) written in the Greek language by early Christians, who were almost all Jewish as well. They speak to events that occurred from about 6 BC to AD 100. Though we don't have the specific dates for these texts, they were written in the latter half of the first century AD. The New Testament is grouped into three major categories: the narrative writings, which are the Gospels and Acts; the Pauline Letters; and the General Letters and Revelation.[11] Though these Old and New Testaments of the Bible are distinct, the Bible narrates a unified story of God's work in the world, as Irenaeus showed us.

Deuterocanonical Texts (i.e., the Apocrypha). In Roman Catholic and Eastern Orthodox Bibles, a collection of eighteen (or so) other books are included with the Old Testament writings. These books were also written by the Jewish people. Indeed, they were written before Christianity arose. These Jewish texts recount how the Jews attempted to remain true to their faith in spite of the challenges by gentile domination and persecution in the timeframe following the Old Testament period (i.e., Second Temple Judaism).[12] These texts were primarily written in Greek and were included in the **Septuagint**, which contains the Greek translation of the Old Testament (from Hebrew) and these deuterocanonical texts.[13] Since most early Christians did not know Hebrew, the Greek Septuagint collection became the Bible for the early Christian church (and therefore for the medieval Catholic and Orthodox traditions). In the Protestant Reformation, the Reformers followed the path *ad fontes* (to the sources) and translated the Old Testament from Hebrew. They decided that the deuterocanonical texts were not inspired because they did not form a part of the Jewish Hebrew Bible. They still encouraged believers to read them, and these texts were still printed in (all) Protestant Bibles until the early 1800s under a separate heading called "the **Apocrypha**." Following Catholic and Orthodox practice, Some Protestant traditions continue to use these texts in their **liturgy** through the **lectionary**.

---

10. We address differences with Roman Catholic and Eastern Orthodox Bibles below.

11. This last group is sometimes called the "Catholic Epistles," since they were addressed to the universal (Greek: *catholikos*) church.

12. This timeframe is called Second Temple Judaism because it relates to the time after Babylonian exile when the second temple was in use in Jerusalem until AD 70 when it was destroyed by the Romans.

13. The term "deuterocanonical" relates to a "second" canon.

Inspiration: How Are These Human Words Also God's Word?

The doctrine of inspiration allows us to call the human words in these writings the Word of God. By *inspiration* we mean the supernatural influence of God (through the Holy Spirit) on the writers that enabled them to record an accurate account of God's revelation. In addition to 2 Timothy 3:16–17, 2 Peter 1:19–21 also shows God the Holy Spirit as the divine influence on those who wrote Scripture. Even though we have been emphasizing the Spirit's work, we can easily see from a variety of texts in the Bible that the human authors did not merely go into a trance as the Spirit dictated words to them. Rather, the process was more subtle and hidden. Ultimately inspiration is a mystery, not unlike the Trinity, where we affirm the full reality of two aspects: these are 100 percent human words and 100 percent God's words.[14] Because it is the Word of God, we come to it expectantly, knowing that we will hear God's voice. It is truth. For this reason, many speak of the *verbal plenary inspiration* of the Bible—each word is fully inspired. And yet because they are human words, these texts reflect the influence of human culture and language.

Both voices are there (divine and human), but whose voice do we hear more clearly? How much do the human authors influence the output? Do the human authors, because they are not omniscient, introduce problems or errors into the text? Often these questions work from a zero-sum understanding of inspiration—100 percent God and 0 percent human, or 50 percent God and 50 percent human. We affirm that it is 100 percent of both. Scripture's authorship was a noncompetitive experience of divine and human action (or divine and human **agency**) working in cooperation.

In the twentieth century, a disagreement arose about how to speak about God's voice in the Bible. While still holding to the Bible's inspiration, two primary views have been used to describe the truth claims in the Bible: inerrancy and infallibility. For those who ascribe to *inerrancy*, the Bible (in its original manuscripts) has no factual errors in anything it refers to—historical, scientific, and so on. For those that ascribe to *infallibility*, the Bible will achieve God's purposes (that is, it will not fail) to communicate the truths of ultimate reality, but it may reflect errors due to the limited understanding of the human authors.

Canonization: How Do We Know Which Books Are Inspired?

The Old Testament documents were written over a period of about one thousand years, and the New Testament over a period of about fifty years. These texts were not simply dictated by God to the human authors, nor were they written on special paper to show they were to be immediately recognized as Scripture. The believing community went through a process of canonizing (selecting and vetting) different texts. More texts were omitted than selected; it was not a simple or short process. Eventually the church came to believe that only the canonized books were inspired by God.

---

14. For a similar paradigm, see the discussion on Jesus being fully God and fully human.

The scope of the Hebrew Bible was settled in the second century AD, generally speaking. Yet Christians have recognized different canons for the Old Testament (e.g., some Christians accept the Apocrypha). We have a greater clarity about the canonization process of the New Testament and the implicit criteria used to decide which books should be included. Even though the New Testament documents were written between AD 50 and 100, it was not until AD 367 that we have a canonical list of texts that corresponds to the twenty-seven books we recognize today.

Various factors influenced whether a book was included in the New Testament canon: the texts were evaluated based on whether they were *inspired* (communicated God's voice), *apostolic* (written by the apostles or their close associates), *catholic* (recognized and used "universally" by churches around the ancient world), and *orthodox* (presented theological vision in accord with the church's historic teaching). Just because a text possessed some of the factors did not mean it was included. For example, the Apostolic Fathers met many of these informal criteria, but they were not canonized.[15]

Interpretation and Illumination

When we are talking about revelation, it might seem as if determining what is in the canon of Scripture is the biggest hurdle. But just as significant is the question of how we interpret what the Bible says. Both of us authors grew up in traditions that often said: "The Bible says it; I believe it; that settles it." If the meaning and interpretation of the Bible were so straightforward and unquestionable, why are there distinct Christian confessions—Protestant, Catholic, and Orthodox—that all claim the Bible as the basis of their theology? Or, better still, why are there thousands of "Bible-believing" Protestant denominations? There are core elements of biblical truth that have withstood the test of denominational squabbling, such as the Nicene Creed, but other aspects are much more debated and debatable.

INTERPRETATION IS ALL AROUND US

While many think of interpretation as something primarily related to high literature—the Bible or poems—we are involved in the task of interpretation all the time. We (the authors) are regularly approached by students wanting to find new or flexible meaning in the language of our syllabi. The most vocal debates we have at home are not about politics or religion but about how to interpret a rule in a board game that can be read two (or more) ways. Or think of two friends trying to parse the meaning of a note one received from someone they have a crush on: "When he says X, do you think that really means he likes me?"

---

15. The Apostolic Fathers are the earliest Christian texts that we have outside the Bible, with some dating to as early as AD 70, and yet they were not included in the canon.

Revelation and Interpretation

Tuesday

Should Christians baptize infants? Should women be ordained as ministers? Should we even ordain ministers? Should worship services allow speaking in tongues? Christians of good faith hold varying opinions about these questions (and many more!), and all would say they are drawing their views from the Bible. Is the Bible unclear? Are some twisting its meaning? Does this mean that the Bible shouldn't be trusted? If people debate meanings of the Constitution, does that mean it should not be trusted? No, in fact, the opposite. It is because we care so much about God's revelation in the Bible that we argue over its meaning and interpretation. However, it does mean that we should be more cautious about what we call "biblical." That is, we should distinguish between revelation and interpretation. The following table might help us see the differences (see figure 4.2).

FIGURE 4.2: REVELATION VS. INTERPRETATION

Revelation	Interpretation
What God says	What we think the text means
God speaking by the Holy Spirit	Hearing God's voice by the Holy Spirit
Does not change	Can and does change
Infallible	Can be fallible
Approach with assurance	Approach with humility

We trust and rely on the Bible as infallible truth, but we also humbly recognize our own limitations as interpreters. The discussion of interpretation relates to **hermeneutics**, or the practice of interpretation. A few terms are often used in this context: interpretation, **exegesis** (getting the meaning out of a text), significance, and application (appropriating the meaning for your audience). Interpretation takes into account the reader, the text, the author(s), and the audience. It is both art and science, and its practice has shifted over time.

Broad Movements in the History of Interpretation

Sometimes different interpretations come from emphasizing different aspects of a text, but many times different interpretations come from different reading strategies. To help us understand these strategies, we note four basic approaches Christians have used to approach the Bible, because our preconceived expectations highly influence how we find meaning in it.

While we will focus on how these four movements engage the Bible, they reflect broader cultural movements that will help you understand wider worldviews at the time. This is a thirty-thousand-foot view of interpretation, so we are just giving broad summaries and giving you a stereotypical perspective. Of course, individual interpreters will vary from these general models. Before working through these movements, it will be helpful for you to reread the timeline of church history (in ch. 1) in conjunction with the Wesleyan Quadrilateral of Scripture, tradition, reason, and experience (in ch. 2). Regarding the basic issues, the key question is: How much relative influence is (or should be) given to tradition, reason, and experience in readings of the Bible? As we explore these movements, you should note that when one movement begins, that does not mean the previous one ends. For example, Roman Catholic interpretive practices followed in the stream of Ancient methods after the Reformation. Likewise, many protestants followed Reformation methods after the start of the Enlightenment.

Ancient: Scripture with Tradition

The ancient approach to interpretation rose to prominence in the patristic time period and held sway over the Byzantine and medieval Christian interpreters. Reflecting the canonization process, ancient interpreters held the Bible to be inspired by the Holy Spirit. As interpreters encountered these texts, they were specifically interested in reading the Bible along with **ecumenical** tradition (e.g., the rule of faith, the Nicene Creed). This Trinitarian-focused tradition was not only drawn from Scripture but also helped provide a basic interpretive lens for Scripture. Culturally speaking, older things were trusted more than newer ones, so *tradition* was viewed as valuable and necessary to help guide readings of Scripture.[16] One aspect of ancient readings of Scripture is that they recognized multiple senses, or multiple meanings, in passages.

Reformation: Scripture over Tradition

In the 1500s, the Reformation erupted in Europe out of the Renaissance. At the basis of the Protestant Reformation was a reading of Scripture that differed from the medieval Catholic church. In line with ancient (and later) interpreters, Reformation readings of the Bible were based on its being inspired by the Holy Spirit. What changed was their understanding of tradition: tradition was not automatically a bad thing (that's a later Enlightenment perspective), but the Reformers held it as subservient to Scripture—Scripture over tradition. Most still recited the creeds during the service, but they specifically removed other traditions particular to Roman Catholic theology, such as the practice of penance and a requirement that priests be unmarried. With this demotion of communal authority, the role of the individual interpreter and "reason" was promoted, though not in a dominating way.

Enlightenment: Objective Interpretation through Reason

In the Enlightenment (c. 1650–1800), a movement ushering in "modernity," interpreters took the Reformation impulse of questioning tradition further by rejecting tradition altogether, with reason alone as the proper means to approach the biblical

---

16. Some later medieval interpreters may have shifted toward a "tradition over Scripture" model, but the wider medieval church would deny this approach.

Tuesday

texts. With their focus on universal reason, they wanted to remove the influence of any subjective and sectarian factors (like tradition) because tradition skews objectivity. In fact, those thoroughly committed to the Enlightenment project denied the Holy Spirit's inspiration of the Bible because that was just a tradition that could not be empirically verified through objective measures. Higher criticism, or the "historical-critical" method of interpretation, reflects these Enlightenment concerns: the Bible should be read and interpreted like any other book since it was not specifically inspired. (This movement went hand-in-hand with the advent of deism, which rejects special revelation.) By following the historical-critical method, the single meaning of the text was associated with the *human* author's intention.

Of course, not all (Protestant) Christians fully embraced this movement. However, many **low-church** Protestant denominations arose during this time, and they reflect many post-Enlightenment concerns. Evangelicalism, in general, has followed Reformation presuppositions about the inspiration of the Bible, but they have followed the interpretive practices of the Enlightenment, often following a "historical-grammatical" method. In that way, the single meaning of each biblical text was to be found in the intention of the text's *human* author, which in light of inspiration accurately reflects God's intention.

Postmodernism: Subjective Interpretation through Experience

Reacting to the Enlightenment enthusiasm for reason, **postmodernism** (c. 1900–present) has emphasized personal and communal *experience*. Those committed to postmodernism typically believe it would be impossible to get an unbiased and objective interpretation of Scripture. They question whether finite human authors can guarantee readers will grasp their intention. Rather, they place their focus both upon the meaning of the text itself (without consideration of its author) and its meaning within an interpretive community. Without confidence that one right interpretation was intended or can be recovered, they embrace a plurality of readings from different communities. At times it seems there are as many meanings in a text as there are interpreters. With its commitment to **pluralism**, postmodern interpreters often highlight perspectives that have been marginalized or rejected in the past in order to give them equal weight now. Examples of these interpretive methods are postcolonial, feminist, black, and liberationist approaches.

Many evangelicals have had difficulties with postmodernism due to its rejection of fixed truth (or **metanarratives**). While Christians cannot fully accept the skepticism of many postmodern thinkers (nor, for that matter, of modern thinkers), we need not be afraid of the claim that all interpreters are culturally biased. This just means that we have a little humility about our finite attempts to understand God's infinite truth. In distinction to the "God said it; I believe it; that settles it" model, a contemporary T-shirt offers a different reading: "God said it; I interpreted it (as best I could in light of all my filters imposed by my upbringing and culture, which I try to control but you never do a perfect job); that doesn't exactly settle it (but it does give me enough of a platform to base my values and decisions on)."[17] This also speaks to our need to interpret Scripture in the wider Christian community—from around the globe and from the past—to hear how God is speaking and has spoken to others. The broader movement of the **theological interpretation of Scripture** captures this attempt to read Scripture with the historical community of the church while also attending to the plurality with which God still speaks to the contemporary church.

INTERPRETATION NEEDS THE SPIRIT

The Bible speaks to our need for illumination in interpretation. In Mark 4:12, Jesus explains why he speaks in parables by quoting Isaiah 6:9–10:

> They may be ever seeing but never perceiving,
>> and ever hearing but never understanding;
> otherwise they might turn and be forgiven!

In terms of the parable of the sower in Mark 4, even if we have the seed that the farmer scatters (special revelation), we still need God's illuminating work to understand God's revelation. If we need the Spirit's illumination to understand the direct words of special revelation, we should expect little from unaided reason.

Conclusion

The doctrine of revelation is an extension of the doctrine of God, particularly of God as Trinity. Revelation is not merely about our acquired ideas or truths, but we come to know God as he has revealed himself to us. The Nicene Creed highlights the Father's work in creation, through which we encounter general revelation. We receive the central revelation of God through the Son who equally shares the same nature with the Father and Spirit. We also encounter God through the Spirit and his work of inspiring the authors of Scripture and illuminating those who attend to Scripture. Thus alongside Irenaeus we see the unity of God's work in the whole Story of the Bible.

CONTEMPORARY THEOLOGICAL RELEVANCE

Now that we have explored key ideas related to the doctrine of revelation, our goal is to explore a limited number of crucial areas where this doctrine relates to wider issues in the contemporary world and church.

---

17. I (BCB) was pointed to this by my pastor Reagan Waggoner: Brant Hansen, "Best Christian T-Shirt Like, Ever?" *Letters from Kamp Krusty* (blog), October 31, 2009, branthansen.typepad.com/letters_from_kamp_krusty/2009/10/best-christian-tshirt-like-ever.html.

Tuesday

Revelation and Christian Identity

Given the priority of Jesus and the Spirit in the doctrine of revelation, the questions of the place and role of Jesus and the continuing work of the Spirit are central in the debates noted below.

Revelation and Other Christian Traditions

We noted several heterodox groups in our discussion of the Trinity, and since most theological disputes relate to the interpretation of Scripture, the concept of revelation is inherently tied to their separate identities.

- **(Functional) Deists.** As a direct outgrowth of the Enlightenment, traditional deists deny any form of special revelation (e.g., the incarnation or the inspiration of the Bible) because God is not active in the world after creation. This view, predominant in traditional Protestant liberalism, is what Karl Barth so strongly reacted against when he affirmed Jesus as God incarnate. While very few are explicitly deist today, the worldview that God is barely or not at all active in the world is prominent due to an increasingly disenchanted outlook. Hesitance toward God's use of miracles, words of knowledge, dreams, or visions might reflect deistic tendencies.
- **Jehovah's Witnesses** affirm the same canon as Protestant Christians, but they use a specific translation of these texts—the New World Translation—in order to support their **subordinationist** perspective about the Son. While Jehovah's Witnesses affirm the Bible as revelation, they do not identify Jesus as God's self-revelation: God is not fully revealed in Jesus because Jesus is a lower mediator between Jehovah and humanity.
- **Mormonism** affirms, in addition to the Protestant canon, the revelatory value of several other holy writings: the Book of Mormon, the Doctrine and Covenants, and the Pearl of Great Price, most of which were revealed (in various means) to Joseph Smith.[18] These texts are seen as scriptural and authoritative, but Mormons work from the model of an open canon (rather than closed canon) that can grow and change because of a strong focus on continuing personal revelation through the active work of the Holy Spirit. For this reason, the inspired writings of the current living prophet (the President of the Church) are also considered authoritative revelation.

Revelation and Other Religions

Almost every religious tradition has holy writings (scriptures), so as we consider the claims of Christianity, we need to consider the nature and authority of the writings and revelatory divine acts.

---

18. Most well known is the Book of Mormon. According to accounts, in 1830 an angel guided founder Joseph Smith to golden tablets that were buried in AD 421, and the Spirit inspired his translation into English.

The two other Abrahamic religions, Judaism and Islam, overlap with Christianity in ways that others religions do not. While both emphasize texts overlapping with the Christian canon, the most important difference is that Jesus is as much the message as the messenger for Christians. Our comparison will focus particularly on scriptures:

- **Judaism.** Jews hold up the Hebrew Bible, the **_Tanakh_**, as inspired by God (it includes the same texts as the Christian [Protestant] Old Testament). Additionally, they recognize the authority of subsequent "unwritten traditions." These "unwritten traditions" (including teaching, interpretations, debates, and stories) are recounted and codified in the Mishnah (c. AD 200). The two recensions of the **Talmud** (completed between AD 500 and 600) include the Mishnah and expand the interpretive conversation. While Jews believe in inspiration, they generally see the ancient text as the starting point of a conversation. They often explore the text by asking questions of the Bible and comparing it to other stories and wise sayings within the tradition. The result is an expanding _halakhah_ applied to the changing situations of life.
- **Islam.** One of the key affirmations of Islam is belief in the books of God, and the Qur'an is the primary holy book sent down from heaven. They believe that for more than twenty years Muhammad received words from the angel Gabriel and recited them to others who then recorded them. Humans contributed nothing, only recording words that already existed in heaven. Aspects of the Old and New Testaments are incorporated into the Qur'an, though with transpositions of stories and characters. For Muslims, the Qur'an is authoritative revelation only if it is in the original Arabic. A less authoritative but still very important set of materials, called _Hadith_, records sayings and practices of Muhammad. Many Hadith are commonly accepted, but Muslims debate others. Theology and practice come from both sources. Praying five times a day, for example, comes from Muhammad's example in the Hadith rather than from the Qur'an. The Sunnah are a collection of authoritative practices and function similar to legal precedents setting tradition for others to follow. In addition to the Qur'an, three other texts are considered the books of God given through other prophets: Tawrat/Torah (Moses), the Zabur (David), and the Injil/Gospel (Jesus). Christians, due to their commitment to these other forms of revelation, are described as "People of the Book" in the Qur'an.

In contrast to the Abrahamic religions, the writings of the other major world religions are more distinct from Christianity:

- **Hinduism.** Two great collections make up Hinduism's sacred writings. (1) The four _Vedas_ (and appendices called _The Upanishads_) are the most sacred writings because they are _shruti_ ("that which is heard"). The Vedas are not ascribable to any human author but are continually reheard in the cycle of history. These were typically reserved for study by the higher castes. (2) A lower tier of writings (including, e.g., the *Bhagavad Gita* as part of the epic *Mahabharata*) interpret and supplement (or supplant) the earlier sacred texts, and they are *smriti* ("that which is remembered"). These later texts provide the basis for the pantheon of contemporary Hindu devotion today across the castes and are thus functionally the most influential.

- **Buddhism.** The two largest Buddhist traditions—Theravada Buddhism and Mahayana Buddhism—have greatly varying collections of sacred texts. The sacred canon of Theravada Buddhism contains early revelations that came to the Buddha which were gathered in three collections (or "baskets"). Strictly speaking, there are no gods to reveal, only insights to learn. Mahayana Buddhism depends on a larger set of texts, including additional teachings of the Buddha and of different *bodhisattvas* (exalted teachers). While still not affirming a god, this approach to Buddhism embraces divine figures who display mercy or grace when they put aside their own progress to assist others. These texts vary greatly in content and number.

The Practice of Interpretation: Hermeneutics

In the academic discipline of biblical studies, the historical-critical (mainline) or the historical-grammatical (evangelical) methods have been primary, but questions have arisen about the role of the interpreter as well as the role of the Holy Spirit. How much freedom should we have to see the Bible play out in our lives in ways beyond the historical focus of a passage? For instance, New Testament authors regularly interpret the Old Testament with a hermeneutic at odds to ones we employ today in our academic settings. Accordingly, there have been arguments for the greater use of typological and Spirit-based hermeneutics following the pattern of the New Testament authors. In light of these New Testament examples, how do we best attend to the meaning of Scripture? Is there one right hermeneutic to find truth and meaning in the Bible?

A Canon within the Canon

Different parts of the Bible are not always treated equally. With the idea of *progressive revelation*, the New Testament takes precedence over the Old Testament in Christian theology. Different theological traditions often emphasize different aspects of the Bible. While the three major confessions—Protestant, Catholic, and Orthodox—have different canons, the greater difference in theology is how the texts in their common canon are used differently. For example, Catholics, Orthodox, and Anabaptist traditions tend to emphasize the Gospels. The majority of Protestant traditions have tended to emphasize the Pauline letters (e.g., finding the gospel centrally in "justification"). How much diversity do we find in the canon? Is it possible to treat all parts of the Bible equally? Should we emphasize some parts over the others?

Further Questions and Issues

In addition to the topics we have explored above, these further questions are important:

- **Old and New Testaments.** How should we understand the continuities and discontinuities between the Old and New Testaments? Does your understanding of God help you see them as more similar or more different?
- **The Spirit Still Revealing.** How should the church understand the Spirit's work outside the Bible (e.g., in tradition, words of knowledge, prophecy, dreams, etc.)? If God does speak through preaching and tradition, how do we balance that with his more direct and specific revelation in Christ and the Bible?
- **Questions about Inspiration.** How should Christians understand the nature of inspiration and truth? How should we understand the Scripture as both God's Word and human words? What did the process of inspiration look like (a trance, dictation, unseen motivation, etc.)? How does one's view of inspiration shape one's understanding of the text's authority?

PRACTICING THE FAITH

Revelation is not a storehouse of information like the internet or Wikipedia, nor is it a list of rules and duties. Revelation is about God making himself known as Father, Son, and Holy Spirit and calling us into a relationship with him. With this in mind, let's consider how revelation impacts our spiritual life.

Meeting God in the Scriptures

Paul famously declared that all Scripture is "inspired" (2 Tim 3:16). I (RLH) hold the minority opinion that he was borrowing an image from the Bible's first pages. In Genesis "God breathes" into the lifeless body of Adam, and he becomes a living being. With the word "inspiration" Paul claims that Scripture exhibits such an animating power—a life-giving potency by the Holy Spirit. No wonder he goes on to spell out that Scripture is good for correction, teaching, and so on.

Can you bring to mind stories of people who encountered God while reading the Bible? In his conversion experience, Augustine famously heard a voice say, "Take up and read."[19] These stories are everywhere. We have had several students who received Christ or shunned suicide because they felt God addressed them in the Scriptures.

One young man's experience captures what we have heard from others. He was mocking faith, cursing God as he read the New Testament. Despite his anger, he perceived that he was meeting or encountering a living person. The written Word was bearing witness to the living, transforming God we meet in the Son, through the stirring power of the Spirit.

---

19. Augustine, *Confessions* 8.12, trans. Edward B. Pusey, http://www.newadvent.org/fathers/110108.htm.

That God seeks to communicate with us is humbling. We must be valuable to God. His revealing is not a cold mechanical exchange of data. He seeks a personal encounter. This communication calls for personal engagement, not a mastery of concepts. We rightly think of an ongoing friendship and relationship that grows deeper over time. We grasp him better as we learn to love him.

There are any number of methods to meet God in the Scriptures, but the most simple and necessary is just to read them (or listen to them)![20] The practice of daily devotions, or "quiet times," is grounded in reading Scripture in order to hear from God. I (BCB) can attest that committing to this daily practice as a sixteen-year-old was one of the most important decisions in my life. Of course, as an ancient text, the Bible is not always easy to understand on your own. Thankfully, God provides others in the church to help you along the way.

Meeting God in the Scriptures: His Abiding Presence

Christian monks developed a pattern for praying the Scriptures called *Lectio Divina* ("divine reading"). This strategy for praying and reading Scripture seeks transformation so that we may enter the triune communion. We start with (1) *lectio*, a deliberate reading. Ancient people read aloud and ponderously slow. To do this, modern folk must shift gears. We need to be exploring the passage, not mastering content and moving on. Eventually the Spirit will suggest a word, image, or aspect upon which to focus. This focus leads to (2) *meditatio*, or meditation. The reader is like a cow that chews and then rechews. The Spirit guides and speaks to us. (Of course, memorizing Scripture passages greatly facilitates this.) We are prompted to respond with (3) *oratio*, a prayer to the Father concerning what has been taught to us during meditation. We may have learned more about ourselves than the text; we may confess a sin brought to mind; we may give thanks for an image or grace. Following our prayer, we enter into (4) *contemplatio*, or contemplation. Technically this is neither more meditation nor prayer. It is a transverbal experience where we remain in the presence of God. It is a simple, this-worldly version of the communion pictured in the story of the boy on the porch—a foretaste of the abiding with the triune God that is to come.[21] Time in God's presence is life-giving and changing.

Meeting God in the Scriptures: Praying the Psalms

From early on Christians prayed, chanted, and sang the Psalms. This book of prayers is a laboratory. Worshipers learn by absorption that God is the great master and Lord over creation, and we are his servants. The Psalms immerse us in a God-oriented world. We learn to cry out to God when creation is failing; we offer thanks and praise when the world is put right. *Common Worship: Daily Prayer* (the contemporary iteration of *The Book of Common Prayer*) identifies a few psalms to pray through each morning and

---

20. YouVersion, the popular Bible app, has access to numerous free translations, many with audio versions.
21. See ch. 3.

evening.[22] According to this plan, you can read the entire book of Psalms over the course of a month. In a year you can read the book twelve times. No wonder ancient monks could recite the Psalms. My (RLH) pastor prays through one psalm each day. Because of this practice, he recites the psalms freely in his conversations. It is like the air he breathes, the word bank in his head and heart. He even remembers the psalm he read on the day of certain momentous events. Psalms teach us that life is lived before God.

"Doing What Is Right in Their Own Eyes": Questions of Authority

Critical of society, the book of Judges concludes with the observation that everyone was doing what was "right in their own eyes" (Judg 21:25 NRSV). These days, it takes some persuasion to convince people that this was a very bad circumstance. After all, today people tend to think that mature and authentic people decide for themselves. The virtually unquestioned moral good for our culture is for something to be "authentic" and therefore self-chosen. By contrast, we hold up the Bible as an adjudicating source—we are bound to it, defer to it, and entrust ourselves to it. Acknowledging or yielding to authority is unpopular today. But it works in a variety of ways which often intersect. We can be influenced by an external power or consequence. When we obey a traffic sign we are recognizing the claims of a community to regulate traffic. Sometimes we follow instructions because we love the person (or institution) instructing us. Think of a strong young person obeying their feeble grandparent out of love, admiration, or trust. Sometimes we act or obey because a conviction or idea is true or inspiring. If we come to acknowledge the Bible's authority, many things will influence us along the way: we may obey a commandment for fear of punishment or consequence, out of respect for our family or community, out of love and trust for a wise mentor, or because we think the command captures a compelling and true insight. Eventually and most importantly our trust of the Bible will be rooted in a deep love and trust for God and the beautiful and inspiring gospel.

Whom Should I Marry? What Job Should I Take?

Christians commonly seek God's guidance. It is wise to look for answers to pressing questions within the scope of an ongoing pilgrimage of discipleship. The task of learning and loving the God of Scripture comes first. In Proverbs 3:5–6, God promises to set us on a "straight path" (rather than a crooked and immoral one) if we follow his guidance as laid out in Scripture. Taking the right steps daily allows us to be prepared to follow him in the big decisions of life. Like with language learning, you cannot have a conversation unless you are able to say simple phrases.

The larger questions of marriage and jobs build upon this daily quest. God sets general (moral) boundaries, but gives us freedom to choose according to his wisdom. We believe God can and does provide guidance through many means. God could give

---

22. *Common Worship: Daily Prayer* is available on the web and by app for free.

Tuesday

special direction in the words of Scripture beyond their normal meaning. Though New Testament writers often attended to the historical or literary meaning of the text, they modeled this hermeneutic when they found broader meanings from Old Testament passages. Similarly, you may sense God is telling you to leave home when reading Abraham was told to leave home. Some might call reading Scripture in this way under the special leadership of the Holy Spirit a "charismatic" reading. People who emphasize this conversational approach believe that God speaks personally in Scripture.[23] Strictly speaking, biblical authority supports the notion that God told Abraham to leave home but not that you are instructed to leave home; the personal instruction rests on whether you rightly discerned God's voice. Reading the Bible in community helps us confirm our sense of God's guidance (we "test the spirits"). We should read the Bible *for* ourselves, but not only *by* ourselves.

Further Considerations

Knowing God through his revelation is foundational to Christian experience. Let us suggest a few other topics to consider for your personal reflection and application:

- **Memorizing Scripture.** The Scripture that we know and treasure in our hearts is a resource for life. People from almost every imaginable circumstance (the sick, the sad, even prisoners of war) testify to the sustaining power of Scripture. A phrase or word can form or inform a decision, a day, or a lifetime.
- **Community.** God has provided the church and its leaders to shape us (e.g., 1 Cor 12; 14; Eph 4). These fellow wayfarers are indispensable as we learn about and hear from God.
- **Testing the Spirits.** Not every idea or teaching about God or theology is right, so we are called to discern if there is false teaching (2 Pet 2), or "test the spirits" (1 John 4:1–6). One way to test a teaching is to compare it to the teachings of Christ and to the full witness of Scripture. Another important test is to listen to the community of God (both present and past) to see how God has shaped their perspective on the topic.

Every theologian mentioned in this book studied theology in order to know God. Our learning is not an end in itself. Remember the threefold Word of God (the concentric circles)? We must not settle to remain in the content of the church's teaching and preaching (the preached Word). This Word presses us toward the Scriptures (the written Word). Abiding in the Scriptures, as blessed as this is, calls us to move toward Christ (the revealed Word). Revealed Scripture does so much for us, but it should move us finally to embrace Christ, who reveals the triune God working through the whole narrative of Scripture.

---

23. Dallas Willard, *Hearing God: Developing a Conversational Relationship with God* (Downers Grove, IL: IVP, 1999).

CLOSING PRAYER

Blessed Lord, who caused all holy Scriptures to be written for our learning: Grant us so to hear them, read, mark, learn, and inwardly digest them, that we may embrace and ever hold fast the blessed hope of everlasting life, which you have given us in our Savior Jesus Christ; who lives and reigns with you and the Holy Spirit, one God, for ever and ever. Amen.[24]

---

24. Collect, Proper 28, for the Sunday closest to November 16, in "Collects: Contemporary," *The (Online) Book of Common Prayer*, Episcopal Church (New York: Church Hymnal Corporation, 2007), www.bcponline.org/Collects/seasonsc.html (October 20, 2017).

wed.

CHAPTER 5

God and the World

Creator and Creation

INTRODUCTION

Big Idea:
Through the Father's, Son's, and Holy Spirit's holy love, we see that God is active in but distinct from the good world corrupted by evil.

Key Terms:
- Immanence, Transcendence
- Holy Love
- Competitive and Noncompetitive Agency

Key Passages:
Gen 1–3;
Exod 20:2–6; 34:5–7;
Pss 19:1–6; 139;
Ezek 36–37;
Matt 28:19–20;
Rom 3:21–26; 8:16–39;
Jas 4:13–17;
Rev 21–22

When I teach theology, I (BCB) enjoy clarifying different (near) homophones related to theology, such as Arianism (a **subordinationist** view of the Son) and Aryanism (a Nazi white nationalist ideology) or Arminians (people with a particular view about God's foreknowledge) and Armenians (people from Armenia). As we discuss the interconnection between God and the world, three (near) homophones are especially relevant: God is eminent, immanent, and imminent. Eminence points to how someone is different, greater in status and importance. The latter two terms speak to how someone is close or near: immanence means being close in space/location, and imminence means being close in time (about to happen soon).[1] Christians affirm God is majestic and unique (eminent), acknowledge he is also close and active (immanent), and await his restoration achieved in Christ in our lives and the world (imminent). This chapter attends to the specific ways that God as Father, Son, and Holy Spirit has revealed his identity and being, particularly through his acts in the world. Before exploring the identity of God in the arc of history, we will explore the story of a Christian woman who lived according to her conviction that God is Lord over and active in the entire world.

FOR THE LIFE OF THE WORLD: LOTTIE MOON

Call to Faith and Mission

Charlotte "Lottie" Diggs Moon (1840–1912) stands apart from women of her culture. Rather than participating in the faith of her family,

---

1. Note the middle vowel to help distinguish the terms—*a* for space and *i* for time.

Lottie was initially skeptical about her family's faith. Instead of preparing for the task of overseeing a home, she received a first-class education outside the home, as her well-to-do parents sought for each of their daughters. Lottie earned a master's degree from a precursor to the University of Virginia, though the classes for women were segregated. Her sister Orianna was the first female physician in Virginia, served as a surgeon in the Civil War, and was later a medical missionary in Jerusalem. Her sister Eudimonia, or Eddie, was a pioneer among single women going to the mission field. After Lottie came to Christ as a college student in 1858, she first taught school and later acknowledged God's call to become a missionary. Her sister Eddie was instrumental in Lottie going to China in 1873. Unfortunately, Eddie was not suited for missionary work, but she lasted four years with Lottie's help. Eddie's mission ended tragically. After those four years, Eddie returned home due to depression. She converted to Catholicism but found no comfort. She eventually took her own life.

Lottie, however, flourished in the work. She had been a gifted student of language since her childhood. She embraced a theological vision that the God revealed in Jesus was the only God and therefore the God of the entire world. She believed the good news about Jesus was to be preached to every person. People from around the globe could find forgiveness, healing, and restoration through Jesus.

Embracing Her New World as God's World

Lottie's strategy was incarnational: she left the distinct living quarters prepared and protected for Westerners and took a remote missionary post by herself. She adopted Chinese dress and spoke Chinese. She concentrated her attention on hunger relief and creating schools for girls. In time she gave her own inheritance toward the needs of the people.

In another season of life, Lottie undertook an evangelistic tour. She traveled extensively across a ten-thousand-square-mile region. She focused on speaking to women, but men also listened in and occasionally requested an audience. One such male convert, Li Shou-ting, became an evangelist and baptized ten thousand converts. In a variety of settings Lottie stood on a rickshaw and preached in the open air. She later reflected on the long journey and recorded that she sensed the presence of Jesus when entering new territory. Jesus would remind her, "I am with you always." The risen Jesus spoke these words in his commissioning of his apostles to make disciples from all the nations (Matt 28:19–20).

A Woman of Substance: Power, Preaching, and Persuasion

Lottie exhibited an imposing strength and courage despite her tiny stature. She was slightly over four feet tall and avoided being photographed while standing. Lottie called for women missionaries to have an equal voice in policy making and insisted upon contributing to strategy decisions among the missionaries that were typically left to the men.

The mission administrators back home had their hands full with Lottie. On the one hand she was great at public relations. During her infrequent trips home, she captured the attention of mission supporters. Her stories were simultaneously showcases of Chinese culture and missionary fundraisers. Her frequent letters back home inspired women across the South who were interested in missions. Yet her bold **proclamation** raised questions about a woman preaching—which, while not unprecedented among Baptists, had fallen out of favor. She seemed impatient with such concerns and offered spirited responses. She volunteered to surrender her post to any man called to missions in China. Her critique was not subtle; others were not coming. She added that if a man was called into China, she would go farther in and take a new mission site, which she would also yield to the next male missionary.

Passing and Legacy

Lottie served thirty-nine years in China, much of it working independently. In later years she worried about the mission and struggled with depression. She began to forgo her own nourishment fearing her students did not have enough. The mission board sent a nurse to accompany Lottie back to the states to recover. She died in route on December 24, 1912, shortly after her seventy-second birthday.

Lottie is famous for inspiring the Women's Missionary Union (WMU), an organization of Baptist women for mission support. When she was still alive, she recommended that Southern Baptists collect a special missions offering at Christmas (like the Methodists did). After her death, the denomination named the offering in honor of Lottie. This offering has been one of the most effective fundraising ventures in all of Christianity. The Southern Baptist denomination built one of the largest missionary sending organizations ever, and for many years, half of the mission dollars raised among Southern Baptist came from the Lottie Moon Christmas offering.

Why did a single woman in the aftermath of the American civil war leave her home, travel across the globe, and pour out her fortune and her life? She joined her life to God's mission to reclaim his world—one God, one world, one mission.

HOW DO WE UNDERSTAND THE RELATIONSHIP BETWEEN GOD AND CREATION?

As we discuss the topic of God's engagement with the world, we will appeal to two perspectives. First, we will explore the identity of the world in relation to God. In particular, we will consider the world from the flow of history in order to understand how the biblical narrative frames the God-world relationship. Second, we will explore how God's identity is revealed through his activity in the world. Our understanding of these two perspectives—the world's identity and God's identity—coalesce through the narrative of God's interaction with the world. These two perspectives cannot be separated, and their interrelation undergirds this whole book.

The Identity of the World: It Was Created Good, But Is Fallen

The Story of God is unfolding in this world. God's self-revelation in Christ, as mentioned in the previous chapter, is the fulcrum of history, and to understand God and his world, we must understand the world's beginning and goal. This section focuses on the beginning (**protology**), but the end (**eschatology**) is always in mind because the goal is no less important. In fact, as we look at the end of the Bible in Revelation 21–22, when God's kingdom and presence are fully established here on earth, we encounter the imagery of the garden of Eden from Genesis 1–2. The culmination of history is a fulfillment of the beginning, so eschatology and protology go hand in hand. The basic story of the Bible is summarized like this: creation, fall, and new creation. God cares for this world and works toward not only restoring his people but also creation itself. This highlights two points which will be our focus: creation is worthy of being restored, and creation needs to be restored.

God Created a Good World. One of the most basic things we know about God is that he created the world. The first line of the Nicene Creed emphasizes this: "We believe in One God, the Father, the Almighty, maker of heaven and earth, of all that is, seen and unseen." Christians dispute the timing and process of creation as described in Genesis, but few would doubt that God is shown to be the Creator. And according to Genesis, one aspect of creation is central: God created a "good" world. Creation is described as "good" seven times in Genesis 1. Though things quickly go wrong (as we will see), God does not just throw it all away. Creation is good; it is worth being restored.

Yet the World Is Corrupted. Just as the creation narrative in Genesis speaks of the goodness of creation, so too it addresses the introduction of evil into creation, especially in Genesis 3. Sin corrupts people, relationships, and the land itself, exactly undoing God's intention for each. In addition to human sin, the biblical account also includes demonic agents enticing and leading humans into sin. Consider the snake in the garden in Genesis 3, as well as the "sons of God" (also known as the "Watchers" later in Jewish tradition) in Genesis 6.[2] The role and identity of these demonic powers is unclear throughout much of the Old Testament, but their role becomes clearer in the New Testament, particularly through Jesus's ministry of healing and exorcism. Corruption in the world is not limited to human and demonic agents; the physical creation itself is corrupted by human sin (cf. Rom 8:17–23).

God Restores. The Story of the Bible is ultimately about salvation history, starting with the call of Abraham and God's promise to bless the world through him (Gen 12). This was fulfilled through the advent of Christ and the Holy Spirit. In mysterious wisdom, God chose for this restoration, which has been achieved in Christ, to play out over time, so the problems of human, demonic, and physical corruption will not be fully resolved until the end of the age.

---

2. The Watchers gain further attention in Jewish texts like 1 Enoch and Jubilees.

The whole Story is important for Christian theology: God created a good world, which was corrupted by others, and God will bring holistic restoration. Those who focus on part of the story move into heterodoxy. **Gnosticism**, as we discussed in chapter 4, is a clear example. One of the basic premises of Gnosticism is that spirit is good and matter is bad. Accordingly, Gnostics denied that God created the world good in the first place.

While philosophical Gnosticism (and its cousin **Manichaeism**) only truly existed hundreds of years ago, many Christians struggle with functional Gnosticism. Functional Gnostics not only talk about the angry God of the Old Testament as distinct from the loving God of the New Testament (how does that square with **monotheism**?), but they also say, "this world is not my home." Is this world inherently evil? No. Let us give an example: when trash is mangled, sullied, or incinerated, we do not think anything about it. It doesn't matter because it is trash. But we are concerned when we face evil, corruption, sickness, and death in this world. Why? Because we implicitly know that this world is valuable. The world is not just trash. This is why the Bible not only anticipates the forgiveness of sin but also restoration of this physical world. That restoration has started in Jesus's ministry—that's why he healed so many—but it won't be fulfilled until he returns again. And the Bible points to this world as the primary place we will experience that restoration.[3]

Gnostics attempted to protect the goodness of God by separating him from this corrupted creation. They are right that God is not the source of evil. Few would explicitly argue this, but it bears stating. God is good, and all he does is good. Evil is not from God; it comes as a second stage in the Story from demonic and human agents. As a result, **pantheism** (where God is wholly identified with the world) has been rejected by Christians because it ultimately identifies God as much with the evil in the world as it does with the good.

Though it is almost self-evident in the Story, creation (the world) can only be understood in terms of its relationship with God. An example of a focus on the world apart from God can be seen in the naturalist position, which rejects the idea of God and holds that the physical universe is all that exists. But in Christianity, God stands outside of creation, so we cannot limit our discussion to physical, created realities. As we focus on the identity of God in relation to the identity of the world, we will continue to frame the discussion through the lens of God's historical act.

God's Identity and Act: Almighty God's Holy Love

From the first verse of Genesis, we see that the Bible is concerned with the relationship of God and the world: "In the beginning God created the heavens and the earth" (Gen 1:1). The biblical text does not begin with philosophical statements about God's

---

3. For more details, see chs. 9 and 11.

wed.

identity, but his nature is revealed through his activity and engagement with creation. The Nicene Creed reflects similar concerns with its first lines: "We believe in one God, the Father, the Almighty, maker of heaven and earth, of all that is, seen and unseen." The story of God (the economy) is the focus, and two key aspects of this relationship between God and the world are worth highlighting: the almighty God is both (1) active in the world and (2) distinct from it.

God's Holy Love

From the perspective of the Bible, theologians often point to God's "**holy love**" as a way to capture these two aspects. In his holiness, God is distinct, totally "other," different than creation, and different than humans. At the same time, God is fully engaged in love, reaching out, seeking reconciliation with those who are unholy. In the Old and New Testaments, both God's holiness and love are evident. Consider, for example, the giving of the first of the Ten Commandments. In that exchange, God first reminds people of his love (through his saving action) and his concern for holiness (through the commandments and their consequences):

I am the LORD your God, who brought you out of Egypt, out of the land of slavery. You shall have no other gods before me. You shall not make for yourself an image in the form of anything in heaven above or on the earth beneath or in the waters below. You shall not bow down to them or worship them; for I, the LORD your God, am a jealous God, punishing the children for the sin of the parents to the third and fourth generation of those who hate me, but showing love to a thousand generations of those who love me and keep my commandments. (Exod 20:2–6; cf. Exod 34:6–7)

We see love and holiness together in the Mosaic **covenant**, namely through the tabernacle and then the temple. God grants access to his personal presence and to the forgiveness of sins in the temple, both of which display his immense love. At the same time, everything about the temple is structured according to his standards of holiness. This pairing of holiness and love drive the rest of the Old Testament.

As we come to the New Testament, the combination of God's holy love continues to be evident in the Trinitarian work of Father, Son, and Spirit. We see the balance of holy love through the destiny of those who follow or reject God's invitation through Christ.[4] And like the Old Testament, the New Testament shows a serious punishment for those that reject God (expressed in terms of eternal judgment), as well as love and forgiveness for those who seek his grace. God's holiness meets this love in the crucifixion of Jesus, where God's holy demands are equivalently fulfilled by God's love (see, e.g., John 3:16; Rom 3:23–26). At the same time, we should not miss the identification of the Spirit

---

4. See ch. 11 for further details on the variety of perspectives on how this punishment takes place.

with holiness and love. As a full and equal person of the Trinity, the Spirit is most often described as the *Holy* Spirit, and it is his manifestation with the people of God that mediates God's presence and sanctification to us. And alongside the Spirit's holiness, the Bible and Christian tradition identify the Spirit with love (cf. Rom 5:5).

Holiness speaks to God's unbounded life and power, as well as God's moral difference from humanity. For humans to be in the presence of this power, we must share in the holiness that he lovingly imparts to those who seek him. His holiness does not hinder his love, and his love does not hinder his holiness. Both exist together and shape our engagement with him. Holiness and love capture the character of God's engagement with the world. Theologians also refer to another pair of terms to capture the nature of God's engagement: **transcendence** and **immanence**.

Transcendence and Immanence

Theologians use the words *transcendence* and *immanence* to describe God's difference and his nearness, respectively. When we affirm God's transcendence, we are saying that God is almighty, standing apart from creation, not dependent upon it. When we affirm God's immanence, we are saying that God is engaged with creation. Christian theology holds these two ideas in mysterious tension, and for orthodoxy neither can be fully affirmed without the counterbalance of the other.

Transcendence

As transcendent, God is wholly other. He is not just a better or higher version of humanity; rather, he has eternally existed before creation and exists in himself rather than being dependent on another. The philosophical term for God's self-sufficiency is ***aseity***. Closely connected is the idea that God created *ex nihilo* (Latin for "out of nothing"). Some ancients (such as Plato) and moderns (such as naturalists) assert that the material world has existed eternally, and that if God exists, he only provides shape and order to this preexisting material. In contrast, orthodox Christians have asserted that only God is eternal, and he created the world "out of nothing." Therefore, the world is and has always been dependent upon him.

Since God is distinct from creation, theologians often note attributes of God that mark him out as different from creation. Based on various biblical texts, Christians affirm that God is eternal (Ps 90:2; Rev 1:8), self-sufficient (Acts 17:25), omnipresent ("all-present"; 1 Kgs 8:27; Matt 18:20; Acts 17:24), omnipotent ("all-powerful"; Job 38–41), omniscient ("all-knowing"; Ps 139:1–6; Matt 10:30; 1 Cor 2:10–11; 1 John 3:20), and spiritual (i.e., immaterial; Ps 139:7–8; John 4:24). Ultimately, these are various ways to speak about the infinite nature of God; he is not bounded in any way. In the Nicene Creed, God's unboundedness is captured in the single term "all-mighty," which (via Latin) is *omnipotent*. God can do whatever he wants to do because he stands outside creation and is not limited by anything in it.

PSALM 139 AND GOD'S IMMANENT TRANSCENDENCE

Though the verses that most people focus on from Psalm 139 are about the reader (e.g., being wonderfully made), the psalm clearly emphasizes God and his immanent transcendence.[5] The psalm features a progression of the exploration of God's knowledge, presence, and power: omniscience (139:1–6), omnipresence (139:7–12), and omnipotence (139:13–18). We call this God's immanent transcendence because even though he is beyond human categories, he is still intimately involved. The last quarter of the psalm explores the problem of evil (139:19–24). Though evil remains a mystery in the face of an all-powerful God, David still trusts in God's immanent transcendence.

Immanence

God's transcendence, his difference from us, is only part of the story. The focus of the Bible (and the Nicene Creed) is that this holy and loving God created the world and continually reaches out to bring restoration to it. A central premise of this book is that God (Greek: *theos*) is essential to *theo*-logy, so if the most basic identity of God is Trinity, then our perspective on God's immanence should be directly influenced by our understanding of God as Father, Son, and Holy Spirit. In our discussion of the Trinity, we already described the view of God's activity in the world with the terminology of the **economic Trinity**, and discussions of God's immanence are really an extension of discussion about the economic Trinity where we see Father, Son, and Spirit at work.

GOD'S IMMANENCE AND THE IMMANENT TRINITY

In theology, context matters. The term *immanent* means different things in different contexts. In chapter 3, we described the immanent (perspective on the) Trinity as a description of the timeless and eternal relationships between the members of the Godhead—that is, how the divine persons relate (by generation and procession, while sharing the same nature) before the world was created. The economic Trinity is a description of the Godhead from the perspective of how the three persons of the Trinity engage the world in history. These are two perspectives—immanent and economic—on the one God.

When we come to the topic of immanence and transcendence in the context of God and the world, the language is transposed. The view of God as eternally existing outside time (the **immanent Trinity**) is here a description of God's transcendence, whereas the view of God as actively engaged with the world in history (the economic Trinity) is here a description of God's immanence. The immanent Trinity is transcendent, but the economic Trinity is immanent!

---

5. Ken Gore, "Does Psalm 139 really teach about the sanctity of life?" *Arkansas Baptist News* 114.5 (March 12, 2015), 5.

God the Father: Creator and Covenant Maker. The Bible begins with the Father's work of creation and explores his continued engagement, particularly through the covenants. God created the world good, but humans introduced sin and corruption into the world. In response, God makes various covenants with the Jews to bring redemption through them to the whole world. While God is recognized as the Creator, his ongoing work of covenant faithfulness and renewal is the focus of his activity in the Old Testament (cf. Num 23:19; Deut 7:9; Ezek 36–37; Hos). This same God is also at work in making and renewing this *new covenant* in the New Testament. Remember, the term *testament* is merely Latin for "covenant." But now we see God working in and through Christ and the Spirit more specifically.

God the Son: The Incarnate God-Man. God was clearly immanent in the world through his work of creation and covenant making, and the Bible (and the Nicene Creed) notes the Son's coworking with the Father in the act of creation (1 Cor 8:6; Col 1:15–20). However, the most unique aspect of the Christian understanding of God is that God the Son truly took on humanity in the **incarnation**. God did not send an angel or snap his fingers to take care of our problems, God himself bridged the gap between God and the world and "moved into our neighborhood" (John 1:14 MSG).

God the Holy Spirit: God's Empowering Presence. The Bible notes the Holy Spirit's presence in creation (Gen 1:2) and the Spirit's empowering presence among the Israelites in the Old Testament. God's identity as Spirit points to his transcendence (cf. John 4:24); he is not limited to physical creation. And yet, God's unboundedness as Spirit means that as the Holy Spirit God can be present in every believer. This was the key promise of the new covenant texts (Ezek 36–37; Joel 2). Indeed, the focus of Acts via the Pentecost experience (Acts 2) and the rest of the narrative is the worldwide presence of God with his people through the Holy Spirit (cf. Acts 1:6–8).

God's holy love is made known through his consistent personal action in the world. He is not an abstract idea, force of history, or figment of imagination. Rather, God as Father, Son, and Spirit is personal and relatable. God is not driven by passion and whims, but he does care when you break the covenant—he is grieved and jealous. Love and wrath only make sense in light of his creation and covenant.

Affirming Both Transcendence and Immanence: Finding Balance?

The Story of God's work in the world grounds our understanding of God's identity and the identity of the world as God's creation. As Father, Son, and Spirit, God is distinct and transcendent but also active and immanent. We affirm both. Either/or perspectives lead to heterodox positions. Traditions such as *deism* have so emphasized God's disengagement from the world (transcendence) that they do not fit within the biblical narrative that points to his immanent presence.[6] On the other side, traditions such as *pantheism* have so emphasized God's identification with the world (immanence) that they do not fit within

---

6. Some describe deism as God's immanence in creation since we can only know him through general revelation and natural theology.

the biblical narrative that points to his distinct nature and identity. With immanence and transcendence, it is not one or the other but both/and, and thus for some a mystery. This tension becomes clearer when we consider God's providence over a corrupt world.

Providence, Agency, and the Problem of Evil

Providence and Agency

God not only created the world but also sustains it through his grace. God's providence is his oversight, care, and governance over the world. We spoke earlier of God's holy love as a description of the intersection of his act and being; the question of what God does involves the question of who God is. We must remember God's character when we speak about God's **agency**, his working to bring his preordained will into fulfillment. Many conceive of God's providence on a spectrum, with some only speaking of God's general providence and others speaking of God's specific providence. *General providence* refers to God superintending the general laws of nature (and "destiny") but allowing free agents to impact the flow of history. *Specific providence* refers to God superintending not only the general flow of history but also individual decisions and actions that undergird it. The introduction of sin and evil into the world complicates our understanding of God's providence, because we must ask how evil from humans and other spiritual agents relates to God's foreordination of actions and decisions. The balance of human and divine agency—human free will and divine providence—are most evident in discussions of creation and evolution (more on this below) as well as of faith and salvation (see ch. 9).

WHAT PROVIDENCE IS NOT

Providence corresponds to God's act of creation. It means that God not only freely made the world to share his love but also keeps and directs the world. Providence is *not* consistent with:

- pantheism because God is distinct from his creation;
- deism because God is not distant or aloof;
- dualism because God has no true rival force or principle;
- Gnosticism because God creates a good creation (that suffers injury);
- indeterminism because God directs creation to a goal;
- chance because God directs creation to his goal;
- fate because God personally and benevolently governs creation;
- fixed determinism because God's order makes responsibility possible but does not rule it out.[7]

---

7. Adapted and amended from Thomas Oden, *The Living God, Systematic Theology: Volume One* (San Francisco: HarperCollins, 1987), 277–78.

Thurs.

This general picture of God acting in the world sounds well and good, but things do not appear to be as nice and tidy when we bring these broad theological concepts into contact with more specific discussions. Instead of thinking in terms of God and the world, you might think in terms of other related pairs: faith and science, creation and evolution, divine providence and human freedom. Many consider these pairs to be antonyms.

Those who see these as antonyms often hold a view of *competitive* **agency**—that is, God's activity is seen as in competition with the agency of the created order. In the Western world, this separation of God's agency from the world (sometimes called "disenchantment") is parallel to the rise of deism and naturalism, where natural processes are seen to work independently, and God is pushed to the margins or not included at all. This is known as the "God of the gaps" perspective. It works off a zero-sum model in which everything adds up to 100 percent. The God of the gaps view says that if science can describe 90 percent, then God is allocated 10 percent, and if science covers 100 percent, then God 0 percent. Fundamental to this perspective is that God's agency works in the same way (or we might say on the same plane) as that of creation. Even though this zero-sum game works against a faith perspective, many Christians (even conservative ones) buy into this model. They just reverse the percentages: science covers 10 percent, and God 90 percent; or science 0 percent, and God 100 percent.

CHRISTIAN PERSPECTIVES ON GOD'S WORKING IN THE WORLD

- **Supernaturalism** (Westminster Confession; C. S. Lewis)—a system of nature (order, regularity, cause and effect) is affirmed. Nature is the creation of God, the effect of God sustaining, and the instrument of God's governing the world. God works beyond and even against nature when he works supernaturally.
- **Providentialism** (Cornelius Van Til)—a system of nature is assumed as above. God does not and needs not work supernaturally beyond what he accomplishes through nature. Every miracle and event have a natural explanation.
- **Occasionalism** (George Berkeley; G. C. Berkouwer)—a system of nature is not articulated by the Bible. God governs and acts at each moment. The things that appear to follow the ordered regularity of nature are occasions of God acting (consistently).
- **Self-Limiting Providence** (John Polkinghorne)—God limits his providence to avoid being a spectator or tyrant.[8]

When, however, we work from a creational perspective of divine transcendence, we have a way out of this dilemma because we conceive of God's agency as being different than creational agency. God stands outside and over creation, so the two are not in competition.

---

8. Adapted and amended from C. John Collins, *The God of Miracles* (Wheaton, IL: Crossway, 2000), 20–22.

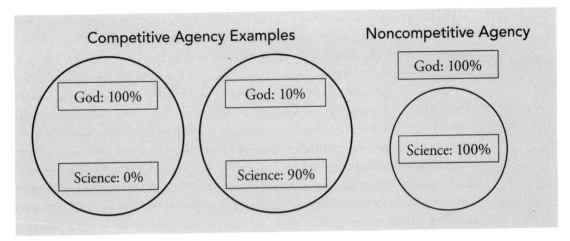

Figure 5.1
Competitive and Noncompetitive Agency

We can affirm that God is 100 percent involved and, at the same time, affirm that humans, science, and so on are 100 percent involved. This is a *noncompetitive* form of agency. Sin is what breaks nature. When God acts, the laws of nature are not broken; rather, nature runs according to its divinely intended goal.

Problem of Evil and Theodicy

When we consider evil in the context of providence and agency, fundamental problems arise for those who think, as Christians do, that God is good and all-powerful. In reality, however, all religions have tried to make sense of evil, whether they attribute it to fate, illusion, demons, or otherwise. Christians have traditionally considered the topic of evil in light of the biblical narrative rather than being limited by philosophical quandaries.

In the Old and New Testament, God's people faced evil from the perspective of a covenant encounter with God. God's deliverance of the Jews from the oppressive evil of slavery was a defining moment in the Old Testament. The exodus narrative does not explain evil straightforwardly; instead, it focuses on God's active agency to save his people from evil, especially in response to the people's prayers. We see, for example, prayers for God's action against injustice in the psalms of lament (e.g., Pss 3; 13; 17; 22). The book of Job is an extended lament and exploration of God's sovereignty in the face of unjust suffering. Fundamental to the narrative is that Satan and his demonic minions actively perpetuate evil. The Bible sometimes explains suffering as a punishment for sin, but often the two are unrelated. Scripture tends to focus not on the source of suffering but on the eschatological hope of restoration when God overcomes evil. Following this model, the New Testament focuses on Jesus as the **Messiah** who conquers evil through a new exodus (his death during Passover) and establishes the hoped-for kingdom.

Thurs.

Modern people process evil in a distinct fashion. Unlike biblical writers who saw evil as inevitable, moderns see themselves as entitled to "pursue happiness." When evil and injustice disrupt life, they feel someone must be held accountable—a ruler, a doctor, or God. The ancient believer knew that evil was derived from the Devil. God stood over them, but they still wondered why he mysteriously delivered some people but not others. Modern persons, by contrast, have expunged the Devil from the system so only God ultimately takes the blame for evil. They think they stand over God, deciding whether "God" is a concept they will embrace or reject. Evil and suffering count as evidence against the idea of God. If God is powerful (able to help) and loving (wants to help), then there must be some explanation as to why God permits suffering. Crudely, we must ask, "Can we defend the just character of God in the face of evil?" The term **theodicy** (Greek: *theos*, "god" + *dike*, "justice") is fashioned in the modern period to convey this question.

Defenders of God have created numerous arguments. They borrow ideas from ancient Christians, who ironically never framed theodicy in these modern terms. From Irenaeus, they borrow a notion that some evil is required for humans to progress as mature souls. From Augustine, they adopt the idea that evil emerged when creatures misused their God-given freedom. Some add that freedom was essential for genuine fellowship. Others craft sophisticated defense strategies to show that a loving and powerful God can logically coexist with evil.

Some see this as an exercise in logic or philosophy that must be settled before we can study theology. Irenaeus and Augustine show greater wisdom. They describe God's victory over evil as unfolding in history and centered in his Son. The gospel is a Christian answer to evil.

Conclusion

In the face of this evil, we can lose sight of the wonder of creation and more so the wonder of the Creator. Though God is distinct from the world, the narrative of Scripture demonstrates his continual triune engagement with the world. With the immanent Trinity we see God's uniqueness from creation, but with the economic Trinity the focus is specifically upon God's action in the world. The Father is Creator, the Son becomes incarnate, and the Spirit is present with his people. Though we at times struggle to reconcile how evil relates to his providential care, the incarnation of Christ and the life-giving presence of Spirit reveal God's holy love.

CONTEMPORARY THEOLOGICAL RELEVANCE

Now that we have explored some important ideas related to God's interaction with creation, we will explore a few ways this doctrine relates to wider issues in the contemporary world and church.

Thurs.

God, the World, and Christian Identity
God and the World and Other Christian Traditions

The discussion of God's interaction with the world could encompass the whole of theology, so we will limit ourselves here.

- **(Functional) Deism.** Classical deism argues that God created the world and will actively judge it, but in the meantime he passively allows it to run according to the laws he designed. This means that his active involvement, such as the incarnation or other miraculous interventions, is ruled out as impossible. While only a few classical deists exist, functional deism is pervasive in Western Christianity, as reflected by a disenchanted worldview: a mechanistic view of nature, a distant generic God, the lack of demonic agency, and an emphasis on personal autonomy.[9] This is captured by the common description of American Christianity as "moralistic therapeutic deism."[10] For example, Christians can embrace the phrase "In God we trust," but many (even most) would balk at replacing the phrase with "In Jesus we trust," which for Trinitarians should mean exactly the same thing. Have we bought into the generic supreme being "God" and lost out on the Father, Son, and Spirit as revealed in the Bible?

- **Jehovah's Witnesses.** Generally speaking, Jehovah's Witnesses have views of God's action in the world that are not substantively different than orthodox Christianity. However, since the Son is not God himself acting (but a subordinate archangel), God's transcendence is emphasized more than traditional Christianity. That is, he is not immanent in the world in the same way we have described above. Notably, they also affirm that the world was created good but is now corrupted by sin.

- **Mormonism** views the Godhead as transcendent and immanent very much like orthodox Christianity, though a couple of ideas distinguish their theology. Matter, Mormons argue, was not created _ex nihilo_; it eternally existed and was formed and shaped by God in creation. Also, while Heavenly Father is viewed as perfectly expressing now the attributes of power, knowledge, and so on, he was once a man like us who became exalted, and he continues to have an (exalted) body. So with regard to Heavenly Father's current state, LDS views of his transcendence are similar to orthodox Christianity, but the process of growth and exaltation stands at odds with the orthodox affirmation that God is eternally perfect. Though creation was not _ex nihilo_, they do affirm that evil entered through human sin.

---

9. See especially James K. A. Smith, _How (Not) to Be Secular: Reading Charles Taylor_ (Grand Rapids: Eerdmans, 2009).

10. Christian Smith with Melina Lundquist Denton, _Soul Searching: The Religious and Spiritual Lives of American Teenagers_ (Oxford: Oxford University, 2005).

Thurs.

God and the World and Other Religions

The numerous ways that other world religions conceive of God/god/gods' engagement in the world is dizzying. Each tradition might hold to some general tenets, but there are numerous debates within each about how these issues play out in creation, providence, and so on.

- **Judaism and Islam** have direct overlaps with Christianity in ways that others do not because of their explicit focus on monotheism. Both maintain God's transcendence and some means of immanence through God's creation and acts of providence. Each religion has its own variation. With regard to Jewish theology, God's immanence is connected to his active providence.[11] With regard to Islam, God's providence is a distinct factor, as evidenced by the phrase *insha'Allah* (or *inshallah*)—"if God wills it"—when speaking about the future. Further details about how Islam understands the God-world engagements are explored more in other chapters, particularly 6 and 11.
- **Hinduism.** Within its various traditions, Hinduism presents an interesting case. Perspectives on how the gods/god engage the world are highly dependent on one's approach within Hinduism. In some ways Hinduism is polytheistic with millions of gods, and in other ways it is monotheistic with Brahman, a single uniting reality. The emphasis on many gods, known as the *bhakti-marga* (or the path of devotion), is the most prominent, and it focuses on the immanence of these many gods. They actively engage the world, often through avatars, or incarnations of the gods. The focus on Brahman, with its more philosophical emphasis is the *jnana-marga* (or the path of knowledge). For some in this tradition, Brahman is so transcendent that we cannot even speak of Brahman having properties (i.e., *nirguna Brahman*).
- **Buddhism.** Buddhism is technically nontheistic, so one would not talk about a god's interaction with the world. Ultimate reality is fundamentally about emptiness (*sunyata*), and humans that recognize this are able to achieve *nirvana* ("blowing out"). However, some can be misled by the language of emptiness. Just as humans exist in this world, so can gods and spirits. These gods do not serve as the basis of ultimate reality. In Mahayana Buddhism, different Buddhas and *boddhisatvas* (exalted teachers) can take (semi-)divine roles with their aid of others.

God and Change: Passibility and Time

Does God change (or suffer) on account of his encounter with the world? In other words, is God passible? The term *passibility* derives from the Latin *pathos*, and thus "passion," in this context, refers to suffering and change. Until the late 1800s, most theologians took God's impassibility, his freedom from the vagaries of change and suffering,

---

11. In biblical times the temple was an important way to experience God's immanence—his glorious presence.

Thurs.

as a given. Indeed, in the debates of the early ecumenical councils (like Nicaea), those on both sides of the Trinitarian and christological debates assumed God's impassibility. Though this presumes a God very distinct from creation, God's active involvement in creation, especially in the incarnation of Christ, maintained his connection to this suffering world.

In response to the utterly transcendent God of modernity's deism, much more immanent views of God arose in the postmodern twentieth century. In *process theology*, for example, God remains distinct from creation, but he grows and changes along with it. In this model, God does not exist independently of the world and time but is bound up with it. According to **panentheism** (pan-en-theism), God and the world are distinct (unlike pantheism), but since love is so much a part of God's identity and nature, creation becomes an inevitable overflow of God's love. Some forms of panentheism appear to be a type of process theology, whereas others appear closer to orthodoxy. For instance, Jürgen Moltmann and others argue for a mediating position on God's passibility when it is related to the suffering of Jesus and the **revelation** of God: God does not have to suffer (as in process theology), but he lovingly chooses to suffer for our sake voluntarily.[12] In Moltmann's model, God is passible not by nature but by grace. Another model of passibility has been advanced under the title of ***open theism***. This perspective tries to take seriously the biblical passages where God does things like regret (e.g., Gen 6:6) or change his mind (e.g., Exod 32:14). On the basis of passages like these, open theists challenge traditional views of foreknowledge that are, they say, based on Greek philosophical views of impassibility and timelessness.

Whether they identify explicitly with these contemporary theologians or movements, many today are quite willing to accept views of God's passibility. This will surely be a matter of debate for years to come since this position challenges the traditional perspective.

Creation and Evolution

By what process did God create the world? Many in the church affirmed the surface reading of the creation material in Genesis (along with New Testament discussions about Adam in passages like Rom 5) that God created the earth in seven (literal) days. The church has more readily embraced scientific insights about **cosmology** (the nature of the universe) regarding the center of the solar system and now is reconsidering its **cosmogony** (how the universe began). Alternative reading strategies and approaches to Genesis have been considered, namely reading the initial chapters as more about *who* created the world than *how*. As a result Christians promote several different models of how God created. As we discussed above, appeals to contrastive agency (science vs. faith) are unwarranted since we can equally affirm God's agency and scientific reality. Just because we can

12. See, for example, Moltmann's well-known *The Crucified God: The Cross as the Foundation and Criticism of Christian Theology* (Minneapolis: Fortress, 1993).

explain scientifically why rain falls from clouds, that does not exclude God's simultaneous providential agency.

In assessing views on the relationship of creation and evolution, Christians incorporate different **sources of theology** (see ch. 2) balancing the witness of Scripture with reason (i.e., science). The first three views represent the broad range of positions held by Christians, whereas the last rejects Christianity:

- **Young-Earth Creationism.** This position holds that God created the earth a few thousand years ago with the appearance/reality of age (e.g., Adam was not a newborn). A question for this view is how to make sense of things that do not easily fit this timeframe model, such as dinosaurs.
- **Old-Earth Creationism.** This position holds that God created the earth progressively over billions of years, but he specifically created Adam and Eve more recently. This balances the progression in Genesis with scientific propositions about the age of the earth. Questions for this model relate to (1) the origin of death before Adam and Eve and (2) the possibility of a single ancestor couple.
- **Evolutionary Creation.** This position holds that God created the earth progressively over billions of years through a process of evolution (superintended by God), and Adam and Eve are metaphorical or covenantal figures representing humanity as a whole. This view places great weight on scientific arguments while still asserting God's providence and creation *ex nihilo*. Questions arise about (1) the origin of evil and death if God was superintending the process and (2) the biblical characterization of Adam and Eve.
- **Naturalistic Evolution.** This non-Christian position holds that biological life progressively evolved over billions of years solely through natural processes, such that we cannot speak of "creation" since that term presumes an act of God.

Virtues of Embrace and Renunciation

Pursuing the goodness of the things of the earth means embracing its goodness as God's gift to us. As we celebrate creation and embrace it, the Bible also warns us against substituting creation for the Creator. Take marriage and celibacy as examples. God has given us family as a basic means to flourishing. Yet, while extoling marriage and sex, Paul speaks of a temporary renunciation to pursue prayer (1 Cor 7:5). He also speaks of some who have a lifelong calling of renunciation through celibacy in order to commit themselves to a life of service (7:8, 32–35). The virtues of embrace and renunciation are not just reserved for sex but regard many if not all areas of life, such as food (feasting and fasting), relationships (community and solitude), work (service and rest), and so on. Due to concerns about a two-tier spirituality, most Protestants rejected vocations of renunciation (like monasticism) and communal practices of renunciation (like Lent) and thus celebrated the ordinary virtues of embrace (like marriage and vocation). Luther, in particular, strove to honor the sanctity of daily vocation as expressing the virtues of embrace. What do we lose if we have a two-tier spirituality? What do we lose if we ignore the virtues of renunciation? Is there a both/and approach, celebrating the ordinary virtues of embrace and the extraordinary virtues of renunciation?[13]

Further Issues

- **Providence.** To what extent does God's providence guide human and natural events? Does God superintend (or determine) all, some, or none of the world's events?
- **Acts of God.** Evil generated by people can be difficult to understand, but we can seem to explain it. What about natural disasters? A great tsunami in 2004 killed more than 220,000 people. Do these "acts of God" (as insurance contracts call them) influence faith? Why do modern people see natural disasters as evidence against God more than ancient people did?
- **Our Place in Outer Space.** Would life on other planets make Christianity less plausible? Does our world's displacement from the center of a simple solar system influence our theology? Or are we left with the same wonder before God: "what is mankind that you are mindful of them, human beings that you care for them?" (Ps 8:4).

PRACTICING THE FAITH

The following items explore various shifts in thinking, loving, and doing that might attend to the God-World relationship.

Creation Not Chaos

Is creation and its story important to you? The Bible begins with God creating an orderly and beautiful world. It is the act of a good and sovereign God. In the ancient Near East, each people group had its own story of creation. While these stories share images and vocabulary with the biblical story, they paint a different picture. To them the world is made of chaotic stuff that is always breaking out of control. These stories portray the world as the byproduct of the gods fighting with one another. If you live in violence, and your stories teach that the world originates in violence, then you have little reason to think life could be any other way. Violence is just the way of the world. If the Bible is your guiding image, two different things emerge. (1) Since a single God of order—rather than gods at war—created an orderly, stable, world, we can pursue knowledge and science impossible in a capricious, chaotic world. This, in fact, is why Christians were the first promoters of the great universities: to explore that order. (2) Even though we acknowledge that the world has suffered a gone-wrong-ness, we have reason to hope. The God who

---

13. See for example, Richard Foster, *Celebration of Discipline: The Path to Spiritual Growth* (San Francisco: HarperCollins, 1988).

Thurs.

created the world will also restore its goodness. How can you participate in the vocation of humanity to bring order to this world (Gen 1:26–28)?

Engaging Creation

One of the central messages of the creation narrative in Genesis 1 is that creation is "good," even "very good," as this is repeated over and over. The goodness of creation is also affirmed at the very end of the Bible, as this world is renewed by the restored presence of God. While evil enters the world, this framing shows that evil is not inherent to physical creation and that God's goodness is experienced through physical creation. However, this good creation needs care and concern: humanity was given a vocation to rule and expand the order of Eden to the wider world (Gen 1:26–28; 2:8). As a result, Christians have the obligation to care for the physical world and the life within it. What is the nature and extent of our responsibility? How might you attend to the needs of the environment by attending to the goodness of creation?

Recognizing Transcendence: Worship and Beauty

Worship is one of the most basic ways of living out our proper orientation to God. As we discussed in chapter 3, Scripture ties belief in God directly to a life of worship and obedience (Exod 20:1–21; Deut 6:4–5). The Psalms regularly point out how creation itself cries out in worship (Pss 19:1–6; 148). Some live according to the natural order of causes and effects. But those who have been and are being engaged by a transcendent God respond in worship.

We do not worship created things, but the beauty of the created world often points beyond itself to God. Indeed, God told the people of Israel to fill the Old Testament tabernacle and temple with beautiful art, much of which displayed garden of Eden imagery, to help lift their hearts to him (Exod 25–31; 35–40). This worship fully engaged all five senses. **High church** traditions often use all five senses, but **low church** traditions often focus just on one or two.[14] How can you more fully pursue beauty and art to recognize and to communicate to others how God stands above the mundane?

God Acts in History: Prayer for the Kingdom

Worship and beauty point us to God, and prayer brings us in line with God's action in our lives. God the Father, Son, and Spirit has been, is, and will continue to be active in the world. The heart of the prayer Jesus taught his disciples to pray is "your kingdom come, your will be done, on earth as it is in heaven" (Matt 6:10). When we pray, we enter into fellowship with the triune God and into the work of God. Although the battle for this world may seem too large for us, God calls us to pray persistently and plead for his kingdom and purpose. We pray for God's victory over the gone-wrong-ness of the world.

---

14. See ch. 10 for further detail.

We are encouraged to pray for our own cares and struggles because creation is off-kilter wherever evil is present. But when God works, creation flourishes as he intended it.

Trusting God in Hard Seasons

God's providence doesn't mean we are insulated from difficulty. If fact, Ecclesiastes 7:14 seems to indicate that we will not always understand specific pictures of providence. The hope given by providence rests elsewhere. Romans 8:28 does not claim that all things are good; it teaches that no matter what comes your way, nothing will keep God's purpose for you from being realized. We must learn to trust God and grow in confidence that he is faithful and present. When difficulty strikes, immerse yourselves in eschatological texts like 1 Peter and the lament psalms, and they will guide you through these dark paths.

Does God Care What Color Socks I Choose?

As we considered God's active role in creating and sustaining the world through his providence, we noted that obedience is an important form of worship. Accordingly, obedience to God in all things is important to Christian discipleship, but does God care what color socks I choose? How specific is God's will for my life, and how closely do I follow it? There are differing opinions about how God's providence works, whether it allows plenty of room for human freedom or includes God's intending even minor details, down to the color of our socks. Even if God does superintend this level of detail in our lives, he does not reveal that knowledge to us, and so we are not judged by that standard. We are called to walk in holiness and obedience, and as we choose between options that are equally holy, we can walk in freedom and creativity like the God we serve.

Further Considerations

- **Engaging a God of Holy Love.** When speaking of providence, people can sometimes project a mechanistic perspective on God's process of willing and acting. However, the Bible is clear that we are engaging a personal God. How could you better relate to him personally?
- **God Willing.** James reminds us that we do not control the future and commends the practice of adding "God willing" when we speak of the future since he is provident (Jas 4:13–17).
- **The Liturgical Calendar and the Active God.** The holy days and seasons of the liturgical calendar remind us that we serve a God who was and is active in history. These rituals related to Easter, Advent/Christmas, Pentecost, and so on draw us into the story of his action as Father, Son, and Spirit and train us to expect his continuing action in our lives.
- **Sacramental Prayer.** We find God not only in the transcendent but also in the ordinary aspects of life, like the bread and wine of communion. We can encounter

Thurs.

God in ordinary places by taking an ordinary practice and transforming it into a prayer—like washing dishes, making the bed, or drinking coffee. For example, you might pray, "As I hold this cup and feel its warmth, may I feel your warmth in my soul."

In the Bible we see the story of the creator God intimately engaged with the world, filling it with his goodness. Even when evil is introduced, he works to provide for the world's restoration, not by separating from it but by becoming part of it, taking humanity on himself in the Son. Accordingly, we can trust that he is still active in his creation.

CLOSING PRAYER

May this eternal truth be always on our hearts,
That the God who breathed this world into being,
Placed stars into the heavens
And designed a butterfly's wing,
Is the God who entrusted his son
to the care of ordinary people,
became vulnerable that we might know
how strong is the wonder of Love.
A mystery so deep it is impossible to grasp.
A mystery so beautiful it is impossible to ignore.[15]

15. John Birch, "Prayers for God's Created World #1," Faith and Worship, 2016, www.faithandworship.com/creation_prayers.htm#ixzz5MqPgQgsp.

CHAPTER 6

Jesus the Christ

The Incarnate Messiah

INTRODUCTION

As we get to roughly the center of this book on theology, we are arriving at what is often seen as the center of Christianity—Jesus the Christ. His first advent stands as the fulcrum of history, and it separates the current Western calendar into its two eras: BC (before Christ) and AD (*anno Domini*, in the year of the Lord). His second advent will mark the next great transition in history.[1] As someone so central to Christianity, Jesus has inspired an almost innumerable array of conceptions regarding his person and work by those in and outside the church. Increasingly, in this age of skepticism we have students who think he is a figment of imagination. Yet others follow him as the **incarnation** of God. We will explore some of these perspectives on Jesus to gain a better grasp on who he is and what he came to do. We begin with an account of Cyril of Alexandria, a patristic writer who contended for orthodox **Christology**.

CYRIL OF ALEXANDRIA: CAN GOD BECOME HUMAN?

Cyril and His World

Cyril (c. AD 378–444) was raised in the proud city of Alexandria, Egypt. An ancient center of Christianity and economic hub, Alexandria contended with another important center of Christianity—Antioch in Syria. The church in the new Roman capital of Constantinople was also growing in prestige, and in Cyril's mind imperial politics were eclipsing

---

Big Idea:
Through his incarnation, death, resurrection, and exaltation, we come to know the Son as the Messiah, who is one person existing in two natures—fully God and fully human.

Key Terms:
- Christology
- Messiah/Christ
- Incarnation
- Subordinationism
- *Homoousion*

Key Passages:
2 Sam 7:8–16;
Ps 2;
Isa 52:13–53:12; 60:1–3;
Dan 7:9–14;
John 1:1–5;
Phil 2:5–11;
Col 1:15–20;
Heb 1:1–4

---

1. See ch. 11 for more details.

the authority of the apostles who had founded the ancient churches—Saint Peter in Rome and Saint Mark in Alexandria.

Cyril was groomed to rule as bishop over the church in Alexandria. His uncle Theophilus became bishop in 385 and gave Cyril a first-class education to match his knowledge of Scripture. Cyril observed his uncle's firm rule as his assistant for nine years. Cyril was present when his uncle was instrumental in deposing the famous preacher John Chrysostom as bishop in Constantinople. At his uncle's passing in 412, Cyril became bishop despite some protest. Once in charge, Cyril—like his uncle—sought not only to rule firmly over his churches but also to confront weak theology.

Cyril's rule was indeed controversial. He confiscated a church building belonging to the Novatians (a group the church rejected for being overly strict). He also was hard on the Jews and the pagans. Socrates Scholasticus, a Christian historian with hard feelings toward Cyril, recorded the murder of the noted pagan philosopher Hypatia by a radical Christian group of monks. Cyril is commonly blamed for executing the philosopher because she thought freely about matters both sensual and philosophical. In truth Hypatia was well regarded among Christians and had numerous wealthy Christians as her students. Though Cyril did not direct the event, he may bear some responsibility for not intervening or condemning the violence.

The first phase of Cyril's theological study was given to struggling against Arianism, a **subordinationist** view that the Son was created and a lesser god. Like theologians of his time, he focused on Scripture. His massive commentary on the Gospel of John shows his attentive reading of the text and demonstrates his theological and intellectual rigor.

Two Approaches to Christology

With his acumen for theology, Cyril became concerned about careless explanations of Jesus's identity from some teachers in Antioch—namely, Diodore of Tarsus and Theodore of Mopsuestia. Following the councils of Nicaea and Constantinople I, both theologians affirmed that Jesus is fully divine and fully human. But one question remained: How should we understand these natures working together? The debates were nuanced, but it will still be useful to understand the differences between the Antiochian and Alexandrian approaches to Christ. Antiochians typically held that the divine and human natures of Jesus were distinct. You might picture these natures as separate airtight compartments. They thought the eternal Word of God was paired with and partner to the individual human man named Jesus (Word-man). Likewise, the Alexandrians affirmed the two natures, but typically they viewed the divine nature invading humanity. They pictured the eternal Word of God becoming flesh (Word-flesh). The significance is that the Word genuinely entered the human realm.

Diodore (an Antiochian) worried that Alexandrian believers ignored the humanity of Jesus. For example, he questioned the popular title *theotokos* ("the one who gives birth to God," or "mother of God") used to describe Mary the mother of Jesus. He worried about losing focus that she was the mother of the *human* Jesus. Were the Alexandrians intentionally ignoring the humanity of Jesus? Theodore (another Antiochian) believed that salvation was at stake; salvation rested on this crucial idea—the man Jesus was the perfect and willing partner with the Word at every moment of his life. The man Jesus got it right—he lived in harmony with God's will. He is our champion and example to inspire us. Theodore worried the Alexandrians thought salvation happened just because the Word became flesh—God doing it all with a human puppet.

Enter Nestorius

A well-spoken student of Theodore named Nestorius became bishop over Constantinople in 428. He was an effective preacher and sincerely wanted to reform the capital. He was idealistic like John Chrysostom, a former bishop with Antiochian connections who had been torpedoed by Cyril's uncle. Cyril was angry when the emperor assigned Nestorius to oversee a citizen appeal against Cyril. Controversy in Constantinople spread when Nestorius rejected the well-entrenched term *theotokos* (Mother of God) to describe Mary. Cyril offered various theories why Nestorius would not embrace such a common piece of Christian **liturgy**. He protested how Nestorius divided the person of Jesus: Jesus's human nature was at work when he asked for water or cried, but Jesus's divine nature was at work when he raised the dead. Cyril complained that in practice Nestorius had two Jesuses. In a setting where all agreed that God was impassible (does not suffer), Nestorius's approach had some superficial advantages; this separation allowed the eternal Word (who was thought to be above suffering) to be clearly distinct from the human man (who suffered and died). The problem had to do with the nature of spirituality: If the divine and human could not work together in Christ, what hope did believers have for truly experiencing the divine presence?

The Verdict and Legacy of Ephesus

The theological disputes became political, but later councils vindicated the theological vision that undergirded Cyril's work. Both sides read and argued uncharitably; both sides achieved advantage by seeking political favor with imperial and church officials. After numerous regional meetings, each condemning the other, the powers aligned with the verdict of the Council of Ephesus in 431 at which Nestorius was condemned and exiled for the remainder of his life.

Cyril's weighty engagement with Scripture guided him to a more biblical verdict. Nestorius's multiperson Jesus was not the Jesus of the New Testament. Cyril insisted that there was one person, the Son of God incarnate, not two persons. The same Son who was tired and slept also raised the dead and walked on water. Jesus was not merely in tune with the Son of God; he was the Son of God. With great wisdom, Cyril acknowledged that the Son even suffered: the Son of God before the incarnation could not suffer, but the incarnate Son of God could suffer impassibly. Cyril's view also makes sense of

Jesus welcoming us to share in his Sonship: only the genuine Son could make room for adopted children. The New Testament does not celebrate a man who climbed up to God or claimed divine status; it pictures a God who comes down to save humanity and unite heaven with earth. Though Cyril and the councils who followed him made use of the philosophy of their day, they rejected Nestorius's position, which attempted to fit the Bible into a philosophical view of God's impassibility. Rather Cyril accepted a position that did not make clean philosophical sense—God suffered impassibly in Christ—because it was what the Bible presented. Like Cyril, our discussion focuses on the biblical narrative to explore how Jesus unites heaven and earth.

JESUS CHRIST IN THE BIBLE AND THEOLOGY

Biblical Approaches to Christology

In our chapter on **revelation**, we talked about progressive revelation, the idea that God progressively reveals knowledge about himself and his plan. Nowhere is this more evident than in **Christology**. The biblical narrative presents a picture that develops and has multiple sides and perspectives. To organize the biblical data we will consider these three perspectives: Christology *from behind*, Christology *from below*, and Christology *from above*. Some theologians use these frameworks in opposition to one another, often to present a one-sided picture: Christology from below as a "low Christology" (Jesus as just a man) or Christology from above as a "high Christology" (Jesus as really God). We, however, see these three perspectives as mutually reinforcing each other. They help tell the story of Jesus without being fixed, separable categories.

Christology from Behind: Old Testament Messianic Expectations

The idea of Christology does not start with Jesus and the New Testament. Like almost all things theological, the Old Testament sets the framework for the ideas that the New Testament (re)interprets and shapes. The term *Christ* is a Greek word that means "anointed" and is a translation of the Hebrew term **Messiah**. Today anointing is often metaphorical, but in the ancient world it literally referred to the practice of pouring oil on leaders' heads, setting them apart as ordained by God. Kings (1 Sam 10:1; 16:12–13; 1 Chron 29:22) and priests (Exod 28:41; Lev 8:30) were anointed most commonly, but prophets were anointed too (1 Kgs 19:16; 1 Chron 16:22). These were all messianic—that is, anointed—leaders. They were all fallible, but the Jewish people expected God to send a special messianic leader who would faithfully guide the people in the ways of the Lord.

Among the various roles expected for the messianic leaders, the role of king was prominent. We see the expectation of a future king with the Davidic **covenant** in 2 Samuel 7. At the heart of this covenant is a promise for David's heirs: "I will establish the throne of his kingdom forever. I will be his father, and he will be my son" (2 Sam 7:13–14). Being a "son of God" came to be a title for kings in this setting (cf. Pss 2; 89). The Old Testament prophets extend this hope for a coming leader. Isaiah, for example, has several "Servant Songs" that describe the coming servant (Isa 42:1–7; 49:1–6; 50:4–9; 52:13–53:12). The last of these is most well known because it speaks vividly of the suffering servant. In addition, Daniel 7:9–14 speaks of a "son of man, coming with the clouds of heaven" who will have an eternal dominion and kingdom. In light of these texts, many Jews continue to look forward to the coming of a messiah who will bring restoration. Christians in the New Testament see these expectations fulfilled in Jesus.

OLD TESTAMENT AND SECOND TEMPLE JEWISH MESSIANIC EXPECTATIONS

A variety of Jewish writings explain what their expectations are for the coming Messiah and help us understand how the New Testament writers understood Jesus:

- **Old Testament Passages:** 2 Sam 7:9–16; Pss 2; 89; 110; Isa 7:14; 9:6–7; 11:1–5; 42:1–7; 49:1–6; 50:4–9; Jer 33:14–22; Ezek 34:22–24; Dan 7:9–14; Mic 5:2.
- **Second Temple Passages:** 1 Enoch 46; Psalms of Solomon 17:26–46; 4 Ezra 13.

Christology from Below: New Testament Messianic Fulfillment

Four first-century biographies of Jesus are called "the Gospels": the Gospel according to Matthew, according to Mark, according to Luke, and according to John. The term *gospel* (Greek: *euangelion*) means "good news," and the center of that good news is evident from the beginning. Mark, likely the first of the four to be written, starts with "the beginning of the good news about Jesus the Messiah, the Son of God" (Mark 1:1). Jesus being the "Messiah/Christ" is the good news. (We must remember that "Christ" is not Jesus's last name: Joseph and Mary Christ did not have little baby Jesus Christ.) He is the culmination of the hope for a messianic leader.

The association of Jesus with the *kingly* messianic ideas is evident in the Gospels. Besides being called the Messiah/Christ by the narrator and later by his disciples (Mark 8:29), one of the first accounts in the Gospels is Jesus's baptism, in which the Spirit descends on him and God says, "You are my Son" (Luke 3:22). This confirms his identity as "Son of God," and Jesus interprets this Spirit-experience as his anointing (Luke 4:16–21). Not only is he the Son of God but the "Son of David" (Matt 1:1; 12:23) as well. He also calls himself the "Son of Man" repeatedly, even quoting the Daniel 7 passage to describe his kingly self-understanding (Mark 14:61–62). Even the gentiles understand his role as the messianic King when they write his charge over his cross as "Jesus of Nazareth King of the Jews" at his crucifixion.[2] That Jesus was the messianic King is perhaps the clearest element of the Gospels, and just as evident is that the **kingdom of God** was at

---

2. In Latin this is "Iesus Nazarenus Rex Iudaeorum." In iconography related to the cross, the first letter of these words (INRI) is often seen.

the heart of his ministry. His preaching and teaching focused on the kingdom (e.g., Mark 4) and his miracles demonstrated it (e.g., Matt 12:22–32).

Unexpectedly, this King died, even put to death as a criminal on a cross, and was raised from the dead. This surprising mystery consumes the imagination of the rest of the New Testament. People considered following a crucified messiah foolishness in the ancient world (cf. 1 Cor 1), and it remains foolishness today.[3] Indeed, it is his death (on a cross) that most definitively reveals his full humanity. Jesus ate and drank (in fact he spent a lot of time eating and drinking with people). He got tired, thirsty, and hungry. He grew in wisdom and maturity (Luke 2:52). He was human just like us. And like us, he was subject to death. Yet even this mystery of death fits within God's plan, as the various texts speaking of the suffering messianic servant in Isaiah 53 show. The story does not end with his death; God raised him from the dead. The celebration of his death and **resurrection**, with Good Friday and Easter Sunday, thus serves as the most important weekend in the Christian calendar. Indeed, his resurrection was so central that Christians worshiped weekly on Sunday, the day of his resurrection, rather than on the Jewish sabbath as would have been expected. After his resurrection, he ascended to heaven, and his ascension and exaltation to the heavenly throne further confirmed his messianic identity (Luke 24:50–53; Acts 1:9–11). Jesus's death and resurrection not only shape our understanding of *his* identity but also *our* identity as his disciples, as we are called to walk in that same path of suffering obedience (e.g., Mark 8:29–38; 9:30–37; 10:32–45).

JESUS'S HUMANITY IN THE GOSPELS

According to Luke Timothy Johnson, "The Gospel writers interpret Jesus' sayings and deeds from the perspective of a deeper understanding of him given by the experience of the resurrection and the rereading of Scripture in light of his death and resurrection. What remains remarkable, in view of this, is how vividly human Jesus remains in their respective portraits of him: a man totally at home in the Judaism of first-century Palestine, with the words and gestures that fit that time and place. The Gospels should stun us most, not because they see Jesus as somehow divine, but that they so steadily and convincingly portray him as also utterly human."[4]

In terms of the Christology from below, we meet a very human Jesus. But he is not a generic human. He is the long-awaited messianic King bringing in the kingdom of God. He is not only a human messiah who died and raised (Christology from below) but the embodiment of God (Christology from above).

---

3. For example, while Christians proclaim the power of the cross, many of them also think the path of nonviolence is foolish.

4. Luke Timothy Johnson, *The Creed: What Christians Believe and Why It Matters* (New York: Image, 2005), 110.

Christology from Above: The Divine Son Becomes Incarnate

Through the narrative of the Bible, we progressively learn the breadth and depth of God's identity. In Christology from below, it is important that we see the resurrected and exalted Christ as no mere human—he embodies the God of Israel. Some biblical texts, rather than giving us this slow reveal, work with the whole picture at once: they narrate how God himself came to earth as human (has become incarnate) for us and our salvation as Jesus the Christ. As we discussed in chapter 3, this experience of the God of Israel as Father, Son, and Spirit meant that theological categories had to be expanded, so Trinitarian theology was developed to make sense of this biblical revelation.

In addition to narrative indicators about his divine identity (e.g., the Lord in Mark 1:1–3 or Immanuel, "God with us," in Matthew 1:23), several biblical passages are explicit.[5] They start with the divine identity of the Son and then explore his incarnation, death, and resurrection in light of that (John 1:1–18; Phil 2:5–11; Col 1:15–23; Heb 1:1–4). John 1 has had a large influence in the history of theology. Its iconic beginning intentionally reflects Genesis 1: "In the beginning was the Word [the *Logos*], and the Word was with God and the Word was God" (John 1:1). We see the unity of the Word with God (the Father) while also showing some kind of distinction. Later, Christian theologians will express that unity through the term *nature* or *being* (Greek: **ousia**) and the distinction through the term *person* (Greek: **hypostasis**). We derive the term *incarnation* from John 1:14, where the text says, "the Word became flesh"—he came *in carne*. Jesus did not "reincarnate." He was not human before, died, and then came back as another human, as we find in Eastern religions. He was only incarnated once for eternity. Thus, his resurrected body remains immortal today, sitting on his heavenly throne.

Different Christology-from-above texts highlight other aspects of the incarnation. For instance, Colossians 1:15–23 shows the divine Christ creating and descending to reconcile heaven and earth through his death on the cross. Hebrews 1:1–4 highlights the elevated identity of Christ over humans and angels; he both sustains creation and reconciles it to God. In Philippians 2:5–11, Christ Jesus, who is God, becomes human and submits himself to death on a cross, but he is raised and exalted. All will recognize Jesus as "Lord," the divine name—"the name that is above every name" (2:9). In each of these settings we see the divine Messiah not only coming to earth but also dying to bring reconciliation. God himself gets his hands dirty fixing our problems.

Putting Together the Biblical Story about Jesus

A balance between the Son's divine and human identity is maintained throughout all these passages. This is not abstract or speculative theology about divine and human

---

5. For an excellent introduction to these OT interconnections, see Richard B. Hays, *Reading Backwards: Figural Christology and the Fourfold Gospel* (Waco, TX: Baylor University Press, 2014).

natures but the narration of a story about how God himself comes to unite heaven and earth. However, we need theological categories to make sense of this; otherwise, we must affirm the worship of humans or the worship of multiple gods. As we make sense of the Bible, we must remember that not every text focuses on the same aspects of Christ's identity: some focus on his human vocation (*Christology from below* in conjunction with *Christology from behind*) and others on his incarnation from heaven to reconcile the world to God (*Christology from above*). Different biblical images bring these perspectives together. For instance, as the **image of God**, Christ reveals God (Col 1:15; Heb 1:3). As the image of God, Christ also is the model for human salvation—the image into which believers are transformed (Rom 8:29–30; 2 Cor 3:18). So these three perspectives reinforce rather than oppose one another. The multiplicity of these three larger biblical perspectives left the door open for theological discussion in the early church, and that historical discussion will be our focus now.

Historical Debates

All three perspectives tell part of the story, and so the view we get from each is not static. When we consider the debates in church history, the *narrative* of Jesus remains central, as the christological section of the Nicene Creed shows, yet at the same time the identities of the *characters* in the narrative come into focus. Accordingly, the issues of Christ's divine and human natures will serve as a lens to examine how best to understand and interpret the Story of God, who is restoring our broken world.

The recognition of Jesus's identity in the church did not begin as theological pronouncement, but as worship. Early Christians incorporated the worship of Jesus into their worship of God, and their experience of God in Christ (and the Spirit) required that their theology evolve to make sense of the story of Jesus's death and resurrection. The Scriptures describe and explain this Jesus-experience. By doing so they further shape the language and categories that the early church used to describe Jesus. The broad consensus of the church was that Jesus embodied God's presence on earth in human form. In short, they affirmed that Jesus was fully God and fully human.

JESUS AS GOD IN THE SECOND CENTURY

In chapter 3, we discussed how Jesus was affirmed as God at the Council of Nicaea in AD 325. It is not uncommon to hear popularly (e.g., on *History Channel* documentaries) that this is when the church hierarchy invented this view. However, we have very clear evidence from patristic writings that Christians regularly called Jesus "God" two hundred years before Nicaea, following the pattern we already see in the New Testament (John 1:1; 20:28; Tit 2:11–13; Heb 1:8). The following snapshots reflect the church's perspective on Jesus as God in the second century:

1. Non-Christian sources point to Christians worshiping Jesus as a God (e.g., Pliny the Younger; Letter to Emperor Trajan c. AD 113, Letters 10.96–97).
2. As Ignatius of Antioch (c. AD 115) was heading to martyrdom, he wrote that he was "to be an imitator of the suffering of my God" (Epistle to the Romans 6:3).
3. In *Dialogue with Trypho*, Justin Martyr (c. AD 150) wrote several times that Jesus is both Christ and God (36; 63; 126).
4. In the Acts of Paul (c. AD 175), Thecla praises Jesus as God for saving her from martyrdom (4.17).
5. Irenaeus (c. AD 177) argues for Jesus being fully God and fully human (e.g., *Against Heresies* 3.17–19).

While the affirmation that Jesus was divine was common, that does not mean it was always interpreted in the same way. In polytheistic cultures, the term *god* can be flexible, so over time Christians worked out what that meant to affirm Jesus as God (and as human). As we progress through the second and third centuries, we see various ways to make sense of the balance of divinity and humanity in Christ, choosing both/and positions. Some heterodox groups, however, chose either/or positions, such as the **Gnostics**, who focused only on Christ's divinity, or others, who only focused on his humanity.[6] The orthodox maintained some sense of both. The story of Christ's death and resurrection as reconciling humans with God was what united Christians. This point of unity is clear from the various versions of the **rule of faith**.[7] The various rules of faith were Trinitarian in structure, and when they described the Son, they usually focused on the story of Jesus like we see in the second paragraph of the creed quoted below ("For us and our salvation . . .").

With the Arian controversy in the fourth century, the church decided to address the issue of Christ's divinity more formally, though the story of his death, resurrection, ascension, and return still remained central.

THE SECOND ARTICLE OF THE NICENE CREED (COUNCIL OF NICAEA, AD 325)

We believe in one Lord, Jesus Christ, the only Son of God,
eternally begotten of the Father,
God from God, Light from Light,
true God from true God,
begotten, not made, of one Being [*homoousios*, "consubstantial"] with the Father;
through him all things were made.

---

6. Some attribute this position with the Ebionites, an early group of Jewish believers in Jesus. The common thinking is that they tended to follow what is described as an "adoptionist" view (see below), though this is now disputed by many scholars.

7. See Michael Kruger, *Christianity at the Crossroads: How the Second Century Shaped the Future of the Church* (Downers Grove, IL: InterVarsity Press, 2018), 135–45.

> For us and for our salvation
> he came down from heaven,
> was incarnate from the Holy Spirit and the Virgin Mary
> and became truly human.
> For our sake he was crucified under Pontius Pilate;
> he suffered death and was buried.
> On the third day he rose again
> in accordance with the Scriptures;
> he ascended into heaven
> and is seated at the right hand of the Father.
> He will come again in glory to judge the living and the dead, and his kingdom will
>   have no end.

Arius and his spiritual children promoted a subordinationist position which viewed Jesus as divine but not fully God as the Father was God. According to various biblical texts, the Son was "begotten" (or "generated"; see, e.g., John 3:16). Arians wrestled with these texts and argued that the Son had to have a beginning in time; he was created. Yet they argue that he was the first and highest of all God's creations and so should not be merely considered our equal.

In response to this subordinationist position, which makes the Son lower than the Father, the church drafted the Nicene Creed. Starting with the traditional rule of faith, they added a paragraph to clarify the relationship of the Father and Son ("eternally begotten of the Father"). The Son is "begotten" (as the Bible affirms) but "not created." Rather, he is God in the same way the Father is God; he shares the same nature or being (Greek: *ousia*), so he is "of one Being," or "consubstantial," (Greek: *homoousion*) with the Father. Further nuances and debates arose after Nicaea (see ch. 3), but the affirmation that the Son is fully God as the Father is fully God has remained the central position of the church.

JESUS AS DIVINE AND HUMAN

Contemporary people tend to consider Jesus as being more human than divine. That is, the base cultural assumption about Jesus is that he was a good man pointing people to God but not divine himself (an "adoptionist" position; see below). The opposite was true in the early centuries of the church. The second-century church was tempted to see Jesus as more divine than human, as Gnosticism shows. Accordingly, when describing the events surrounding Nicaea, New Testament scholar Luke Timothy Johnson argues: "The innovation was not the 'imposition' of high Christology by the orthodox bishops of the fourth century, but rather the denial of that high Christology in the early fourth century by the Alexandrian priest Arius and his followers."[8]

---

8. Johnson, *The Creed*, 111.

Though you may get lost in all the discussion of natures and *homoousion*, do not miss what these patristic theologians are trying to affirm: when you see Jesus, you see God; what Jesus does is 100 percent a reflection of God. Jesus is the clearest revelation of God we will ever get because he is God. Reread the second paragraph of the creed quoted above with this in mind. God the Father is not up in heaven, angry, needing to be convinced to love us, requiring Jesus to come and appease him. Rather, Jesus is God himself, who gives himself "for us and our salvation." That is why the church fought so hard over this seemingly overtechnical language: the Son is eternally "of one Being with the Father." While this is argued from a slightly different tack than the biblical texts, even with their Christology-from-above perspective, the purpose is the same. As is common in "from above" views, the life and ministry of Jesus is not so much the focus as is his incarnation, death, resurrection, ascension, and return. For a creed to be short enough to be an outline, it cannot include a bunch of details.

As the creed narrates this Christology from above, it does not gloss over the reality of Jesus's humanity. He was incarnate (i.e., he took on flesh) and "became truly human." What does it mean to be human? This question followed Nicaea quickly. Apollinarius, a bishop of Laodicea (a city in Asia Minor / Turkey), was an ardent supporter of Nicaea. He argued for the divinity of Christ and affirmed with Nicaea that the Son took on flesh (cf. John 1:14) and became human, but for Apollinarius this meant that Jesus only took on a human body—not a human mind. The Old and New Testaments are very unsystematic in their approach to human composition (see ch. 8): What is the difference between the mind, soul, conscience, heart, will, emotions, and spirit? The distinctions are not clear, yet most agree that humans have both a physical and spiritual aspect. Why then would Apollinarius question Jesus having a human mind/soul?

With that question, we are brought into a central issue at the heart of the incarnation: How can divinity and humanity exist together? Are they at odds? Is the humanity absorbed into the divinity? Apollinarius, it appears (since hardly any of his writings are still extant), was concerned that if Jesus had a human soul, it would function in contrast with the divine Word, leading Jesus into sin—after all, to err is human. Apollinarius affirmed that Jesus had a real human body but that the divinity of Christ functioned in lieu of a human soul. The Council of Constantinople (AD 381) condemned this position, affirming that Jesus had a human body and a human soul because he is fully human. This is not just abstract metaphysics about what makes up a human; it points to the question of how humanity and divinity work together.[9] If the human soul or mental facility cannot work together with the divine in Jesus, then it seems implausible or impossible that we as humans could conform to God's purpose. We would not be able to follow God in obedience and live in union with him. But since we see humanity and divinity in harmony in Jesus, our Christology has implications for our discussion

---

9. See our discussion of noncompetitive **agency** in ch. 5.

of spirituality. We will now detail what have been deemed insufficient models and how the church responded to them.

Chalcedon and Heterodox Christologies

At the Council of Chalcedon (AD 451), the bishops of the church responded to a number of challenges from all sides. Accordingly, they developed what has become the standard by which christological perspectives are measured. They affirmed the main thrust of Cyril of Alexandria's work, with a slight modification. We can boil down their conclusions to this: *Jesus Christ (after the incarnation) has two natures—fully divine and fully human—that exist as one person.* The Definition of Chalcedon says it this way:

> We, then, following the holy Fathers, all with one consent, teach people to confess the one and only Son, our Lord Jesus Christ, the same perfect in deity and also perfect in humanity; truly God and truly man, with a rational soul and body; consubstantial [of the same being] with the Father according to deity, and consubstantial with us according to the humanity; in all things like unto us, except without sin; begotten before all ages of the Father according to deity, and in these latter days, for us and for our salvation, born of the Virgin Mary, the Mother of God, according to humanity; one and the same Christ, Son, Lord, only begotten, to be acknowledged in two natures—without confusion, without change, without division, without separation. The distinctiveness of the natures are by no means taken away by the union, but rather the property of each nature (*ousia*) is preserved, and concurring in one Person and one Subsistence (*hypostasis*), not parted or divided into two persons, but one and the same Son, and only-begotten God, the Word, the Lord Jesus Christ; as the prophets from the beginning [have declared] concerning Him, and the Lord Jesus Christ Himself has taught us, and the Creed of the holy Fathers [Nicene Creed] has handed down to us.[10]

Oftentimes, excluding false positions (what something is not) is easier than spelling out fully what we affirm (what something is). With Chalcedon we have an "orthodox box" that derives from this belief that Jesus is one person in two natures—human and divine (see figure 6.1). The box shows that different things on opposite sides of the box are held in tension—one person in tension with two natures and divinity in tension with humanity. These are not in opposition since orthodox theology holds that both are true about Jesus simultaneously; he is both one person and two natures, both divine and human. Orthodox theology has a both/and approach, whereas heterodox theology has an either/or approach. The various either/or heterodox positions (1) overemphasize what

---

10. Slightly modified from Philip Schaff, *The Creeds of Christendom*, vol. 2, *The Greek and Latin Creeds* (New York: Harper, 1877), 62.

the orthodox affirm and therefore (2) deny some other aspect the orthodox affirm. We'll go through the six christological heresies.[11]

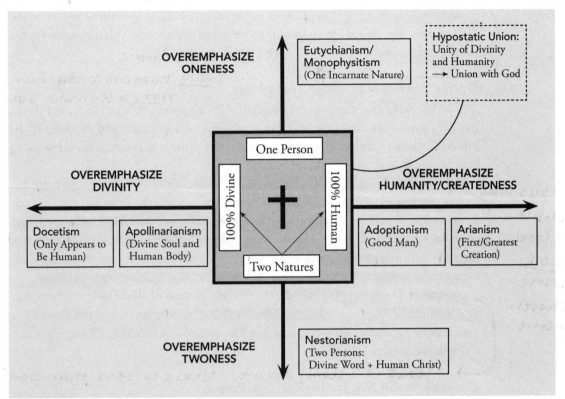

FIGURE 6.1
The Orthodox Box—Christology in Light of Chalcedon

Overemphasize Divinity

The following two positions overemphasize Jesus's divinity and therefore deny something fundamental about his humanity. Docetism and Apollinarianism try to protect Jesus from too close an involvement in this broken world. Both falsely assume that passible things (humanity) cannot be truly united to the impassible (divinity).

Docetism. Deriving from the Greek term *dokeo*, which means "to seem," Docetism argues that the divine Son only seemed to be human. This position is often associated with Gnostic traditions, which affirmed the goodness of spiritual and immaterial existence and the evilness of the material existence. Thus they would not want the savior to have a physical body, which by nature is evil. There were two ancient versions of this:

- divine Son → only human   · Jesus was not material

11. Often heresies are labeled by a theologian who did not fully hold to the position that his followers promulgated, but for shorthand we continue to use the initial person's name to label the doctrine.

· As a ghost or
divine Christ possesed
Jesus left after bapt

(1) Jesus, like an angel (or ghost), only appeared to have a human body, or (2) the divine Christ possessed the human man Jesus at his baptism and left before Jesus was crucified.

Apollinarianism. This position affirms that Jesus was fully divine but only had a human body not a human soul. This is sometimes called Logos-Christology, since the divine Logos (the "Word," from John 1) serves as the main source of Jesus's agency—his willing and action.

[handwritten: ° Jesus = fully divine]
[handwritten: ° only human body but NOT a human soul]

Overemphasize Humanity/Createdness

The following two positions overemphasize Jesus's humanity/createdness and therefore deny something fundamental about his divinity. Adoptionism and Arianism try to protect Christian theology from its perceived polytheistic tendencies, and both want to preserve the uniqueness of God the Father.

[handwritten: ° Jesus was 'adopted' by God • NOT divine • chosen by God]

Adoptionism. The man Jesus had a normal human birth like any other human, but he was called to serve God and lead God's people, much like the other men and women mentioned in the Bible. The Bible calls him a "Son of God" metaphorically, much like other ancient (biblical) kings. In that sense, Jesus is "adopted" as God's son. He is not divine by nature or divine in any way at all. He is a good man, who was chosen by God, in much the same way that an adopted child is not a child by nature but by choice.

Arianism. The Son is (semi)divine, the first and greatest of all of God's creatures, but he is not fully divine in the same way that God is divine. Arians argue this semidivine Son became incarnate, died, and rose just like orthodox Christians affirm. They just claim he was created first.

[handwritten: ° Jesus is (semi) divine   ° Jesus is less than God]

Overemphasize Two Natures or One Person

The first four heterodox positions are fairly easy to understand, and their deficiencies have been well studied and documented. The next two, however, are much more nuanced and difficult for students to grasp, not least because modern churches often speak in terms similar to these positions! Both monophysites and Nestorians affirmed the Nicene Creed, that Jesus was fully divine and fully human, but the question was how this union works. Students often feel this is where theology seems to take a highly speculative turn: How do we know what was going on in the mind of Christ? The Bible does speak to these issues, so they are not entirely speculative. While we affirm Jesus's unique place in history, the patristic writers who hammered out their theology about these issues were pastors as well as theologians, so their Christology always related to spirituality.

Before discussing these, we need to examine or remember a few terms. We have talked about the focus on *nature* (Greek: *ousia*) as what unites the three persons of the Trinity, but as the discussion developed in the fourth century, the church searched for a good term (or set of terms) to express the diversity in the Trinity. The term *person* (Greek: *prosopon*; Latin: *persona*) is most commonly used today, and it had some sway in the ancient church. However, *person* could also refer to an inconsequential distinction, as when an actor wears a mask, and so it had the potential to point to **modalism** (the view that God is one person who shows himself in three roles, or modes). Instead, the ancient church chose *subsistence* (Greek: *hypostasis*) as the term to represent the persons. Thus God has one nature (*ousia*) and is three persons (*hypostases*). The Son is one hypostasis of the Trinity, and when his humanity is united to his divinity this is described as the *hypostatic union*. These two views—Nestorianism and monophysitism—are narrations of how the hypostatic union works.

Nestorianism. Nestorius and his spiritual heirs so emphasized the distinction between the divinity and humanity in Christ that they argued for not only two natures but two persons in Christ—the divine Son and the human Jesus. Nestorius was trying to protect the distinct reality of each of the two natures in Christ, namely because passible humanity cannot truly unite with impassible divinity. But by overemphasizing the twoness of Jesus's natures, he therefore denied something fundamental about the oneness of Jesus's person.

[margin note: → • Two persons in Jesus • Divine son and human Jesus]

Eutychianism/Monophysitism. Rejecting Nestorius's stark division between the divine and human in Christ, Eutyches took Cyril of Alexandria's theology a step further and argued too strongly for an indivisible unity. He argued that there is only one person, one substantive reality, after the two natures came together in the incarnation. Eutychianism was condemned at Chalcedon, and those in general agreement with Eutyches who rejected Chalcedon became known as monophysites (from the Greek for "one nature"). Variations of this view argue that either the two natures were mixed and created a new third nature or there is a functional absorption of his humanity into his divinity. Eutyches was trying to protect the unity of the narrative of the God-man Jesus in the Bible, but in doing so, he overemphasized the oneness of Jesus's person and therefore denied something fundamental about the twoness or distinction of his natures.

[margin note: → • Only one person • Two natures as 'one']

Orthodoxy stands between these extremes. By considering how the hypostatic union serves as the ground for our spirituality (our own union with God), we can see how monophysitism and Nestorianism go wrong. We are not absorbed into the divine (as the monophysites), nor is the divine so incompatible with humanity that they cannot truly interact (as the Nestorians). Rather, like a sword placed in a fire, the steel and the fire remain distinct, but the sword is transformed by the union. They are not incompatible, and the union of the divine (fire) and human (sword) transforms Christ's humanity, but they are never fused or destroyed. As it is in Christ, so too it is possible with us when we encounter the divine.

While most Protestants end their discussion of Christology with the fourth ecumenical council at Chalcedon, the later ecumenical councils directly address Christology as well—the fifth, Constantinople II (AD 553); the sixth, Constantinople III (AD 660); and the seventh, Nicaea II (AD 787). Constantinople II attempted to mediate between the monophysites and Chalcedonians, while still affirming Chalcedon. Constantinople III, in response to imperially mandated attempts at reconciliation that rejected biblical and theological discussion, affirmed (in line with Maximus the Confessor) that Christ's full humanity means he has not only a human mind but also a human will (in addition to a divine will). Nicaea II addressed the use of icons (paintings of holy figures) in the church. Since God has revealed himself through his icon, or image (Greek: *eikon*), Jesus, God has opened the door for the use of icons, as long as they are not worshiped.

Historical and Modern Issues

While some minor changes took place over the medieval period and the Reformation, the core christological perspective of the church did not change. In the Reformation a shift did occur, not in the doctrines related to the hypostatic union but with a new form of Christocentrism (*solus Christus*), which came in contrast to the mediatorial work of the church. A much stronger challenge arose in the Enlightenment with the historical-critical method of biblical studies from the mid-1800s. In simple terms, this led to a focus on Jesus's humanity (a Christology from below) divorced from discussions of his divinity (Christology from above). This adoptionist Christology, influenced by a deistic view of God, became central to traditional Protestant liberalism. In response, Karl Barth helped recapture a Christology from above in the twentieth century by emphasizing God's direct personal act in Christ. This reclamation of Christ as the self-revelation of God generated a revival in Trinitarian thought. Theologians, such as Jürgen Moltmann, developed this further by emphasizing the voluntary suffering in the person of Christ (as well as in the person of the Father) as central to this divine self-revelation. How we understand the hypostatic union still has room for exploration, but as theologians continually return to the story of Christ's incarnation, death, and resurrection, this always generates fresh interest in what Christ's story reveals about God acting for us.

Conclusion

In discussing Christology, the focus can easily shift toward philosophy with all the talk about natures and persons. These ideas are important, but the primary focus of the biblical narrative is that Jesus is the Spirit-anointed Messiah bringing in the kingdom of God. Early Christians knew he was not just a mere man because when they encountered him, they encountered God. Thus the affirmation that the Son is *homoousion* (shares the same nature) with the Father simply describes early Christians' encounter with the divine Messiah, who suffered death and was raised to bring salvation to the world.

CONTEMPORARY THEOLOGICAL RELEVANCE

Now that we have explored key ideas related to Jesus the Christ, we will explore a few key areas where these doctrines relate to wider issues in the contemporary world and church.

Jesus Christ and Christian Identity

Jesus plays a crucial role in a few world religions, so he might seem like possible place for concord. Yet views about Jesus are often a source of distinction rather than unity.

In other words, Jesus is the sharp end of the spear of theological divisions. It is fundamental to orthodox approaches to Jesus that he is the fullest and greatest revelation of God in the world because he is God. From this perspective we address other religious traditions.

Jesus and Other Christian Traditions

- **(Functional) Deism.** Traditional deism (often associated with traditional liberal Protestantism) argues that God actively created the world but passively allows it to run according to his laws. His active involvement, seen through the incarnation or other miraculous intervention, is ruled out as impossible. Therefore, traditional deists typically hold an adoptionist Christology. More prevalent in Western Christianity, functional deism does not explicitly reject Jesus's divine identity but does minimize the necessity of the divine activity of grace. Success is sought through moral effort rather than through the power of the cross. As such, **human flourishing** comes from the world's power rather than through sacrifice and **cruciformity**.

- **Jehovah's Witnesses** hold that the Son is "a god" (John 1:1 New World Translation) and divine only metaphorically. That is, the Son is not equally God with the Father, because the Son is the Father's first creation. Jehovah's Witnesses argue that the Son is none other than Michael the Archangel. This is a subordinationist Christology, like that of Arianism. Though the Son is not God (but a subordinate archangel), they affirm that he preexisted (though not eternally) in heaven before becoming incarnate by a virgin birth in order to establish his messianic kingdom through his death and resurrection.

- **Mormonism** holds that all sentient beings share the same nature, so there are not two natures in Christ, just one. In that way, Jesus is of the same nature as the Father and of the same nature as humans (as the ecumenical councils affirm), because all humans are of the same nature as the Father (which the councils do not affirm). In short, Christ is one person with one nature. According to the *Book of Mormon*, after Christ's ascension as narrated in the New Testament, he revealed himself to Jewish believers who had come to North America.

Jesus and Other Religions

Several world religions mention Jesus, though when he is incorporated, his role is never distinctly formative to these traditions in the same way as Christianity. The two other Abrahamic religions have been influenced by the developments in Christian theology, and both address it more and less directly depending on the context. Yet the Christian affirmation that Jesus is God incarnate is difficult if not impossible to incorporate in their monotheistic traditions. Steven Prothero describes Christianity as a "soft monotheism" and the other Abrahamic religions as more of a "hard monotheism."[12]

---

12. Stephen Prothero, *God Is Not One: The Eight Rival Religions That Run the World* (New York: HarperOne, 2010), 36.

- **Judaism.** Jesus was a Jewish man who lived primarily among Jews. His earliest followers were Jews who interpreted Jesus according to Jewish categories like **monotheism**, **election**, **eschatology**, and (especially) messianic hopes. What separates Christianity from Judaism is not belief in a messianic figure but whether Jesus is that Messiah. Various groups within Judaism have hailed numerous ancient and modern figures as the Messiah, though very few have achieved widespread acceptance. Since the fullness of the messianic age of peace has not begun through these figures (including Jesus, as it is argued), most are still waiting for the Messiah. Given the interpretive diversity in Judaism, many interpret the future messianic age more figuratively, without focusing on an individual Messiah.
- **Islam.** To the surprise of many Christians, Islam has a high view of Jesus, or Isa (the Arabic pronunciation).[13] (Most Arabic Christians call Jesus Yasu rather than Isa.) The Qur'an has several *surahs* (chapters) that describe Jesus as the Christ (Messiah) who was born of the virgin Mary. He is one of the major prophets, along with Abraham, Moses, and Muhammad, and therefore worthy of great honor. Even so, Jesus is only a man like the other prophets. In this way, Islam holds an adoptionist Christology. As a "hard monotheist" position, Islam avoids any language about Jesus that would hint toward or affirm Jesus's divinity, such as the title "Son of God."[14] Most Muslims reject the theology that Jesus died on a cross and was resurrected from the dead (though there is some ambiguity in the Qur'an on the matter), but they do hold that he ascended to heaven and will return again.

The main non-Abrahamic traditions arose before the advent of Christianity, so they do not formally engage with Jesus; however, in interactions with Western Hindus and Buddhists, we have found them proactive about including Jesus in their description of things, as an incarnation of the gods or as a *bodhisattva*.

- **Hinduism.** In the more philosophical versions of Hinduism, the manifestations of the gods are less important than Brahman, the single uniting reality. In the *bhakti marga* or the path of devotion, the most prominent path among contemporary Hindus, the focus is on the **immanence** of the gods. These gods, such as Vishnu and Shiva, actively engage the world, often through avatars, or incarnations. While these incarnations provide a parallel to that of Jesus, his incarnation is once for all.
- **Buddhism.** While most Buddhist traditions hold to the idea of mediator figures, these figures do not create the path to salvation. Rather, the Buddha and gods point the way to enlightenment for those who would follow their way so they too

---

13. For a list of verses from the Qur'an that mention Jesus, see Carl Medearis, *Muslims, Christians, and Jesus* (Minneapolis: Bethany House, 2008), 70–77.

14. At a popular level, this can be misunderstood by some Muslims to understand that God had sex with Mary and Jesus was their son. Of course, Christians reject this idea as well.

can achieve *nirvana*. Theravada Buddhism focuses on the singular role of the Buddha, whereas with Mahayana Buddhism there are a wide variety of *bodhisattvas*, people on the threshold of *nirvana* pointing the way to others, in addition to the Buddha. For Pure Land traditions, merit achieved by Amida (or Amitabha) Buddha can be transferred to those who meditate on him and chant his name.

Jesus and (Original) Sin

Within Christianity itself, there are debates surrounding Jesus. The question "Did Jesus sin?" is pretty straightforward from a biblical perspective since several passages clearly state that he never did (2 Cor 5:21; Heb 4:15). But could Jesus have sinned (i.e., was he "impeccable")? This question, almost like no other, helps probe the boundaries of Christian thought about Christ as fully human and fully divine. As fully human, Hebrews 4:15 argues that Jesus "has been tempted in every way, just as we are—yet he did not sin." Yet if he is fully God, could he have sinned?

An important and related question concerns whether Jesus had **original sin** like all other humans.[15] Virtually all theologians argue Jesus did not have original sin, though it is not a common topic of discussion and the method of argumentation varies. A traditional line of interpretation focuses on sin being passed through the human father, and since he was born from a virgin, he is immune.[16] Focusing on human solidarity and not genetics, others emphasize Adam's covenantal relationship ("federal headship") with humanity. Christ is the second or last Adam (1 Cor 15:45–48), so he creates a new covenantal headship. These explanations must also account for Jesus's mortal body, which points to his participation in a humanity that still reverberates with the consequences of sin, even if Jesus did not sin himself.

A More Christlike God

"God is Christlike and in him there is no unChristlikeness at all."[17] The affirmation that the Son eternally shares the same nature with the Father and Holy Spirit (they are *homoousion*, or consubstantial) grounds a basic theological premise: when one encounters Jesus, they encounter God; what Jesus does is what God does.

This radically undercuts the notion that the loving Jesus dies on the cross to appease an angry God. As the fullest revelation of God, the love of Jesus reveals God's love. What then about the parts of the Bible that speak of God's wrath and anger? A number of contemporary theologians have critiqued models of theology that separate God and Jesus, with many affirming (perhaps incorrectly) that the doctrine of **penal substitution** (see ch. 9) is a sign of that division. Another area of reassessment is the place of violence

---

15. See full discussion of original sin in ch. 8.

16. The doctrine of the immaculate conception in Roman Catholic teaching technically relates to the Virgin Mary and not Jesus, and it argues that since she was not born with original sin, Christ would not have been either.

17. A. M. Ramsey, *The Christlike God* (London: SCM, 1992), v, as cited in Rowan Williams, *Tokens of Trust: An Introduction to Christian Belief* (Louisville: Westminster John Knox, 2007), 70.

in the Old Testament: If Jesus shows that God nonviolently engages the other, what do we do with divinely commanded violence in the Old Testament? In the Old and New Testaments, we should remember that God's love is a holy love. For example, about 75 percent of the mentions of hell in the Bible come from Jesus. How should we understand the balance between God's love and judgment? While we would not affirm all of these criticisms and moves, the impulse to view God in light of Jesus is a good place to start.

Further, could the God who is incarnated in Jesus be impassible (above suffering) and immutable (above change) if Jesus suffers? Considering Jesus's two distinct natures, Christians have typically answered in the affirmative—God is impassible because he stands outside of time and space. However, many recent theologians argue that God is passible by his own choice, not from necessity. How does the finite incarnation reveal the infinite God?

Further Issues

- **What Did Jesus Know?** New Testament scholars and theologians regularly debate the extent to which Jesus was conscious of his divine identity. Did Jesus know that he was fully God?
- **Two Wills?** In the sixth ecumenical council, Constantinople III (AD 681), the church fathers affirmed that Christ had both a human and a divine will, which work in absolute harmony, since he is 100 percent of both natures. A minority perspective has recently rearisen, rejecting this by affirming that the will relates to the person (or hypostasis) rather than the natures.
- **Jesus and the Oppressed.** With the advent of liberation theology and black theology in the late 1970s, some theologians emphasize Jesus's special connection with those who are oppressed. He is Savior of all but a friend to the oppressed. How do we understand the balance of God's special concern for and identification with the marginalized while also appreciating he is Savior of all?
- **Sacraments.** In **sacramental** traditions, Christ is affirmed to be (literally) present in the bread and wine of the communion (see also ch. 10). Is Christ present in communion, and if so, in what way?

PRACTICING THE FAITH

These are practices to take theology from your head into your heart and hands.

Following a Christlike God

The deep theological discussion about Jesus being of the same nature (*homoousion*) with the Father can feel a bit abstract, but it speaks to a fundamental premise at the heart of Christianity: Jesus reveals God. From a New Testament lens, to engage God means that we must engage Jesus, and vice versa. Our student Lora Doremus once told us a great exercise to get at potential divisions we have in our theology. List the attributes you associate with Jesus and those you associate with God. If your list about God is at odds with your list about Jesus, then the doctrine of the incarnation requires that you change your view of God because Jesus fully reveals God like nothing before or since.

If God has become human, this is a sign of his enduring love. God's advent reveals his desire to engage and repair. We are not abandoned, even when facing the gone-wrong-ness of the world. God's instinct or inclination to restore the world is not a fluke but is in concord with his creation of the world. The world is not irredeemable; we are not irredeemable.

If God has become human, the Son of God gives us a concrete vision or image of God. We are not left to interpret God's messages or messengers; we have seen and encounter God. The Son provides the best picture of who God is. I (RLH) met a convert who had read the Gospels as an angry atheist. He dismissed almost everything he read but felt like he kept meeting a real person. Jesus is a tangible expression of God.

If God has become human, that can encourage us. Jesus is "God with us," even in our brokenness. The Son became a human like us and was even tempted like us. We walk our life's journey knowing Jesus has walked where we walk.

If God has become human, the cross shows us the true value structure of the divine economy. The hierarchies of power and wealth in the world's economy are subverted and inverted. The poor as well as the rich are important to Christ's ministry. Sacrifice for others—rather than the sacrifice of others—is the measure of discipleship.

Faith in Christ

As the incarnation of God, Jesus has a unique identity and role. He once stated, "I am the way and the truth and the life. No one comes to the Father except through me" (John 14:6). Jesus's unique identity brings a challenge to respond and engage. His first sermon (in the Gospel according to Mark) explains, "The kingdom of God has come near. Repent and believe the good news!" (Mark 1:15). The New Testament repeatedly calls on people to respond to Jesus in "faith/belief/trust."[18] The basic idea is not simply believing a set of ideas but committing yourself to Jesus and his kingdom. Consider faith as allegiance to the King. That is why the Gospels combine faith with repentance—a change in action. It is one thing to believe a tightrope walker can make it across a ravine; it is another to be willing to ride on his back. As Dietrich Bonhoeffer reminds us, ideas do not demand that we become disciples, but Jesus does: "Christianity without discipleship is always a Christianity without Jesus Christ."[19]

Kingdom of God

To be a Christian is to be a kingdom person, since to follow Jesus as the Messiah/King is to follow in his kingdom. What does the kingdom look like? The first two-thirds

---

18. We use different terms because of the Latin and German roots that come into English, but they all mean basically the same thing.

19. Dietrich Bonhoeffer, *Discipleship* (Minneapolis: Fortress, 2003), 59.

(or more) of each of the Gospels spell out what the kingdom of God is about: Jesus's preaching, teaching, and healing point directly to the kingdom. Note how often he is preaching "the good news of the kingdom" (Luke 4:43), or teaching parables about the kingdom (Mark 4), or casting out demons in the Spirit as evidence of the kingdom (Matt 12:28). Jesus's followers are to live out the kingdom in which the life of new creation is overcoming the brokenness of sin. We are to pray that God's "kingdom [will] come and [his] will be done, on earth as it is in heaven" (Matt 6:10).

United with Christ

This union of heaven and earth, of divinity and humanity, is what we find in Christ as he brings together both natures in one person. A common description of the Christian life in the New Testament is that believers are "in Christ." As we participate in Christ, we share in his story—that is, we live out his death and resurrection, beginning with baptism (Rom 6) and throughout our lives (Rom 8). As believers "die with Christ," we walk his path of suffering obedience (e.g., Mark 8:29–38; 9:30–37; 10:32–45; 2 Cor 4; Phil 3). This path of **cruciformity** (living a cross-shaped life) is expressed in love for one's enemies, nonviolence, patience, faithful endurance, and the like. And yet the life of Christ is also evident in our lives now, even as we walk in the expectant hope of experiencing a bodily resurrection like his (e.g., Rom 8; 2 Cor 4–5). As we are united with Christ, we therefore partake of and walk in the very union of heaven and earth that he came to bring.

Christ and His Body

Several times in the New Testament, Christ identifies his community of followers with himself. In one description of the final judgment, Jesus describes the different paths of those who serve the needy and those who do not (Matt 25:31–46). He tells them, "Whatever you did for oen of the least of these brothers and sisters of mine, you did for me" (Matt 25:40). In a different setting, the risen Jesus asks Saul, the persecutor of the church, "Why do you persecute me?" (Acts 9:4–5). Paul describes the church several times as the "body of Christ" (1 Cor 12:12–14; Eph 4:1–16). To be a follower of Christ, then, means that one should be connected to his body, the church.

Further Issues

- **Spiritual Disciplines.** Even in his divine fullness, Jesus pursued spiritual disciplines, such as prayer, fasting, and solitude, in order to pursue depth in his spiritual relationship. If Christ needs these things, surely we in our weakness do even more. Check out Foster's *The Making of an Ordinary Saint*.[20]
- **Jesus Prayer.** A prayer drawn from the Bible but most commonly known from the Byzantine tradition is the Jesus Prayer: "Lord Jesus Christ, Son of God, have

---

20. Nathan Foster, *The Making of an Ordinary Saint: My Journey from Frustration to Joy with the Spiritual Disciplines* (Grand Rapids: Baker, 2014).

mercy on me a sinner." Though simple, this connects believers with God through their dependence on him.

- **New Creation Reality.** In the incarnation, Jesus shows that the material world can truly embody the spiritual because he is God in the flesh. This means that our life in this body now matters and that we have a hope for a bodily resurrection. Our Creator is also Savior, so we know the end is a fulfillment of the beginning.
- **Avenues of Grace.** This idea that the material can communicate the spiritual is at the basis of sacraments and other spiritual realities. Consider the use of icons in worship by Catholics and the Orthodox. Their practice is not just from theological speculation but comes from the seventh ecumenical council, Nicaea II (AD 787), which is one of the major christological councils.

In the life, death, and resurrection of Christ, we encounter the climax of God's saving work for us. The more philosophical-sounding claims, such that he shares the same nature with God and with humanity, are important for helping us narrate his work of salvation properly. As fully God (*homoousion* with the Father), he is the greatest revelation of God in history. As fully human (*homoousion* with us), he lived an authentic human life. Thus in his one person (the hypostatic union), Jesus united heaven and earth in himself and shares that union with us.

CLOSING PRAYER

This is a portion of Saint Patrick's Breastplate, an old Irish prayer attributed to Saint Patrick:

> Christ, shield me today
> Against every poison, against burning,
> Against drowning, against wounding,
> So that there may come to me abundance of reward.
> Christ with me, Christ before me,
> Christ behind me, Christ in me,
> Christ beneath me, Christ above me,
> Christ on my right, Christ on my left,
> Christ when I lie down,
> Christ when I sit down,
> Christ when I arise,
> Christ in the heart of every man who thinks of me,
> Christ in the mouth of everyone who speaks of me,
> Christ in every eye that sees me,
> Christ in every ear that hears me.

I arise today
Through a mighty strength, the invocation of the Trinity,
Through belief in the threeness,
Through confession of the oneness,
Of the Creator of creation.[21]

---

21. Thomas Cahill, *How the Irish Saved Civilization: The Untold Story of Ireland's Heroic Role from the Fall of Rome to the Rise of Medieval Europe* (New York: Anchor, 1995), 118–19.

CHAPTER 7

Holy Spirit

The Lord and Giver of Life

INTRODUCTION

When I (BCB) was in seminary, I surveyed Protestant churches in northern Dallas about their Trinitarian theologies. The various denominations approached the Father and the Son quite uniformly but had little consistency in their understanding of the Holy Spirit.[1] If the Spirit is God and thus one of the three persons who share the one divine nature, why is there so much diversity of thought and lack of clarity? Beyond establishing the core ideas that the Spirit is fully God and is truly a person at Constantinople I,[2] there was not a particular historical debate regarding the Spirit to define the doctrinal boundaries (like Nicaea and Chalcedon did for **Christology**). Therefore, people have a more amorphous perception of the Spirit. We often form mental pictures of the Father and the Son, but the Spirit is "God without a face," as one book has described.[3] As a result, personal experience is central to how Christians have understood the Spirit. William Seymour, an early Pentecostal preacher, had powerful experiences of the Spirit that have shaped worldwide Christianity, so we will begin with his story.

Big Idea:
From creation to new creation we encounter the Holy Spirit as God's active and empowering presence in the world.

Key Terms:
- Pneumatology
- Kingdom of God
- *Filioque* ("and the Son")
- Spiritual Fruit and Spiritual Gifts
- Pentecostalism

Key Passages:
Isa 44:1–8;
Ezek 36–37;
Joel 2:28–32;
Matt 12:28;
John 14:26;
Acts 1:1–8;
Rom 5:5; 8:10–11;
2 Cor 3:17–18;
Gal 5:22–23; 6:7–8

---

1. Some Christian groups still primarily refer to the Holy Spirit as the "Holy Ghost," using language from the King James Bible. Even though the terminology is different, it does not signal a different theology.

2. In comparison, the Son (after the incarnation) is affirmed as one person existing in two natures.

3. Najeeb Awad, *God Without a Face? On the Personal Individuation of the Holy Spirit* (Tübingen: Mohr Siebeck, 2011).

WILLIAM SEYMOUR AND THE ACTIVE SPIRIT

Given the circumstances of his life, William Seymour (1870–1922) was likely to be forgotten by history. He was born in Louisiana to former slaves and raised in the era of Jim Crow laws. Finding better opportunities in the Midwest, he worked as a railroad porter and waiter. Seymour converted to Christianity in Indianapolis under the ministry of Methodists and afterward attended holiness churches. In Cincinnati he lost sight in his left eye from a near fatal battle with smallpox. After that, he kept a beard to hide the scarring on his face. Surviving the experience, he acknowledged that God was calling him as a minister.

In 1903 Seymour relocated to Houston. There he received guidance from and shared ministry with his holiness pastor, Lucy Farrow. More importantly he received instruction from a former Methodist pastor and healing evangelist, Charles Parham. Though the practice of segregation did not allow Seymour to be seated in the same room with the white students, he continued to listen to Parham's teaching, which emphasized that God was ready to pour out the Spirit on the church like he did to the earliest Christians at the Jewish festival of Pentecost (Acts 2). In Kansas Parham had already seen the Spirit poured out as evidenced by people speaking in tongues.

Holding on to that anticipation, Seymour left Houston for Los Angeles to minister in a holiness church there, but they rejected his vision. Among other criticisms, they found it odd that Seymour proclaimed an outpouring of the Spirit and speaking in tongues that he himself had not experienced. Seymour took residence in a member's home, and a small group prayed for the Spirit. Finally, in 1905 the Spirit stirred a parishioner to speak in tongues, and Seymour soon followed—the outpouring had begun. Within a year, the small gathering had become a revival and relocated to a former Methodist church building on Azusa Street. Fervent worshipers saw the Spirit manifested in gifts of healing, prophecy, and speaking in tongues. This last gift was identified as the "sign" that the person had received the Spirit. For another three years, thousands came from across the nation and around the world, sharing in three services a day seeking a personal Pentecost as the outpouring of the Spirit.

Most came from holiness movements that believed in a two-stage spirituality. Salvation begins when the convert is declared to be righteous in the eyes of God. A second experience then awaits believers. This second blessing is a gift of complete purity or empowerment. Pentecostals later came to understand the second blessing (or added a third blessing) to be the gift of the Spirit, or "baptism of the Spirit."[4] Speaking in tongues accompanied a person's baptism of the Spirit, and the experience awakened the believer to a previously unknown spiritual dimension.

These events in the early 1900s sparked a revival that is part of one of the most

---

4. This is not a literal water baptism, but an experience of immersion in the Spirit's presence and power.

phenomenal religious movements known in all of history. Far less than one percent of Christians were Pentecostal or charismatic in 1900. One hundred years later, their numbers had grown to include at least one in four Christians globally. Charismatic historians report numerous outpourings internationally at about the same time as the Azusa revivals. Yet one can hardly underestimate the importance of this revival; hundreds of denominations have their origin or inspiration in the experience of Azusa Street.

At the heart of the phenomena was its pastor, leader, and spokesman, William Seymour. He believed the Spirit had left a legacy, breaking down the barriers of race and gender. The Spirit had moved people to love profoundly and to embrace a missionary and evangelistic vision. He was a one-eyed black man born in the unreconstructed South with a meager education in a freedman school in Centerville, Louisiana. He endured poverty, injustice, serious illness, and racial snubs from the very people who taught him about the Spirit. He was remarkably patient; ironically he even waited for his own experience with the Spirit. He preached, wrote, and published a newsletter that influenced countless others. Numerous witnesses claim he was a strong, wise, generous leader without jealousy. After revival fires declined, his congregation saw division and decay. While he did travel to speaking engagements, he remained the pastor of this small church until he died. His gravestone humbly reads, "Our Pastor," but it could rightly claim that he was a pioneer in matters of the Spirit that profoundly changed the landscape of worldwide Christianity.[5]

Not all Christians equally identify with Seymour's experience of the Spirit, but the Holy Spirit remains central to ancient and contemporary traditions in various ways.

THE SPIRIT IN CHRISTIAN THEOLOGY

Throughout history the church has relied on the robust description in the Bible as well as their experience of the Holy Spirit to develop their **pneumatology**.

The Holy Spirit in the Bible

The Spirit is often seen as the hidden member of the Trinity, but he is prominent and active in the biblical narrative, even showing up in the second verse of the Bible as part of the creation account (Gen 1:2). The primary biblical terms for *spirit* (Hebrew: *ruach*; Greek: *pneuma*) have flexibility and can refer to the divine Spirit, the human spirit, wind, or breath. Our focus will be on the divine Spirit. There are many ways to describe the Spirit's work in the Bible, and one scholar has given this phrase to summarize them all: God's empowering presence.[6]

---

5. Timothy C. Tennent, *Theology in the Context of World Christianity: How the Global Church Is Influencing the Way We Think about and Discuss Theology* (Grand Rapids: Zondervan, 2009), 163–64; Gastón Espinosa, *William J. Seymour and the Origins of Global Pentecostalism: A Biography and Documentary History* (Durham, NC: Duke University Press, 2014).

6. Gordon Fee, *Paul, the Spirit, and the People of God* (Grand Rapids: Baker, 1996).

THE SPIRIT AS FULLY GOD AND TRULY A PERSON

The proposition that the Spirit is fully God and is truly a person derives from the witness of Scripture. We find various references to the Spirit as God (e.g., Acts 5:3–4, 39; 1 Cor 2:10). As we noted in chapter 4, the Spirit reflects the fact that God is both transcendent (e.g., John 4:24; Heb 9:14) and immanent (e.g., Luke 12:12; Rom 8:15). Those aspects are easier to understand, but how can we understand the Spirit as a person? Several passages highlight the distinct work of the Spirit that reflect his being a person like the Father and Son: he was lied to (Acts 5:3–4), grieved (Eph 4:30), made choices (1 Cor 12:11), was blasphemed (Matt 12:31–32), is an advocate (John 14:16–17), and intercedes (Rom 8:26–27). Since the Spirit is a person, we use the pronoun *he* rather than *it* to refer to him.

Old Testament

The Spirit appears throughout the Old Testament. In the Old Testament, the Spirit seems to be more of a way to speak about God's action rather than a person distinct from the Father. However, we see hints of personal distinction in passages like Isaiah 48:16 and 63:10–14 in which the Spirit is sent and can be "grieved." The term *ruach* implies movement and action, and the people of God often know the Spirit best through his work as God's empowering presence.

One of the Spirit's primary works is to endow God's people with gifts and leadership abilities. The Spirit fills and empowers people to achieve their divine purpose, including craftsmen (Exod 31:1–5), judges (Judg 3:10; 6:34; 14), kings (1 Sam 16:13), and prophets (Num 11:25; Deut 34:9; Ezek 2:2; 8:3). The **inspiration** of the prophets by the Spirit *as God* is the primary reason for seeing the Bible as the Word *of God*.[7] This empowering through filling helps frame expectations of the "new **covenant**" restoration of Judah after the exile. God's people were suffering the covenant curses because they and their leaders had turned away from God, yet God promised to remain faithful to his covenant by bringing restoration through the Spirit. The Spirit would work through the messianic servant (Isa 42:1–9; 61:1–11) and bring eschatological restoration to God's people (Isa 44:1–8; Ezek 36–37; Joel 2:28–32; cf. Jer 31:31–40). Therefore, the outpouring of the Spirit was expected to be both a cause and a marker of the coming of the new age, a time of new creation and new covenant, when God's kingdom will be fully established. Since the Spirit relates to the hope of future renewal, we speak of the Spirit's presence as an eschatological reality.

---

7. See ch. 4.

New Testament

Continuing with this expectation, the Spirit fits directly in New Testament's eschatological theology. The new age of the **Messiah** and the Spirit overcame the brokenness of sin in this age. Rather than an immediate fix to the problem of sin and death, the **kingdom of God** is instituted in two stages: the first coming of Jesus (the kingdom is "already" here) and his second coming (it is "not yet" or "not fully" here).

Jesus's First Coming

The Spirit distinctly marks out Jesus's life and the lives of his followers. The Son became incarnate through the Holy Spirit (Matt 1:18, 20; Luke 1:35), and Jesus fulfills his messianic role as King by bringing in the kingdom of God through the Spirit. This begins with the Spirit coming down on Jesus at his baptism at the Jordan river (Luke 3:21–22). His baptism does not embody his repentance from sin but his anointing as King, making him the Messiah (i.e., the "anointed one"). The Spirit leads him (Luke 4:1, 14), and Jesus explains the purpose of his ministry by quoting a key Old Testament passage: "The Spirit of the Lord is on me, because he has anointed me to proclaim good news to the poor" (Luke 4:18; see Isa 61:1–11). Jesus's ministry to bring the kingdom of God—healing, liberation, social justice—is a Spirit-inspired ministry, which is framed as a battle with the kingdom of Satan (Matt 12:22–32; cf. Luke 4:1–2).

The Spirit is for Jesus's followers as well (Luke 3:16), and through the Spirit they do the same kind of kingdom ministry as Jesus (Luke 9:1–9; 10:1–24). Jesus tells them that the Spirit's work will be even greater after he leaves (John 14–16): he will send the Spirit as another Advocate/Helper (Greek: *paraclete*) like himself who will teach, encourage, and empower Jesus's followers and convict the unbelieving world. In fact, it is better for Jesus to go away so the Spirit can be with his followers (John 16:7). After Jesus's death and resurrection, the disciples ask about the kingdom, and unsurprisingly Jesus answers with expectations about the Spirit (Acts 1:1–8). Where the Spirit is, there is the kingdom. As before, they will go out in the power of the Spirit to share the story of Jesus with the whole world, thus expanding the kingdom. The rest of Acts is a witness to the Spirit's increasing presence with the church: first the Jews at Pentecost (Acts 2), then the half-Jewish Samaritans (Acts 8), and finally the non-Jewish Gentiles (Acts 10). As expected from the Old Testament, the Spirit is the sign of the beginnings of the eschatological restoration—not only of the Jews but of the whole world.

At the heart of the story of Acts and the rest of the New Testament is miraculous empowerment by the Holy Spirit. In particular, the Spirit allowed believers both to speak in tongues and to speak in their own language more boldly. At Pentecost Peter associates this experience of the Spirit with the Old Testament promise in Joel 2 that the Spirit would be poured out on all types of people (Acts 2:14–41). As with Jesus's story, Peter identifies water baptism with the experience of the Spirit (Acts 2:38). Surprisingly, the "all" in Joel 2 included the gentiles (Acts 10), who did not follow the **Torah** commandments. It was primarily through the gentile experience of the Spirit that the early believers recognized and accepted these outsiders into the community of faith as equal members. The Spirit is thus a marker of **election** (that they are the people of God) as well as **eschatology** (that the kingdom is already here).

SPEAKING IN TONGUES (GREEK: *GLOSSOLALIA*)

There are two basic understandings of *glossolalia*. (1) A person speaks in a human language by a God-given gift without knowing the language (technically called xeno-lalia). Listeners can understand these languages normally because they are everyday languages (like German or Spanish). (2) A person speaks not in a human language but in ecstatic speech by a God-given gift, sometimes called "tongues of angels." The listener receives understanding or the interpretation only by God's help. The second of these marks the vast majority of contemporary experiences. Often, the experience of tongues is through the practice of personal prayer with no interpretation.

The Spirit's presence with the people of God is a recurring theme in the rest of the New Testament. Paul, in particular, emphasizes the new covenant expectation from the Old Testament that the Spirit will restore God's people by bringing heart transformation and new life (Rom 2:28–29; 2 Cor 3). The Holy Spirit empowers believers to follow God by liberating them from the power of the flesh (Rom 8; Gal 5–6) so they can experience the flourishing that God intended for them: love, joy, peace, and so on. Since he is the *Holy* Spirit, this work of transformation by the Spirit in believers' lives is often described as *sanctification*, or becoming *holy* (from the Latin *sanctus*). Of course, the life in the Spirit is not an instantaneous victory over our weaknesses.

THE SPIRIT AND SPIRITUALITY

The term *spiritual* has come to mean any generally godward or religious orientation, particularly inward feelings (in distinction to outward or physical practices). However, biblical writers did not understand *spiritual* in this way (cf. 1 Cor 3:1; 12:12). Almost every time you see *spiritual* in the New Testament, you need to capitalize it—*Spirit-ual*—because the biblical authors are talking about something specific to the Holy Spirit, not a generic religious feeling.

In addition to this sanctifying transformation by the Spirit, which is often called the "**fruit of the Spirit**," the Spirit provides special "gifts" to believers so they can serve others and build up the community of faith, much like the Spirit did in the Old

Testament. There are three listings of gifts (1 Cor 12; 14; Rom 12), and we believe these lists are representative and not necessarily comprehensive. These gifts, which may or may not correspond to a person's natural talents, include uncontroversial practices like faith, teaching, and encouragement, as well as miraculous empowerment like healing, speaking in tongues, and prophecy. Christians who emphasize the present work of the Spirit through miraculous gifts (Greek: *charismata*) are called "charismatic."

As in Jesus's kingdom ministry, the Christian ministry of *liberation*—spiritual, physical, and social/communal—is part of God's work of restoration through the Spirit (Rom 8:1–22; Cor 3:17). Since this liberation will not be complete until Christ returns again, the Spirit intercedes presently for believers as we wait for the eschatological fulfillment (Rom 8:26–27).

Jesus's Second Coming and the Eternal State

The presence of the Spirit is eschatological, bringing creation toward new creation. As with Christ's present kingdom, the Spirit's presence will be a sign of the fullness of the kingdom to come when God promises that believers will be liberated from the problem of death through resurrection—when their bodies are raised from the dead like Christ's.

The Spirit's presence is particularly linked to future resurrection in two ways. First, his current presence is a guarantee, a down payment (Rom 8:23; 2 Cor 1:22; 5:5; Eph 1:14). Since believers have life now through the Spirit, they will have life even more surely in the future. Second, as the Spirit of life, he brings resurrection (Rom 8:6–11; 2 Cor 5:1–10; cf. Ezek 37). In fact, the longest discussion in the Bible on resurrection—1 Corinthians 15—focuses on the transforming presence of the Spirit as the basis of bodily resurrection.

This New Testament account of the Spirit as God's empowering presence gave the church a foundation for their even more developed theology, which we will now address.

THE SPIRIT AND SPIRITS

In addition to the Holy Spirit, the Bible mentions a variety of other "spirits," referring to angels and demons. Christianity describes angels and demons as personal spiritual beings that exist in addition to God and humanity. They are especially prominent in the New Testament.

The Spirit in the History of the Church

Early History

In the patristic church, a full conversation about the Spirit waited until the Council of Constantinople (AD 381), after the language about the Son had been articulated at Nicaea (AD 325). Even so, the earliest church used the triadic formula of "Father, Son, and Spirit" in worship from the outset. Irenaeus (c. AD 140–202), for example, represents many who incorporated the Spirit deeply in his theology with his earthy image of the Son and the Spirit as the two hands of the Father. Irenaeus was not concerned to specify the relationship between the persons but to counter a heresy called **Gnosticism**. Gnostics believed that a weak divine being created this horribly evil world, separating the physical and the spiritual. Irenaeus answered that the Father as Creator was elbow deep in the world—through the Son and Spirit—uniting the work of creation and new creation and integrating the physical and the Spirit-ual.

While Irenaeus represents a more mainstream position, Montanism (a movement launched in about AD 160 by Montanus) was more marginal. Though the movement's history and makeup are disputed, Montanus reportedly argued that the Spirit was being poured out again. Along with Maximilla and Prisca, he spoke words of prophecy and may have claimed to be the incarnated Spirit. He criticized the church for being morally lax, abandoning a vivid expectation of the in-breaking kingdom of God, and ignoring the gifting of all believers (e.g., the poor and women). The movement was eventually condemned by the church. At stake in the debate was the balance between the Spirit's present work (like prophecy) and the Spirit's past work (like Scripture and tradition). Montanus neglected the Spirit's past work of the Bible in favor of the present work of prophecy. For the church, the Spirit's work to inspire the biblical writers is the foundation for the unique divine authority of these texts (e.g., 2 Pet 1:19–21), and so the Scriptures remain the primary source of theology.

Focusing on the Father-Son relationship, the Council of Nicaea (AD 325) issued a creed ending with the simple affirmation of belief: "We believe in the Holy Spirit" (without commentary). Later, Gregory of Nazianzus, a famous Cappadocian Father,[8] sought to specify the Spirit's solidarity with the Father, as Nicaea had affirmed for the Son. What we now know as the Nicene Creed is really the creed reworked by the bishops at the Council of Constantinople (AD 381), which adds the "Third Article" of the creed (see below). Gregory wanted an even more explicit affirmation of the Spirit, but what was said proved sufficient to defeat the *pneumatomachians* (those "fighting against the Spirit" as fully divine).

THE THIRD ARTICLE OF THE NICENE CREED
We believe in the Holy Spirit, the Lord, the giver of life,
who proceeds from the Father,
who with the Father and the Son is worshiped and glorified,
who has spoken through the prophets.
We believe in one holy catholic and apostolic Church.
We acknowledge one baptism for the forgiveness of sins.
We look for the resurrection of the dead,
and the life of the world to come. Amen.

---

8. See further on him in ch. 8.

Each aspect of these later lines was seen as a pneumatological doctrine. That is, reflecting the New Testament witness, the Spirit was affirmed to be central to Scripture (by prophets), **ecclesiology**, baptism, and resurrection. In addition, patristic theologians connected the Spirit with **theosis** and with love. Augustine, in particular, focuses on love and describes the Trinity as a tripersonal relationship with the Father as the Lover, the Son as the Beloved, and the Spirit as the Bond of Love between them. While some, perhaps rightly, have critiqued Augustine's love model for depersonalizing the Spirit, this characterization of the Spirit as the Bond of Love is one of the most repeated descriptions of the Spirit in Western Christian theology.

FULLY DIVINE AND FULLY HUMAN?

If the Spirit is fully God and truly a person, does that mean that the Spirit, like Christ, is fully divine and fully human? No, only Christ became incarnate as a human. The Spirit is a person but not a human. Not all persons are humans. Angels are persons and not human. If the Father is a person, and the Son is a person, the Spirit is just as much a person (and not an "it"!).

Filioque *and the Great Schism*

For a millennium, the church enjoyed a substantial diversity of beliefs and cultures under a general unity. But in 1054 the Christian communion was rent in two when the church of Rome excommunicated the Eastern church in Constantinople. The precipitating issue was a debate over the Holy Spirit, though the dispute included the use of leaven in the communion bread (East, yes; West, no) and the nature of decision making and authority.

WORSHIP, AUTHORITY, AND THE CREED

The *filioque* debate seems like needless theological hairsplitting. However, the issue is ultimately about **liturgy** and authority. Think about contemporary issues, such as those involving liturgy (what kind of music is played?) or authority (who gets to make decisions?). Unfortunately, the same issues continue to cause churches to split.

When the creed describes the relationship between the Father, Son, and Spirit, it distinguishes the three by their relationships: the Son is eternally begotten (or generated) by the Father and the Spirit proceeds from the Father. Christians in the West inserted the Latin term *filioque* (meaning "and the Son") into the Nicene Creed: the Spirit proceeds from the Father "and the Son." The idea has some theological support. For example, the risen Jesus breathed out the Spirit on his followers in the upper room (John 20:22). Additionally, by claiming the Spirit proceeds from both the Father and Son, the West actually emphasizes the coequal divinity of the Son (the topic had still been of dispute in some places in the West) while also defending the place of the Spirit (e.g., the Council of Toledo in AD 675). On the Eastern side of the argument, the proposed double procession (from the Father *and the Son*) discounted the Father as the unique source of divinity. Jesus seems to picture a single procession (John 15:26). Procedurally, the Eastern church objected to the West adding the phrase to the ecumenical (church-wide) creed without ecumenical consent. A proposed mediating position has been "through the Son," but rapprochement was never achieved.

THE TRINITY AND INTERPRETATION

If you look back at chapter 3, you will notice that we discussed the difference between the **economic Trinity** and the **immanent** (or ontological) **Trinity**. These were not two different trinities but two ways of viewing God. The question with the *filioque* is whether we should read the language in John 15:26 with the East as referring primarily to God's act in time in this world (the economic Trinity) or with the West as God's timeless interrelationship between Father, Son, and Spirit (the immanent Trinity).

Late Medieval Era and Reformation

Christian theologians have generally focused upon Christ, though some are notable for their focus on the Spirit. For example, medieval Italian priest Joachim of Fiore (c. 1135–1202) divided history into three ages, one each for the Father, Son, and Spirit. He foresaw the new age of the Spirit was just dawning. Later, the Spiritual Franciscans saw themselves as the catalyst of this new age.

As Reformers, Luther and Calvin noted the Spirit's work, particularly his role in sanctification (becoming holy) and regeneration (gaining new life). They also acknowledged how the Spirit uniquely inspired **revelation** in Scripture (central to their *sola Scriptura* claim) and helped believers embrace Scripture. Luther suggested that the Scriptures may lay lifeless until the Spirit enables the reader; Calvin also claimed that the inner witness of the Holy Spirit convinced readers of its authority—only God can vouch for God.[9] Besides separating the Spirit from justification, the Reformation did not change the general shape of pneumatology, though some Radical Reformers ventured into mysticism and revolutionary prophecy.

John and Charles Wesley, known for founding Methodism, greatly emphasized the

9. Alasdair Heron, *The Holy Spirit* (Philadelphia: Westminster, 1983), 105.

Spirit in their theology. The Spirit's sanctifying and transforming work was (and has been) central to their focus on holiness and the experience of God. Holiness movements were influenced by Wesleyan theology and later shaped **Pentecostalism**, as we noted above.

Modernity and Enlightenment

Modernist scholars generally moved away from thinking of the Spirit as a personal identity within the Trinity. To them the Spirit is a potency or sense of belonging or identity you could feel at work in a community. For German philosopher G. W. F. Hegel (1770–1831), the spirit was not a distinct divine or human being; he saw a larger spirit (German: *Geist*) that takes in persons, communities, and even an age or era. For example, a single era in time saw struggles for liberty in England, France, and the United States—it was the spirit of the age, a Zeitgeist. For Hegel, the spirit was working itself out in the progress of history; the spirit was the highest expression of God, surpassing the Father and the Son. Friedrich Schleiermacher (1768–1834) and others linked the Spirit to the shared experience, a consciousness present in the church.

Contemporary theologians speak of the Spirit with great variety: they may address him as a person, as the bonding agent in communal solidarity, or as a force behind the work of justice and liberation. In response to deism, Karl Barth pioneered a renewed emphasis on the Trinity and the Spirit. Likewise, Jürgen Moltmann protested against the idea that God was absent or distant from his creation, though he more strongly emphasized the presence of the Spirit within creation.[10] Of course, Pentecostalism's emphasis on the Spirit is continually shaping theological discussion in greater ways.

Pentecostalism and the Question of the Spirit's Present Work

The question of the Spirit's miraculous gifts arose strongly at the turn of the twentieth century with the advent of Pentecostalism. With the rise of the Enlightenment and deism, expectations of the miraculous waned. Even Christians who affirmed God's continued work in the world often lived as functional deists; they did not expect God to work or viewed his working as an intrusion from a typically remote God. Scholars describe this as a disenchanted view of the world. The doctrine of **cessationism** arose in the church and challenged reliance upon the miraculous. Traditional cessationism argues that miraculous gifts described in the Bible were given by the Spirit in order to verify the preaching of the apostles in the first century, and they "ceased" with the closing of the biblical **canon**. God may still do miraculous things, but they are not associated with **spiritual gifts**. Pentecostalism arose as a challenge to this environment. It emphatically asserts that God is still very active in the world, particularly through the miraculous gifts of the Spirit.

---

10. See the discussion of **panentheism** in ch. 5.

WHO ARE CHARISMATICS OR PENTECOSTALS?

These two terms overlap in popular use. Practically speaking, if someone shares in the exercise of the more dramatic gifts (*charismata*) of the Spirit such as speaking in tongues, healing, or offering words of prophecy in public worship or private devotion, they are charismatic. Scholars identify "Pentecostals" as those who are members of Pentecostal denominations (16 percent), "charismatics" who practice their Spirit-driven faith within traditional denominations (39 percent) and "neocharismatics" within nondenominational or independent churches (45 percent).[11]

The charismatic movement is the fastest growing segment of the church today, and some have mapped out a three-wave progression in its growth and influence, particularly in the United States. The first wave refers to the outpouring of the Spirit at Azusa and the emergence of the major Pentecostal denominations that followed. The second wave denotes a sweeping encounter and embrace of charismatic life spilling over into other Protestant denominations and Catholicism in the 1960s and early 1970s. The third wave began in the 1980s and saw the embrace of signs and wonders by neocharismatics, those wanting an integration of charismatic theology with more traditional theologies of Spirit baptism (i.e., they do not hold a two-stage spirituality). Thus not all charismatics are alike in their theology and practice.

In response to these movements, some (arising from traditionally cessationist groups) have taken on the moniker "open but cautious" to describe their position. They have come to agree biblically with the idea of miraculous gifts (and so reject cessationism) but do not actively pursue these gifts.

DISPUTES OVER BAPTISM OF THE HOLY SPIRIT

Traditionally, Christians have linked conversion and water baptism with the receiving or being "baptized" in the Spirit. The biblical phrase, "baptism of the Spirit," was attributed to an inward reception of the Spirit by every believer upon joining the faith (cf. Rom 8:9–11; 1 Cor 3:16; 2 Tim 1:14). Following the book of Acts, traditional Pentecostals embraced another position: people became Christians first and then received the Spirit in an independent and likely subsequent experience (cf. Acts 2; 8; 10; 19). This latter "baptism of the Spirit" is accompanied by speaking in tongues. (Churches that affirm this theology are often self-designated as "Full Gospel" churches.) However, numerous charismatics today (particularly third-wave or neo-charismatics) hold the traditional view linking baptism of the Spirit with conversion.

---

11. Espinosa, *William J. Seymour*, 1.

Conclusion

Although much Christian theology tends to focus on the Father and the Son, we have seen that the Holy Spirit is just as integral to the identity of God and the narrative of Scripture. The Spirit plays an active role in engaging the church, both now with his personal presence and in the future as he ensures our hope of resurrection. Accordingly, as the church lives in the fullness of the Holy Spirit, it lives in the fullness of the kingdom of God and experiences the Spirit's fruit and gifts.

CONTEMPORARY THEOLOGICAL RELEVANCE

Now that we have explored ideas related to the doctrine of the Holy Spirit, our goal is to explore a limited number of areas where this doctrine relates to wider issues in the contemporary world and church.

The Holy Spirit and Christian Identity

The Spirit and Other Christian Traditions

Doctrines about the Spirit are diverse in the traditions outside orthodox Christianity.

- **(Functional) Deism.** Traditionally, Christians have affirmed the Bible as **special revelation** because of the Spirit's inspiration. Classical deists do not view God as active in the world, and thus they reject special revelation since it requires God's distinct action. Deists minimize the Spirit's role when they treat "the Bible like any other book" or restrict meaning to the intention of the human author (rather than the divine author). As a result, the Spirit's identity and activity are reinterpreted, and the Spirit is considered primarily as a personification rather than a person. With their disenchanted worldview, they reject or minimize the possibility of God's miraculous acts, especially through spiritual gifts, as well as human need for the Spirit's help obeying God's commands.
- **Mormonism** builds strongly upon the Spirit's work. The Spirit reveals the Bible as well as additional texts and prophecies (see ch. 4). Thus, he is active in guiding new revelation, particularly through the current living prophet (i.e., the President of the Church). They see the Spirit's presence and leadership of all believers as confirmation of the church's teaching.
- **Jehovah's Witnesses** focus on the sole divinity of the Father, so that Jesus is an angel-like figure and the spirit is an impersonal force or activity of God and not a person. An outpouring of this spirit will signal the arrival of the millennial kingdom.
- **United or Oneness Pentecostals.** While most Pentecostals are Trinitarians, a minority of Pentecostal believers deny the Trinity. "Oneness Pentecostals" (also known as "Jesus-Only" or "United" Pentecostals) promote a form of **modalism**

and argue that the Father, Son, and Spirit are three modes of the same person, Jesus. They recall that Jesus called for baptism in the singular "name" of the Father, Son, and Spirit, while Peter called for baptism in the name of Jesus alone (Matt 28:19–20; Acts 2:38). Like other Pentecostals they focus on speaking in tongues as the primary sign of Spirit-baptism.

The Spirit and Other Religions

Other religions' assessments of the Spirit's work vary greatly. Some have sought to find the unboundedness of the Spirit as a place for opening discussion between Christians and other world religions because the Spirit is working among them, even if incompletely. Paul's preaching in Athens (Acts 17) or the noble searcher Cornelius (Acts 10) may illustrate that. Others are less optimistic since the Spirit helps discern that false gods are supported by the demonic (1 Cor 10:19–21).

In monotheistic traditions the Spirit of God is seen primarily as a figurative description of God's work, like the arm of the Lord.

- **Judaism.** In the Hebrew Bible the Spirit is primarily a way of talking about God's inspiring and empowering action, as discussed above with regard to the Old Testament. However, in light of Judaism's commitment to **monotheism**, the Spirit is not considered a person distinct from the Father.
- **Islam.** Similar to Judaism, the Qur'an and Hadith can speak of the (Holy) Spirit as a description of God's action without speaking of a distinction of persons. In other times the language of the spirit refers to the Angel Gabriel, particularly in his support of Mary and Jesus. The Qur'an implies that some Christians believed in the Trinity as the Father, Mary, and the Son, excluding the Holy Spirit, which is something Orthodox Christians have never maintained. Muslims believe in lower spirits, such as the Jinn, which are more like angels than the Holy Spirit of Christianity.

In non-Abrahamic traditions, parallels with the Spirit become more tenuous:

- **Hinduism.** There is no direct correlation to the Holy Spirit in Hinduism. The Spirit could be seen as the unity of reality, Brahman. In different schools of thought, Brahman is viewed differently,[12] sometimes seen as utterly transcendent, beyond distinct properties (*nirguna Brahman*) and sometimes as God with properties (*saguna Brahman*). In either case the outlook is a form of nondualism, which has pantheistic leanings.

---

12. See Timothy C. Tennent, *Christianity at the Religious Roundtable: Evangelicalism in Conversation with Hinduism, Buddhism, and Islam* (Grand Rapids: Baker, 2002), 37–61.

- **Buddhism.** The role and identity of the distinct person of the Spirit is without comparison in Buddhism. While functionally various gods have different roles in many Buddhist traditions and emptiness (*sunyata*) defines the ultimate reality rather than the fullness of the Spirit. For Christians, the Spirit grounds ultimate reality as God, and he gives life in creation and new creation.
- **Animism**, often associated with indigenous tribal religions, generally views all of nature as imbued with spiritual reality. Some tribal religions speak of the Great Spirit as supreme deity, which can be identified with a divine Father figure and/ or Mother Earth.

Distinguishing the Spirits and Blasphemy of the Spirit

Several passages speak of testing (1 John 4:1) or discerning the spirits (1 Cor 12:10). The Bible is especially concerned with those falsely speaking on behalf of God, namely, false prophets (e.g., Deut 18:20; Matt 24:24; 2 Pet 2:1–3), and believers need discernment to evaluate these teachings and other spiritual experiences. The central test whether an experience is really Spirit-ual, as opposed to just a spiritual feeling, is whether the experiences leads to faith in and obedience to Christ (1 Cor 12:3; cf. 2:1–16). One should also measure these experiences by the Spirit-inspired revelation in the Bible.

Many experiences are still contested. For instance, a variety of unique practices have been associated with (Pentecostal) revivals (e.g., people speak in tongues, laugh uncontrollably, or are "slain in the Spirit," that is, falling down due to being overwhelmed by God's presence). In following God's command to discern and test these, some have condemned them as unspiritual and even demonic. The tension in these assessments is that Jesus did miraculous works in the power of the Spirit, and some of the Jewish leaders falsely called these miraculous works the works of the devil (Matt 12:22–32). In response, Jesus describes such "blasphemy of the Spirit" as the unforgivable sin. So while not every charismatic event is necessarily of God (Matt 7:21–23), we should be cautious of strong negative claims about acts and events that we cannot explain. How do you know what is the Spirit's activity and what is not?

What is "blasphemy of the Spirit," and what if you commit this "unforgivable sin"? The best way to describe *blasphemy* is a person's state of resolved slander and rejection. If you are concerned that you have committed this sin, then you almost certainly have not. Jesus was referring to those who have totally and finally rejected God and his work through the Spirit in Christ.

The Spirit and Gender

In Acts 10, the experience of the Spirit by the gentile "outsiders" was a primary reason Jewish Christians knew gentiles were part of God's people too. However, a positive experience alone does not make something "Spirit-ual" because experience can be contrary to the Spirit-inspiration of Scripture.[13] How do we balance these two works of the Spirit—new experience and Scripture? This tension is present in two contemporary conversations: women in ministry and the LGBTQ community in the church. In both cases, each side appeals to the Spirit's work.

While males have historically played a primary role in ministry, the Spirit's indiscriminate endowment to both men and women with spiritual gifts such as prophecy (cf. Acts 2; Joel 2) has led various traditions to support and affirm equal participation of women in ministry. Likewise, LGBTQ Christians testify to the Spirit's work in their lives and ministry. The difference between these debates relates to the role of Scripture in testing this experience. Biblical texts support women in leadership/preaching roles (e.g., 1 Cor 11:1–12), even while some texts seem more limiting (1 Cor 14:33–35; 1 Tim 2:11–12), but the Bible is consistent in its disapproval of homosexual behavior (e.g., Rom 1:24–27). Discerning the Spirit's voice requires careful (theological work) and caring (pastoral work) conversation. How do we discern when the Spirit is leading the church into new truth? What role should experience play?

Spirit's Liberation and Justice

The Spirit's liberating work through Jesus's ministry is evident (e.g., Luke 4:16–21; cf. Isa 61:1–2). Jesus transforms daily practical realities such has health and poverty by the Spirit, and today Christians who live in cruel political and economic oppression often claim that the stirring for justice is moved by the Spirit. Popular American pastor-theologians, such as Francis Chan and David Platt, have seen the dire circumstances of Christians in the Majority World and have called Christians to change their lifestyles to give and work for justice everywhere. Is the Spirit's work of liberation only for individuals or also for communities? How might you see a Spirit-empowered kingdom ministry at work in your setting that seeks to transform communities as well as individuals?

The Spirit, Health, and Prosperity

The Spirit brings freedom (Rom 8:1–2; 2 Cor 3:17), and for charismatics this liberation is not just "spiritual" (relating only to release from shame or the power of sin) but physical and social. Are there any limitations then on the blessing poured out on believers through Christ and the Spirit? Can all sicknesses be healed? Will faithful believers experience financial prosperity? In the "already" and "not yet" eschatology of the New Testament (see ch. 11), we recognize the powerful effect sin and mortality have on this current age, even though the kingdom of God is already present here. While not all will be healed in this age, no matter how faithful they are, we may fail to acknowledge God's powerful activity or see it as evidence of the kingdom (e.g., Matt 12:28). How should we understand the tension between prosperity and brokenness in the church?

13. See ch. 2.

Further Issues

- **Questions of Authority.** Protestants and Catholics separated over the nature of authority. In distinction to Scripture and tradition from the Catholic perspective, Protestants affirmed the ultimate authority of Scripture alone. Both sides appeal to the Holy Spirit, because it is the Spirit who works in the church and who inspired Scripture. How do we appropriately understand the Spirit's work in both?

- **Baptism and Filling.** Traditionally, the church has identified the "baptism of the Spirit" with conversion and "fillings of the Spirit" with temporary experiences throughout one's life. How should we think about these? Is there a baptism of the Spirit distinct from conversion?

- **Ongoing Miracles.** Though an openness to the Spirit's work is growing among Christians outside of charismatic circles, many noncharismatics are cessationists. What should we think about the miraculous today? How should cessationists pray and minister in ways that do not reinforce a functional deism?

- **Justification.** In Protestant theology justification has been primarily viewed as a christological phenomenon: Christ's blood covers our sin, and his righteousness is imputed to believers—removing their guilt. However, in patristic theology the Spirit's work to transform believers is also central since righteousness is linked with holiness. Is there room for a more pneumatological, that is, Trinitarian, view of justification in light of passages like Romans 8:10; 2 Corinthians 3:6–9; and Galatians 2–3?

- **Interpretation.** The Bible is inspired by the Spirit, and Paul says that Spirit-ual things can only be understood by the Spirit (cf. 1 Cor 2–3; 2 Cor 3). So we need the Spirit's help in interpreting the Bible. If we have a good understanding of historical issues (language, culture, rhetoric, etc.), to what extent is the Spirit necessary for understanding the Bible?

- **The Spirit's Presence.** As God, the Holy Spirit is omnipresent in the world. However, it is common in churches to pray things like "Come, Holy Spirit," seeking his filling presence. How do we balance these two ideas?

- **The Spirit and Gender.** Though we traditionally use the pronoun "he" for the Spirit, the term "Spirit" is feminine in Hebrew and neuter in Greek. Some promote seeing a greater diversity in God, even using the pronoun "she" for the Spirit (e.g., the popular book and movie *The Shack*). How should we evaluate these moves?

PRACTICING THE FAITH

In many ways, our discussion of the Spirit is the most practical topic in this book. The most active and experiential aspects of theology described in the Nicene Creed is in its third article: life, worship, the church, baptism, and resurrection. Since the Spirit is active in the life of believers, Paul says that we should not "grieve the Holy Spirit" (Eph 4:30) or "quench the Spirit" (1 Thess 5:19) by ignoring his work in us.

The Spirit Calls Us to Faith in Jesus

Jesus's farewell address in John's Gospel includes two very similar speeches; they differ the most, however, when describing the legal work of the Spirit, as he takes two different roles as an attorney (Greek: *paraclete*). In John 14, the Spirit is believers' *defense attorney*, encouraging, teaching, empowering us to share in the Son's work (vv. 12–13, 16–17, 26). In John 16, the Spirit is a *prosecuting attorney* pressing for the world to change its judgment or verdict on three issues (vv. 8–11):

1. On the sin of unbelief. Refusing the Spirit's witness to the Son or the Son's witness to the Father is a culpable failing before God.
2. On the righteousness of Jesus. By declaring Jesus is alive (victorious over death) and is truly God's Son, the Spirit works to change the hearts and minds of unbelievers who conclude Jesus is merely dead or justly condemned.
3. On the judgment of the ruler of this world (Satan, in John's lingo). The Spirit reveals condemnation and judgment as the true destiny of the chief rebel Satan and, implicitly, those who follow him.[14]

Will we listen as the Spirit guides us into all truth and instructs us to follow Jesus in faith? When we share the gospel, has the Spirit already been at work before us?

Kingdom Living Is Spirit Living

Wherever the Spirit is at work, there is the kingdom (cf. Matt 12:28). The kingdom of God is not merely a prediction about the future—it concerns the world running according to God's design and control. The kingdom was present in the ministry of Jesus and the early church. In the book of Acts, early believers were willing to share the news of Jesus as Messiah and demonstrate that reality through healings and miracles, all in the power of the Spirit. As Spirit-people, Christians should be "naturally supernatural" as one author describes.[15] A friend once told me that faith is spelled R-I-S-K. Faith is the ability to trust in God's empowerment and direction by taking a step. Will you take the risk to pray supernatural prayers (for healing, etc.), not just for those in the church but for those outside the faith?

The Spirit Transforms People

In the Roman empire, ancient Christians may have resembled philosophers more than religious folk. Roman religion paid tribute to the gods but seldom aspired to moral transformation. The philosophers, however, focused on moral progress but typically believed it was only realistic for well-raised, well-off, intelligent people with strong wills and time for study. For philosophers, moral training was for experts and champions,

---

14. Raymond Brown, *The Gospel According to John XIII–XXI* (New York: Doubleday, 1970), 711–14.
15. Gary Best, *Naturally Supernatural: God May Be Closer Than You Think* (Cape Town: Vineyard International, 2008).

but Christians witnessed the Spirit transforming all sorts of people (e.g., 2 Cor 3). The philosophers thought Christianity was like a get-rich-quick scheme, but Christians knew that God works through the Holy Spirit in internal and transformative ways to overcome our weaknesses of the flesh and give life (Gal 5–6). This Spirit transformation is from God, not ourselves. And by dependence on the Spirit, we avoid the "moralistic therapeutic deism" (i.e., **Pelagianism**) that happens when we try harder on our own.[16] How can you better rely on the Holy Spirit for your sanctification?

The Spirit Confirms Our Identity as God's Children

The Spirit works within us to create our identity as children of God. This intimacy is revealed when we cry out to God as Father with the tender words of a child—Dad, or *Abba* in Aramaic (Rom 8:15–16; Gal 4:4–6). The Spirit unites us with the Father and establishes our deepest identity found in him. Several times Paul reminds us that our present experience of the Spirit, however faint, guarantees our inheritance, that God will bring us to restoration in the coming age. Because of the Spirit, we can trust our dad to fulfill his promises, now and in the future, even when life is difficult. How has the Holy Spirit confirmed your identity? How can you find assurance in this confirmation?

The Spirit Provides Gifts and Fruit

At the heart of a Spirit-led life is the experience of the "fruit of the Spirit," which Paul describes as "love, joy, peace, forbearance, kindness, goodness, faithfulness, gentleness and self-control" (Gal 5:22–23). This is the fullness of life as God intended it to be.[17] We may seek fullness on our own terms (even in the desires of the flesh), but true flourishing is found in the work of the Spirit. As we sow seeds of the Spirit, the fruit of the Spirit grows (Gal 6:7–8).

Paul also mentions the "gifts of the Spirit," or Spirit-ual gifts (Rom 12; 1 Cor 12–14). In 1 Corinthians 12–14, Paul says that love (1 Cor 13) is more important than gifts (1 Cor 12, 14). In that way, the fruit of the Spirit is more central than the gifts of the Spirit,[18] though they are not in opposition. In fact, God gives the gifts in order that Christians may love and support their community. Believers receive the gifts in order to serve and bless others. No one has every gift, so we need others to live the Christian life fully, sharing our gifts and receiving theirs. There are various ways to discern your gifting, but a practical way is just to try different ways of serving. You will eventually (through the encouragement of others and your own discernment) find places that best fit. It is as easy as asking God where you can join him in ministry and then trying it out.

Sometimes, Christians in traditions that emphasize (miraculous) gifts believe that the Spirit is missing from traditions that do not experience these gifts. However, if the

---

16. See chs. 8 and 9.

17. It is the pinnacle of human flourishing (a pursuit of "*eudaimonia*" as the ancient Greeks called it or "happiness" by the founding fathers).

18. The fruit of the Spirit (love, patience, etc.) are spelled out in ch. 13, though without the term "fruit."

fruit (love, joy, peace, etc.) of the Spirit is there, then the Spirit is there, even though we should pursue all the gifts.

The Spirit Fills Believers

The Bible, especially Acts, gives several examples of Christians "filled with the Spirit," and the focus is often on miraculous signs and wonders. Other times, the filling is less miraculous but still extraordinary, as in Ephesians 5:18 when Paul commands Christians to "be filled with the Spirit." In one very long sentence (5:18–21 in the Greek), Paul links the command "be filled" with five participles, and these participles show what Spirit-fullness looks like in real life. In particular, Spirit-filled people

- *speak* to one another in songs, hymns, and Spirit songs
- *sing* and *make music* in our hearts to God,
- always *give thanks* to God for one another in the name of our Lord Jesus Christ,
- and *exercise a yielding disposition* to one another in respect for Christ.

This Spirit-filled experience of wholeness, with God and one another, reorients all relationships around Christ (Eph 5:21–6:9).

The Spirit Creates the Church by Reconciling People

Paul never envisions a private, Lone Ranger convert. Reconciliation must be learned and practiced in life together—especially in the life of the church. Though the human family was divided at the tower of Babel (Gen 11), the book of Acts highlights how the Spirit reunites us and breaks down ethnic barriers between Jews, Samaritans (half-Jews), and gentiles (Acts 2, 8, and 10). With each outpouring, the Spirit's presence is evidence that God intends to build a people for himself from every tribe and nation. The Spirit, rather than ethnicity or race, distinguishes God's people. Thus racism obstructs the purpose of God. In 1 Corinthians 12–13, we see the Spirit uniting believers in the church in love, though they are different and have different gifts. If there is division in the church, this is not of the Spirit (1 Cor 1–2). Seek the unity of the Spirit!

The Spirit Works in Scripture and Tradition

Fundamental for understanding and living out a relationship with the Spirit is listening to his voice and watching how he is at work. In chapter 4, we detailed the way the church has understood the Bible to be God's Word, because the authors of Scripture were inspired by the Spirit. Accordingly, to live as if the Spirit is real and active, we should heed what the Spirit is saying through Scripture. Just as the writers of Scripture were inspired by the Spirit, Paul reminds us that the truths of God can only be discerned by the Spirit (1 Cor 2:6–16). We must be just as dependent on the Spirit in our interpretation and application of the Bible.

While tradition is not equal to the Bible as revelation, that does not mean that we cannot hear the Spirit's voice in it. Just as we hear and experience God's work personally, we can learn his voice from other Christians (i.e., "tradition") who have heard and experienced God before us. In particular, there is much interest in patristic writers today, and their works are more accessible than ever.[19] You may be refreshed to see how they integrate Scripture with theology and practice and challenged since their worldview is shaped by factors different than ours.

Further Considerations

- **The Spirit and the Cross.** Often Spirit people are considered "enthusiasts," looking to experience the fullness of life now. While the presence of the Spirit is a sign of the already present kingdom of God, a Spirit-driven life also makes sense of the "not yet" of the kingdom, the time of suffering while God's people await Christ's return. In 1 Corinthians 1–3 and Romans 8:14–30, Paul argues that Spirit-people will live out the foolishness of the cross and follow Christ in the path of suffering and service.
- **Getting Spirit-ual.** We're often tempted to think that our soul, with its immaterial ideas and feelings, is more spiritual than the body and other physical stuff. That is, we can be functional Gnostics like those early heterodox Christians who said, "the material is unimportant (even evil); it is the spiritual that matters." But when Christians get Spirit-ual, they do not escape from the material world. Instead they reveal the transforming work of the Spirit in the concrete world, both now and later, as with the resurrection of our bodies.
- **Sacraments. Sacramental** traditions affirm the Spirit's work of grace in baptism and the **Eucharist**.

In conclusion, when we encounter the Holy Spirit, we encounter God. The Spirit, like the Father and Son, is a person of the Godhead. Every encounter with God is transformative, and we see this especially as we engage the Holy Spirit. Through his transformative grace, believers live more fully in the flourishing that God intended, and this flourishing is captured in descriptions of the kingdom of God.

CLOSING PRAYER

Come, Holy Spirit, fill the hearts of your faithful and kindle in them the fire of your love. Send forth your Spirit and they shall be created, and you will renew the face of the earth. O God, who by the light of the Holy Spirit, did instruct the hearts of your faithful, grant that by that same Holy Spirit, we may be truly wise, and ever rejoice in your consolation, through Christ our Lord. Amen.[20]

---

19. Check out the Popular Patristics Series by St. Vladimir's Seminary Press.
20. "Traditional Prayers—Holy Spirit," *Compendium of the Catechism of the Catholic Church*, 2005, http://www.vatican.va/archive/compendium_ccc/documents/archive_2005_compendium-ccc_en.html#MOTU%20PROPRIO.

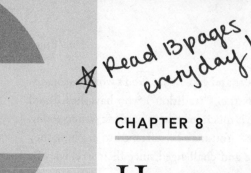
*Read 13 pages every day!

MON

CHAPTER 8

Humanity and Sin

Human Flourishing and Failure

INTRODUCTION

In a book filled with abstract (and at times confusing) academic terms, **anthropology** is one of the few that you will have already come across. You might have heard of the academic study of cultural anthropology, which is similar to sociology in that it focuses on people within communities, but this chapter focuses on *theological* anthropology. Community still plays a vital role, but the primary question is how our interaction with God determines and shapes what it means to be human. Debates over theological anthropology were central to the life of Gregory of Nazianzus, a patristic writer given the nickname Gregory the Theologian because of his influence on the life and thought of the church.

GREGORY OF NAZIANZUS AND APOLLINARIANISM

Gregory of Nazianzus (AD 329–89) and two brothers, Basil the Great (bishop of Caesarea) and Gregory of Nyssa (Basil's brother), are known as the Cappadocians.[1] They greatly influenced theology in the patristic period, but we should not skip the impact of their sister, Macrina. She embraced the life of celibacy and prayer when her fiancé died. Later, when her brother Basil returned to Caesarea after receiving a world-class education with stops at Constantinople and Athens, it was Macrina who appealed to him to abandon his vanity and serve others. Eventually, Basil answered his sister's plea. He renewed his study of theology and

---

1. Cappadocia is a region in Asia Minor (Modern Turkey). Calling them the Cappadocians is like calling the two authors of this book the Texans or the Houstonians.

received spiritual direction from his sister. The Cappadocians, along with Macrina, contributed significantly to the spirituality of the Eastern church.[2] They inspired distinctive forms of communal life for both men and women, with a special emphasis on serving humanity. The life-changing fruits of their labor included one of the earliest hospitals. A view of anthropology with a higher destiny (communion with God) led to a higher view of human life.

Gregory of Nazianzus stood shoulder to shoulder with this holy family. He struggled with several competing inclinations: the life of contemplation (private and communal), the theological orthodoxy concerning the Son and the Trinity, the demands of serving the church, and loyalty to his family and friends. Attending to one of these callings was done at the expense of the others. He felt coerced into assisting his father, who was a bishop, to restore sound theology and fellowship to a divided city and congregation. Similarly, his friend, Gregory of Nyssa, coerced him to become bishop for a remote city, in part for political advantage.

Legacy in Constantinople

In AD 379 Gregory of Nazianzus went to revive the church in Constantinople, which had been in the grips of Arians for thirty years. He served a fledgling congregation named "Resurrection," which met in his home. The congregation was aptly name, for it was dead and needed to be brought to life. They had been beaten and pelted with stones, since the orthodox positions that he held were in the minority, but Gregory answered with perseverance and preaching. He corrected three false teachings: (1) Arianism (Jesus was a lesser god), (2) Apollinarianism (Jesus was truly God but not completely human), and (3) Macedonianism (the Spirit of God was a lesser god).

The great Council of Constantinople in 381 was Gregory's triumph. The persecuted preacher standing up for the truth was elected bishop over the great city. The bishops reaffirmed the Son's complete deity (against Arius), the incarnated Son's complete humanity (against Apollinarius), and the Spirit's divine standing (against Macedonius). The language of the Cappadocians was adopted to affirm the language of the Trinity. The Nicene Creed, as reworked by the Council of Constantinople, stands today as the key statement of Christian orthodoxy and ecumenical unity.

When Gregory arrived in the city, a true believing congregation could not be found; by the time he was elected bishop, a heretical church could not be found. A famous story tells of a beam of light falling on Gregory and the crowd spontaneously shouting his name to be the new bishop. But this sudden inspiration ended sadly. Gregory had not presided long when critics challenged him on numerous grounds including his controversial transfer of office from his previous city.

---

2. Their contribution includes early versions of the *Philokalia* (a compilation of important spiritual writings) and Gregory of Nyssa's *The Life of Moses*.

Disputes with Apollinarius over the Incarnation

One might be surprised to find the name of a champion of the Nicene cause, Apollinarius, attached to a false teaching. Being orthodox in one area, even a central one, does not automatically lead you to be orthodox in other areas. Apollinarius declared that the Son shared the divine nature of the Father completely. In fact, his view of the incarnate Son was too divine. Apollinarius could not imagine how the fully divine Son could have possessed a human mind. Since human thinking jumps from one thing to another, it lands upon thoughts that are inappropriate. His solution was that the divine Logos (the Word) did all the work normally done by a rational human soul; Jesus had a true human body but no human soul.

Gregory and the Constantinople council ruled decisively against Apollinarius, arguing that Christ had both a rational human soul and a human body. They rejected Apollinarianism not just because of its deficient view of anthropology but also because of its implications for salvation and spirituality, as expressed in the doctrine of **theosis**.[3] Theosis refers to humans becoming divine metaphorically, becoming like God as they are transformed into the image of Christ. It may sound strange to modern Western believers, but for patristic (and now Eastern Orthodox believers) it was the primary view of salvation. God left uncorrupted experience to share in our corrupted experience so that believers can then share in the divine communion. We do not displace or rival the Father, Son, and Spirit by becoming God in nature, but the destiny of believers is to share in the love, fellowship, and life of the Trinity. Apollinarius's theology misses this goal by not recognizing that the Son shares completely in humanity. The patristic response to Apollinarius was "what he [the Son] did not possess, he cannot heal/restore."[4] In other words, if the union of divine and human cannot work in Jesus, the model of perfection, why would we think it works in our salvation? The hypostatic union is thus a model for our own spirituality of union with God.

Gregory and the Cappadocians show the importance of understanding who we are as human persons. The incarnate Son is completely and genuinely divine and completely and genuinely human. God created humans to share a higher destiny of communion with God, but we are also disoriented and damaged by wrongdoing and the gone-wrong-ness of the world. Being restored to this divine fellowship awakens in us a care and respect for the human family. Sharing in the life of God (aka theosis) means experiencing true **human flourishing** in relationship with God, ourselves, and others. Becoming like God makes us better humans—fully human—and this is why it matters that Christ was fully human and fully God.

---

3. See further discussions of this in ch. 9.

4. Adapted from Gregory of Nazianzus, Letter 101, in *On God and Christ: The Five Theological Orations and Two Letters to Cledonis*, Popular Patristics Series, trans. Lionel Wickham (Crestwood, NY: St. Vladimir's Seminary Press, 2002), 158.

THEOLOGICAL ANTHROPOLOGY: FOLLOWING THE NARRATIVE

By starting with this account of Gregory of Nazianzus and his views on **Christology**, we are following the time-honored path of beginning with the end in mind. While the majority of this chapter focuses on the beginning accounts of humanity and how that sets the narrative going forward, it is important to know that theological anthropology is shaped by the goal of humanity as modeled by Christ, not just its beginnings as modeled by Adam and Eve. The story that follows is a story of how God created us for a purpose, to live and flourish as those made in God's image, but because of sin, humans have turned away from their purpose, languishing and withering in our rejection of God.

Exploring Our Purpose as Image of God

One of the most fundamental affirmations about human identity within the Christian tradition is that we are made in the **image of God** (Latin: *imago Dei*). The nature of this image is a matter of some debate, as we will see below, but one aspect is undisputed: Jesus, the incarnate Son of God, is the image of God par excellence. The climax of the biblical Story in Jesus Christ both reveals God and the telos, or goal, of humanity (cf. Col 1:15; Heb 1:1–4). Patristic interpreters highlight the fact that Jesus *is* the image, whereas Adam and other humans are made *according to* the image of God. The apostle Paul captures this christological thrust when he describes the purpose of humanity as being conformed or transformed into the image of Christ by the Spirit (Rom 8:28–30; 1 Cor 15:49; 2 Cor 3:18). To understand this restoration of the image of God, it will help to explore the original purpose that God set for humanity and how that purpose has been thwarted by human sin and evil powers in the world.

Our discussion here builds on chapter 5, where we discussed how the story of the Bible is framed by God's loving act of creation and redemption, often described as the "history of salvation" (German: *heilsgeschichte*). Therefore, everything in existence is the creative work of the eternally Trinitarian God. As the climax of the Genesis creation account, God creates humans:

> Then God said, "Let us make mankind in our image, in our likeness, so that they may rule over the fish in the sea and the birds in the sky, over the livestock and all the wild animals, and over all the creatures that move along the ground."

> So God created mankind in his own image,
>   in the image of God he created them;
>   male and female he created them.

God blessed them and said to them, "Be fruitful and increase in number; fill the earth and subdue it. Rule over the fish in the sea and the birds in the sky and over every living creature that moves on the ground." (Gen 1:26–28)

In distinction to other animals, humans are made "in the image of God." With this image language and the later mention of giving humans the "breath of life" (Gen 2:7), there has been much discussion in the Christian tradition to determine what biblically grounds human identity, and especially what makes us distinct from animals.

Perhaps the most widely held position about the "image of God" (popular among patristic theologians as well) is that it reflects human possession of a soul or a rational mind. This is known as a "*substantive view*" of the image. While this view connects some philosophical discussion to theological debates, it cannot be demonstrated exegetically from the Genesis passage since nothing related to souls or rational thought appears in these verses or the context more broadly, beyond the ambiguous "breath of life" (Gen 2:7).

If the biblical context of the Genesis passage is determinative for the meaning of the image, the "*functional view*" has much more to commend it. In this view, God creates humans in his image "so that they may rule over" his creation as his stewards. In the creation account it seems that chaos was still over most of the earth, except in the garden, and the task of humans was to bring the divine order of the garden to the rest of the earth. To the extent humans fulfill that vocation, they are embodying the image of God.

MALE-FEMALE MUTUALITY

God declares in Genesis 2:18, "It is not good for the man to be alone. I will make a helper suitable for him." Men and women need each other, and they are presented as mutual partners. While "helper" (Hebrew: *ezer*) might seem like a subordinate role, the term *helper* is most often used in the Old Testament to describe God, who comes to help his people (often in military contexts), and God is surely not subordinate to his people.

Another exegetically founded perspective is the "*relational view*" of the image, which focuses on the nature of community in the passage. To be fully human is to be in relation with one another: "So God created mankind in his own image, in the image of God he created them; male and female he created them. God blessed them and said to them, 'Be fruitful and increase in number.'" The immediate focus of the passage is the family—husband, wife, and lots of children. What makes us fully human is the wider human community standing in relation to God together. As we are in relation with one another and, of course, with God, we most fully reflect the image of God. One foundation for this relational perspective is that God himself is grounded in relationship between Father, Son, and Spirit. So if relationality is fundamental for God, we should expect to see this as the ground of human identity as well.

Rather than seeing all these perspectives as competing, the text presents an integrated picture of humanity within creation, a creation that includes individuals, a community, and place (see figure 8.1). Each of these is oriented to God but also integrated (working in harmony) with one another. That is, individuals are in relationship with God, but also in relationship with the community as family and set in the location God placed them to rule and steward. Our contemporary culture offers us many models of human flourishing, but Scripture presents us with a holistic picture of flourishing grounded in God's purposes.

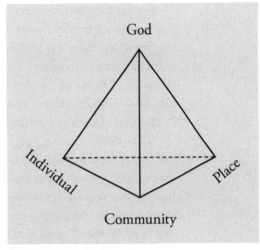

FIGURE 8.1
Holistic Biblical Theology

Of course, this account of wholeness and flourishing is not the end of the story. This sets up our understanding of the purpose of blessing and life for humanity. Yet why do we see disharmony instead of harmony, disintegration instead of integration? The good creation has been corrupted. It is to this gone-wrong-ness that we now turn.

Lamenting Our Brokenness: Genesis 2–3

The introduction of sin in Genesis 2–3 shapes the theological frame for understanding our brokenness throughout the Bible. Since humans and creation were described originally as "good," the events in these two chapters clearly introduce something evil, that is, not good. The introduction of evil into creation is often described as "the fall" of humanity from grace because of their disobedience to God. That is, that human beings *fell* from their high place of obedience and life with God into sin, shame, and disobedience.

TERMINOLOGY OF THE FALL

In addition to the term **hamartiology**, which is the theology of "sin" (Greek: *hamartia*), a couple more key terms show up in theological discussions related to the fall. Both derive from the idea that humans "lapsed" into sin. Prelapsarian things relate to aspects of life "before" (pre-) the fall, whereas postlapsarian things relate to aspects of life "after" (post-) the fall.

The Genesis narrative sets up a basic association between sin and death in 2:16–17 that continues for the rest of the Bible: "The LORD God commanded the man, 'You are free to eat from any tree in the garden; but you must not eat from the tree of the knowledge of good and evil, for when you eat from it you will certainly die.'" Of course, Adam and Eve eat of the fruit, yet they did not immediately drop dead. Did God lie? No, death invaded the entire creation, but the furthest extent of death did not occur immediately. God's grace mitigated their experience of sins' consequences.

While not spelled out fully in this initial account, sin is not just a human issue. With the serpent in Genesis 3 and later the troublesome "sons of God" in Genesis 6,[5] we see the beginning of a complex interchange between demonic powers and complicit humans. Indeed, this continues throughout the rest of the Bible and into the New Testament. Consider the prominence of Jesus's exorcisms in the Gospels, the role of demonic "authorities" and "powers" (Eph 6:12), "the god of this age" who "has blinded the mind of unbelievers" (2 Cor 4:4), and the final judgment for Satan (Rev 20). In addition to these personal powers, Paul often speaks of Death, the Flesh, and Sin as personified powers over us. Evil has a both/and quality: it comes from humans and demonic influence, and both are held responsible.

The effects of sin are easiest to see in Genesis 3 (especially 3:14–19) in terms of the individual, community, and place framework we saw earlier. On an individual level, Adam and Eve do not die immediately. Instead, they become mortal and will return to the dust someday (3:19). While the term *cursed* is reserved for the ground and the serpent in this passage, this experience of death from sin is one of the most fundamental descriptions of the **covenant** curses for sin (e.g., Deut 30:15–20). Death is not only at work in individuals, but it corrupts the community as well: husbands and wives are at odds, and there is pain in childbearing. Similarly, as the humans engage the land, they now toil and are even removed from the garden. Rather than the harmony and blessing that pervaded creation, human sin introduced disharmony and cursing to every part of creation. Figure 8.2 helps show the contrast between God's intention and sin's disruption of that intention.

FIGURE 8.2: CREATION AND FALL COMPARED

	Individual	Community	Place
Creation	Blessing / (Flourishing) Life	Family / Community	Land / Garden
Fall (through sin)	Cursing / Death	Broken Family / Conflict	Exile / Toil

When we consider the two stages of creation and the fall together, we see how sin disrupts God's good purposes for creation. While God's active judgment is certainly involved,

---

5. These "sons of God" are known in later Jewish writings as the "Watchers."

most of the negative consequences from sin are inherent in sin itself. In Genesis 3 (cf. Rom 1), we see that in turning away from the God of life, people instead turn to death. We are meant to flourish, but apart from God we languish.

These two strands of reality—of good and evil, life and death, harmony and disharmony, integration and disintegration—now frame the human story. God is present in his creation, but we are separated from him. Humans are neither totally good nor totally evil; we see both aspects in everyone. Families can be our greatest source of joys and greatest source of pain. Evil, with all of its varieties of suffering and its climax in death, pervades every aspect of life. It is this problem in which the Christian hope of restoration stands.

Glance at Restoration

Our next several chapters more fully spell out a vision of salvation, but for now we will note one key connection between the original picture in creation and the restoration God brings through Christ and the Spirit. Just as sin infects us holistically—individual, community, and place—the biblical story also provides a holistic hope in terms of a restored and renewed creation. The New Testament describes the restoration of the image of God through Christ and the Spirit. With regard to the restored image, often passages focus on individual restoration (e.g., 1 Cor 15:49) or the individual in community (e.g., 2 Cor 3:18), but other times the individual, community, and place are drawn together (e.g., Rom 8:14–30). The Trinitarian focus of these New Testament passages about the image is unmistakable: believers are in relationship with the Father, conformed to the image of the Son, and transformed by the presence of the Holy Spirit. Another notable insight about these passages is that we share not only in Christ's life but also his death through the power of the Spirit. This is a place where the Trinity and **eschatology** directly shape our theology. Human flourishing is fundamentally about sharing in the life of God in the context of a restored community in the world.

KEY PASSAGES ON IMAGE AND LIKENESS IN THE NEW TESTAMENT
- Rom 8:14–30
- 1 Cor 15:35–49
- 2 Cor 3:1–4:6
- Col 1:15–21
- Heb 1:1–4
- 1 John 3:1–6

Sometimes sin and restoration are only viewed in terms of individual consequences, particularly in postmodern Western contexts. James Cone, known for his immense influence on black theology in the late twentieth century, shows how a relational view of the image of God means that the community cannot be abstracted from theological anthropology and therefore **soteriology**. Cone writes,

Theology is the exposition of the meaning of God's liberation. For to affirm that human beings are free only when that freedom is derived from divine revelation has concrete political consequences. If we are created for God, then any other allegiance is a denial of freedom, and we must struggle against those who attempt to enslave us. The image of God is not merely a personal relationship with God, but is also that constituent of humanity which makes all people struggle against captivity. It is the ground of rebellion and revolution among slaves. . . . Human fellowship with God is defined as Jesus' work of liberation.[6]

Christians do not have to convince the world of its brokenness with regard to individuals, communities, and the world. The question is whether the Christian perspective on the goal of wholeness and flourishing should frame our discussion of brokenness.

The remaining chapters of this book explore the holistic nature of restoration—with attention to the individual (salvation), community (church), and place (eschatology). While the topics of restoration and hope are important, one cannot grasp restoration as a solution without understanding the nature of the problem. We have introduced the basic account of the problem of sin and its effects, but the historical discussion about sin is important for understanding salvation.

HISTORICAL VIEWS OF SIN

One historical debate regarding the questions of free will and determinism plays a distinct role in discussions of sin. In the West the debate was framed as a binary between Augustine and Pelagius, but Greek theologians conceived of the effects of sin in different ways.[7] Though many variations exist within each perspective, we offer three representative views: **Pelagian**, Greek patristic, and Augustinian (see figure 8.3).

FIGURE 8.3: EFFECTS OF ADAM'S SIN

Pelagius	Greek Patristic	Augustine
(Heterodox Position)	(Orthodox Options)	
No Corruption	Corruption	Corruption
Not Liable	Not Liable	Liable

(Free will ←———————————————→ Determinism)

(Individual ←———————————————→ Communal)

---

6. James H. Cone, *God of the Oppressed*, rev. ed. (Maryknoll, NY: Orbis, 1997), 134.

7. Early Western theologians such as Tertullian also follow this pattern exemplified by the Greek patristic tradition.

While Pelagius's position was condemned by the church, orthodox theologians have had huge debates about different views on Greek or Augustinian views of sin.[8] While each of these positions has a wider discussion of sin, the focus of the debate relates to how Adam's sin relates to the rest of the human race.

By *corruption*, we are referring to the inborn inclination toward sin, having corrupt desires that are innate from birth because they were passed down from Adam to all his progeny due to Adam's sin. By *liability*, we are speaking of each person's accountability before God for sin. Christians from virtually all perspectives agree that people are liable for their own sins. The question this table describes is whether the liability of sin is passed down to Adam's children for Adam's sin. Arising from passages like Romans 5:12–21, the theological debates revolve around how our sinfulness relates to Adam and his first sin.

LIABILITY OR GUILT?

Many describe this liability or accountability for sin as "guilt." While capturing part of the problem, guilt is also a loaded term that can skew one's perception of the doctrine. For instance, many think of guilt as a feeling rather than a reality. And the word *guilt* is primarily a legal (or judicial) term today. Augustine (and the biblical tradition more generally) does address the legal aspect of sin at times but does not limit it to this area. For instance, the problem of sin is also described using other metaphors such as impurity, slavery, uncleanness, disease, enmity, separation, and so on. *Liability*, therefore, is our preferred term to capture this wider scope of the problem so that we do not import different ideas about guilt into the picture.

Pelagius

Pelagius (c. AD 360–418) was a British monk living contemporaneously with Augustine, and he, along with many of the clergy, was troubled by the increasing moral laxity of Christians. Since Christianity had become the culturally acceptable religion of the Roman empire, many were called "Christian" without living as committed Christians. It was not so much Pelagius's assessment of this problem but his solution that the church found difficult. Pelagius, like all the best heretics, paid close attention to the Bible, and he noted all the commands in the Old and New Testaments about obeying God. His fundamental premise is that God would not give those commands if people did not have the ability to obey them. Thus he emphasized individual free will and independent human agency. Pelagius argued that we sin because of our own choices as we follow bad

---

8. See ch. 9 for a more detailed discussion of Augustine and Pelagius.

models, not because of innate corruption. Pelagius preached a message of moral rigor: you not only should but can follow God because you already have the ability within you. Since we have no innate corruption from Adam, we are not liable before God for Adam's sin. This position was rejected in the ancient church because it makes grace for salvation helpful but unnecessary.

Since Pelagius's position has been roundly condemned within the church, few explicitly trumpet his position, but functional **Pelagianism** is constantly vying for the hearts and minds of Christians. Pelagius was motivated by moral rigor, whereas many today are much more influenced by the Enlightenment emphasis on the moral neutrality of creation. The *Tabula Rasa* ("blank slate") view of humanity championed in the Enlightenment points directly to the "no corruption" ideal proffered by Pelagius.

Augustine

Augustine (AD 354–430) was also a monk and later the bishop of Hippo in North Africa, and he was one of the Latin patristic theologians who most influenced medieval theology. He wrote about many things, but he is perhaps most well known for his theological debates with Pelagius. Augustine, like Pelagius, was concerned by the lax moral condition of many Christians, but unlike Pelagius, Augustine viewed sin as much more pervasive and corrosive to humanity. It is not that he was pessimistic about what humans could become or achieve; he was pessimistic about what they could become and achieve *without grace*, without God's act within them to transform and empower them.

To understand this need for grace, you need to understand his view of sin and its effects. In simple terms, Augustine affirms that all humans, due to our family connection to Adam, are corrupted by sin and personally liable for this sin within them. With inherited corruption we might say that everyone is infected with an incurable virus that perverts their desires and turns their hearts away from God. Since this corruption originates from Adam, the tradition describes this as **original sin**.

With individual autonomy and responsibility championed by **modernism**, many contemporary people find Augustine's view difficult: can the entire human family be liable before God from birth because of the sin of the first man? Augustine's more communal view on human identity is obvious: all humans fully share in Adam's corruption from sin and his accountability before God from birth. The individual and their personal choice is not the sole basis of their liability before God; rather, the disposition to sin and the responsibility for sin is passed down to all of Adam's family. That is, the children are responsible for the action of parents and predecessors. This communal way of thinking is common in the Majority World but has been largely rejected in the (post) modern West.

POSTMODERNISM AND COMMUNAL DETERMINISM

A primary focus of contemporary culture is being an "authentic" individual. Books and movies regularly vilify how society puts individuals into specified roles or positions and heroize those who break out of these boundaries. We regularly tell ourselves that the most authentic people do not follow the norms set by the community. We see this play out in subtle and not so subtle ways in society. Take names for children as an example. Many parents don't want to follow the conventional communal norms and so give unique names or spellings. We therefore have a cultural aversion to views like Augustine's in which our individual identity is inescapably bound by our communal identity. (Ironically, we may be more socially manipulated than ever since media algorithms so carefully mold the information we receive.) The important question is whether our cultural bias leads us to ignore aspects of the Bible that might have a more communal focus or emphasize external agency.

In addition to this more communal focus, Augustine emphasizes a form of determinism, where external agency or causation is at work. One cannot follow God's will apart from grace because sin pervades every part of us, an idea captured by the phrase **total depravity**. This idea does not mean that people separated from God do as much evil as they can but that sin touches every area of life. Some prefer the term *radical corruption* to communicate the same idea: since all human action apart from grace is rooted in sin, we are enslaved to sin.[9] Augustine recognizes both human ability and desire, but those who have not been transformed by the Spirit will not desire the things of God (cf. Rom 8:4–8). One cannot do good if one does not desire the good in the first place. So we are stuck unless God changes us.

The medieval church followed Augustine's perspective in many respects, and his vision has set the terms for most discussion since. One influence in the church practice that was already starting to change was the move to baptize infants. Due to Augustine's theology that infants bear the full weight of the liability for human sinfulness, the practice of infant baptism (i.e., paedobaptism) became the common practice in the West. Baptism, it was argued, wipes away original sin and restores human agency before God.[10] Based on this renewed agency, Catholic theology is more synergistic—with divine and human agency working together—than most Protestants are comfortable with, but it is important to understand that this happens after the sanctifying grace of baptism.[11]

---

9. The term *radical* comes from the Latin for "root" (*radix*).

10. The Eastern church also baptizes infants but does not hold to Augustine's view about infant accountability.

11. In some ways, Catholic theology often functions similar to the Greek patristic model *after baptism*, but the theological system is grounded in categories established by Augustine.

MON.

The Protestant Reformation has been seen as a return to Augustine's direct challenge to any agency for unredeemed humans. Today many Catholics and Protestants find Augustine's perspective on sin hard to swallow.

Greek Patristic

The debate in the Western (Latin) church has primarily proceeded as a binary opposition between Pelagius and Augustine, but another position predates this debate by a couple of centuries, and it holds on as the primary position in the Eastern (Greek) church. Since it is the general position held by those in the Eastern tradition, we have labeled this the Greek patristic perspective, though several in the Latin tradition (such as Tertullian) held a position like this. Some in the West who only work with the Pelagius-Augustinian binary will describe a mediating position between the two views as "Semi-Pelagianism" (though the title did not arise until after the Protestant Reformation). We, however, prefer a title that speaks to the origination of the view rather than something anachronistic and pejorative.

Since the church was primarily Greek-speaking for the first several centuries, the Greek patristic tradition arose from early developments in Christian theology. These theologians affirmed human sinfulness and the need for God's grace to experience life; however, this was challenged by **Gnostic** traditions. Gnostics were among the earliest heterodox movements in the early church, and versions of Gnosticism were often hyper-deterministic (a step beyond Augustine): one was born inescapably into an identity as a spiritual, natural, or fleshly person (almost like a caste system but without reincarnation). This challenge helped early orthodox Christians clarify their position. They affirmed that all humans (not just the "fleshly" group) were corrupted by Adam's sin. However, they also affirmed that each person is liable before God only for their own sins, not for Adam's sins too. This tradition therefore holds to "original sin" and "depravity," but some might hesitate to use the term *total depravity* to describe it.

THE PROBLEM OF SIN

We might think of the Greek patristic view of sin from the view of a therapist: what your parents did is not your fault, but it is your problem.

The various Eastern Orthodox traditions follow the tracks laid by their theological forebearers. They affirm that grace is necessary to escape the problem of sin, so this has been considered an orthodox option. (That said, many Augustinians find it deficient.) In the West direct affirmation of this kind of position arose with the Anabaptists (those who pushed only for believer's baptism, or credobaptism) and the Radical Reformation. Most contemporary baptistic traditions functionally follow this perspective, though without any explicit affirmation of the Greek patristic tradition or even knowledge of it.[12] This is evident through the concept of "the age of accountability." Children are not, in this theological perspective, accountable for Adam's sin. But when they reach a certain maturity (perhaps somewhere between seven and twelve years old), they become accountable before God for their own actions. This perspective vies for supremacy among lay Christians even if theologians are more mixed between Augustinian and Greek patristic positions. Fed by the influence of baptistic and revivalistic (e.g., Pentecostal) traditions within Protestantism, this perspective also accords more easily with the modernist impulse toward individual freedom.

Heterodox Imbalance

We will not adjudicate between the Augustinian and Greek patristic views since different traditions will find different evidence compelling. What unites both views is their ability to maintain the balance between the creational goodness and the fallenness of sin. As with other doctrines, orthodoxy is found in a both/and balance rather than a stark either/or. Several heterodox positions have been excluded from orthodox Christianity because they do not maintain that balance.

Some heterodox positions overemphasize the goodness of creation and minimize the effects of sin (therefore minimizing our need for grace). **Pelagianism** is one example. We noted how heirs of the Enlightenment repeat some of the key tenets of Pelagianism because of their penchant to see humans as blank slates. Likewise, the Enlightenment-inspired view of *naturalism* (as expressed through **secular** humanism) rejects the idea of inherited sin and therefore holds to a generic goodness of nature.

Just as there are those who underemphasize the role of sin's corruption, there are those who overemphasize it, and the church has excluded these positions as well. We noted earlier how Gnostics claimed that some people were by nature irredeemable. Another form of Gnosticism that unfortunately holds a huge sway over popular Christianity is that the body ("flesh") is irredeemable. This can be seen in those with a singular focus on the soul going to heaven after death rather than affirming the resurrection of the body—with restored people living on a restored earth. We will spell out in more detail how the body (and soul) experience restoration in the salvation and eschatology chapters. However, this raises an important topic in theological anthropology: How should we understand the different parts of the person, like the body, soul, and spirit?

HUMANS AS PHYSICAL AND SPIRITUAL

Like with other aspects of theology, our primary consideration is what the Bible says about the various parts of the person, such as heart, soul, body, and spirit. The authors in the Old Testament used a variety of terms without much discussion on how they relate,

---

12. By baptistic traditions, we are referring to those that follow believers' baptism.

whereas in the New Testament these terms become a little more defined. One reason for the difference is the increased eschatological awareness, that is, what happens after death and what happens when Christ returns. While we can see a basic distinction between the material and immaterial parts of the person, the wide and diverse use of terms makes coming to a neat systematic perspective on human components difficult.

While the term *body* seems pretty straightforward, the majority of biblical terms are much harder to pin down. *Flesh*, for instance, relates to the body but also speaks to bodily appetites. On top of that, the Bible has a variety of internally focused terms, such as soul, spirit, heart, mind, will, and conscience. Are these distinct parts, overlapping parts, or simply different words for the same thing?

Generally the church has affirmed that humans have both a physical (material) aspect and a spiritual (immaterial) aspect. While this broad perspective undergirds Christian discussions, the church has allowed a wide variety of interpretive diversity on how this plays out. The three primary positions about this are dichotomy, trichotomy, and holism (see figure 8.4).

Dichotomy: Body and Soul

With dichotomy, the focus is on the two constituent parts of the person. A key passage that illustrates this perspective is 2 Corinthians 4:6–18, which speaks of the distinction between bodily suffering and inward renewal. Ultimately, Paul describes this as related to the "outward" and the "inward" aspects (4:16), not as if there are two persons vying for power within each of us but as a figure of speech to describe the duality of physical and spiritual at work. This perspective was the primary view that patristic theologians used when they described Jesus as being fully human as we are human: he had a rational soul and a body (as in the Definition of Chalcedon).

Trichotomy: Body, Soul, and Spirit

With trichotomy, three different parts are constituent of the person: the body, soul, and spirit. This three-part perspective seems to inform key passages such as Deuteronomy 6:4–5 and 1 Thessalonians 5:23. Both of these passages use a three-part structure, but note that the terminology used is different with each! And it is interesting to note how Matthew 22:37 adapts Deuteronomy 6:5 such that the body does not appear. While these issues can present a challenge for this position, the distinction between mind and spirit is supported by passages like 1 Corinthians 14:14–16 where Paul describes praying with his mind (in a human language) and praying with his spirit (in tongues).

Holism: Irreducible Parts

With holism, the focus is on the unity of the person rather than the diverse parts. In light of biblical anthropology (particularly Old Testament anthropology) and modern neuroscience, this position questions easy distinctions between the body and soul (even more so, soul and spirit). For example, where do we draw the line between physical brain functions and the immaterial soul? Some outside the church do not affirm a soul but assign all consciousness to physical processes, sometimes described as reductive physicalism. Christian versions of holism are often identified as *nonreductive physicalism* because they emphasize bodily functions (physicalism) but do not reduce human identity to physical processes alone (nonreductive). These interpreters of the Bible do not deny or reject the language that points to the various parts of human composition; rather, they reject the position that these are somehow separable, almost independent pieces.

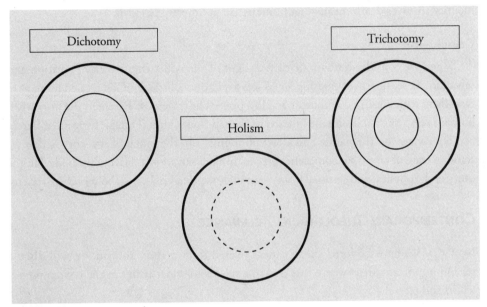

FIGURE 8.4
Views on Human Consitution

Each of these three options maintain a both/and balance between the physical and spiritual aspects of humans, but each view has a slightly different emphasis. We hold the key affirmations about the goodness of creation and the pervasiveness of the fall in tension. All parts of us—physical and spiritual—are part of God's good creation, and likewise all parts of us are corrupted by sin. While this sets the frame, it still leaves open the main question of how the different parts of us work together.

Those who fell into heterodoxy so overemphasized the rational/spiritual that they denigrated the body of flesh as inherently evil. *Gnostics*, as we saw earlier, did this by denying that the body was part of God's good creation and that it has any place in God's restoration from sin. This position is often reflected in popular Christianity. For instance, it was not uncommon for me (BCB) to hear illustrations like this one when I was growing up: "Think of yourself like an astronaut in a spacesuit. The real you is the you on the inside (the spiritual you) and not the outside (the bodily you), which you will lose when you go to heaven." We talk more about the role of heaven as our hope in our chapter on eschatology, but this illustration is a functional reappropriation of the Gnostic rejection of the body. However, God cares just as much about our bodies as he does our souls. He created us with bodies, and Jesus's ministry of healing and the hope of resurrection show that physical restoration is essential to Christian hope.

On the other side, the *naturalist* position claims that humans are just chemical machines. It affirms one aspect of humanity, the physical, but makes it the only aspect by rejecting the spiritual or immaterial part. And yet the fact that something of human identity survives death means that humans are not merely physical.

Conclusion

When we consider human identity in light of the wider framework of creation and salvation, we see how a relationship with God works out holistically. God created humans to bless them with life, in a community and in a place. The tragedy of evil enters the story when humans reject this God-ordained means to human flourishing. Though there are different orthodox views on the nature and effect of original sin, the moral of the story is that we stand in need of salvation. Sometimes people think of salvation as leaving the body, but the unity of the physical and spiritual from creation shows that God cares about every part of us.

CONTEMPORARY THEOLOGICAL RELEVANCE

Now that we have explored the key ideas related to humanity and sin, we will discuss several important areas where this doctrine relates to wider issues in the contemporary world and church.

Theological Anthropology and Christian Identity
Theological Anthropology and Other Christian Traditions

- **(Functional) Deism** emphasizes human's God-gifted agency, such that they have the freedom and ability to follow an ethical path without divine help, which is necessary because of God's inactivity. Highly influenced by the Enlightenment, this tradition rejects the role of inherited human sinfulness and resorts to a form of Pelagianism. This inherent goodness or blank-slate model creates the possibility for human moral effort without God's grace. With this high view of moral agency, this perspective raises the probability of increased anxiety for those who cannot live up to the expectations.
- **Mormonism** affirms that humans are the children of Heavenly Father, and like the Father they have a spirit and a body. With regard to sin, Latter-day Saints hold a position very similar to the Greek patristic model in which corruption is passed from Adam, but humans are only accountable for their own sins, not Adam's.

- **Jehovah's Witnesses** affirm that humans are made in the image of God by reflecting his moral character. They hold a position similar to holism in which the body and soul/spirit are not separate from one another. For Jehovah's Witnesses, *soul* is a general term that means "life" (cf. Mark 8:34–38).[13] A distinctive element of their practice is that they do not accept blood transfusions since the Bible commands people to abstain from blood, which is associated with life. With regard to sin, they hold an original sin position similar to Augustinian views of total depravity.

Theological Anthropology and Other Religions

The two other Abrahamic traditions frame the role of humanity in light of creation and the effects of Adam's sin.

- **Judaism and Islam.** Both traditions highlight humanity as the climax of creation and point to humanity's role in stewarding God's creation. With regard to sin, both traditions reflect a similar position to Christianity that sin is a rejection of God's command. In contrast to Christianity, these traditions hold that humans have not been given by Adam a corrupt inclination to sin that is unsurmountable by free will. For Judaism, the evil inclination (*yetzer hara*) is balanced by an equally innate good inclination, and people have the ability to choose between them. Both traditions also reject any notion of inherited liability for Adam's sin, as people are only accountable for their own actions.

The Eastern religions hold to a cyclical understanding of existence that shapes their views of humans within it.

- **Hinduism.** In the great wheel of existence all creatures are linked through the cycle of *karma* and reincarnation, called *samsara*. This cycle of *samsara* is viewed as a fundamental problem, as bondage (not as a continual cycle of second chances that Westerns often imagine). There is a hierarchical system (of sorts) not just for humans but for all creatures, and humans stand at the very top. Hinduism speaks not of sin as an offense against a personal God but rather of good or bad *karma* (merit). As persons individually accumulate *karma*, this determines their next reincarnation in the hierarchy of beings. Fundamental to this system is that a person bears their own *karma*, so no corruption or accountability would be passed from another (e.g., as from Adam in Christian traditions). *Atman* refers to the eternal self as an unchanging reality, which allows personal continuity in rebirth, though not through personal memory.

---

13. Importantly, many orthodox translations of the Bible also translate certain occurrences of *soul* as "life."

- **Buddhism.** Similar to Hinduism, Buddhism affirms the unpleasant cycle of *samsara*, of reincarnation and *karma*, with good *karma* leading to higher levels of reincarnation and vice versa. This cycle of rebirth is seen as fundamentally negative. A key point of distinction with Hinduism is the teaching of "no self" (*anatman* or *anatta*). Since the liberation from the cycle of rebirth (i.e., *nirvana*) is identified with emptiness (*sunyata*), the goal is release from desire. Some form of personal identity (consciousness) exists for *karma* to pass on after death, but maintaining hold of the past is not a goal, or even achievable.

Human Identity

Christians have several internal disagreements concerning humanity. Contemporary culture bombards us with calls to know yourself, find yourself, be true to yourself. This raises the question of what really serves as the basis of our identity. We believe identity is found in knowing and loving the triune Christian God, yet we are embodied creatures who occupy a place and experience elements of embodiment like social status, culture, and gender. In Galatians 3:28, Paul teaches that these aspects of identity are transformed and transcended by belonging to Christ. How do these embodied realities fit with being Christian? When do these different identities complement one another and when do they stand in conflict? This issue has always required attention and discernment. For example, most Christians do not see an inherent conflict with being both female and Christian or Asian and Christian. It gets a little more complicated with national affiliations like American Christian or German Christian, when national identities can take precedence over the Christian one, as the story of Dietrich Bonhoeffer in chapter 10 explores. These debates hang on the premise of whether the identity should be seen as part of creational goodness or the fallenness of sin. Is identity something you construct or something you receive? When does an identity marker interfere with finding one's core identity in Christ through the Spirit? Are there times that the church allows social, cultural, or sexual identity markers, among others, to limit its ministry rather than seeking to reach all?

Human Modification

We are quickly moving into an age where science fiction is becoming science fact. Through the use of biomedical technology, we are steadily increasing the variety of ways that human life, and particularly the human body, can be augmented. Some of these are seen as extremely helpful, such as pacemakers and artificial limbs. However, as the variety and capability of these augmentations grows, we will be faced with increasing questions about the nature of human identity. Movements known as transhumanism or posthumanism have the stated goal to move humans beyond their intrinsic physical limitations, primarily by means of technology. Questions about identity will only advance more quickly when the augmentation is not external but internal, made through manipulation of our genetic code. A central question is this: How much change is acceptable? We will face a host of other questions: What is the fate of all the embryos used to perfect the process of modification? How will nonmodified children and adults be treated? How will the church and society treat clones?

Hierarchy of Sins: Before God?

We have been focusing on original sin, not the different types of sin. While different punishments for sin were commonly understood as part of Christian theology in the **patristic era**, the rise of the penitential system and the doctrine of purgatory heightened discussions about different types of sin. The medieval Catholic church ultimately made the basic distinction between mortal and venial sins as a description of two broad categories. Generally speaking, for a mortal sin a believer will lose their salvation, but for a venial sin they will not. However, consistent, unrepentant venial sins can ultimately have mortal consequences.[14] In response to this distinction, most Protestants affirmed that all sins are equal before God. Various Old Testament and New Testament texts complicate this simple affirmation. For example, Jesus notes a couple of times that there are worse sins (John 19:11) and worse punishments (Matt 11:20–24). While all sins create the need for God, that does not necessarily mean they are all equal. How should we understand the tension between the equal need created by sins and the reality of the difference between serious and minor sins?

Hierarchy of Sins: In Society?

While most Protestants will affirm the equality of sins, all sins are not treated equally in contemporary social discourse, both inside and outside the church. For example, homosexuality and abortion garner lots of attention, with political and financial backing from Christians. However, other issues that damage the church and society receive little attention: gluttony, divorce, pornography, violence against one's enemies, the mass incarceration of people of color, and the rampant abuse of the poor through payday lenders, to name a few. Unfortunately, the church seems more driven to condemn other people's problems rather than focusing on our own issues. Are these distinctions appropriate?

How should we choose what to focus on? First, we must remember that sin is both individual *and* communal/structural, so we should be concerned with issues in both areas. Second, we should follow the focused attention of the Bible. Some hot-button issues are only mentioned a handful of times, but there are over two thousand verses on the use and abuse of wealth. The Old Testament prophets in particular consistently critiqued idolatry, social injustice, and religious formalism. In the New Testament, the sins of anger, jealousy, racism, and social injustice are pictured destroying communal integrity.[15]

---

14. See *Catechism of the Catholic Church* on "Sin," §1852–1864, http://www.vatican.va/archive/ccc_css/archive/catechism/p3s1c1a8.htm.

15. We recommend Richard Hays, *Moral Vision of the New Testament: Community, Cross, New Creation: A Contemporary Introduction to New Testament Ethics* (New York: HarperOne, 1996).

Further Issues

- **Image of God.** What does it mean for humans to be in the "image of God"?
- **Humans and Animals.** What is the difference between humans and animals? How does this shape our views of human rights and animal rights?
- **Origin of Evil.** What is the origin of evil in the world—demonic (via serpent) or human? Does the agency of demonic forces influence human action? If so, how?
- **Individual and Corporate Responsibility.** How responsible are you for others' actions? Traditional views of total depravity extend liability to the community—to Adam *and* his family. To what extent are we (as individuals) responsible for the wider sins of our local, national, and global communities? What if we did not actively pursue these sins? What if we did not actively oppose them? (Consider Dan 9; Neh 9; and Ezra 9–10.)
- **Individual and Corporate Sins.** How might the church better balance its focus between individual and corporate sins? How might this shape our views on disputed issues like social justice, abortion, euthanasia, human trafficking, and civil rights?
- **Repentance and Therapy.** With the rise in awareness of mental health issues, a potential tension has arisen on how to view mental problems—are they sins or conditions? Should we prescribe repentance (for sin) or therapy (for a condition)? How do we maintain a balance between the two without ignoring the realities of either?

PRACTICING THE FAITH

The most authentic way to be human is to be authentically like Christ, since he is the true and perfect image of God, the goal toward which God's creative blessing is shaping us by the Spirit. The following thoughts are offered with that goal in mind.

Spirituality of Earth and Vocation

In the midst of our focus on the problems down here (sin, disease, death) and our focus on escaping these problems (up in heaven), we sometimes lose sight of the intrinsic goodness of the earth God created. The fundamental affirmation of creation in Genesis 1 is that "it is good," even "very good." Our locatedness on earth is directly tied to our human vocation to serve as stewards of the earth in community with one another. The idea of work is inherent to human identity as created by God—even before the fall. But the fall changed work; our work is now frustrated by our struggle with ourselves, others, and our world. Enjoying creation and pursuing work in community with others is fundamental to human flourishing. When work is distorted by sin to become oppressive, Christians should seek justice. Even in the brokenness of this age, however, Christians can discern and give thanks for the dignity and pleasure of work as we pursue the things we were created for.

Personal Identity through Community

We have spoken of work as a means to encounter God in creation. Just as working in the place God situates us fulfills our vocation as his image bearers, being in community reflect his image as well. Historically community was built around one's blood relatives. But as we come to the New Testament, the community is a family of faith—the church. We are most complete, most human, when we are connected to this multiethnic community of God. Our culture tells us that we are most authentic when we go it alone and break out of the boundaries set by the community. Yet, this model of life not only disconnects us from others but from ourselves. Our increasing isolation without communal support is contributing to increased troubles with mental health and even suicide. To be fully human according to a biblical model does not mean being absorbed into an undifferentiated sea of people. Actually, the Christian church is the only truly global religion, with a balance of populations across Africa, Asia, North and South America, and Europe, in distinction to the other major world religions that are primarily focused in one geographic region.[16] Christians are called to embrace the diverse global church by committing to a local church community.

Confession of Sin

In spite of the suffering, death, and corruption that sin introduces to our lives, the message of Christianity is hope. The experience of that hope is found in faith and repentance from sin. Essential to repentance is confessing sin before God and others. Confession is often framed as a prayer directly to God, as John tells us, "If we confess our sins, he [God] is faithful and just and will forgive us our sins" (1 John 1:9). James 5:13–20 speaks of our communal help to one another and commends the practice of confessing our sins to each other. Theologically, we describe this role we play for one another as the priesthood of all believers. If human identity is both corporate and individual, then human sin is communal and individual too. We must confess our communal sins communally. There are several examples of communal confession in the Bible, notably in the "nine" chapters: Daniel 9; Nehemiah 9; and Ezra 9–10. Pastoral wisdom may keep public confession from being manipulative.

Further Issues

- **Honoring the Image.** The most important fact about any human being is that he or she is created in the image of God. If so, then James says we need to be careful to honor others and not curse them in our speaking (Jas 3:9). Paul also speaks of honoring all those in the image of God (1 Cor 11:7). This has huge implications for how we should honor those who are marginalized.

---

16. Douglas Jacobsen, *Global Gospel: An Introduction to Christianity on Five Continents* (Grand Rapids: Baker, 2015), 9–11.

- **Brains on a Stick?** Noted author James K. A. Smith rightly critiques the quasi-Gnostic view that humans are just brains on a stick, that is, our minds and thinking is what really matters (against a holistic view of humanity).[17] We are called to embody the reality of the kingdom, not just think about it.[18]
- **Embodied Image.** We spend huge amounts of money on things related to our bodies—clothing, tattoos, diet, cosmetics, and exercise. If our focus is imbalanced, these can become problems, but they also reveal a natural concern for our embodied state and personal identity. Our self-image will never be fulfilled until we let the image of Christ be embodied in us through these things.
- **Human Rights.** In a world where everyone is defending their own rights, Christians are also called to defend rights—the rights of others. We recognize the inherent dignity of all persons from birth, through school, adulthood, and death. Christians are to sacrifice our own rights and freedoms in defending the rights of others; serving others not seeking power for ourselves (cf. Rom 14–15; 1 Cor 8–9).
- **In the Image of the Creator.** One way we reflect the image of God is to reflect his role as Creator, bringing order out of chaos. So go and do likewise: be creative!

In conclusion, we see that human flourishing is found in relationship with God, participating in the wholeness of life that he intended in creation and is restoring in salvation. God-intended flourishing is holistic, and sin counteracts this flourishing in a holistic way—in us individually, in our communities, and in the land where we live. Though we often limit the focus of human identity and of the nature of sin to the individual, the vision of theological anthropology is much more integrated with the world around us.

CLOSING PRAYER

Most merciful God, Father of our Lord Jesus Christ, we confess that we have sinned in thought, word, and deed. We have not loved you with our whole heart. We have not loved our neighbors as ourselves. In your mercy forgive what we have been, help us to amend what we are, and direct what we shall be; that we may do justly, love mercy, and walk humbly with you, our God. Amen.[19]

---

17. See James K. A. Smith, *You Are What You Love: The Spiritual Power of Habit* (Grand Rapids: Brazos, 2016).

18. For more on kingdom theology, see chs. 6, 7, and 11.

19. "Forms of Penitence," *Common Worship: Daily Prayer*, Church of England, www.churchofengland.org/prayer-and-worship/worship-texts-and-resources/common-worship/daily-prayer/forms-penitence.

CHAPTER 9

Salvation

Participating in New Creation

Introduction

At the most basic level, Christianity is a rescue religion. That is, the fundamental Christian message is the Story of how God is setting things right after they have been broken by sin. God's work in Jesus the Christ to secure salvation is at the heart of that Story. We see this right at the beginning of the New Testament as an angel announces Jesus's birth: "You are to give him the name Jesus, because he will save his people from their sins" (Matt 1:21). Jesus is the Greek pronunciation of the Hebrew name Joshua [or *Yeshua*], which means "Yahweh saves." The first letter to Timothy also captures this: "Here is a trustworthy saying that deserves full acceptance: Christ Jesus came into the world to save sinners" (1:15). The key theological term that relates to salvation is **soteriology**. At the heart of this salvation (Greek: *soteria*) is grace, and our account of Augustine and Pelagius that follows is a debate about what grace is and how it works.

Augustine and Pelagius on Grace

Setting the Stage

Augustine (AD 354–430) was born in North Africa to parents of modest status who provided their exceptional son with an education. He took up teaching and eventually moved to Rome and then Milan. His mother was a devout Christian who wished to influence his sanctity and success, though he did not follow her faith until later in life.

Augustine did not know what he was searching for, but he was inspired by Cicero's noble philosophical quest for truth and integrity.

Big Idea:

In response to sin's corruption of the world, God achieves salvation through Jesus's death and resurrection and applies that restoration to people of faith through the Spirit.

Key Terms:
- Soteriology
- Atonement
- Divine and Human Agency
- Monergism
- Synergism

Key Passages:
Gen 12:1–3;
Deut 30:1–20;
Isa 52:13–53:12;
Jer 31;
Luke 4:16–21;
John 3:16;
Rom 3:21–26; 5:12–21;
Eph 2:1–10;
1 Tim 1:15;
Rev 21–22

He tried out a succession of approaches. Early on he associated with a particular version of **Gnosticism** called **Manichaeism**. They taught that humans were victims of a crude warfare of two roughly equal powers of good and evil matter. Augustine used this battle as an excuse for his inability to reform his life. The group eventually proved intellectually disappointing. Later, as he adopted Neoplatonism, Augustine found clarity on several matters that helped him embrace faith. He realized that God could be pictured in spiritual (not physical) terms, that creation could have a single source, and that evil resulted from distorting the good creation. But the Neoplatonic nameless "One" that unified all things was not a personal God and thus was not satisfying.

The final pieces for his Christian faith came together when Augustine began listening to the famous preacher Ambrose. He realized that the need for communion with God is ingrained in humans as their highest goal. Freedom from sin is not enough, creatures must learn to love God. While struggling with the desire to convert to Christianity, he was walking in a friend's garden and heard a childlike voice telling him to read. As he picked up the Bible, his eyes fell on Paul's exhortation to put on Jesus Christ and make no provision for satisfying the desires of the flesh (Rom 13:13–14). This changed his life.

Augustine followed the example of several prominent converts to Christianity and adopted the life of study, devotion, and celibacy. Ambrose baptized him on Easter in 387. His life of contemplation and study was short-lived when he was forcibly drafted as priest and soon after made bishop in North Africa. He served the church with its many administrative demands for forty years. His preaching and writing made Augustine the single most important voice for the next millennium of Western Christianity.

As a contemporary of Augustine, Pelagius (c. AD 360–418) was born in Britain. Sometime before 390 he arrived in Rome to study law. He made a name for himself, however, as a spiritual director among Christian social elites. Following the traditional philosophical calls for self-mastery that had typically characterized aristocrats, he challenged believers to live a holy and disciplined Christian life. With Rome faltering in 410, he moved to North Africa and became embroiled in a debate with Augustine about grace and holiness. Eventually his teaching becomes difficult to distinguish from the views of his supporters, such as Celestius, who took up Pelagius's cause.

Debates about Sin and Grace

Pelagius believed that God gave grace to humans before he asked them to respond to God, but he thought of grace as the standard equipment all humans possess, something inherent in the created order. Suffering from sin and evil circumstances does not disable or excuse the human family, because God gives people freedom of choice and a moral conscience. Each person should be able to do what God tells them to do, so the ten commandments and the teaching of Jesus are achievable instructions for living. He argues that God would not command something humans could not do.

Not unlike Pelagius, the early Christian Augustine insisted on human freedom in contrast with the fatalism of the Manichaeans. Later, Augustine discerned that sin disoriented humankind more than he had previously acknowledged. Sin was not simply a wrongdoing but was a corrupting presence within humans. In *Confessions* he observes, "The malice of my act was base and I loved it. . . . I loved the evil in me."[1] A person, he argued, must receive an enabling and restorative grace to allow them to turn to God and perform good works because humans were born with **original sin**—the corrupt disposition and liability humans share with Adam.

Pelagius was offended when Augustine asked God to "grant what you command and command what you will."[2] Pelagius thought Augustine's *Confessions* recklessly promoted indifference to God's commands by suggesting our inability to obey without God's intervention; this amounts to a license to sin without accountability. In Pelagius's view, God gave persons the ability to respond, but humans had to exercise their choice or will. By his reckoning, a person who always obeyed would not need Jesus to die on the cross. However, Augustine emphasized the grace provided in the cross: if people could obey just on their own, why did Jesus die to provide us grace?

Two images help us understand this crucial conversation about the human struggle with sin. Pelagius's view of the life of faith is like a person seeking weight loss. He says they just need to break away from bad examples and environments and make the tough choices to reform their life. Augustine views the life of faith more like recovery from drug addiction or mental illness. In these great afflictions, victims testify that recovery is not a matter of willpower. Such a victim is not in charge of their faculties and needs serious intervention. Effective external help is required to restore responsible behavior.

PATRISTIC YOUTH TALKS

Can you imagine the worst caricatures of Augustine and Pelagius speaking to a church youth group? Would parents and sponsors be happy?

Augustine: "By now some of you are stuck in reckless behavior including drugs, alcohol, and sex. You are stuck in sin until God gives you grace. Okay, that's it for tonight."

Pelagius: "I know some of you are struggling with alcoholism, but you don't need rehab. Come on, pull yourself together. Snap out of it. Okay, that's it for tonight."

The Secret to Success

These perspectives on grace are related to different visions of a successful Christian life. The heroes of faith were important for Christianity's self-image. The martyrs were celebrated like today's rock stars because they maintained their testimony to Christ

1. Saint Augustine, *Confessions*, trans. F. J. Sheed, 2nd ed. (Indianapolis: Hackett, 2007), 2.4 (p. 29).
2. Augustine, *Confessions*, 10.37 (p. 222).

WED.

when facing death. Christians also admired virgins—groups of women who had forgone marriage and motherhood to pursue the life of devotion and service. Some monks were revered for facing Satan in deadly battles for the soul. With great self-denial, these champions had found victory over sin's grasp.

Pelagius challenged ordinary Christians to engage the heroic battle, to become champions among us. In contrast, the *Confessions* recount how Augustine lived recklessly and rebelliously on his own and how God's grace was necessary to bring change. With worshipful adoration, he praised God for directing and achieving God's purpose in his life. God deserved the credit; he put people in Augustine's path and brought good from things Augustine had sought for vain and selfish reasons. Augustine found faith and liberty because of God's stubborn interventions of grace.

This retelling is groundbreaking. For one thing, it creates an altered vision of the hero. As a high-profile convert to Christianity, Augustine claims that his victory was not due to heroic human effort but to the healing infusion of grace. Augustine reminded common Christians that grace, not heroic strength of will, empowered obedience. It was God's grace at work in Augustine that enabled him to renounce his driving ambition and desired status and serve the church where common people encountered the grace that restored their humanity.

These debates highlight the issues at the heart of the discussion about soteriology: brokenness from sin, the need for grace, and the reality of transformation as humans encounter God.

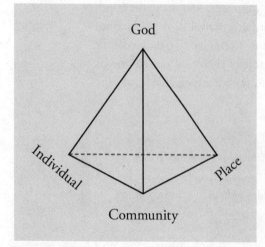

FIGURE 9.1
Holistic Biblical Theology

SALVATION IN BIBLICAL AND HISTORICAL PERSPECTIVES

Framing the Big Picture

In the previous chapter we detailed how the foundational narratives in Genesis frame the holistic nature of human experience. God created us to flourish holistically—as individuals, in community, in a geographical place (see figure 9.1). And sin, we discovered, is a corruption of all three of these aspects. Most Christians tend to only think about salvation as an individual issue, but a fully biblical perspective on salvation views the individual, community, and place as coordinate. This chapter focuses on individual salvation, but the chapters on the church and **eschatology** round out the picture of this holistic restoration.

This holistic view is captured in the Nicene Creed, which reminds us that the purpose of Jesus's **incarnation**, death, and resurrection was "for us and our salvation." This salvation relates more widely to the **kingdom of God** and the work of the Holy Spirit in the church, and the "life of the world to come." Note how salvation shapes the second and third articles of the creed:

> We believe in one Lord, Jesus Christ, the only Son of God, . . .
> For us and for our salvation he came down from heaven,
> was incarnate from the Holy Spirit and the Virgin Mary
> and became truly human.
> For our sake he was crucified under Pontius Pilate;
> he suffered death and was buried.
> On the third day he rose again
> in accordance with the Scriptures;
> he ascended into heaven
> and is seated at the right hand of the Father.
> He will come again in glory to judge the living and the dead,
> and his kingdom will have no end.
>
> We believe in the Holy Spirit, the Lord, the giver of life. . . .
> We believe in one, holy, catholic, and apostolic church.
> We acknowledge one baptism for the forgiveness of sins.
> We look for the resurrection of the dead, and the life of the world to come.

Exploring soteriology, we see a basic shape described by the creed: Christ's death and resurrection *achieve* salvation for us and the Spirit's presence *applies* salvation to us. This model of *salvation accomplished* and *salvation applied* will guide our discussion below, but before we arrive there, we need to see how the holistic nature of salvation fits within the biblical narrative.

Wider Biblical Narrative

In the wider biblical narrative, we see a basic problem-solution progression: God created the world good so we would share in his life and blessing, but sin corrupted the world through the fall of Adam and Eve. In response to this problem, God has taken the initiative in Jesus Christ and through the Spirit to deliver us from sin. However, God's activity to restore creation began long before Jesus died on the cross. Like an expert chess player, God began to set up his checkmate move dozens of moves in advance. We can see these early moves to restore creation to God's intended purpose clearly in Genesis 12. In other words, salvation history began with God's calling and **election** of Abraham and his family, and the salvation accomplished by Christ and applied by the Spirit is a culmination of this wider Story of Israel and the people of God.

In the previous chapter on **anthropology**, we saw in Genesis 1–3 how God's good intention and sin's corruption affected individuals, the community, and the place, such that sin exactly reverses God's plan (see figure 9.2).

FIGURE 9.2: CREATION AND FALL COMPARED

	Individual	Community	Place
Creation	Blessing / (Flourishing) Life	Family / Community	Land / Garden
Fall	Cursing / Death	Broken Family / Conflict	Exile / Toil

Abrahamic Covenant. In response to the downward spiral of humanity in Genesis 3–11, God called Abraham (and his family) to restore blessing to the world as part of the **covenant** God made with Abraham:[3]

> The LORD had said to Abram, "Go from your country, your people and your father's household to the land I will show you.
>
> "I will make you into a great nation,
>   and I will bless you;
> I will make your name great,
>   and you will be a blessing.
> I will bless those who bless you,
>   and whoever curses you I will curse;
> and all peoples on earth
>   will be blessed through you." (Gen 12:1–3)

Perhaps you noticed a repeated term? Blessing! Just as in creation, God's intention for his people is to bless them, not to curse them. Likewise, we see God's activity to establish a family for Abraham (he will be a "great nation"), and God will give him a place to live. God started the work of salvation.

This promise of restoration is not just for Abraham, but as verse 3 points out, God's goal is to bless "all peoples on earth" through him. Christians, therefore, see the work of Christ and the Spirit as the fulfillment of this global blessing that God had promised through Abraham's family. This establishes the shape of Christian views about salvation because God's work through Abraham only makes sense in light of Genesis 1–3. What do you notice about figure 9.3?

Salvation is primarily a restoration of God's exact plan from creation! God intended the blessing of life in all its fullness, and when sin interrupted that plan, God acted to fulfill his original purposes through restoration. Salvation is about fixing what sin

---

3. Abraham is called Abram in this part of the narrative. Later God changes his name.

broke, not throwing away what is broken and starting over somewhere else. Salvation is not just about individuals flourishing; it is also about a new flourishing community in a renewed place.

FIGURE 9.3: CREATION RESTORED

	Individual	Community	Place
Creation	Blessing / (Flourishing) Life	Family / Community	Land / Garden
Fall	Cursing / Death	Broken Family / Conflict	Toil / Exile
Restoration / Renewed Creation	Blessing / (Flourishing) Life	One Family → Whole World	Promised Land

SALVATION HISTORY AS THE STORY OF THE BIBLE

The Story of the Bible moves in three parts:

- Creation—The world is created good (Gen 1–2)
- Fall—Sin has corrupted God's creation (Gen 3–11)
- Salvation / New Creation—God is working to restore humans (Gen 12–Rev 22)

This salvation climaxes in Jesus Christ through his death on the cross, his resurrection from the grave, and the restored presence of the Spirit within creation. Salvation history is a history of covenants:

- Abrahamic Covenant (Gen 12:1–3; 15; 17; 21)
- Mosaic Covenant (Exod 19–20; Deut 30)
- Davidic Covenant (2 Sam 7; Ps 2; 89)
- New Covenant—New Testament (Jer 31; Ezek 36–37)

The rest of the Bible plays out the various moves in God's chess game against sin and evil through Abraham's family. We see this through the progression of covenants God makes with this people. Each covenant builds on the previous ones but with new iterations, displaying God's holy love.

Mosaic Covenant. After Abraham, the next major step in the story of Israel centers on God's rescue of his people from Egypt through Moses. There are several key themes to note: (1) God's liberation of his people from Egypt (as celebrated in the annual festival of Passover) becomes the paradigmatic lens for interpreting his saving activity. The exodus is perhaps the most defining event in Old Testament theology. (2) God calls the people to obedience (as with the Ten Commandments in Exod 20:1–17), but it is important to note that God's saving deliverance happened first (e.g., Exod 19:3–6). That is, God shows his love for his people first, and their obedience is a response to his love, not an attempt to earn his love. (3) God provides the tabernacle and temple as a gracious means for the community to experience his presence. (4) If the people break the covenant, they will face covenant curses. These curses look much like consequences of the fall, climaxing in exile from the land.

Exodus and Passover

The exodus is the rescue of the family of Abraham from Egyptian slavery. God won their liberty by breaking the will of the Egyptian rulers through a series of plagues and finally providing for Israel's miraculous crossing of the Red Sea. Later, Israel celebrated this rescue with the feast of Passover. Passover commemorated God protecting Israel from the judgment of the plagues and mighty deliverance. Jesus was crucified (and raised) at Passover, so Christians celebrate salvation offered by Jesus as in continuity with God's previous Passover deliverance.

Davidic Covenant. The covenant God makes with David furthers the same ideas, but with a focus on the kings of Judah. David wanted to build the temple, thus showing his faithfulness to the Mosaic covenant. As a result, God promises to establish David's family as kings over the people so that they can be a flourishing community in the land. This is the basis for Jewish hopes for a *messiah*, as a fulfillment of the Davidic covenant.

New Covenant. The kings and the people of Israel and Judah eventually wander from their covenant commitments and therefore experience the covenant curses. Though they are unfaithful to God, he promises to restore them by bringing them back from exile, forgiving their sin, and restoring their communities. (This is an eschatological hope: things are broken now, but God will come in the future to bring restoration.) At the heart of this hope is the promised presence of the *Holy Spirit* to be with the people to renew their hearts so they will walk in covenant obedience. They will share in the fullness of God's life again.

These covenants find their fulfillment in Jesus the Messiah. He comes to share the restoring presence of the Spirit with the people of God. The word for "covenant" in Latin is *testamentum*, and so when we speak about God's work through Christ and the Spirit in the *New Testament*, we are speaking about the fulfillment of God's eschatological restoration in the new covenant. This is the context for understanding God's climactic act of salvation, his checkmate move through Christ against the power of evil in the world. With the new covenant, we see the dual focus of salvation accomplished in Christ and salvation applied by the Spirit. We will now address those topics in turn.

SALVATION ACCOMPLISHED: ATONEMENT

God's holy love drives his action in salvation: in his holiness he takes sin seriously, and in his love he goes to the furthest extent to resolve our problem. God set the stage for restoring the world in the Old Testament, but the decisive and transformative event in the history of salvation is the death and resurrection of Jesus the Messiah. That said, this is not a naturally anticipated progression of events. Someone suffering the ancient equivalent of the electric chair as the focus of God's climactic redemptive act in history is surely odd and unexpected. Paul calls the cross the "foolishness of God" from the perspective of the world, and yet he argues that God's "foolishness" is filled with more wisdom and power than anyone can fathom (1 Cor 1:18–25). This beautiful mystery of the death and resurrection of Christ is thus our focus here.

One of the most basic statements about Christ comes from 1 Corinthians 15:3: "Christ died for our sins according to the Scriptures." His death resolves a fundamental human problem related to sin, and the focus of *salvation accomplished* is that God, not us, has worked to fix broken people. We should not miss the "according to the Scriptures" aspect because it shows that the earliest Christians saw the death and resurrection of Jesus as part of the larger scriptural narrative. The chief resonance driven by the biblical text is the recapitulation of the exodus since Jesus's death and resurrection happened at Passover, the annual celebration of the exodus.

We have already explored Jesus's identity as the God-man in our chapter on Christology, so here we focus on what his death and resurrection achieved. The key theological term that describes this is **atonement**, initially popularized by the first major English translator of the Bible, William Tyndale. This term points to the reconciliation of humans once separated from God by sin who now can become "at one" with him again. While there is a great unity in the Christian tradition about the identity of Jesus, there is diversity in the tradition about why Jesus had to die to bring salvation and how his death and resurrection achieved salvation for the world.

This diversity comes from the plethora of metaphors and images the Bible uses to describe the Christ event (his incarnation, death, and resurrection). Over time theologians have come to speak of different "models of the atonement" to describe these various perspectives.[4] Since there has never been an ecumenical, creedal pronouncement about the atonement, there have been many debates over time whether there is one correct model of the atonement or if the various models might work together. The New Testament scholar Scot McKnight has helpfully used the metaphor of a bag of golf clubs to describe the relationship of the different models.[5] Instead of having one real model

---

4. It is also common for these to be described as "theories" of the atonement. The term *theory* is not bad, but since it connotes an unproven or speculative idea, we prefer to avoid it in this context.

5. Scot McKnight, *A Community Called Atonement* (Nashville: Abingdon, 2007), 35–43.

and several others as illustrations, McKnight argues that each model (like each golf clubs) has a necessary purpose.

With no set number of models, a host of positions have been offered. In the following account, we give three primary family groupings under which several models lie: divine restitution, victory over evil powers, and transforming vision. This obviously limits the detail of our discussion, but we think it provides a helpful introduction. In figure 9.4 we summarize the key elements of each, namely that each family has similar perspectives on how the problem-solution relation works.

FIGURE 9.4: PRIMARY ATONEMENT FAMILIES

Atonement Family	Problem	Solution	Specific Models
Divine Restitution	Offense against God (Violation)	Restoration of Moral Order (Requirement Fulfilled)	Satisfaction Penal Substitution
Victory over Evil Powers	Enslavement to Evil Powers (Death)	Liberation/Redemption (Life)	Ransom Christus Victor Recapitulation/Deification*
Transforming Vision	Corrupt Desires [Ignorance]	Transformed Desires [Knowledge/Revelation]	Moral Influence Moral Example

* The recapitulation/deification model is more of a hybrid in that it works from a combination of the victory over evil and transforming vision families.

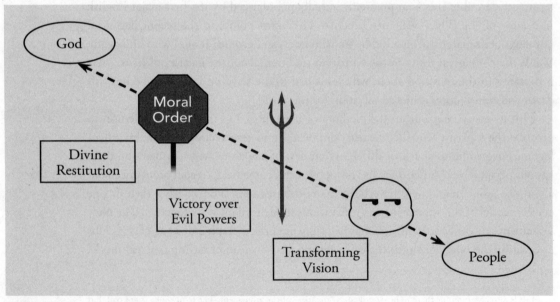

FIGURE 9.5
What Is Separating People From God?

KEY TERMS RELATED TO ATONEMENT

Propitiation and **Expiation.** These two terms describe sacrificial imagery. With propitiation, God (as a person) is the object of the action, such that his anger is appeased. With expiation, sin (as a thing) is the object of the action, such that sin and its related problems are removed.

Objective and **Subjective.** In theological discussions, the terms *objective* and *subjective* are often used to describe different models. Models that focus on the transformation of individuals are described as "subjective," whereas those that achieve a change in God's perspective are described as "objective."

Divine Restitution

While the victory over evil powers models attracted early attention in patristic theology,[6] the divine restitution family draws the most attention today, particularly in Catholic and Protestant traditions. As Creator, God ordained humanity to live and serve him in obedience. By pridefully rejecting God's priority, humanity perpetrated an offense against God and violated the ordered system he created. God did not leave humanity in a state of separation and brokenness but brought restitution to the ordained order through the death of Christ, thus fulfilling the requirements they owed.

The two main versions of this family are the satisfaction and the **penal substitution** models. The basic distinction between the two models is which requirement of God's order needs to be fulfilled, his honor or his justice. According to the *satisfaction model*, humans created an infinite offense against God's honor (because to sin against an infinitely great God creates an infinite offense). Humans were obliged to correct the problem, but only God had the ability. Accordingly, Jesus, the God-man, offered himself to restore God's honor. Anselm is a notable proponent. In the *penal substitution model*, the focus shifts from God's honor to his justice. Humans in their sinfulness are due a just penalty (hence the term *penal*) of death, but Christ dies in their place as a substitute, taking their just punishment upon himself so it would not fall on them. In light of Trinitarian theology, the Father is not being appeased by the Son; rather, the Father and Son are working in union together to bring salvation to humanity (see Isa 52:13–53:12; John 1:29; Rom 3:23–26). Proponents include John Calvin and John Wesley.

Victory over Evil Powers

In our scientific age, we rarely think about spiritual agents like angels and demons, but in the biblical and postbiblical world, evil powers were very much seen as a threat.

---

6. When Anselm of Canterbury set out one of the first comprehensive arguments for a divine restitution model in his work *Cur Deus Homo* (*Why Did God Become Human?*), he explicitly wanted to remove the devil from the equation and set God himself as both the actor and receiver of Jesus's death.

Indeed, in most non-Western contexts people are still open to the activity of spiritual powers, much like what we find in biblical contexts. In addition to the directly personal agents like Satan and demons (e.g., Eph 6:10–20), we also find personified powers like Sin and Death that rule over humans.[7] What unites this atonement family is a focus on the enslavement by evil powers that keeps us from God. Jesus's death and resurrection, however, defeat these powers and liberate his people. The biblical term *redemption* informs this atonement model. It is a metaphor for liberation from slavery that also brings to mind the liberation in Exodus.

The three main models of this family are the *Christus Victor* (Christ the Victor), ransom, and recapitulation/deification models. The basic distinction between the models is how the Christ event interacts with the evil powers. With *Christus Victor*, the more commonly held of the three, Christ's death and resurrection are an assault on humanity's evil captor Satan, and he is defeated by Jesus's resurrection from the dead, which empties Satan's power over death (see Rom 5:11–21; 1 Cor 15:20–28). Proponents include Martin Luther and Gustav Aulén. With the *ransom model*, Satan (or Death) has kidnapped humans, and Jesus's death on the cross is the ransom paid to redeem them from their captor (see Matt 20:28; Mark 10:45; 1 Tim 2:5–6). Proponents include Origen, Gregory of Nyssa, and Augustine. The ransom model is often associated with the "fishhook" model, where God tricks Satan into taking the bait (Jesus's cross) that serves to undo his power (see 1 Cor 2:7–8). The *recapitulation/deification model* takes the *Christus Victor* framework and combines it with a transforming vision account (as described below).

Transforming Vision

The transforming vision family focuses more on humans. As a result, these models are often labeled "subjective" models of atonement because they effect change within humans. From this general perspective, the fundamental problem is that humans have turned our focus away from God. The solution, therefore, is not about repairing our status before God or defeating the evil powers but realigning our attention on God. Jesus's death and resurrection are the ultimate display of God's love that draws our wayward attention back to him. Take an example of a married couple where one of the spouses turns their attention to others. In this model, the faithful spouse reaches out in sacrificial love to restore the wayward spouse and restore the relationship.

The two main models in this family, particularly from the Western tradition, are the moral influence and the moral example models, but the earliest is the patristic recapitulation/deification model, which is a hybrid of the *Christus Victor* and transforming vision approaches.

The *recapitulation/deification model* addresses the dual issues of the cosmic corruption of sin and the personal effects of that cosmic problem. Humans turned away from the

---

7. We intentionally capitalize these terms because passages like Romans 5–6 treat these as powerful adversaries.

source of life and introduced death into the cosmic order. To remedy the problem, God not only needed to refocus our attention on him, but he also needed to expunge corruption from creation. Through the incarnation, death, and resurrection of Christ, the immortal God overcame mortality and at the same time revealed himself to those who had strayed. Jesus recaps the human story,[8] but in this retracing or reliving the story, he gets it right and fixes the problem of sin. With the conditions for life restored, believers who come to know God through the **revelation** of Christ become like him.[9] Jesus's death and resurrection reveal the true nature of God and his love for humanity in such a way that when we truly encounter this revelation in Christ and through the Spirit, we are transformed to become like God (immortal, holy, etc.) through our knowledge and experience of him.[10]

We might say that the basic distinction between the other two models is how they exert pressure on humans; however, the dividing lines between the two are not always firm. We might say that the *moral influence model* is more of a "pull" model, in that the revelation of God's love pulls unredeemed humanity into a reconciled relationship (see Luke 19:10; John 18:37; 1 John 4:10). Proponents include Augustine and especially Peter Abelard. The *moral example model* is more of a "push" model, in that Jesus's sacrifice exerts an outward pressure on his disciples, creating the primary model for how they should live. Christ suffered, so they should follow Christ in suffering for others. This is the primary ethic of the whole New Testament (see especially Mark 8:27–9:1; 9:31–37; 10:32–45; 2 Cor 4:7–18; 1 Pet 2:21–25). Those that hold to a Pelagian view of sin regularly hold to *just* a moral example model of atonement to the exclusion of other models. We affirm that Christ's sacrificial suffering is the primary model for New Testament discipleship, but limiting atonement to a moral example model is insufficient.

All of these models capture important aspects of the cosmic and personal work of Christ on the cross as described in the Bible. Yet none present the whole picture by themselves. Having explored how Jesus the Messiah accomplished salvation, we now turn our attention to how salvation is applied through the Spirit.

SALVATION APPLIED

Sin does not automatically disappear because Jesus died and rose again. Salvation achieved must be applied to people, so we are now attending to what salvation looks like in a person's life and how they access this saving work. Looking back at figure 9.3,

---

8. Recapitulation is a long term for summing up a story at the end or recapping it.

9. They held an ancient philosophical tenet that "like knows like" (or "like is a friend to like"). We cannot truly know God unless he became like us, but also we cannot truly know God unless we become like him (through grace).

10. For a brief illustration, see the quotation by Irenaeus regarding the rule of faith in ch. 3. See also Irenaeus, *Against Heresies* 3.16–19. For a more extended but still accessible and enlightening example of this perspective, see Athanasius, *On the Incarnation*: He begins with a clear Christus Victor discussion in §1–10 and seamlessly combines it with a Transforming Vision approach in §11–19.

we remember that salvation reverses the problems of sin. The multivalent curse of sin requires a multivalent blessing for believers to share in the life of God.

Much of this book has been focused on doctrinal unity, with attention given to Christian "essentials." When we come to the question of salvation applied, Christians hold differing opinions about this important doctrine. Accordingly, we will begin to explore much more diversity among Christians. We will first look at the primary metaphors or descriptions of salvation, and then we will look at issues of agency—how divine and human purposes work together.

Salvation Applied: New Creation Images and Metaphors

We began our discussion in this chapter by walking through the main Story of the Bible: creation, fall, and renewed creation (or salvation), using the biblical covenants as the foundational structure of that history of salvation. God created us for blessing and the fullness of life, but sin brings cursing and death; salvation is ultimately about restoring and bringing greater fullness of life.

Metaphors

As we focus on the pictures of salvation in the Bible (and primarily the New Testament), we discuss different images and **metaphors**. By using the term *metaphors*, we do not mean something unreal; rather, we are merely recognizing that theologians employ imagery drawn from their cultural forms to explain their experience. We will first explore several of these metaphors and then note how different interpretations of these metaphors (and the texts that undergird them) influence the confessional differences in Christianity. As with models of atonement, no one picture captures the fullness of the restoring work of Christ and the Spirit, so these are like different facets on a gem:

- **Justification/Righteousness (Law Court):** We were condemned before the judge, but now we are forgiven and declared "not guilty."
- **Reconciliation (Relationships):** We were estranged from God, but we are now reunited.
- **Adoption (Family):** We were without a family, but now we are God's children, heirs with an inheritance, and coheirs with Christ through the Holy Spirit.
- **Sanctification/Holiness (Temple):** We were impure due to sin, but now we are being made holy and pure through the Holy Spirit.
- **Resurrection (Death):** We were dead in our sin, but we now walk in new life and have the hope of bodily resurrection through the Holy Spirit.
- **Glorification (God's Presence):** We were mortal because we were separated from the presence of the immortal God, but now we are united with him and will ultimately share in his resurrection glory through the Holy Spirit.

- **Theosis/Deification (Creation):** The **image of God** in humanity was corrupted by sin, but now we are transformed into the image of Christ and share in the divine life. Theosis refers to "being made a god" (metaphorically) or becoming "like God." Believers become "gods" by grace (by adoption), in distinction to the Trinity who is God by nature. The Greek patristic and Orthodox theologians' use of the term *theosis* allows them to speak about not only the anthropological change in salvation but also God's salvation-historical purposes in creation and new creation.

Metaphors and the Confessions

It would be hard to overemphasize these metaphors' role in the history of Christianity. Many secondary differences exist between Protestants and Roman Catholics, but one of their primary differences regards the relationship between justification and sanctification. Our description below gives only the broadest of outlines of Protestant, Catholic, and Orthodox views of salvation (see figure 9.6).

A starting point for our discussion is the idea that salvation happens in three tenses—past, present, and future. Those in our evangelical tradition often only speak in the past tense when they talk of getting "saved" (e.g., "When were you saved?"). Yet each person's struggle with sin does not end at conversion; rather, God's saving work began in the past, continues in the present, and will not be consummated until the future when we are finally free from the problem of death. So we can and should speak of past, present, and future salvation.

FIGURE 9.6: METAPHORS OF SALVATION IN THE CONFESSIONS

	Past	Present	Future
Protestant	Justification (Point)	Sanctification (Process) ⟶	Glorification (Resurrection)
Roman Catholic	Justification Sanctification (Process) – – – ⟶		Glorification (Resurrection)
Eastern Orthodox	Theosis/Deification (Process) – – – ⟶		(Resurrection)

The present and the future expectations are similar across the three confessions. The present is marked by progressive sanctification, or the process of becoming more holy by means of the transforming work of the Holy Spirit. Each tradition might emphasize different things, but the macro perspective is similar. Likewise, all three share the hope of glorification for the future, where believers share in God's divine life primarily through the resurrection of the body (reuniting the body and soul) when Christ returns again.

WED.

The main Western dispute centers on how to understand the relationship of justification and sanctification. The distinction between these relates partially to the international roots of theological language noted in the sidebar below. While Paul only uses one family of Greek terms centered around the root *dikaios*, English Bibles translate this with two sets of terms—as "righteous" and as "just." This distinction gives a window into the Catholic-Protestant debate: Is the righteousness (i.e., justification) that Paul describes more focused on morality or on a legal status? Most Protestants have emphasized the legal aspect (in conjunction with their view of penal substitution), so the focus is on God's pronouncement of "not guilty" as a new status, which is forgiveness (as in Rom 4). Catholics have historically emphasized the moral aspect, seeing God's gracious act of setting believers right as enabling them to live in a holy manner, hence its basic identification with sanctification (as in Rom 6).[11] In contrast to the progressive nature of justification/sanctification in the Roman Catholic confession, Protestants have focused on finding assurance of salvation, so it is central that justification happens at a point in time (i.e., it is one-and-done).

INTERNATIONAL ROOTS OF THEOLOGICAL LANGUAGE

English, as a language, is derived from two primary roots: German (through the Angles and Saxons) and Latin (through the French). As we do theology, this double source creates all sorts of trouble for us since many theological terms from the Greek New Testament get filtered to us through these two different branches. For example, the Greek term *dikaios* is translated as both "righteous" (via German) and "just" (via Latin). Those two translations, while correct, have different nuances—one more moral (righteous) and the other more legal (just)—which the original Greek held together.

While we agree with the Protestant reading, it is important to note that Catholics base their theology on an interpretation of the biblical text and on a doctrine of grace. While the differences between Protestant and Catholic theologies are not insignificant, the primary Catholic teaching on justification is focused on those who are already members of the church, that is, those who have experienced baptismal regeneration. So the Roman Catholic call to moral holiness is calling believers to walk progressively closer to God and is not a way to earn an "admission ticket to the party."

---

11. An important and accessible source for engaging Roman Catholic theology is the *Catechism of the Catholic Church* on "Grace and Justification," §1987–2029, http://www.vatican.va/archive/ccc_css/archive/catechism/p3s1c3a2.htm.

JUSTIFICATION IN AN ECUMENICAL CONTEXT

There has been a growing rapprochement between Protestants and Catholics over the last fifty years regarding the issue of justification, as evidenced by the "Joint Declaration on the Doctrine of Justification" (1999). In that statement, the historical condemnations promoted by Lutherans and Catholics against one another were deemed no longer applicable. Beyond these original two participants, the statement has now been ratified by the Roman Catholic Church, the Lutheran World Federation, the World Methodist Council, and World Communion of Reformed Churches. Many Protestants, even among the traditions just noted, disagree with the Joint Declaration, but the interest in ecumenical discussion and agreement will impact theological discussions for years to come.

The Eastern Orthodox tradition uses the terms sanctification and glorification, but they subsume the whole salvific experience under the term ***theosis***, meaning that the consistent thread in each stage is that believers become like God by sharing in the divine life. Some (usually Protestants) simplistically gloss the idea of theosis as if it were merely sanctification, but to do so misses the holistic nature of the term. The Roman Catholic tradition also speaks of theosis, or its Latin-based equivalents deification and divinization, though it is less central. Thus the Orthodox may use a different terminology and emphasize different things, but their overall perspective is not at odds with the two Western confessions.

This distinction between the three traditions is often framed as a debate about the efficacy of grace in relation to works. The discussions build upon underlying doctrines about divine and human agency, that is, how God's willing interacts in, with, and/or against human willing. Does God do everything in salvation? Are God and humans partners? Does that divine-human relationship shift after conversion? If so, how?

Salvation Applied: Divine and Human Agency

In the previous section about salvation applied, we explored what salvation looks like. Now we are focusing on the process of how that salvation is experienced.

Wider Perspectives: Synergism and Monergism

As we discuss agency, you might be familiar with the related debates about nature versus nurture, or free will versus determinism. These types of issues arise when we discuss the topic of **agency**, and the two primary Christian approaches fall into the categories of **synergism** and **monergism**. These terms derive from the Greek root *ergon*, which relates to the idea of work. In synergism, the divine and human wills are working together in cooperation. In monergism, only one (hence "mono") will is functionally operative: God's will. What is important about these approaches is that they build on particular views of original sin that we explored in the previous chapter: Pelagian, Greek patristic, and Augustinian.

The Greek patristic and Augustinian perspectives (the two primary orthodox options) are distinguished from **Pelagianism** by the affirmation that all humans have been corrupted by sin as passed to them by Adam. The difference between the two orthodox traditions relates to whether there is a personal liability that is also inherited with that corruption. Since both of these perspectives recognize a universal problem, they agree on the most basic aspect of divine and human agency—humans need divine grace. Those following the Greek patristic tradition (namely, the Eastern Orthodox but also some [Ana]baptist Protestant traditions) affirm a view of synergism as a free human choice in response to God's grace and prompting. With an Augustinian approach (represented by traditional Catholic and Protestant teaching), monergism is the focus: the human will and desires are corrupted by sin's depravity, and so the Holy Spirit must lead believers to faith (see figure 9.7).

FIGURE 9.7 SYNERGISM AND MONERGISM IN RELATION TO MODELS OF SIN

	Pelagius	Greek Patristic	Augustine
Sin (vis-à-vis Adam)	No Corruption Not Liable	Corruption Not Liable	Corruption Liable
	Heterodox Option: *Priority of Human Faith over Grace*	Orthodox options: *Priority of Divine Grace + Response of Human Faith*	
Salvation (agency)		Synergism	Monergism

Note shift along spectrum:

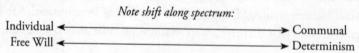

Individual ← → Communal
Free Will ← → Determinism

It is best to view these views of sin as existing on a spectrum because certain subtraditions and theologians will emphasize divine or human agency more. For example, in the Catholic tradition they affirm what might be considered a softer monergistic, or possibly synergistic, tradition. That is, they affirm **total depravity** in original sin, but the Holy Spirit erases the problem of original sin for infants and adults who are baptized. That baptismal experience of the Spirit moves them more into a focus on cooperating with God's grace and thus a synergist model after entering the faith. Some Catholics, such as the **Jansenists**, tend toward the monergist end of the spectrum and focus much more strongly on divine determinism (as with predestination). Many Protestants also affirm a version of monergism, but some are considered softer and others harder depending on how they balance divine and human agency/willing. Also, many are more monergistic regarding initial conversion but regard the Christian life in synergistic terms because believers cooperate with grace after conversion since the encounter with grace restores ability. In particular, several in Wesleyan traditions have commented to us that they are comfortable with the language of synergism, if properly qualified.

PROTESTANTS, THE *SOLAS*, AND MONERGISM

The term *sola* is a Latin term for "alone" (or "only"), and it is common to point to five *solas* of Protestantism: *sola Scriptura, sola gratia, sola fide, solus Christus,* and *soli Deo gloria.* They all point in some way to monergism, that is, divine agency over against human agency. Scripture alone is divine revelation, not human tradition. Salvation is "by grace alone" and "by faith alone," so not by human effort. This is achieved by Christ alone, not mediated by the church. All this is to God's glory alone rather than to any human agent.

MONERGISM, SYNERGISM, AND THE AGE OF ACCOUNTABILITY

Many Protestants are uncomfortable being described as "synergists," which shows their monergist inclinations. Those in baptistic traditions, however, often follow a perspective on sin described as the "age of accountability." In many ways this is like the Greek patristic view of sin: one is corrupted because of Adam's sin but not accountable for Adam's sin; rather, people are only accountable for their own sins once they reach an (undefined) age of accountability. Greek theologians have had almost no direct influence on baptistic theological traditions, but they share a common perspective. This model fits closest to a synergist position, but with the Protestant inclination toward monergism (at least for conversion), those Protestants holding this position will sometimes affiliate explicitly with a synergist or monergist position.

Protestant Perspectives: Calvinism and Arminianism

The varieties of synergism and monergism are numerous, and it goes well beyond the scope of this book to explore all of them. To get a window on the topic, we will focus on the main debate within the Protestant confession. The two perspectives are Calvinism and **Arminianism**, and several issues distinguish them, but a simple question serves to introduce the debate: Do we experience salvation because God chooses us or because we choose him? These two positions answer this differently, and both of these traditions appeal directly to Scripture to ground their positions. Our goal here is to explain the systems rather than advocate for one. Each has much depth that we will not explore, so if you do not quite understand something in one view, compare it to the other view, and it might help clarify things.

Calvinism

Calvinism (and the broader **Reformed** tradition) is primarily represented by writings like John Calvin's *Institutes of the Christian Religion* and later the *Westminster Confession of Faith*. A helpful five-point theological acronym describes Reformed theology: TULIP. This five-point structure was developed in response to Arminian questions.

> **T – Total Depravity.** Humans are infected with the corruption and accountability of Adam's sin. Sin is like a black hole, and we cannot escape its gravity on our own.[12]
>
> **U – Unconditional Election.** God chooses ("elects") and predestines those who will be saved. This election is not based ("conditioned") on God's foreknowledge of human faith in God. That is, God chooses based upon his mysterious and inscrutable will, not on human willing.
>
> **L – Limited Atonement.** The atoning effects of Christ's death are applicable ("limited") only to those who are elect.
>
> **I – Irresistible Grace.** When humans encounter the truth and beauty of God's grace, they do not resist because they always bend to God's will.
>
> **P – Perseverance of the Saints.** God's (irresistible) grace is equally relevant to past, present, and future salvation. Those that are truly members of the faith will persevere, experiencing the reality of present sanctification and the sure hope of future glorification. (This is not merely "once-saved-always-saved" but an expectation of seeing God's transformative work in each believer.)

PAUL'S CALVINISM IN ROMANS 9?

Romans 9 stands as the lynchpin for many who hold a Calvinist perspective. The passage focuses on God's agency with its discussion of God's making some for his glory and others for his wrath, evidence that God loves some and hates others. We, however, contend that many misread Paul's focus in this text. It might still support Calvinism, but its focus is not so much on God choosing individuals as God choosing people groups, namely Jews and gentiles. These groups are the focus of the whole of Romans 9–11. In Romans 9, Paul undercuts Jewish presumption of election based on their genealogy; likewise, in Romans 11, Paul undercuts gentile presumption of election based on their current position. In the middle (Rom 10), he shows that Jews and gentiles equally find salvation in Christ alone.

---

12. See the fuller explanation in ch. 8.

How does Paul undercut Jewish presumption in Romans 9? His argument is that God's promises to Abraham do not come through the firstborn (Ishmael or Esau) but surprisingly through the second born (Isaac and Jacob). With his wider concern about Jews and gentile Christians, he is pointing out that the Jews are the firstborn, whereas the gentiles are the second born. So when Paul gives the quote that "God loves [second-born] Jacob and hates [firstborn] Esau" (9:13), he's rhetorically arguing that God has rejected the (firstborn) Jews in favor of the (second-born) gentiles. Obviously, God does not hate the Jews, because Paul reverses the argument in Romans 11, even stating that "all Israel will be saved" (11:26). So Paul is not talking about God choosing/electing individuals but people groups as part of his salvation-historical grace for both Jews and gentiles.

Arminianism

Arminianism arose from within the Reformed tradition and derives its name from Jacob Arminius (1560–1609). This tradition has affinities with aspects of the synergist position, and so many will be happily affiliated with that term as long as we recognize the priority of grace. Other Arminians would be uncomfortable with the language of synergism and would describe Arminianism as a soft monergism—humans are active agents but they cannot contribute in any way to their salvation. In this way, they want to highlight the assurance of salvation, which the Catholic and Orthodox traditions do not emphasize. Parallel to the Reformed TULIP, this five-point structure captures Arminian distinctives:

Total Depravity but Prevenient Grace. While humans are fully affected by sin (as described above in the Calvinism discussion), God's grace comes to humans and enables them to make a free decision. This grace is "prevenient" because it "comes before" any human willing.

Conditional Election. God chooses ("elects") those who will be saved, but his choice is based ("conditioned") on his foreknowledge of human faith in God. That is, the focus is upon human freedom to choose based on prevenient grace.

Unlimited Atonement. Since Christ died for the whole world, the benefits of Christ's death are not applicable ("limited") only to the elect but available to all.

Resistible Grace. The encounter with God's grace provides humans with an authentic choice, and they can (and sadly do) often reject this grace in their freedom provided by God.

Assurance of Salvation. The gratuitous provision of grace encountered in Christ and sealed in the Holy Spirit gives those of authentic faith an assurance that God will keep his promise of salvation. For some Arminians, this authentic assurance does not preclude the possibility of human apostasy, the rejection of God, and the loss of salvation.

So Which One Is Right?

These two positions—Calvinism and Arminianism—give a picture of the tensions of monergism and synergism that the wider Christian tradition has lived with since its earliest days. Ultimately, both of these orthodox positions affirm an asymmetry of divine agency and human freedom. This is asymmetrical because God stands above and outside human powers. By accepting this tension they rejected the two heterodox extremes: (1) forms of Pelagianism in which humans had so much freedom they did not need grace and (2) **hyperdeterminism** in which God so ordains everything that he ultimately causes people to sin and thus becomes the origin of evil himself. Neither of these reflect the biblical witness.

The affirmation of both divine and human agency is a mystery, not unlike the other central affirmations of the Christian faith—God as three persons with one nature, Christ as two natures in one person, the Bible as fully God's Word and fully human words. These are not tensions to be solved; the dialectical or paradoxical affirmation is actually at the center of orthodox claims. Rather than an either/or approach, both/and theologies tend to better capture the orthodox spirit. In this vein, one should likely avoid models which are solely based on a zero-sum game: 100 percent God vs. 0 percent human, or 51 percent God vs. 49 percent human, where the balance has to be 100 percent. The danger of this thinking is that it basically sees God as just another being in the created order. However, if God stands outside of the system, then his ways of acting are beyond our conceptualities. In that way, salvation is both 100 percent God's agency in the grace of election and 100 percent human agency in faith as a response to his grace.[13]

Conclusion

Humans sinfully rejected God-oriented flourishing, but through the death and resurrection of Jesus, we have the hope of restoration. Though the Christ-event is the focus in discussions about salvation, the story of salvation forms the narrative arc for the whole Bible. As the climax of God's covenant promises, he provided atonement through Christ, and in response to the grace of God, humans are called to respond in faith to experience a transformative encounter with God through the Holy Spirit, which brings a holistic renewal.

CONTEMPORARY THEOLOGICAL RELEVANCE

Now that we have explored ideas related to the doctrine of salvation, we will explore a limited number of key areas where this doctrine relates to wider issues in the contemporary world and church.

---

13. See our discussion of **noncompetitive agency** in ch. 5.

Salvation and Christian Identity

Salvation and Other Christian Traditions

- **(Functional) Deism** downplays the role of human sinfulness and almost always resorts to a form of Pelagianism. Christ is often simply a moral example, not the avenue for the Spirit's transformation; therefore, humans must have the freedom and ability to follow an ethical path without divine help. Benjamin Franklin's maxim captures this heterodox position fully: "God helps those who help themselves." With this version of "moralistic therapeutic deism," the temptation to just try harder in your own power is common in the contemporary Western church.

- **Mormonism** emphasizes the role of Jesus in bringing salvation to the world through his death and resurrection, and the primary atonement model they highlight is similar to penal substitution (divine restitution). Mormonism places a high value on the individual freedom of each human as a child of Heavenly Father. Holding a view of sin akin to the Greek patristic model, they also follow a view of divine and human agency that would fit closely with the synergism model described above. Mormonism uses the language of deification for ultimate salvation, but what sets their view apart from Orthodox and Catholic theology is that Mormons hold to the idea that Heavenly Father and his children have the same nature, whereas traditional Christians make a firm distinction between God's uncreated nature and humanity's created nature.

- **Jehovah's Witnesses** emphasize the atoning effect of Jesus's death and resurrection, and they also highlight a penal substitution (divine restitution) model of the atonement. Though Jehovah's Witnesses appear to have a view of sin more similar to the Augustinian model, they do not think it limits human ability to respond to the grace found in Christ. So their position about divine and human agency is similar to the synergism model, where faith is exemplified through obedience.

Salvation and Other Religions

- **Judaism.** The Hebrew Bible (the *Tanakh*) focuses on salvation for the community rather than the individual, particularly since the *Tanakh* makes almost no mention of life after death. There are expectations for eschatological restoration of the community through the Messiah, as promised in the prophets, but most do not hold that the Messiah has come yet. At the same time, when the language of "salvation" is used, it has mostly come to be associated with discussions of the afterlife, for those who are faithfull, based on God's forgiveness.

- **Islam.** In Islam, "salvation" is an afterlife-focused idea rather than something that has already occurred. Allah is just and merciful, and those who come to him seeking mercy in faith receive forgiveness. This faith is embodied in submission to Allah's commands. While this seems to place a large focus on human agency in obedience, a strong undercurrent in Islamic theology is Allah's sovereign freedom to direct and determine human affairs, and thus we see a similar tension between monergism and synergism like in Christianity.

In both of the Eastern religions, the fundamental problem facing humanity is *samsara*, the cycle of *karma*, and reincarnation. Salvation is framed as escape rather than restoration.

- **Hinduism.** *Moksha* is the Hindu term that describes liberation (or salvation) from the odious cycle of *samsara*. The liberation from *samsara* that *moksha* speaks of depends on which subtradition one follows, but often it is considered the absence of suffering and oneness with Brahman. Since people are born into different roles, their pursuit of a particular path (*dharma*) is individualized. In popular Hinduism, devotion to the gods allows for union. This devotion, often through *murti darshan*—viewing the statues of the gods as worship—builds good *karma* to aid in better reincarnations and ultimately *moksha*. As release, *moksha* dissolves all individuation.

- **Buddhism.** The liberation from *samsara* in Buddhism is called *nirvana*, and it is identified with "emptiness" (*sunyata*). The goal is achieved through release from desire. A key point of distinction from Hinduism is the teaching of "no self" (*anatman*), so Buddhism usually does not focus on personal identity in liberation. Various meditation practices are the primary method to eliminate attachment. While there are mediator figures, gods (*devas*) or teachers (*bodhisattvas*) who help, they do not interrupt the *karma* cycle for an individual. Rather, they show humans how to live and act in a way that will lead them to accumulate good *karma* and ultimately achieve enlightenment. That said, accumulated karmic merit can be transferred to others, most often deceased relatives, to aid in their next rebirth.

As we will see in the next section, there are several debates within Christianity regarding salvation.

The Extent of Salvation (in the Present)

Believers share in the life of God through Christ and the Spirit, and they have the hope of transformation in their lives. A tension, however, exists in the eschatological experience of that new life—it is already here but not yet fully here until Christ returns. This raises the question of which benefits can be experienced now and which only later. Some affirm that Christ's benefits *now* are mostly interior—peace in one's soul, loving interpersonal relationships, and more—but others point to Christ's physical healing ministry, social transformation for the poor, and wider material blessings in this age. Some within this latter perspective think no believer should be sick or poor now if they have enough faith. This is often labeled the "prosperity gospel," and extreme versions often have trouble finding a place for the call to suffer with Christ. How do we promote a gospel of holistic restoration—spiritual and material—so that we are neither Gnostic (just spiritual) nor drawn into simplistic views of prosperity (too material)?[14]

The extent of sanctification in this life is another key aspect of this debate: How holy can we expect someone to become before Christ returns? Those in Wesleyan traditions, such as the holiness movement, have traditionally held to a view of "entire sanctification," or "Christian perfection." John Wesley wrote about this, but he did not claim to have experienced it himself. It was not that a person that reached this point would never sin but that they would never consciously sin. Those in Reformed and Lutheran traditions still expected holy living but tended to have a less sanguine view of one's ability to achieve that in this life. Luther's *simul iustus et peccator* ("at the same time justified and a sinner") was not only a rejection of Catholic views of justification but also a description of the continual struggle with sin that believers will maintain in this life. To what extent should we expect to experience holiness? Have we set the bar of sanctification too high or too low?

Can You Lose Salvation?

For synergistic traditions that hold to cooperation between God and humans, apostasy, turning away from or the outright rejection of faith, is always a possibility. If humans are free to choose to enter, they can choose to leave. For monergistic traditions, the question of whether you can lose your salvation is much more challenging. A few might say the apostate lost their salvation (the soft monergists), but most monergists say it cannot be lost: it was not their choice in the first place, so those who turn away were never really saved. How should we make biblical sense of these issues?

Rejecting one's faith (apostasy) is not the same as struggling with sin, which is something all Christians deal with. Our friend, pastor, and professor, Mike Skinner, once shared a helpful analogy. The struggle with sin is like losing your keys in the couch cushion, but apostasy is like throwing your keys in a pond—totally and intentionally rejecting the faith. Lost keys are no good, but it is the radical and intentional rejection of God that leads to questions of lost salvation. Can salvation be lost? What happens if you lose faith?

Exclusivism, Inclusivism, and Pluralism

In our postmodern setting with increased global awareness and interreligious interaction, questions easily arise about those who practice other faiths and those who have never heard of Christ. There are traditionally three perspectives offered to these questions—exclusivism, inclusivism, and pluralism. *Exclusivism* holds that only those who have explicit faith in the grace offered through Jesus's death and resurrection will be saved.

---

14. We explore these issues more fully in ch. 11.

Generally, this means that those who have not heard of Jesus cannot be saved, but many are unsure how God will treat them. A minority of exclusivists hold to the possibility of postmortem faith (i.e., faith after death but before judgment). *Inclusivism* holds that Christ's death and resurrection are necessary for atonement but that humans must only have faith in accordance with the revelation they received. Thus those who have only received **general revelation** and believe in God will be covered by Christ's grace even though they do not believe in Christ explicitly. *Pluralism* holds that all religions are equal and adequate means for humans to express faith in God. The last option is often considered heterodox (why would there be so much concern with idolatry if all religions were equal?), so the issues of exclusivism and inclusivism generate the most discussion. What happens to those who have never heard of Jesus? Is there salvation for them? Can some be saved if they sincerely follow another religion?

Further Issues

- **Models of the Atonement.** Does one of the models of the atonement garner more biblical emphasis? What do we learn about God through the various models? Is one right, or do we need them all?
- **Divine and Human Agency.** In light of the discussions about monergism and synergism, which of these models best captures the relationship between divine and human action?
- **Justification.** The language of righteousness and justification is important to Jesus's and Paul's teaching. Considering Matthew 5–7, Romans 3–8, and Galatians 2–3, should we consider the biblical language as "legal" reasoning focused on God's gift of a "not guilty" status (as the Protestants), or is it "moral" reasoning focused on God's making believers more holy (as the Catholics)? Is there a reward for righteousness?
- **Baptism for Forgiveness of Sins.** The Nicene Creed's statement about baptism and forgiveness is developed directly from Acts 2:38—"Be baptized . . . for the forgiveness of your sins." How does baptism relate to receiving the grace of forgiveness? Consider also John 3:5; Romans 6:4; 10:9–10; 1 Peter 3:21.

PRACTICING THE FAITH

The call of salvation is the call to respond to the grace God offers through Christ and the Spirit. In other words, Christians are granted the gift of embodying the kingdom of God.

Faith and Baptism

The gift of divine grace calls for the response of human faith. As Jesus calls, "The kingdom of God has come near. Repent and believe the good news!" (Mark 1:15). The act of faith is a confession that we need God's help to fix our brokenness and a dependence on God's help found in the grace supplied through Christ and by the Spirit. Baptism is the sign or marker of faith and the experience of grace in the New Testament. The original practice of immersion in water captured the participation in Christ's death and resurrection but also the reception of the Holy Spirit (as with Christ's baptism). Faith does not end after this initial step. The first step merely begins your walk in faithfulness to the God of holy love. Have you trusted in Christ and been baptized?

Grace with No Strings?

In our contemporary conception, the perfect gift has no strings attached. The problem is that almost nobody in the ancient world of the Old and New Testaments thought that way. When biblical writers speak of God's gratuitous and free grace, we only partially understand it if we use modern categories. We rightly understand that people do not deserve this gift from God (Rom 5:6–8), but we think of it as a no-strings-attached gift. Every gift of grace in the Bible came with a responsibility to respond to God's gift in faithfulness and obedience. Take **spiritual gifts**, for example. They are not for us, with no strings attached. They are gifts that come with a responsibility to love and serve others. God's grace is free, but it is not just "fire insurance" that lets us do whatever we want. We have a responsibility to walk in that grace and grow in sanctification.

Relying on Grace

Grace features prominently among all three Christian confessions. As we speak about the need to walk in faith beyond conversion, there is therefore an equal need to continue to rely on God's grace. Even though many formally reject the crass Pelagianism of salvation by human effort, we are constantly tempted in our post-Enlightenment world to live and work according to a functional Pelagianism: we get in by grace but continue by works. This has been called a "moralistic therapeutic deism." It's a just-try-harder mentality: God helps those who help themselves. That's wrong! We always need grace.

The new covenant hope (Jer 31; Ezek 36–37; Rom 8; 2 Cor 3) shows us how relying on grace works. Grace brings restoration to what was broken, as life to what was dead. As we participate in the life of God, this "life" is not just flying to heaven someday; rather, it is the ability to walk in wholeness now, through Christ (Rom 6:4) and the Spirit (Gal 5:25). The transformation of our lives (i.e., sanctification) is a new covenant hope based on the Spirit's transformation of our heart. It is described as a fruit *of the Holy Spirit* (Gal 5:22–23), not moral effort. This is why salvation applied is a Holy Spirit doctrine. Just as we need the Spirit to get in, we need the help of the Spirit to continue in the life of faith (Gal 5:1–6). See chapter 7 on the Spirit to consider how to walk in the fullness of grace from the Spirit.

Further Issues

- **Discipleship and the Cross.** While we would not want to narrow the atonement to moral example alone, it is surely a model of the life of the disciple to follow Christ in his suffering (see ch. 6).
- **Evangelism.** Since God offers the true path to **human flourishing** through faith in Christ, it is not just an obligation but a privilege to share the call with others to experience a life-giving relationship with God.
- **Salvation and the Church.** Christians debate about the role of the church in salvation. We will argue in the next chapter that the church is necessary for our progress in sanctification and discipleship and therefore present salvation.
- **Trust in God's Providence.** I (RLH) recently heard a testimony of a doctor who converted after my friend had witnessed to him for thirty-five years. He told my friend, "Looking back on it, I didn't have a chance. Everywhere I moved God put someone there to show me Jesus loved me." God was at work in his life even when he was unaware.

In this discussion of salvation, we have explored one of the hinge doctrines of Christian theology, as different perspectives on this topic greatly influence the diversity of church traditions today. In this doctrine, we see the priority of divine grace in the work of Christ on the cross which calls for a response of human faith. Salvation is not just something that happens in the past, but it also includes the process of God's gracious transforming work in the present and the reality of resurrection life in the future.

CLOSING PRAYER

O God, who for our redemption gave your only-begotten Son to the death of the cross, and by his glorious resurrection delivered us from the power of our enemy: Grant us so to die daily to sin, that we may evermore live with him in the joy of his resurrection; through Jesus Christ your Son our Lord, who lives and reigns with you and the Holy Spirit, one God, now and for ever. Amen.[15]

---

15. Prayer for Easter Day, in "Collects: Contemporary," *The (Online) Book of Common Prayer*, Episcopal Church (New York: Church Hymnal Corporation, 2007), https://www.bcponline.org/Collects/seasonsc.html.

CHAPTER 10

The Church

The People of God

INTRODUCTION

In our postmodern culture, several themes have become so prevalent that they have almost become trite: money, sex, and power make you happy; violence solves problems; and communal boundaries destroy authentic individuality. For this last theme, think of recent movies where the protagonist breaks free from the oppressive roles society puts them in. This distrust of community makes discussing the **church** (Greek: *ecclesia*) one of the most difficult topics in this book. Our default cultural position deifies "authenticity" through individual autonomy. We see the fruit of this in the institutional and denominational disaffection among Christians. There was already a dizzying array of views about the role and purpose of the church before this shift, but now the challenge to understand the church is even greater. Before we explore these diverse interpretations, we will look first at a pastor and theologian who grasped the church's unique identity: Dietrich Bonhoeffer.

DIETRICH BONHOEFFER: SOLIDARITY WITH THE HOLY CHURCH

Dietrich Bonhoeffer (1906–45) was born into a well-to-do German family. His father was a distinguished professor at the University of Berlin, and his mother descended from noted pastors. Famous artists and academics were regular guests for dinner. Although the children were baptized, the family rarely went to church. His mother provided instruction that was as much moral and patriotic as it was Christian. Therefore, some family members were surprised and disappointed when Dietrich announced at the age of sixteen that he would study theology.

Big Idea:

Through Christ and the Spirit, God makes a people for himself from among all the peoples of the world for them to experience and embody his presence.

Key Terms:

- Ecclesiology
- Election
- High Church, Low Church
- Ordinance, Sacrament

Key Passages:

Gen 11:1–9; 12:1–3;
Ezek 16;
Exod 19:3–6;
Acts 2:42–48;
1 Cor 11–14 (esp.,
    11:23–34; 12:12–20);
Gal 3:26–29;
Eph 1:18–21; 2:11–22

217

In Germany, pastors trained for ministry in state universities since the Lutheran Church was the state church. These universities had dismissed much of traditional Christianity and embraced a general theological skepticism, as we noted in Karl Barth's story (see ch. 2). More challenging was the rising German patriotism intertwined with Christianity: Germans developed a national version of Christianity, which saw German identity as a superior pathway to Christ, replacing and dismissing Judaism. Christianity had been co-opted into propaganda for German nationalism with the result that serving as a minister was reduced to being a civil servant.

Along with others like Karl Barth, Bonhoeffer broke with this framework. He called the church to embody its holy calling rather than just serving as a mouthpiece for political parties. Against the skepticism of the universities, he read the Bible as God's real **proclamation**. He also took interest in the great traditions of Christianity with the ecumenical goal of seeing the churches across the world cooperate and unite.

The Communion of Saints

Bonhoeffer began to write his dissertation when he was only nineteen years old and submitted it eighteen months later. He titled it *Sanctorum Communio*, the Communion of the Saints. This work presented the church from the perspectives of both theology and sociology, and he noted several interconnected themes: the Son's **incarnation**, the human person, the church, and the world. Bonhoeffer rejected modern efforts to define personhood as an isolated and insulated self. He claimed that a person is defined by their place before God and with other persons. Relationships are crucial to personhood.

Expanded Experiences of Community

Though most of his time was spent lecturing in Germany, Bonhoeffer also spent some time at Union Theological Seminary in the United States. He initially saw Americans as theologically weak but came to appreciate the attention given to social justice. He attended Abyssinian Baptist Church in New York for six months with his friend Frank Fisher. They shared in the sense of community and were moved by the music that had been forged in the suffering of the black church. While traveling with Frank, who was African American, Bonhoeffer was refused service and witnessed racism first hand. Bonhoeffer had known tensions between nations (Germans hated the French), but this experience stimulated his thinking on race.

Bonhoeffer also learned to read Jesus's Sermon on the Mount (Matt 5–7) as simple instructions for following Jesus. Many had viewed the sermon as instruction for the spiritual elite or as an impossible standard intended to prove we are moral failures (as with Bonhoeffer's own Lutheranism). However, through a friendship with Frenchman Jean Lasserre, Bonhoeffer saw this as Jesus's direct address to the church. Embracing the pacifism presented in the sermon, he especially saw the danger of a nationalist church.

Underground Seminary: Finkenwalde

Meanwhile, the Nazis had co-opted the German Lutheran Church, with many pastors believing it was their patriotic duty to support the "German Christians."[1] Influenced by Karl Barth, an opposition movement called the Confessing Churches arose, whose basic theology is represented in the Barmen Declaration (1934). In 1935, Bonhoeffer was asked to direct an illegal and underground seminary for this movement after he returned to Germany, and he worked for two and a half years on the project before the Nazi powers shut it down. The students may have anticipated an accelerated course of study to correct the error of Nazism. In addition to challenging Nazism head on, Bonhoeffer created a communal form of life rooted in classic Christian practices. They slept in a common room, observed structured mealtimes, took private devotions, meditated on Scripture, confessed their sins, practiced silence, and such. The focus was not merely learning theological information but also experiencing a transformation as Christ followers. His most famous book, *Discipleship*, based on his reading of the Sermon on the Mount, emerged from lectures given here.[2] His experience of seeing and learning Christ in the life of community prompted *Life Together*, his most popular book during his lifetime.

The Hit on Hitler

After several run-ins with the Nazis, Bonhoeffer was in danger of being drafted into the army, a significant problem for a pacifist. Remarkably, he joined the Abwehr, the German military intelligence. His connection with church leaders around the world gave him opportunity to spy for the Germans, but Bonhoeffer operated as a double agent and informed others about the Nazis. He also used connections to rescue Jews. Later, suspicions prompted Nazi officials to restrict Bonhoeffer to his parent's home in Berlin. Ironically, the Abwehr was the center of anti-Hitler forces in Germany, and his parent's home was ground zero for an unsuccessful plot to assassinate Hitler.

There are different assessments of Bonhoeffer's participation in this plot. Often, he is seen as a hero who bravely shares in the evil of violence in order to avoid greater evil. Others see him as a champion of a new kind of Christianity, who set aside traditional piety to make a difference in the world—a hero who got his hands dirty. We (the authors) share an alternative perspective. Bonhoeffer's plotting represents a loss of vision, not a new vision. He had it right at his seminary when Scripture was his basis for engaging culture rather than culture (and pragmatism) being his basis for engaging Scripture. The job of the church is not to outsmart the world or kill the enemy; our job is to obey the commands of Christ. This concrete sharing in Christ's life is the testimony the world desperately needs.

Bonhoeffer was imprisoned for his part in the assassination attempt and was hanged

---

1. For their nationalist theology, see "The Guiding Principles of the Faith Movement of the German Christians." A. C. Cochrane, *The Church's Confession under Hitler* (Pittsburgh: Pickwick, 1976), 222–23.

2. Many will know it through the partially abridged printing in the United States known as *The Cost of Discipleship*.

with Hitler's personal approval weeks before Hitler took his own life at the end of the war. Bonhoeffer's life and death were a witness to Christ among those under the rule of death. Hitler's life testifies to a mad tyrant's quest to rule; Bonhoeffer testifies to the rule of Christ. Hitler sought a perfect community and tore the human family to pieces. Bonhoeffer sought an obedient community, uniting the human family in radical service to others. As we will see below, Bonhoeffer was calling for the church to be holy (set apart) and catholic, not co-opted by political interests and nationalism.[3] This challenge is still relevant for the church today, and it draws from the biblical foundations we now address.

The People of God in the Bible

In biblical theology we see God's ordering of three interconnected aspects of life—individuals, communities, and places (see figure 10.1). As we have explored the biblical narrative, communal aspects have consistently played a part. Though they have been more in the background, they will now be in the foreground.

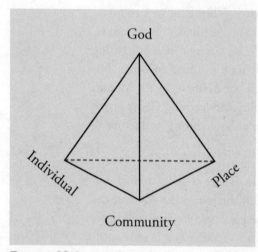

Figure 10.1
Holistic Biblical Framework

God's Chosen People: Abraham and His Family

To speak of the people of God, we need to return to the broader narrative of Scripture that places the formation, disfigurement, and re-formation of the people in the context of God's greater salvation-historical purposes. We noted earlier in our chapter on salvation, God responds to the problem of sin (Gen 3) and human divisions at the tower of Babel (Gen 11) by calling Abraham (then named Abram) to bless restored individuals among a restored community in a restored place:

> The Lord had said to Abram, "Go from your country, your people and your father's household to the land that I will show you.
>
> "I will make you into a great nation,
> and I will bless you;
> I will make your name great,
> and you will be a blessing.
> I will bless those who bless you,

---

3. Note the lower case "c" in catholic. He is pointing to the "universal" nature of the church.

and whoever curses you I will curse;
and all peoples on earth
will be blessed through you." (Gen 12:1–3)

This holistic vision of **human flourishing** can be seen in figure 10.2, which shows that salvation is a restoration of God's initial, holistic, creational intent. While the Abrahamic **covenant** contains all three aspects, we'll focus here on Abraham's family, the covenant community. The theological term central to this discussion of this community is *election*. God is electing or choosing Abraham and his family to be his people—the chosen people.

FIGURE 10.2: CREATION RESTORED

	Individual	Community	Place
Creation (Genesis 1–2)	Blessing / (Flourishing) Life	Family / Community	Land / Garden
Fall (through sin) (Genesis 3–11)	Cursing / Death	Broken Family / Conflict	Toil / Exile
Restoration / Renewed Creation	Blessing / (Flourishing) Life	One Family → Whole World	Promised Land → Whole World

The rest of the Bible is the story of Abraham's family, the Jews, serving as the people of God. In figure 10.3, the hour glass shape shows how God chose Abraham's family out of the whole world. God chose them not because they were special or that he loved them more.[4] Rather, he chose them for a special role—to be a conduit of his blessing to the rest of the world (see Gen 12:3; cf. Exod 19:3–6). The hope is for the whole world, not just the Jews. Gentiles could experience this blessing, primarily by joining the Jewish covenant community. In figure 10.3 this movement toward Israel is shown with the arrows pointing to the one people.

We spoke in the early chapters of God's holy love. In love he delivered his people from Egypt, and he desires covenant holiness for his

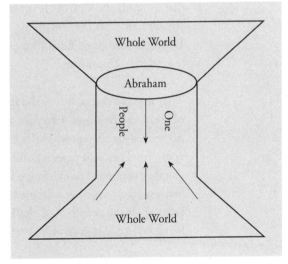

FIGURE 10.3
Old Testament Election

people because unholiness leads to separation and brokenness. Ultimately the people were unfaithful to the covenant, and the covenant curses come into effect, resulting in exile and control by pagan nations. Through the prophets God promises to restore his people.

---

4. See the sidebar discussion of Rom 9 in ch. 9.

This includes a return to the land, but the deeper promise is God's repeated claim: "I will be their God, and they will be my people" (e.g., Ezek 37:27; cf. Jer 31:1). The Jews only experienced a partial restoration in the Old Testament, and they maintained an eschatological hope that God would fulfill his promises. This is what we see more fully in the New Testament—through Christ and the Spirit.

One Family, Many Nations: Election in Christ and through the Spirit

With the coming of Jesus as the **Messiah**, his kingdom ministry ultimately shifts the focus for the people of God to the nations, particularly through the widening experiences of the Spirit. Jesus's kingdom ministry promotes a love ethic within the Jewish community that made greater space for those who were socially and ethically marginalized. His community of disciples joins in that mission. In fulfillment of Jesus's kingdom ministry (Acts 1:3–8), the Spirit is poured out on these disciples at Pentecost (Acts 2). As they speak in tongues, they reverse the confusion that scattered those at the tower of Babel (Gen 11:1–9). After the miraculous event, Peter's sermon climaxes with this call: "Repent and be baptized, every one of you, in the name of Jesus Christ for the forgiveness of your sins. And you will receive the gift of the Holy Spirit" (Acts 2:38). This common commitment to Jesus instantiated through the experience of the Holy Spirit (in baptism) is what grounds the church. It is for this reason that the Pentecost experience in Acts 2 is often described as the "birthday" of the church.

Luke, the author of Acts, immediately records other distinguishing practices of the early Christian community:

> They devoted themselves to the apostles' teaching and to fellowship, to the breaking of bread and to prayer. Everyone was filled with awe at the many wonders and signs performed by the apostles. All the believers were together and had everything in common. They sold property and possessions to give to anyone who had need. Every day they continued to meet together in the temple courts. They broke bread in their homes and ate together with glad and sincere hearts, praising God and enjoying the favor of all the people. And the Lord added to their number daily those who were being saved. (Acts 2:42–47)

Practices like these persist in later Christian traditions: worship, sermons, Bible study, the Lord's Supper, common meals, home groups, sharing financial support, and God's continued miraculous work.

Key movements of the Spirit in Acts reveal that sharing in the life of the Spirit defines the church rather than Jewish ethnicity. We must remember that all these early church members were Jewish. Jesus was the Jewish Messiah, who had come to restore the **kingdom of God**, and those who responded were Jews coming to Pentecost, this large national festival. The big shift comes a few chapters later when others receive the Spirit:

first the half-Jewish Samaritans (Acts 8:4–25) and then the non-Jewish gentiles (Acts 10). The Spirit and the gospel break down the ethnic boundaries.

Texts like Acts 15, Galatians 2–4, and Romans 4 show that believers from any nation can participate in the blessing of Abraham without becoming Jewish. Rather than being Abraham's children by birth, these were adopted children, not just of Abraham but also of God. Thus anyone who has faith in Christ and has experienced the Spirit belongs to Abraham's family. This passage from Galatians captures the point well:

> So in Christ Jesus you are all children of God through faith, for all of you who were baptized into Christ have clothed yourselves with Christ. There is neither Jew nor Gentile, neither slave nor free, nor is there male and female, for you are all one in Christ Jesus. If you belong to Christ, then you are Abraham's seed, and heirs according to the promise. (Gal 3:26–29)

See figure 10.4 and note the direction of the arrows have changed from figure 10.3. God's intention is still the same: the blessing of Abraham is passed to the whole world, and the church is now the climax of that multinational blessing.

The breaking down of ethnic boundaries is fundamental for understanding the notion of reconciliation within Christian communities (cf. Eph 2:11–22). Since God's Spirit explicitly worked outside human divisions, the church has an inherent theological pressure pushing it to reject any and all forms of ethnic and social hierarchies (1 Cor 11:17–22; Gal 2:11–16). Of course, the church often fails at this foundational ideal, living according to the world's model of racism, nationalism, and economic hierarchicalism rather than the narrative of Christ and the Spirit. But the fundamental vision of the church is unity and reconciliation.

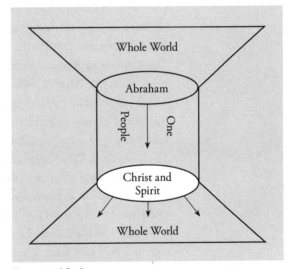

FIGURE 10.4
Old Testament Election

Ecclesial Metaphors

In this discussion of the church, we have focused on one primary metaphor: the church as family—the family of Abraham as the family of God. This is prominent in the New Testament, but there are several other metaphors worth exploring as well. One particular thing to note about these metaphors is that they shape the way one views church structure, leadership, and practice in different ways.

1. **The Church as Family.** We explored one aspect of the family metaphor above, but we should note another familial metaphor: the church is the bride of Christ (2 Cor 11:2; Eph 5:22–33; Rev 19:6–10; 21:2, 9–10). In addition, some traditions have seen their leaders as authorities in the family and therefore call them "father" or "mother" (e.g., Roman Catholic and Eastern Orthodox). In **low church** traditions (see below), leaders (though perhaps older and wiser) are ultimately seen as equals and are often called "brother" or "sister."

2. **The Church as Flock.** Jesus, in the pattern of Psalm 23, describes himself as the Good Shepherd who leads his flock through sacrificial love (John 10:1–21; 21:15–19; 1 Pet 5:1–11). "Pastors" also help lead and care for the flock. Another common title related to this metaphor is an "overseer," often appearing as the term "bishop" (Greek: *episcopos*). In **high church** traditions, bishops hold a staff called a "crosier," which was modeled after a shepherd's crook.

3. **The Church as Temple.** While the Jewish people did not limit God's presence to the temple, it was the primary place to experience him. The believing community is now pictured as the temple, with holiness a key emphasis (Eph 2:19–22; 1 Pet 2:4–10). The temple metaphor is prominent in Roman Catholic and Eastern Orthodox traditions since their leaders are called "priests," whereas Protestants highlight the priesthood of all believers (though ministers are called "priests" in a few Protestant traditions).

4. **The Church as Body.** The life and direction of the community flows from its head, who is Christ (1 Cor 12:12–31; Eph 1:18–23; 4:7–16; 5:23; Col 1:24). There is a diversity of parts of the body, but they are united together in a common purpose. The goal of leaders is to guide the body to maturity, though no particular leadership title seems to draw from this metaphor.

5. **The Church as City/Kingdom.** Christians are not fundamentally identified with local or national identities according to human political maps; rather, their ultimate citizenship is heavenly, with Christ as the King in the kingdom of God (Phil 3:17–21; 1 Pet 2:11–17). As a result, believers are called to live as foreigners, strangers, and aliens (or exiles, 1 Pet 1:1) among human kingdoms. As citizens of this heavenly city-state, Christians follow the wisdom and leadership of "elders" (Greek: *presbyteros*), who help guide and administer. Additionally, "apostles" (or emissaries) help communicate God's kingdom realities to those outside the community of faith.

The New Testament uses a variety of terms for leaders, often interchangeably, so parsing distinctions between roles is often difficult. Instructions for appointing elders and overseers are very similar (1 Tim 3:1–7; Tit 1:5–9). And both overseer and elder are used interchangeably with pastor/shepherd (e.g., Acts 20:17, 28; Tit 1:5, 7), but early in the history of the church, the bishop/overseer came to have authority over the elders/priests.[5] In addition to these leaders, the church also has "deacons," who help in the ministry of the church (see Acts 6:1–7; 1 Tim 3:8–13). This term is derived from the Greek term *diakonos* meaning "servant."

The diversity of perspectives by the biblical writers provided much fodder for an even greater diversity of interpretation and approach to **ecclesiology** through history.

THE CHURCH IN HISTORICAL AND THEOLOGICAL DISCUSSION

The Church in History

The church is the tangible representative of Christ on earth and has been committed to embodying his rule in many places throughout history. This community of faith has been continually challenged to respond to new circumstances and events, so the scope of its history is staggering. Despite its failures, the church has set the stage for remarkable achievements and moral standards for the human family. Several events influence our understanding of the church.

Constantine and the Challenge of Social Christianity

The Roman Emperor Constantine converted to Christianity in AD 312 and consolidated the empire in 324. Though he was a benefactor for Christians, it was under a later emperor that the empire officially embraced Christianity. However, with Constantine the die was cast. Previously, being part of the church produced serious disadvantage or even danger, but in a matter of decades belonging to the church became a shrewd political move.

A contrast emerged. Before Constantine *the church was visible*. A person could see this gathering of believers following Christ in the face of persecution and suffering—visible to the naked eye as a present reality. After Constantine *the church became invisible*. Throngs of citizens came into the church with nominal conversions. For example, Augustine acknowledged his congregation was comprised of genuine believers mixed with the unconverted—invisible to the naked eye. The genuine church would be visible again at the end of time.

Before Constantine *the kingdom of God was invisible*. It took an act of faith to claim that this persecuted church served the true King of the world, who would one day bring his kingdom in undeniable victory (as pictured in the book of Revelation). After Constantine *the kingdom (or pseudo-kingdom) was visible*. Jesus's name is plastered over all kinds of empire stuff—buildings and armies and such. Some saw this as Christianity

---

5. And the "see" is the area of oversight (i.e., jurisdiction) of the overseer/bishop. E.g., the "Holy See" or the "See of Rome" is the area of oversight the Pope has over the Roman Catholic Church.

conquering the empire,[6] whereas others believed that the empire co-opted Christianity (so said many monks).

The church-state tensions introduced here, which reflect wider church-culture tensions, will plague Christianity throughout history. The use of papal armies or Protestant collusion with the Nazis are key examples of the clear problems of a church too embedded in its culture and too willing to sacrifice its holiness for a seat at the table of power. Secular authorities constantly push the church into a role subservient to the civic structure. Eventually, the church defines itself in terms of the civic group (like a chaplaincy service). Others, however, rightly see the church as pursuing its holy identity visibly distinct from civic structures and political aspirations toward power.

The Great Schism: Eastern and Western Christianity Divide

After the fall of Rome in AD 476, there was an increasing linguistic division between the Greek churches in the East and the Latin churches in the West. This was matched by periodic theological divisions leading to temporary excommunications, which would then be resolved. In 1054, visiting Roman Catholic delegates and Byzantine Orthodox officials exchanged mutual condemnations and excommunicated one another. The event revealed that the long distinct churches of the East and West had grown to be separate churches; this rupture is known as the Great Schism. Later attempts to facilitate rapprochement were unsuccessful, and ultimately the Western failure to render aid when Constantinople fell to invading Muslim armies in 1453 solidified the division. This break meant there were now two distinct branches of Christianity.

The Reformation: The Western Church Divides

Martin Luther, a Roman Catholic monk and scholar, initially protested pastoral malpractice within the church with no intent to sever the Western church. However, the theological, personal, and political divisions proved to be too great. Luther's (German) voice was joined by Ulrich Zwingli (Swiss) and John Calvin (French/Swiss). These "Magisterial Reformers" undertook reform in cooperation with civic officials, i.e., the magistrates. Emerging alongside these were "Radical Reformers" (Anabaptist, Free Church), who formed churches independent of civic authority and comprised of voluntary members only. The efforts by the Radical Reformers to re-create a visible body of believers were seen as socially dangerous and met brutal persecution from Catholics and other Protestants. These early Reformation movements sparked a wave of Protestant activity that has spawned thousands of denominations worldwide, as well as nearly innumerable independent churches. The break meant the church was now comprised of three confessions (families of profession): Eastern Orthodox, Roman Catholic, and Protestant.

---

6. Eusebius, for example, was happy with the emerging Christian empire and found the coming kingdom pictured in the book of Revelation unnecessary.

WARS OF RELIGION OR NATION BUILDING

Europe was torn apart for three decades (1618–48) as Catholic and Protestant forces battled for turf. As commonly told, nation-states emerged in order to provide a larger, religiously neutral nation where Protestants and Catholics could coexist. Zealous believers had to be restrained from enforcing their social policy and practices upon other citizens. Generic concepts of God came to serve as a public standard: a judge may be required to believe in "God" but must agree to never let his distinctive religious views interfere with his public duty. Recent voices claim that the wars were less about religion and more about the founding of the nation-state, where commerce could grow without interruption. Westerners now take it for granted that religion is a private matter, and the church is a place for "supplemental" activities. The public-private divide, now common in the West, appears strange to non-Westerners. Muslims, for example, do not readily privatize their religion.

Contemporary Movements

The history of the church is mostly the history of division, but one of the distinct shifts over the past century is a real interest in unity. Several factors have influenced the rise of ecumenical efforts, and historic steps have been taken to foster discussion and heal divisions. This was especially aided by Vatican II. A significant example is the "Joint Declaration on the Doctrine of Justification" (1999) in which the Roman Catholic Church and the Lutheran World Federation recognized continuing differences but also rescinded the mutual anathemas (or charges of heresy). Though other Protestant bodies have since joined in the "Joint Declaration," theological tensions persist among the various denominations. These ecumenical conversations are encouraging, but the general move toward churches that are independent from denominations means that organizational disunity is on the rise.

The Church in Theology and Practice

In the midst of all this diversity, is there a place for a unified approach to ecclesiology? Let's consider the Nicene Creed:

We believe in one, holy, catholic, and apostolic church.
    We acknowledge one baptism for the remission of sins.

With these words from the third article (about the Holy Spirit), the Nicene Creed declares the Spirit is at work in forming the church. We see here a dual focus on a common confession (the church is one, holy, catholic, and apostolic) and a common practice (baptism). Though there is a common confession and common practice, how traditions understand and interpret these varies.

High Church and Low Church Perspectives

In order to get a grasp on the different views and practices of the many traditions that exist today, we propose using the nontechnical and heuristic categories of *low church* and *high church*.[7] Importantly, these titles point to a wider spectrum, not just fixed categories, because there is a great deal of variation within the broader low and high church groupings. The Roman Catholic and Eastern Orthodox confessions fall directly in the high church group, whereas Protestants are split between high and low. The oldest Protestant traditions have high church roots (e.g., Lutheran and Anglican/Episcopal). The majority of Protestants, however, follow low church approaches (e.g., Baptists, nondenominational, and Pentecostal/charismatic). Presbyterian and Methodists are situated in a hybrid or mediating position within Protestantism. For example, both of these are still **sacramental** in their approach to theology (high church), but they often do not take communion weekly (low church).[8]

What is the basis of the distinction? High church traditions are marked by emphasis on the sacred, tradition, and formal **liturgy**. High church ministers almost always wear robes. Low church traditions are marked by less formality and reject the idea of holy objects. Low church ministers almost never wear robes, and these days are just as likely to be wearing jeans and a T-shirt.

Beyond these outward signs are more fundamental matters, particularly the role of hierarchies. One of the main shifts in the history of the Western church is a move from greater forms of hierarchy (as in the **patristic era**) to no hierarchy (as in **postmodernism**), at least in concept if not always in practice. With its origination in the patristic era, the high church model respects and even expects hierarchies as necessary to the functioning and identity of the church. The low church model, coming to the fore much later, thinks hierarchies are unnecessary (even harmful) to the functioning and identity of the church.

The distinction is reflected in how tradition is treated in the two versions. Tradition is a form of **epistemological** hierarchy because the views of some are given preference over others. In our discussion of the history of biblical interpretation (ch. 4), we saw a progression when it came to the role of tradition: Scripture with tradition in the ancient/medieval church, Scripture over tradition in the Reformation, and then the outright rejection of tradition in the Enlightenment. The move away from tradition is a move away from hierarchy. It is no surprise, then, that low church models flourish in postmodernity, where hierarchies and tradition are culturally out of vogue. While not the sole factor, these various approaches to hierarchies and tradition help explain the high and low church views.

---

7. These designations originally arose as descriptions of Anglican worship, but they are helpful in discussing issues more broadly.

8. There are other traditions, like the Church of Christ, that are hybrid in a different direction—low church in their worship style but take communion weekly like high church models.

FINDING BALANCE WITH TRADITION

As Protestants, we (the authors) agree that the Reformation rightly considered the Bible to be above tradition (i.e., over the church). However, we fundamentally reject the Enlightenment denunciation of tradition (i.e., denunciation of the church) in its push toward individual autonomy, which is even stronger in postmodernism. In other words, we can read the Bible for ourselves, but this does not mean we should read it by ourselves.

Exploring Low Church and High Church Distinctives

The following discussion explores the low and high church distinctions which are summarized in figure 10.5. This includes the four marks of the church (one, holy, catholic, and apostolic) as well as church practices and structure.

FIGURE 10.5 DIFFERENT VIEWS OF CHURCH

	Low Church	High Church
		Roman Catholic, Eastern Orthodox
	Protestant	
Apostolic	Apostolic Teaching (i.e., Bible)	Apostolic Teaching via Apostolic Succession of Bishops
One/Catholic	Common Faith (Invisible)	Common Faith via Structures and Practices (Visible)
Holy	Equal for all (Lay = Ministers) Credobaptism	Levels (Lay vs. Leaders) Paedobaptism
Practices	Ordinances (Memorial)	Memorial via Sacraments (Means of Grace)
Worship	Revivalist (Sing and Preach)	Word and Table
Church Government	Congregational	Episcopal

Apostolic. To be apostolic is to follow the core message and intentions of the original followers of Jesus. The message of Jesus has been passed on to the world through the apostles' writings, the New Testament.[9] For those in a low church tradition, being faithful to the apostolic teaching (the Bible) is the sole condition. Those in high church traditions also seek to be faithful to the apostolic teaching in the Bible, but they argue

---

9. Some contemporary denominations and groups use the term "apostle" for contemporary leaders as well as the earliest church leaders.

that the God-ordained leadership of apostolic succession (of bishops or elders) provides a legacy and tradition that rightly guards Scripture.

One. The biblical witness claims that since God is one, his people must also be one. Indeed, Christ himself prayed for the church "that they may be one as we [Jesus and the Father] are one" (John 17:20–23). This unity is found in a common faith, such as the ecumenical statement of faith like the Nicene Creed. Low church traditions emphasize the unity in a common faith, but do not demand there be structural or institutional (denominational) unity. High church traditions also base their view of unity on a common faith, but they see that faith carried out through particularly ordained structures and practices, such as the succession of bishops and **eucharistic communion**.

Catholic. This mark speaks of the church's universal identity. The term *catholic* comes from the Greek word *catholikos*, which means "universal" (or "of the whole").[10] In distinction to schismatic groups, who usually reside in one place, the true church is "of the whole." Catholicity does not claim there are Christians everywhere; it claims the church is comprised of and for people from everywhere rather than a select few.

Holy. When the creed claims the church is holy, it means that the church is God's distinct people and project. In one sense, all believers are already holy; the term *saints* (holy ones) is one way that the New Testament writers describe every believer. Yet members are still called to progress toward holiness: "Be holy, because I am holy" (1 Pet 1:16). Low church movements seek purity in all members of the community by only baptizing those who have made personal confession of faith, a practice called credobaptism, or believer's baptism. High church traditions practice infant baptism (paedobaptism), and confirmation provides opportunity to complete the process of baptism and embrace faith for themselves. These traditions often recognize a higher standard of holiness for persons devoted to holy callings, such as priests, monks, and nuns. These persons are signs (**sacraments**) of God's holy purpose for the church.

Practices. Key practices such as baptism and communion embody the truth of Christ and the Spirit, and they draw believers into God's narrative. Low church traditions view these practices as **ordinances** and emphasize their memorial function. That is, primarily the ordinances help believers remember what Christ already achieved. High church traditions view these practices as sacraments. They too have the purpose of helping believers remember, but these practices are a means of grace. That is, aspects of grace are missed if these are not practiced. Given their importance, we explore the interpretations further below.

---

10. Note the lower case "c" in catholic. When used with an upper case "C," the term usually refers to the Roman Catholic Church. In that sense, the RCC is the *Roman* (or Latin) expression of the universal church.

UNDERSTANDING SACRAMENTS

Sacraments can be difficult to understand. The Eastern church uses the language of divine "mysteries" to refer to their liturgical practices. The West used the term *sacrament*, which also referred to a soldier's oath of allegiance; it was a public sign of yet unseen loyalty. Since the time of Augustine, a sacrament has been a "visible sign of invisible grace." Other conceptions were also added. Sacraments must resemble the spiritual grace they picture; we are baptized or washed in water, not mustard. Eventually sacraments were seen not only picturing grace but as accomplishing grace: baptism cleans the stain of sin and the Eucharist spiritually nourishes. Grace took on a tangible quality as well, functioning like medicine or a spiritual vitamin. In time, Catholics restricted the number to seven sacraments, which were delivered through the ministry of the church. Important rites of passage are marked by sacraments: (1) birth (baptism), (2) adulthood (confirmation), (3) marriage or (4) celibacy (a gift supporting ordination), and (5) death (extreme unction). Receiving the (6) Eucharist and (7) reconciliation (confession/penance) are done throughout your life.

Sacramental theology builds upon the noncompetitive nature of the spiritual and physical. It is both/and rather than either/or. As a result, charismatic traditions are not often counted as sacramental, but their willingness to see the spiritual at work in the physical serves as a bridge between these traditions.

Worship. Weekly worship recognizes God's glory and orients believers to a proper approach to life. High church traditions follow a Word and Table model to the worship service: the first half is devoted to the Word through Bible readings from the **lectionary**, prayers, and a sermon/homily, and the second half is devoted to preparation and celebration of the Lord's Supper (Table). High church services are colloquially termed the "smells and bells" model because all five senses are usually engaged during this worship. Low church traditions generally follow a revivalist model of the worship service: the first half of the service is devoted to singing, and the second half is focused on the sermon and perhaps a time of response called an "altar call." A hybrid model is common in Presbyterian and some Methodist churches, which we call the reformed model.[11] It arose from the Word and Table model but removes the weekly celebration of communion and devotes that time to a longer sermon.

Church Government. The primary focus of church government (or polity) is proper organization and administration. High church traditions (with their emphasis on the

---

11. Methodist churches are at times difficult to categorize. They originally came from the Anglican church, a high church model, but followed this reformed worship style. However, they were one of the great frontier religions of the American west and many took on the revivalist model along with Baptists. So, you will find high and low church Methodists.

apostolic succession of bishops) follow an episcopal form of government. A bishop has authority over several congregations in a region and oversees the ministry of priests. Low church traditions have generally favored congregational government in which authority rests with the entire congregation, but they feature a huge variety of leadership models since many churches are independent and can set up the leadership structure however they prefer. As with worship, Presbyterians present an intermediate option, with groups of elders entrusted with authority.

Exploring the Key Practices of the Church

Baptism. Baptism had a prominent place in Jesus's experience and ministry. It is a central practice, with the command to baptize at the heart of the church's mission (Matt 28:19–20). The Greek term *baptizo* means to "immerse in water," and early baptisms were the sign of a person's total, immersive commitment to follow Jesus as the Christ. The ritual's submerging and raising up portrays the death and resurrection of Jesus; it embodies dying to sin and rising to new life with Christ (e.g. Rom 6:1–4). The New Testament also associates baptism with the reception of the Holy Spirit (e.g., Mark 1:8–11; John 1:32–34; Acts 1:4–5; 11:16). This connection to the Spirit is why many paedobaptist traditions also describe baptism as "christening." The children are anointed with the Spirit (and oil) like Christ, the "anointed one." Since conversion (or initial faith) only happens once, baptism has historically only been a once in a lifetime practice.

Our earliest records picture baptism as a rite of entry to the church, requiring an intense preparation of disciplined living and learning—up to three years. The early practice was displaced by infant baptism for theological and social reasons. Theologically, parallels were drawn between baptism and (infant) circumcision in Colossians 2:11–12, and baptism was viewed sacramentally. Socially, "the close identification between Church and society as a whole led to Baptism becoming less of a sacrament of conversion to Christ and his Church and more a rite of entry into the wider religious—political—cultural community of Christendom."[12] In time the Western church held that infant baptism removed the stain of Adam's sin and granted a new identity that the child would one day claim. Godparents provided proxy faith in place of the child. The early Reformers maintained the practice of infant baptism for similar theological and social reasons. The Anabaptists, however, broke with infant baptism because they saw it as a social and political strategy lacking in biblical evidence. The last century saw a great global movement of churches practicing believer's baptism.

Lord's Supper. On the night before Jesus's crucifixion, he celebrated a Passover meal with his disciples. Taking bread and wine, he told his disciples to eat and drink because "this is my body given for you" (Luke 22:19) and "this cup is the new covenant in my

---

12. Frederick Christian Bauerschmidt and James J. Buckley, *Catholic Theology: An Introduction* (Malden, MA: Wiley-Blackwell, 2016), 261.

blood, which is poured out for you" (22:20). Not only were they to eat and drink at that meal, but they were to continue to eat and drink "in remembrance" of him (22:19). After Jesus's death and resurrection, Christians quickly began the practice of weekly meetings, and sharing the bread and wine was central to their common allegiance to Jesus. Other terms are used for this meal: *communion, Eucharist, the Lord's Supper,* and *the Table.* The term *communion* emphasizes the unity Christians (the body of Christ) share as they partake of the bread as the body of Christ (1 Cor 10:16). The term *Eucharist* is the Greek word for "thanksgiving" (*eucharistia*) and is related to the Jewish blessing in prayer before breaking bread (1 Cor 11:23–24).

Historically, sacramental views of communion predominated in patristic and medieval theology. The focus was on the "mystery" of divine presence in the practice; believers truly encounter Christ. In the **Middle Ages**, Catholic theologians eventually described the nature of Christ's presence with the doctrine of *transubstantiation*: the outward appearances of the bread and wine remained the same while the substance (genuine character) was transformed into the body of Christ. Early Protestants (and the traditions that still follow them) retained a sacramental theology but were disturbed by the understanding that the Catholic Mass pictured Christ being resacrificed. With his view of *sacramental union* (sometimes described as *consubstantiation*), Luther insisted that Christ is literally present in, with, and under the bread but that the physical bread and wine continued to be bread and wine. With the phrase *spiritual presence*, John Calvin claimed that Christ's presence was mediated by the presence of the Holy Spirit since Christ's literal and resurrected body is in heaven. In distinction to these sacramental views, the Swiss reformer Ulrich Zwingli argued for a *memorial view*, that the bread and wine served worshipers as tangible reminders provoking allegiance and thanksgiving but did not mediate grace. The memorial view is easily the most predominant among Protestants, since it is the standard low church position.

Growing up in the Baptist church, I (RLH) thought it was funny the preacher spent so much energy explaining that Christ was not literally present at the Lord's supper table. Christ was present with us when we gathered but, for some reason, not at the table. I felt deprived of sacramental encounter. But I have come to see that Baptists are very sacramental in one sense. Paul's teaching about respecting the Lord's body does not concern the bread and wine (1 Cor 11:27–32). The body of Christ is the church gathered to worship. For Baptists, the church is the manifest body of Christ.

Conclusion

In the holistic framework provided in the Bible, we see that the restoration of the community, the people of God, is just as important as individual people being saved. The church is this restored community that has been called from all nations to experience the blessing promised to Abraham because they have faith in Christ and have experienced the Holy Spirit. Continuing from the central affirmation that the church is one, holy, catholic, and apostolic, a variety of traditions and interpretations show the unity and diversity of the people of God.

CONTEMPORARY THEOLOGICAL RELEVANCE

Now that we have explored the key ideas related to the doctrine of the church, our goal is to explore a limited number of key areas where this doctrine relates to wider issues in the contemporary world.

Ecclesiology and Christian Identity

Ecclesiology and Other Christian Traditions

- **(Functional) Deism** goes hand in hand with the heightening focus on individual autonomy and rejecting tradition. Since the church holds and passes on tradition, a rejection of tradition entails a minimization of the church. The church becomes more like a social club where people have a common affiliation, like we are all just Jesus's Facebook friends. The goal shifts toward personal experience rather than divine encounter, since God is not really active through Christ and the Spirit. This fits with the "spiritual but not religious" perspective where the church is unnecessary or even stifling of spiritual experience.

- **Mormonism** views orthodox Christianity as experiencing a great apostasy within the first century or so of its history. The true community was restored with the LDS church, arising in the 1800s. Drawing from a variety of ecclesial metaphors, the church is primarily seen as a family of the children of Heavenly Father, but viewing the church as a temple is also very prominent. Men, for example, receive the priesthood of Aaron and Melchizedek to perform the ordinances of salvation. Participation in temple ceremonies is important, and following Paul's statement in 1 Corinthians 15:29, Mormons are known for performing the baptism ordinance for the dead. Local congregations, or "wards," are overseen by a volunteer bishop (rather than paid clergy), and there are levels of organization under the leadership of the first presidency and other leaders, who are also regarded as prophets, seers, and revelators.

- **Jehovah's Witnesses** reserve the term *church* for the people of God, not the buildings: their buildings are called "kingdom halls." They have no paid clergy, as all baptized members are expected to share in the work of ministry. Congregations are led by volunteer leaders called elders, who are spiritually mature men. Like some in orthodox Christianity, particularly Anabaptists, the Jehovah's Witnesses are especially concerned with maintaining the holiness of the church and not offering worship to any but God. They, therefore, respect authorities but generally reject the nationalism related to saluting flags, fighting in the military, or participation in voting.

Ecclesiology and Other Religions

- **Judaism.** The Jewish community is united by both common ancestry and faith. Those who are descendants of the family of Abraham, whether they practice the Jewish faith or not, are still considered Jews. Those who practice the faith are therefore a subset of the wider ethnic community. There is a possibility for those who are not ethnically Jewish to convert and join the community, but Judaism is not a missionary religion. The **Torah** and its commands serve as the basis for communal practices and interaction. In the United States, there are three main branches of Judaism: Orthodox, Conservative, and Reformed.

- **Islam.** What unites the Muslim community is a common faith rather than a specific ethnic grouping. All Muslims are part of the *Ummah Islamiyyah*, the Islamic community. As Torah regulates life holistically for Jews, *Sharia* is the divine law that regulates the life of the Muslim community. The extent to which *Sharia* law is practiced varies widely even in Muslim majority countries, but central practices, such as the five pillars of Islam (faith, prayer, charity, fasting, and pilgrimage), are more universally applicable to the *Ummah*. The unity of the *Ummah* is displayed particularly during the annual pilgrimage (*Hajj*), where all are treated as equals, as evidenced by the common white clothing. There are two main branches of the Islamic community: Sunni and Shia, with Sunnis representing about 85 percent of the worldwide Muslim population.[13]

- **Hinduism.** While the Hindu religion is not limited to those originating from the Indian subcontinent, the majority of Hindus come from that ethnic heritage. To speak of the Hindu community is to consider the disputed role of the caste system among Indian society. Traditionally there have been four main castes (or *varnas*): *Brahmins* (priests), *Kshatriyas* (nobles, warriors), *Vaishyas* (merchants, farmers), and *Shudras* (laborers). In addition, a large number of people are outside (meaning below) the caste system, so they are outcastes, or *Dalits*. As one accumulated better *karma*, they would be reborn in higher castes. In the modern nation of India, the caste system has formally ended since discrimination against lower castes and *Dalits* is proscribed in the constitution; however, the centuries-old distinction still informally shapes social and political realities.

- **Buddhism.** With its consistent missionary impulse, the Buddhist religion is multiethnic, and it distinctly balances individual and communal roles. Though merit is primarily achieved through individual action, it can be transferred to others, particularly dead relatives. In the two main branches of Buddhism (Theravada and Mahayana), there are complementary roles between the laity and the monks (*bhikkhus*). In Theravada Buddhism, the *sangha* ("community") refers primarily to the monks whose devotion means they alone are close to *nirvana*. The laity

---

13. Stephen Prothero, *God Is Not One: The Eight Rival Religions That Run the World* (New York: HarperOne, 2010), 51.

accumulate merit by supporting the monks. In Mahayana Buddhism, the *sangha* includes monks and the laity, and the merit of *bodhisattvas* can assist others in their cycle of rebirths.

Covenant, New Covenant, and Dispensational Theology

One of the major differences between different church traditions relates to how the New and Old Testaments fit together. Should we emphasize continuity (the New is the climax of the Old), discontinuity (the New is a different order than the Old), or see it as a mixture of both? There are three general views that capture these approaches: *covenant* (continuity), *new covenant* (continuity with distinct progress), and *dispensationalism* (discontinuity). Most high church theologians hold some form of covenant theology, where the New Testament is seen as the natural progression of the Old Testament. Therefore, if an Old Testament teaching or practice is not explicitly rejected in the New Testament, then Christians should expect it to be practiced (in some similar fashion) as in the Old Testament. This continuity with the Old Testament explains why, for example, Roman Catholics call their leaders priests and baptize infants. Low church traditions have tended to follow new covenant or dispensational models. Since the focus is on the newness of Christianity or discontinuity, they often work from the inverse of the paradigm just stated: if Old Testament teaching or practice is not explicitly accepted or repeated in the New Testament, then Christians should not expect it to be practiced (in some similar fashion) as in the Old Testament. How should we balance the unity and diversity in the progressive revelation of the biblical narrative?

Social Justice and Social Holiness

In framing biblical theology, we have noted how the narrative includes three aspects—the individual, the community, and place. As the narrative progressed from creation to the fall, we saw how sin exactly reversed God's good creation and intention in each of these three areas. We talk of **total depravity** as sin affecting the whole person, but total depravity in this holistic framework understands that sin affected the whole creation. Viewing sin in this way means we should be on the lookout for comprehensive salvation, reversing the comprehensive nature of sin. Indeed, the scope of salvation or restoration envisioned by the narrative in the Old and the New Testaments includes all three aspects—individual, community, and place. Often the focus of **soteriology** can be only centered on individual restoration, but the call of ecclesiology is to honor the communal as equally important in God's restoration work. God cares not only about justifying individuals or individual holiness but also about social justice and social holiness.[14] That is why the Bible says you cannot hate your brother or sister and then say you love God (1 John 2:9–11; 3:11–18; 4:19–21). Have we limited God's work just

---

14. See Timothy Keller, *Generous Justice: How God's Grace Makes Us Just* (New York: Dutton, 2010).

to heart transformation rather than community formation and restoration? How can we biblically pursue social justice and social holiness? How should the church protect those who are marginalized in our society?

Religion and Politics

Many people put their hope and identity in politics rather than in the church. In the book *To Change the World*, James Davison Hunter provides a helpful summary and analysis of three contemporary approaches to religion and politics by Christians of different persuasions (see figure 10.6 below): the Christian Right (defensive against cultural change), Christian Left (seeks relevance to wider culture), and neo-Anabaptist (purity from corrupted culture).[15] Considering these in a triangular relation, the Christian Left and Right both use state power to achieve their goals, the Christian Right and Anabaptist both are committed to preserve historic values; and the Christian Left and Anabaptist both pursue social justice. Several questions arise: How should the Christian commitment to the church as holy shape its participation in a **secular** (at best) and unholy (at worst) political system? How should Christians balance their political participation in light of their kingdom identity? How can Christians engage politics and political parties without being co-opted and manipulated by them? Which model best represents a healthy and balanced approach to the intersection of religion and politics?

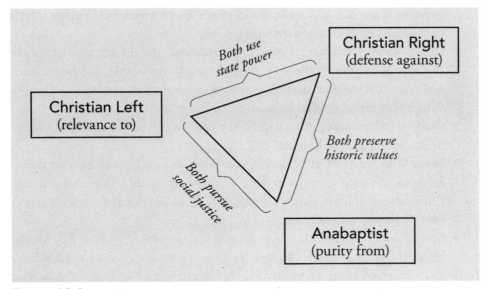

FIGURE 10.6
Christian Approaches to Politics and Culture

15. James Davison Hunter, *To Change the World: The Irony, Tragedy, and Possibility of Christianity in the Late Modern World* (Oxford: Oxford University, 2010), 213–19.

Women in Ministry

One of the major debates within the church today relates to the expected and acceptable role of women in various forms of ministry. Historically, women were limited in ministry roles, but in the last one hundred years some denominations have embraced women's full participation in ministry and even traditional denominations have generally opened more opportunities for women to speak and serve. One primary sticking point remains: key New Testament passages appear to limit women's roles, such as 1 Timothy 2:8–14 and 1 Corinthians 11:2–12. Importantly, in both passages Paul draws from Adam and Eve in Genesis 1–3 as the basis for his argument. With this appeal to these key characters, one would expect the application to be timeless and relevant to all people. But the rub comes when Paul comes to two opposite conclusions: in 1 Timothy he says women should be silent, and in 1 Corinthians he says they should preach (with their heads covered)! This raises the probability that one or both of the passages are speaking to a local or cultural issue rather than a timeless one. The debate is certainly not cut and dry. How do we appropriately balance biblical and cultural factors as we fully engage women in the life and ministry of the church? Could the new covenant be more inclusive?

Further Issues

- **Tradition and Authority.** The role of tradition and authority is hugely important to historical and contemporary approaches to the church. How do we balance the authority of the Bible and tradition? In what ways have we minimized the church because we have minimized tradition?
- **Ordinance vs. Sacrament.** Low church traditions view the key practices of the church as ordinances (focused on remembering Christ's work), and high church traditions view them as sacraments (practices for memory as a means of grace). Which view makes the best sense of the biblical material?
- **Leadership Structures.** Which is the best leadership structure: episcopal, presbyterian, congregational, or other?
- **Saints Who Pray.** In Catholic and Orthodox traditions, it is common for believers to ask departed saints to pray for them. Many would affirm that departed Christians see us from heaven. Do they pray for us like the communion of saints who are present with us?
- **Catholicism.** If the church is truly catholic (i.e., universal, not bound by human categories like political maps), how do we balance a bounded national identity and a catholic Christian identity? Should Christians have a national flag in their sanctuary or say the Pledge of Allegiance at church? Does the church's promotion of things like "Made in America" mean that we think God loves America more than others?
- **Baptismal Regeneration.** The Nicene Creed's statement about baptism is developed directly from Acts 2:38: "Be baptized . . . for the forgiveness of your sins."

How does baptism relate to the reception of the grace of forgiveness and new life? (See also John 3:5; Rom 6:4; 10:9–10; 1 Pet 3:21.)

PRACTICING THE FAITH

The practice of ecclesiology requires engagement with others. Through the community of the church, Christians have the opportunity to experience the fullness of the body of Christ and the reality of the Holy Spirit.

Spiritual but Not Religious? The Countercultural Church

It is very common today to hear someone say they are "spiritual but not religious." This often reflects a rejection of organized religion (i.e., the Christian church) in favor of personal spirituality. That is, the individual is better at figuring out God on their own without the cliché and inauthentic herd mentality of the church. While God's activity is surely not limited to the church, it would seem quite odd that the Bible would invest so much energy describing the purpose, intention, organization, and leadership of this community if it was ultimately irrelevant for encountering God. Consider a passage like Ephesians 1:18–23, which climaxes with the affirmation that the church is the body of Christ and "the fullness of him who fills everything in every way." So if you want to experience the fullness of God, Paul says you will find it in the church (see also Eph 4:11–16). How can we seek a spirituality apart from the people upon whom God poured out his Spirit? It is no easy thing to be committed to a group of broken people, but it is the best thing to serve and be served by others. How committed are you to becoming Spirit-ual through a church and particularly through a small group within it (whether Sunday school or home group)?

Spiritual Gifts: Gift and Task

The Spirit places believers in a church and grants each one special gifts. These gifts are an empowerment and calling to engage in special tasks needed to strengthen the community or enable its mission. The lists of gifts vary (Rom 12:3–8; 1 Cor 12:4–11, 27–31; 1 Pet 4:10–11), so we see them as representative of the various ways the Spirit empowers believers to serve. While these gifts seem like they are for us, they are intended to be employed for the sake of others! They are both a gift (for yourself) and a task (to serve others). You receive the service of others and offer your own gifting to others. It is beautiful to see at work. Remember the following:

- The task may correspond to natural abilities, but it may not.
- Find your gifts by exploring various areas of service.
- Listen to others who sense God at work in you.
- You must be committed to a community of faith to experience this mutual exchange.

Meals and Feasting

Spiritual gifts and serving others sound challenging to many, but one of the most effective ways to invest in your community is just to eat with one another. Meals have an uncommonly significant place in the Bible. They show the most fundamental level of acceptance and a commitment of shared time. This dedication to others, particularly to those who have been socially and ethically marginalized, is directly evident in the life of Jesus. He was committed to spending time with people over meals. Whether you are hosting in your house, grabbing coffee, or sharing a meal together at a restaurant, these are all great ways to invest in the community. However, the challenge Jesus sets before us is not just to invest in those like us or in those that have something to give us. Whom can you invite into your world or whose world can you step into by sharing a meal with them?

Meeting God at Church

One of the metaphors for the church is the temple, the place where God is most present and accessible. Thus, God is most present not in personal Bible reading, in prayer, or on a mountain, but in the midst of community with other (broken) people.

Almost every Christian group speaks of encountering God's presence in the experience of Christ's body. Acclaimed writer J. R. R. Tolkien, as a devout Catholic, spoke of being in Christ's presence every week at the Eucharist. Our students encounter his presence in an extended time of singing. Charismatic Christians witness God working in the power of prophecy or healing through the Spirit. A revivalist Baptist hears God speak and the Spirit's stirring during a fiery sermon. Others are overtaken by God in the quiet routine of high church liturgy. How might you experience God in your local community of Christ's body?

Social Justice

The life of a Christian is communal and demands that we give up our rights for the sake of others. This presented itself in the early Christian community through radical generosity toward those in need. Jesus and the New Testament writers spoke against structures and practices in the community that gave preferential treatment to the wealthy and those of high social status (e.g., Luke 6:17–36; Jas 2:1–13). This follows the same pattern of the Old Testament protections for those that were marginalized (e.g., Exod 22:21–23; Lev 25:39–43; Deut 15:7–11). The church is called to pursue social justice and social holiness. How can you intervene in the lives of others?

Why Is Church so Hard?

It is easy to be skeptical about the church because of people's bad behavior and the daily grind of living with people up close. Paul speaks of treasure in earthen vessels, clay jars: the treasure of the gospel is at work in broken people (2 Cor 4:7). The church is where the theory of faith meets hard facts. It takes faith to believe that God would gather broken people, transform them as a foretaste to a complete future healing, and let them announce an alternative vision and kingdom to the power-hungry world. It has been said that the church is a hospital for sinners, not a country club for saints. Is the hospital an appropriate metaphor for the church? How should the church balance its goal of holiness and grace for those who are broken? What values and practices are necessary for a community to pursue both?

Further Issues

- **Everybody Gets to Play.** The Spirit is gifting people across the whole body. Do the leaders of your ministries represent ethnic and economic diversity? Are we giving preference to the rich by allowing only the well-off to serve in lay leadership roles on boards and committees? Are those who are young, professional, good-looking, well-off, thin, extroverted, or male given preference in leadership or other opportunities? How might the Spirit be working in people we might have missed?

- **Being a Blessing.** At the heart of biblical election is the calling to bless others. Whom can you bless today?

- **Urban Isolation.** We have never been in a more connected world through technology, yet relationships are becoming more shallow and less authentic. The church, even with its brokenness, offers a community of substance and true connection.

- **Otherworldly Worship.** Some complain that worship is abandoning the real world to enter an untrue or alternative world. But if the claims concerning Christ are true, worshipers are abandoning a false distorted view of the world and entering into the true reality that honors Christ as Lord. People in tune with the world of worship make a difference in the gone-wrong world.

- **The Power of "One."** For the church to experience "oneness," the people of God must embody the virtues of grace, forgiveness, kindness, and so on (cf. Eph 4). How might you live out unity in the body rather than just waiting for it to happen?

- **Holy Rollers.**[16] The church serves as a distinct community where people can pursue lives of wholeness, living according to the fullness God intended. This is its calling to be holy.

- **Catholic Hospitality.** A church committed to its catholic nature is one that is committed to breaking ethnic barriers, transcending national boundaries. How might you embrace those of different national or ethnic backgrounds?

- **Apostolic Foundation.** An apostolic church is one that is committed to the faith of the apostles given to us in the Bible. Will you commit yourself to God's Word, not just for your own benefit but for the benefit of the body of Christ?

---

16. For those not from the South, the term *holy rollers* was associated originally with a charismatic experience of being "slain in the Spirit" but is now generally applied to people committed to church life.

We celebrate the church as the center of God's restoration work in the world as he restores a new family, a new community for himself. The people of God have begun to experience this promised restoration, but they still participate in the brokenness of this world. Even in this already / not yet state, the community of faith participates in the reality that the Father has created through the Son and the Spirit.

CLOSING PRAYER

Heavenly Father, you have called us in the Body of your Son Jesus Christ to continue his work of reconciliation and reveal you to the world: forgive us the sins which tear us apart; give us the courage to overcome our fears and to seek that unity which is your gift and your will through Jesus Christ our Lord. Amen.[17]

---

17. "Collects and Suggested Canticles and Refrains," *Common Worship: Daily Prayer.* Church of England, www.churchofengland.org/prayer-and-worship/worship-texts-and-resources/common-worship/daily-prayer/collects-suggested-canticles-refrains#mm11d.

CHAPTER 11

Eschatology
New Creation and the End

INTRODUCTION

Eschatology is about "end" things (Greek: *eschaton*). At a popular level most associate eschatology with end times—apocalyptic events, the Antichrist, the mark of the beast—since these are in the book of Revelation. Some understand these events like a dystopian horror movie, which is more about destruction than salvation. As a result, thoughts about eschatology just generate fear and anxiety. I (BCB) recently met a Christian who was visibly shaken by her family's constant warnings about upcoming apocalyptic events. While the eschatological texts of the Bible do have warnings, this dear Christian's family had missed the central message about biblical eschatology: it is based in hope, not fear, because eschatology is ultimately about restoration, not destruction. That said, in setting our focus on the future, eschatology is not divorced from the present. God is active here and now, and we should therefore live differently if we have an eschatological vision on the world. The story we begin our chapter with is about person whose life modeled that vision—Mother Teresa.

MOTHER TERESA

It may seem odd to think of Mother Teresa (1910–97) in connection with eschatology. She did not write a major book on the topic or produce timeline charts counting down toward the end. Forgive the well-worn turn of phrase, but eschatology is not just about *final matters* but clarity about *what finally matters*. Mother Teresa acknowledged the Son's kingship, both present and coming, and lived profoundly in this age.

Big Idea:
God's ultimate resolution of evil in creation through Christ and the Spirit has already broken into the present, and these future realities shape our lives in the present.

Key Terms:
- Eschatology
- Kingdom of God
- Gnosticism
- Resurrection
- Cruciformity
- Intermediate State

Key Passages:
Isa 40–66;
Jer 31;
Ezek 36–48;
Dan;
Joel 2;
Rom 8;
1 Cor 15;
1 Thess 4–5;
2 Thess 2–3; Rev

Early Influences and Initial Ministry

Mother Teresa was born as Agnes Gonxha Bojaxhiu on August 26, 1910, in Macedonia. She was baptized one day later on August 27 and routinely celebrated this day as her birthday. Her family, of Albanian decent, was somewhat affluent until her father died in 1919. Her mother set an example of generosity despite their more modest circumstance, as the family table was open to any hungry person. They extended care to a needy elderly woman and an abandoned family of six children whose mother could not provide.

Father Jambrekovic, a Jesuit priest from Croatia, influenced young Agnes. He taught her the Spiritual Exercises of Ignatius. The experience called for complete devotion, a mind for missions, and joy. His enthusiasm for missionary stories no doubt marked Agnes, who had previously sensed a call to mission work at age twelve. At age eighteen, she left for Ireland to join the Sisters of Loreto, who did work in India.

In Ireland she learned English and became Sister Mary Teresa after Saint Thérèse of Lisieux (1873–97). What was remarkable about Saint Thérèse of Lisieux was she seemed unremarkable. Her holiness rested in recognition that routine things done with a great love possessed a sacredness; the love of Christ made the ordinary extraordinary. This insight proved crucial for Mother Teresa. Being small and knowing humble circumstance did not defeat her because every moment offered the opportunity to extend the love of Christ.

After only six weeks in Ireland in 1931, she sailed for India to pursue her calling of mission and ministry. Her first station of ministry was at a school in Darjeeling, and it gave her a graphic picture of poverty that almost overwhelmed her. Her next teaching post in Calcutta was more insulated from the worst hunger, but she seemed drawn out from the walls of the boarding school to teach and care for the very poor. She observed that the poor were moved when she would share their lowly circumstance. In the midst of this ministry she took her formal vows in 1937 and was called Mother Teresa (instead of "Sister"). Meager provision and tireless labor marked her service through the years, and doctors ordered her to rest each afternoon when her health began to falter.

Second Calling and Missionaries of Charity

Mother Teresa had a life-changing experience when she was traveling by train to a time of retreat and recovery in 1946. She described the experience as a "call within the call." The episode centered around a devotional pondering of the idea of thirst from the Gospel of John. In Teresa's divine encounter she noted that it was Jesus who was thirsting—he thirsted for the souls of the poor. Jesus challenged her to join him in a pilgrimage of sorts, a journey to reflect the love of God to the poor. The moment is captured in the title of her book *Come Be My Light*. Whenever she saw the desperate poor she would also think of Jesus's desperate thirst—a thirst to share his love and see others join in the cause. Encounters and further insights followed this "inspiration." The most persistent echo of the 1946 event came during communion when she heard Jesus ask, "Will you refuse me?"

Mother Teresa sensed that this special calling to the poor required her to leave the

Sisters of Loreto and form a new order. The path ahead was filled with bureaucratic and institutional roadblocks. She was aided by Father Celeste Van Exem, a Belgian Jesuit priest who had come to serve, although with serious reservation, as her spiritual director. Together they exhibited great faith through times of discernment, intercession, and persuasion. Eventually permission was given to begin the Missionaries of Charity. The work was multifaceted from the beginning, but the popular imagination was most captured by Teresa's care for the dying. The work and organization continued to thrive and the little humble saint who began it received the world's admiration. She was seized by the Lordship of Christ over herself and the entire creation. His Lordship is the great eschatological reality that anchored her life of selfless labor. God's restoration of the world is not just an apocalyptic event in the future, but the kingdom of God is evident even now in the body of Christ (the church) broken for the world. This is a different approach to eschatology than you might have expected, but it is the focus of the New Testament.

Facing Absence and Presence

After her passing, students were surprised to find her letters that bear witness to a spiritual anguish. Scholars of spiritual life call it the dark night of the soul; it is a season where the believer senses a withdrawal of God's presence. Almost every great saint is touched and taught by such a season. Mother Teresa's dark night persisted. Those studying her life with a view to recognizing her sainthood were profoundly touched by the inner suffering as well as the service. She lived an eschatological existence: she yielded to the Lord's presence in devotion and **sacrament**; she cried out for his presence; she enacted and proclaimed the kingdom over all creation (even the darkest places). Even though kingdom realities seemed unseen, she persevered and sacrificed because she trusted God and his eschatological future. It is this theology of kingdom and creation that undergirds the biblical and theological focus on eschatology.

ESCHATOLOGY IN THE BIBLE AND THEOLOGY

Eschatology and the Bible

The fundamental premise of eschatology is this: things are broken and God is coming to fix them. In other words, the whole scope of the Bible is eschatological because salvation did not just happen in an instant but is part of a longer process which will culminate in a final resolution in the future. In that way, eschatology is not just about final events, when the resolution takes place in the future, but is also about the present where God is already at work.

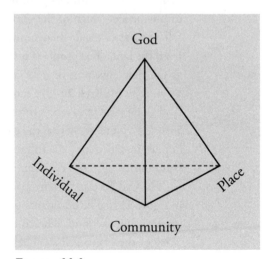

FIGURE 11.1
Holistic Biblical Framework

As with other aspects of biblical theology, we better understand the end if we start with the beginning. That is, we do not fully understand salvation or restoration without understanding God's original goal in creation and the corruption from evil. We have explored the holistic framework in the previous chapters with its three-part perspective on the individual, community, and place (see figure 11.1).

This holistic framework integrates with the creation–fall–new creation progression of biblical theology (see figure 11.2). With the chapters on salvation and the church, we focused more directly on the individual and community respectively, and with this final chapter on eschatology, we will now draw in the issues of place, but the other two topics will continue to be of importance.

FIGURE 11.2: CREATION RESTORED

	Individual	Community	Place
Creation	Blessing / (Flourishing) Life	Family / Community	Land / Garden
Fall (through sin)	Cursing / Death	Broken Family / Conflict	Toil / Exile
Restoration / Renewed Creation	Blessing / (Flourishing) Life	One Family → Whole World	Promised Land → Whole World

Biblically, this renewal of creation begins with the **covenant** promises in the Old Testament. These promises point back to God's creational intent for the world and point forward to a renewed experience of blessing, community, and land. Among these covenants, the Mosaic covenant (and particularly its expression in Deuteronomy) is the primary lens for understanding God's acts of blessing for obedience and cursing for disobedience. Much of the Old Testament rehearses how Israel follows the path of the fall, the way of disobedience, and experiences the covenant curses, which climax in exile from the land. The prophets offer hope after exile, for a restoration sometimes described as the new covenant or new creation. These passages promising restoration (e.g., Isa 40–66; Jer 31; Ezek 36–37) each point to a holistic restoration, a return to the promised land along with forgiveness through inward transformation and flourishing communities and cities. Note, then, that the eschatological vision is not for them to go to heaven. Their hope is to experience the fullness of life in the land God had promised them with their community. *The new covenant is quintessentially eschatological!*

The Old Testament narrative of creation, fall, and eschatological restoration is shown in figure 11.3. The covenants point to the holistic flourishing for individuals, the community, and the land. The climactic event inaugurating restoration is described as the "Day of the LORD." Since it restores justice, the Day of the Lord is both a blessing for the righteous, who are often oppressed by the wicked, and a day of reckoning for those who are unrighteous, since they will be punished. Some passages note apocalyptic battles that accompany the restoration of Israel (e.g., Ezek 38–39; Zech 14) and others speak of cosmic turmoil (e.g., Joel 2:28–32). While these difficult things (or "tribulations"), which we show through dashed lives, are to be expected, the focus of this eschatological vision is hope. The people are currently under the oppression of sin and evil nations, but God will bring renewal to the community through the advent of his messianic King and the Spirit so they can experience the covenant blessings as God intended at creation.

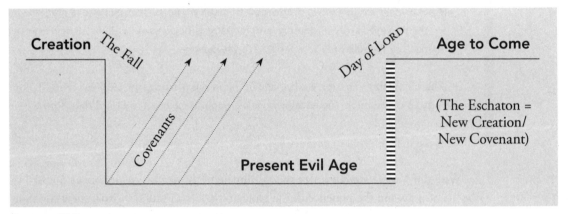

FIGURE 11.3
Old Testament Eschatology

UNVEILING APOCALYPTIC

Apocalyptic can refer to a mindset or outlook as well as a literary genre. The word *apocalypse* means a "disclosure" or "unveiling." Visions unveil God's victorious destiny of the world in order to encourage the faithful. Daniel and Revelation are chief examples of apocalyptic genre in the Bible. Early Christians also found hope in extra-canonical Jewish texts like 1 Enoch and Christian texts like the Shepherd of Hermas.

This genre emerges amid a disorienting, head-on collision between the experience of persecution and the Deuteronomic perspective. Deuteronomy teaches that blessing follows when people keep the covenant while cursing and calamity await those who are disobedient. However, the world is upside-down: the righteous often suffer, and the wicked prosper, especially when oppressive pagan nations are in control. Apocalyptic texts respond by pointing out how God's restoration is coming and is already at work:

- Apocalypses picture the end of time or some crucial omen of the end.
- Apocalypses are comprised of visions. An angelic guide often interpreted the vision for the persecuted.

- The visions are jam-packed with symbols, ornate organizational schemes, and numerology.
- Apocalypses are largely dualistic. They picture a cosmic-scale battle between good and evil, but never lose sight that God is the victorious King of the world.
- A battle among unseen spiritual forces in the spiritual realm is already underway and setting the stage for the battle to come.
- Apocalypses exhibit a two-stage view of history. The current evil age is marked by the powerful sway of demons and monstrous oppressive regimes. A new age marked by the rule of God will displace the evil age.

The big picture: Though we live and suffer in the corrupt age, God will bring the evil age to destruction and establish his new age. Believers are called therefore to remain faithful.

With the *New Testament* we see the fulfillment of the *new covenant* hopes expressed in the life of Jesus and the presence of the Holy Spirit.[1] As a result, Christian new covenant theology is fundamentally eschatological in orientation. As with every other area of theology, New Testament writers expand and adjust Old Testament concepts, while accepting the fundamental structure. See how New Testament eschatology in figure 11.4 is almost the same as figure 11.3. The only major difference is that the Day of the Lord gets split into two.

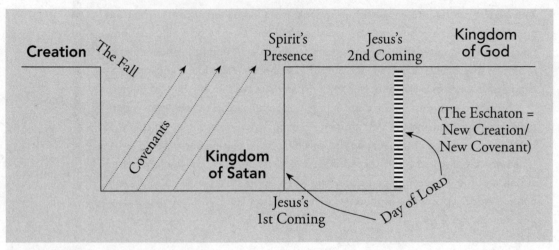

FIGURE 11.4
New Testament Eschatology

---

1. Remember, the term *covenant* comes from the Latin word for "testament," so to speak of the New Testament is really to speak of the new covenant.

The first part of God's "day" of resolution happened through the death and **resurrection** of Christ and through the presence of the Spirit falling on the church. That makes sense in Trinitarian theology since Christ and the Spirit are equally and fully the Lord of the Old Testament. The second part of the Day of the Lord is when Christ returns again.[2] We, of course, are living between Christ's first and second advent.

While there are several passages that mention that we are already living in the eschaton or the "last days" (e.g., Acts 2:17; Heb 1:1–2), the more common term that the New Testament writers use to describe this new age is the **kingdom of God**. Jesus's first sermon in Mark is this: "The time has come. . . . The kingdom of God has come near. Repent and believe the good news!" (Mark 1:15). As we explored in more depth in chapter 6, Jesus is the **Messiah/Christ**, the King who has brought in the kingdom of God. To be the Messiah is to be the "anointed one," and Jesus was anointed not with oil but with the presence of the Holy Spirit (Luke 4:14–21). Therefore, ministry by the power of the Holy Spirit means the kingdom of God is present (Matt 12:22–32; cf. Acts 1:1–8). And as Matthew 12 makes clear, the kingdom of God is overtaking the kingdom of Satan. When Christ returns again, he will end all evil and bring the kingdom of God in its fullness (e.g., 1 Cor 15:20–28).

We have only begun to scratch the surface of New Testament eschatology with this introduction, but it lays out the broad vision for how the various pieces fit together. Since each of these topics brings out further points for discussion, we will now describe the scope, timing, nature, and ethics of eschatology.

Scope: Universal and Personal

While there are the bits about an apocalyptic battle that bring in the whole earth, many just think in terms of personal (or individual) eschatology: Don't we (or at least most of us) just go up to heaven when everything is said and done? Charts like figures 11.3 and 11.4 can help reinforce this idea: If the world we live in is the bottom line, then surely "going up" means "going to heaven," right? Actually, that's wrong. The top line starts with creation (this physical world), so the restoration of creation (i.e., the kingdom of God) is also primarily about this physical world being restored. In other words, eschatology is first and foremost about universal restoration, fixing the whole world, so that when personal restoration occurs, we have a place to experience it.

Look over the last two chapters of the Bible—Revelation 21–22. Surely these last chapters are the most focused on the "last things" of any chapters in the Bible. If you read Revelation 21:1–4 and especially 22:1–5, you see imagery drawn from earlier biblical narrative. It hints at things we saw in Jesus's ministry and the Old Testament covenants, but the clear and unambiguous link with the biblical narrative is imagery from the garden of Eden (Gen 1–2). New creation is a fulfillment of creation (Eden), and we show this

---

2. The Greek term *parousia* means "appearing," and it is often used to refer to the second coming of Christ.

by placing both at the same level in figure 11.4. Of course, new creation will be better than the original, but it will still be a this-worldly place with plants and animals, trees, and rivers. The end (eschatology) is a culmination of the beginning (creation/**protology**).

The difference between the kingdom of Satan and the kingdom of God is not about down here (earth) and up there (heaven) but about death and corruption instead of life and blessing. In other words, the kingdom of God is ultimately about the whole world experiencing the life and flourishing that God intended for creation rather than the death and corruption of sin. God's restoration project in the Bible was calling out a single people to help bring restoration to all nations; the blessing of the church is the inclusion of whole world. Likewise, God called this single people to a single land, a promised and holy land, but his intention was to bring restoration to the whole earth, like he included every nation. Revelation 11:15 communicates this central hope: "The kingdom of this world has become the kingdom of our Lord and of his Messiah, and he will reign for ever and ever."

Heaven does have a role in God's restoration plan. Look at Revelation 21:1–4 again. As John the Seer describes the new creation, it is not that people go up to heaven; rather heaven comes down to earth. God's presence is unmediated with his people here on earth. While Revelation 21 is focused on the union of heaven and earth in the future, other New Testament texts clarify that this heaven-come-down-to-earth kingdom is not only for the future.[3] This kingdom is on display in Jesus's own **incarnation** and ministry. Think also of the Lord's Prayer: "Your kingdom come, your will be done, on earth as it is in heaven" (Matt 6:10). Anywhere that the Messiah is ruling and the Spirit is working, the kingdom of heaven has come down to earth.

In distinction to this vision for a world-focused flourishing, many Christians follow a functional **Gnosticism**, which buys into spiritual/physical **dualism**. This view holds that the physical world and this physical body is inherently corrupted, so salvation is cast in terms of leaving earth and going to heaven when you die. There is a place for heaven in the intermediate state, as we will see below, but focusing on escaping to heaven misses the big picture of the Bible. The Bible shows heaven transforming earth, the spiritual transforming the physical. For personal eschatology, Scripture emphasizes the hope of resurrection—the body being raised from the dead.

Think back to the chapter on humanity: God intentionally created humans with a soul and a body. Living eternally without a body would be a corruption of God's purpose for us. If the soul just floats to heaven at death (once it is separated from the body), why would you need a restored world that looks like the garden of Eden or bodies raised from the dead? But if you have this biblical emphasis on this world, then having a restored body to live in that restored creation makes much more sense. Given that the Bible approaches

---

3. For a great perspective on this, see the video "Heaven & Earth," from the Bible Project, https://thebibleproject.com/explore/heaven-earth/.

theology holistically, it is common to find passages like Romans 8:18–25 where universal and personal restoration are intertwined.

This means that we need to envision salvation as more than just being forgiven of our sins. One theologian noted that there are two primary narrative arcs in the biblical story: from creation to resurrection (new creation) and from the fall to the cross (see figure 11.5).[4] Protestants tell the story of the inner arc really well as the cross bringing forgiveness for the fall, but sometimes we miss the wider story of creation to new creation, which makes sense of the inner arc. We need both, we need Christ's death and his resurrection to experience a holistic salvation. Now that we have explained the scope of eschatology, we will now explore its nature.

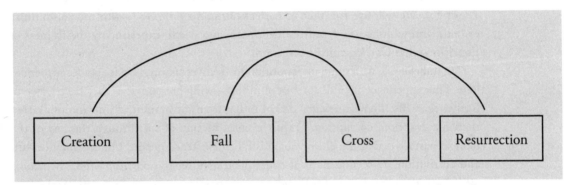

FIGURE 11.5
Two Arcs and the Christ Event

Nature: Blessing and Punishment

The focus of our discussion to this point has been on God's act of restoration, and that accords with the perspective of those who look forward to God's active involvement. The majority of eschatological texts in the Old and New Testaments arise from settings of social, economic, military, and religious oppression that arise from both human and demonic origins. Accordingly, when God shows up to restore justice, this is seen not only as a blessing for the righteous, who are oppressed, but also as a day of judgment for the unrighteous, who are oppressors. The Day of the Lord is both "great and dreadful" (Joel 2:31).

The process of restoring justice is almost never described as a smooth one. Take the exodus as an example. God's ultimate act is to bring about salvation for his people, but the Egyptian oppressors face the plagues and then even drown in the sea. While the nature of the punishment seems harsh and even protracted, the purpose is to give

---

4. Cf. Andrew Louth, "The Place of Theosis in Orthodox Theology," in *Partakers in the Divine Nature: The History and Development of Deification in the Christian Traditions*, ed. Michael J. Christensen and Jeffery A. Wittung (Grand Rapids: Baker Academic, 2007), 32–46.

opportunity for repentance. Will they learn from God's step-by-step revelation, repent, and experience his mercy, or will they continue in rebellion and therefore face the full brunt of the consequences? Unfortunately, most apocalyptic texts note that once people oppose God, they do not repent. Indeed, they are punished along with the demonic powers that spurred them along in their support of the kingdom of Satan.

Numerous texts set the eschatological destiny of the righteous and unrighteous in an either/or binary, leading to blessing or punishment (e.g., Matt 25:31–46; Rev 20:10–21:4). For God's people, his act of blessing includes two interrelated aspects: (1) the gift of grace to any who believe and (2) rewards for those who pursue a sanctified and faithful life (e.g., 1 Cor 3:10–17; 2 Cor 5:1–10). The primary personal hope of eschatological life is resurrection—our physical bodies raised from the dead to live immortally (Rom 8:10–11; 1 Cor 15). We will live together in perfect harmony with God, with the community of faith, and with nature, free from evil, pain, and death, experiencing the fullness of flourishing that God intended in creation.

For unbelievers, who stand in opposition to God's economy, he does not force them to join. They experience the full absence of his life-giving presence that they have rejected. Rather than life, they experience death; rather than integration, disintegration; rather than incorruption, corruption. From the introduction of sin through the rest of the biblical narrative, two dimensions of this fallen existence persist. On one hand, death and corruption are seen as natural consequences of separation from God, the source of life. On the other hand, death and cursing are seen as the active punishment of the Creator, who is due obedience. As we noted, God is patient and gives many opportunities for repentance, but those who do not must bear the unfortunate consequences of their rejection.

This ultimate judgment is described as "hell" (or *gehenna*) in the biblical text.[5] Some Bible versions also translate the Greek term *hades* as hell, but others like the NIV just leave it as Hades.[6] The primary association of hell is with fire (Mark 9:43; Jas 3:6; cf. Rev 20:14) and therefore torment. Several passages describe the experience as "eternal" (Matt 18:8; 25:41; Heb 6:2). As a result, hell has been understood traditionally as *eternal, conscious torment*. In distinction to this view, another perspective called *annihilationism* (or conditional immortality) has gained interest over the last century, though it has had supporters throughout history. Annihilationism holds that punishment is real but that those who are truly and finally separated from God, the source of life, cease to exist. They argue that the fire language is intentional because all things that burn eventually burn up and are gone. And the punishment is still "eternal" because it has eternal consequences.

---

5. Gehenna derives from the phrase "valley of Hinnom" which is on the edge of ancient Jerusalem and which served as a burning garbage dump.

6. We should note that in the Old Testament all humans appear to go to *sheol*, a common holding place for the dead. This seems quite generic to us, but the Old Testament gives little to no discussion about what the afterlife entailed.

OLD TESTAMENT PUNISHMENT VS. NEW TESTAMENT BLESSING?

One popular view is that God in the Old Testament is all about judgment, and when the New Testament comes around, God changes his personality and becomes a God of love. However, God's holy love is the basis of his salvation and punishment in both testaments. God's grace and love are central to the Old Testament (e.g., Exod 34:6–7), and the prospects for God's punishment in the New Testament are striking with its warning of hell. Blessing and cursing are in both; the only difference is the way that love and punishment play out. In the Old Testament, love and punishment are more communal and focused on the present age, whereas in the New Testament love and punishment include more individual elements and are focused on the present and future.

While the promise of blessing for God's people is great, the warning related to judgment is sobering. I (BCB) think it is one of the hardest aspects of Christian doctrine, but it is pervasive throughout the narrative of the Bible. Of course, not all hold the position that people should be punished or that God would punish them. *Universalism* is a heterodox idea that all (or virtually all) will ultimately be reconciled to God, and there are various forms of universalism on offer. On a popular level, many people think God grades on an inverted curve: the worst people in history like Hitler and Stalin will surely be judged, but as long as I'm better than the very worst, God will accept me. This fails because it is basically a form of **Pelagianism**, where salvation is based on human effort rather than on God's grace through Christ's death.[7] More theologically sophisticated versions of universalism focus on passages that say Christ "reconciles all things" to God (Col 1:19–20; cf. Eph 1:10). While these passages (and several others) could be read in this way, the narrative of Scripture is too consistent that punishment is a reality.

As we have discussed the nature of eschatology as salvific blessing or punishment, the focus has been on the afterlife. This is a key component, but another important aspect is that God's eschatological plan is working out even now. Accordingly, we now turn to discuss future and present aspects of eschatology.

Timing: Already and Not Yet

Since eschatology is about the last things, most only associate it with the future—the coming tribulations, the return of Christ, the new heavens and new earth. Theologically, these are items related to the Day of the Lord. Apart from the specific christological focus that shapes the nature of this salvation, this New Testament vision is not drastically different from the Old Testament expectation: when God shows up (i.e., on the Day of the Lord), everything gets set right. The main eschatological transformation of the Old Testament

---

7. See the discussions of Pelagianism in chs. 8 and 9.

structure in the New Testament is that the Day of the Lord is split into two (see figure 11.4 above). God shows up for the first time through Christ and the Spirit, and he will fully assert his presence again in Christ's second coming. This creates an unexpected dynamic: the kingdom of God is present now because of Christ and the Spirit, but we are waiting for its fullness because the kingdom of Satan is still vying for power. God's people already experience life now, but death is still pervasive. This tension created by the overlap of the ages is described as the "already / not yet" (or the "now / not fully") aspect of the kingdom of God.

Already. Right from the beginning of his ministry, Jesus announced that the kingdom is now here. The first two-thirds of each of the Gospels records his ministry, and the focus of Jesus's Spirit-empowered preaching, teaching, healing, and exorcisms centered on the kingdom of God. The important thing is that the New Testament shows that this type of ministry was not just limited to Jesus and his early disciples. Wherever the Pentecost presence of the Spirit showed up, there was life-change, whether spiritually, emotionally, mentally, physically, or communally. To be eschatological people, then, the church should pursue a fully Spirit-empowered kingdom existence.

Not Yet. While the kingdom is here, it has not come in its fullness. Christians still die; they still get sick; their relationships still struggle; they are still oppressed; they still struggle with sin. Evil continues to bear fruit in a variety of ways, thus showing the continuing influence of the kingdom of Satan and his demonic powers on earth. This is why biblical texts continue to point forward to Christ's second coming to consummate the kingdom of God. The events that surround the return of Christ, such as the millennium and the possibility of a rapture, are debated among Christians. We will discuss these issues further among the other debates in the contemporary relevance section.

ALREADY / NOT YET ESCHATOLOGY AND 2 CORINTHIANS 3–5

To see this already / not yet theology clearly at play, check out 2 Corinthians 3–5:

Chapter 3: Already. The present life of transformation by the Spirit
Chapter 4: Not Yet. The present life of suffering with Christ
Chapter 5: Future Glory. The future life of resurrection to come

Until the return of Christ, the church lives in the overlap of the ages where both life and death are at play. This calls for a critical embrace of the tension, not succumbing to an unattainable optimism nor falling into an insurmountable pessimism. We should avoid false optimism, which comes from expecting everything in the kingdom to be present now. Theologians call this an *overrealized (or fully realized) eschatology*. An example of this would be the idea that no Christian should ever be sick because God always heals those with enough faith. On the other hand, we should avoid the false pessimism of an *underrealized eschatology* where the real blessings of the kingdom will not be experienced until Christ returns. This often gets paired with forms of Gnosticism or deism since the current blessings can only be internal but all external blessings have to be future. It ignores Christ's explicit healing ministry, which brought both internal and external healing as a sign of the complete healing that would come later. Thus when any are sick, we should pray in faith and expectation that God will heal, but we also know that many will not be healed. (We do not need to create a false antithesis between God's provision of medical healing or healing through prayer.) Unless they are alive when Christ returns, all Christians will succumb to death, Satan's most powerful tool. This pain reminds us to look forward in hope to the fullness of the already / not yet kingdom.

Ethics: Hope, Holiness, and Cruciformity

If someone asked you what comes to mind when you hear the term *eschatology*, most people think in terms of apocalyptic events or the afterlife. These aspects, as we have explored, are definitely parts of biblical eschatology, but in light of the already / not yet tension and the possibility of blessing or punishment, the primary motivation of eschatological texts is present *ethics*. Having a strong eschatology does not so much mean that you know who the Antichrist is or can parse theories about the rapture; a strong eschatology is one that leads you to live a life of hope, holiness, and **cruciformity**.

The reason the biblical narrative constantly looks forward to God's resolution of the problem of evil is to give God's people *hope*. No matter how bad things are now, God is still in control, and he will restore all things. Many are overcome with fear rather than hope when studying eschatology due to the impending threat of apocalyptic events. There is certainly a strong warning to those who stand in opposition to God's plan, and God's people are not immune to suffering, but the key biblical message is that God brings resurrection life even when things look the darkest.

With the focus on the reality of better things to come, it transforms the life of believers. This future orientation is not just about an attitude of hope but also about action, a life of *holiness*. Consider Peter's admonition: "The day of the Lord will come like a thief. . . . Since everything will be destroyed in this way, what kind of people ought you to be? You ought to live holy and godly lives" (2 Pet 3:10–11). Other texts like 1 and 2 Thessalonians, 1 Peter, and Revelation make the same charge. Since believers are already participants in the kingdom of God, God's people need to pursue kingdom holiness now, not only to receive rewards but also to embody life and wholeness. Following the path of the demonic vices embodies destruction.

Due to the already / not yet tension, believers are called to walk in hope, but God calls them to walk in suffering as well. This path of suffering is often called *cruciformity* since believers are following Jesus in his crucifixion.[8] Perhaps the most prevalent

---

8. This is also called following a "theology of the cross" instead of a "theology of glory."

description of discipleship in the New Testament is this: since Jesus suffered, those who are his true followers will suffer with him and for him as well. Consider this selection of texts that encourages believers to die with Christ: Matthew 5:10–12; Mark 8:27–9:1; 9:30–37; 10:32–45; Romans 6:1–14; 8:17–30; 2 Corinthians 4:7–12; Galatians 2:19–21; Philippians 2:1–11; 3:7–11; Colossians 1:21–27; 3:1–11; 1 Thessalonians 2:13–16; 1 Peter 2:19–25; 4:12–19.

As these passages show, the hope of resurrection with Christ is just as central as dying with Christ. Indeed, this eschatological hope enables us to sacrifice something now. If the here and now is all we have, then we should fight to accumulate and maintain all we can.[9] But if there is more to life than here and now, then we have reason to follow Christ in this way of sacrifice. It is important to note that you will not have to look for suffering. Since we live amid a battle between kingdoms, death and its minions will seek us out, particularly as we walk in obedience to serve others and to follow the path of holiness in an unholy world. In this battle between kingdoms, Christ's death and resurrection was the decisive victory. In that same pattern, as believers follow Christ in that path of sacrifice, they too overcome the power of Satan's kingdom as they unleash the grace of God in everyday aspects of life, just as we saw with Mother Teresa.

HISTORICAL AND THEOLOGICAL DEVELOPMENTS

While the topic of eschatology was never the focus of a specific council and so does not garner the precision of some other doctrines, eschatological debates helped spur the Reformation and have captured the contemporary imagination. Beyond these perspectives an eschatological vision pervades much Christian literature. This was especially true when Christians stood on the margins of society before the time of Constantine. Even so, in the following sections we will treat the general direction of the church on eschatology and then note some key debates regarding the timing of end-times events.

Nicene Creed and General Developments

With the reality of martyrdom and social ostracism for several centuries, the early church was quite interested in apocalyptic material. Besides producing what turned out to be very popular apocalyptic texts like the Shepherd of Hermas, the church was also the main protector of early Jewish apocalyptic material, such as 1 Enoch, that is so informative for helping us understand New Testament Christianity.

In the Nicene Creed, we see a dual focus on eschatology with statements related to both Christ and the Spirit. Based on early Christian theology, it is also important to place these statements about the end in light of the Father's work in creation at the beginning:

---

9. In theological speak, this worldview is only dominated by the immanent because it has no sense of the transcendent.

We believe in one God, the Father, the Almighty, maker of heaven and earth, of all that is, seen and unseen.

We believe in one Lord, Jesus Christ, the only Son of God. . . . He will come again in glory to judge the living and the dead, and his kingdom will have no end.

We believe in the Holy Spirit, the Lord, the giver of life, . . . We look for the resurrection of the dead, and the life of the world to come. Amen.

This captures more of a focus on the **economic Trinity**, how God as Father, Son, and Spirit engage the world through history: Father is Creator, Son is Savior, and the Spirit is Completer. The movement of God's work has a purpose and goal to bring life to the world as the kingdom of God.

In the intervening time before Christ's return, the early church sought to live toward that goal of flourishing. They honored vocations of ordinary flourishing (family and work) as well as vocations of renunciation (monasticism). There was a (healthy) tension between making this world our home and renouncing the things of this world. The various monastic movements through history were often challenges to return to that tension rather than just settling in. These monastic reform movements are not unlike the Protestant Reformation, which also served as a challenge for the church to live in eschatological holiness. Indeed, a specifically eschatological issue of what happens at death set off the Reformation.

Reformation and Debates about the Intermediate State

Before describing the issues in the Reformation, let's briefly describe the **intermediate state** (see figure 11.6). The intermediate state describes the time between death (when the body and soul separate) and resurrection (when the body and soul are reunited).

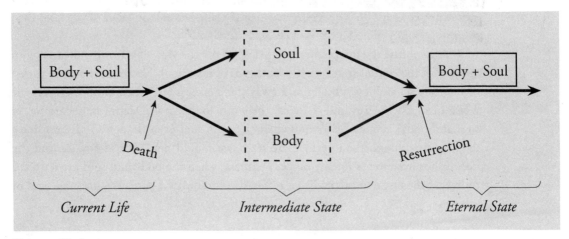

FIGURE 11.6
The Intermediate State

This separation of body and soul, which we call "death," is one of the ultimate evils that sin introduces to humanity.

With this basic summary, we can now turn to the debate that ensued. Living with an already / not yet salvation, Christians are both declared to be holy (as "saints"), but they are also called to become progressively more holy (in progressive sanctification). In the medieval church a question arose: If Christians do not completely master sin at their initial conversion, what biblical evidence do we have that this mastery of sin happens instantaneously at death? In response, the Roman Catholic Church developed a theology of purgatory where, following interpretations of texts such as 1 Corinthians 3:10–15, progressive sanctification would continue after the point of death. In this postmortem process, believers would continue the sanctification process, that is, be purged from their impurities (hence the term *purgatory*). Purgatory is only for believers, whose sins are already 100 percent forgiven, but who are still in need of continued sanctification. As part of that sanctification process, the Roman Catholic Church had (and still continues to use) indulgences, which are declarations related to a reduced time in purgatory for acts of present sanctification. With the "Ninety-Five Theses," Martin Luther challenged the practice of selling indulgences (something the Roman Catholic Church does not do anymore). Though he did not initially reject the idea of purgatory, he quickly did, and almost all other Protestants do as well.[10]

If not purgatory, then what happens when we die? The New Testament regularly speaks of a graced experience at death for believers, so there should never be a place for fear. The traditional position is that believers will be with God *in paradise* awaiting the resurrection of the body at the return of Christ (see Luke 23:43; cf. 2 Cor 5:6–8; Phil 1:23). This view presumes the ability of the disembodied soul to experience heavenly realities. Others prefer a model often called *soul sleep* because the paradise model is perceived to be based on a Platonic dualism of the body and soul. In the soul sleep model, one is not conscious of the passage of time during the intermediate state, like when sleeping, but God maintains their personal identity.

Many confuse the intermediate state (especially the view of waiting in heaven with God) with the eternal state (the ultimate goal of salvation). However, the main thrust of biblical eschatology is by far and away the eternal state, when God re-creates the world in an Edenic way and resurrects believers to live in it. Death (the separation of soul and body) is one of sin's most heinous evils, and even though God gives grace to carry us through the intermediate state, we should not confuse how central the hope of resurrection is for the biblical witness, when the body and soul are reunited to live on the restored earth with a restored community. That is the ultimate goal of salvation.

---

10. For a contemporary Protestant defense of purgatory, see Jerry L. Walls, *Heaven, Hell, and Purgatory: Rethinking the Things That Matter Most* (Grand Rapids: Brazos, 2015).

Conclusion

With the study of eschatology, we see a picture of the narrative arc of the Bible from beginning to end. God's purposes for creation and humanity are ultimately realized through the work of Christ and the Spirit to overcome the evil at work in the world. This creates hope for believers and a warning for unbelievers. This hope for an ultimate resolution is meant to give believers a different perspective on this current age so they are willing to pursue a life of holiness and sacrifice as they experience the reality of the kingdom of God.

CONTEMPORARY THEOLOGICAL RELEVANCE

Now that we have explored a few key ideas related to the doctrine of eschatology, our goal is to explore a limited number of areas that this doctrine relates to wider issues in the contemporary world and church.

Eschatology and Christian Identity
Eschatology and Other Christian Traditions

- **(Functional) Deism.** With its view of an absent God, the language of a spiritual conflict between the kingdoms of God and of Satan was demythologized and renarrated according to the optimism of the **secular** age. This resulted in a (secular) postmillennial perspective (see discussion below) where the expectation of a progress absent of Christ will ultimately lead us forward. Importantly, this progress is grounded not in the saving activity of God but in the indelible human spirit and in the values of free inquiry and democracy. This leads to an ethic of seeking power rather than following Christ in suffering for others. Traditional deism did maintain an expectation of God's final judgment.

- **Mormonism** follows a traditional **premillennial** eschatology (see discussion below) in which Jesus's second coming is associated with apocalyptic events, and he will usher in a time of peace in his millennial kingdom. At the final judgment, believers will be assigned one of the three kingdoms (in descending order)—celestial, terrestrial, or telestial kingdoms—according to their faith and obedience, and unbelievers are cast into outer darkness. For those in the celestial kingdom, exaltation (or deification) is special blessing for a life of faithful obedience.

- **Jehovah's Witnesses** associate apocalyptic events (like wars) with the return of Christ and have determined that in 1914 (the year WWI started) Christ established his kingdom in heaven. When his kingdom is established on earth, it will destroy all human kingdoms as he establishes peace and harmony. An elect group of 144,000 believers will be resurrected to heaven to help Christ rule the restored earth, where the majority of all other believers will live a resurrection life. With regard to personal eschatology, Witnesses reject the idea of a distinct immortal soul. For believers, then, they experience soul sleep at death while awaiting resurrection. For unbelievers, they cease to exist at death, as in an annihilationist model.

Eschatology and Other Religions

In monotheistic traditions the linear progression of time climaxes in God's eschatological restoration:

- **Judaism.** Contemporary Jewish traditions generally hold to the eschatological expectations from the *Tanakh* as the Old Testament description above, though interpretations vary widely. When exploring the topics related to the end of days and the world to come, many look forward to a messianic age when the world will be restored and the promises to the Jews will be fulfilled. Jewish theology appears to focus more on universal restoration than the apocalyptic events that might lead up to them. Beyond general perspectives on blessing for the righteous and punishment for the disobedient, views on personal eschatology are quite diverse, ranging from merely an immortal soul to the hope of resurrection.
- **Islam.** The Qur'an is a very eschatologically oriented book, in that it regularly sets before its readers the options of blessing (through resurrection) in paradise for the faithful and punishment in hell for the disobedient. The Hadith contain a more robust exposition of the events surrounding God's restoration of the world. These include the advent of an antichrist figure who is defeated by Isa (Jesus), who descends from heaven to establish Allah's rule along with the Mahdi, a prophetic figure preparing the way for Isa.

In non-Abrahamic traditions, time is viewed as cyclical rather than linear, and so eschatology is not conceived of as it is above since there is no specific ending (or beginning):

- **Hinduism.** On a personal level, the ultimate goal in Hinduism is release from the repetitive cycle of suffering (*samsara*) inherent in reincarnation. The goal that humans seek is release (*moksha*) by realizing unity with Brahman, the source of cosmic reality, since Brahman is *atman* (one's personal soul). Through the practice of popular Hinduism, this unity is often achieved with one of the gods, who are each an avatar of Brahman. On a cosmic scale, existence is also seen as cyclical rather than linear. One primary model of the cycle of existence features four large epochs (*kalpas*) each with devolving sub-epochs (*yugas*), which cycle through over millions of years and then restart all over again. In this view, the personal liberation of *moksha* is temporary since all life will eventually start over again with a new cycle of *kalpas*.

- **Buddhism.** Also drawing from a cyclical perspective on reality, Buddhism has a variety of eschatological perspectives. While most view the personal goal as *nirvana*, a release from all personal identity, others have looked forward to the Pure Land, a western paradise equivalent to *nirvana*, or at least a pleasant place to achieve enlightenment. When considering a wider universal perspective, the cyclical nature of life drives a devolution of culture. Eventually, the Buddha's teaching will even be forgotten, but this sets the stage for a rebirth of culture through the arrival of new Buddha, who is called Maitreya (or Metteyya).

Views on the Millennium

The Scriptures typically picture the return of Jesus as history's culminating event because it sets the last things (resurrection and judgment) into motion and moves history toward eternity. Though numerous texts speak of Christ's return, Revelation 20 introduces a complicating feature by mentioning a thousand-year reign (a millennium) as an *earthly kingdom* in addition to the eternal state. No other text explicitly mentions the millennium, so incorporating it into other (wider) perspectives can be difficult. It is like having the perfect set of letters in Scrabble and drawing a *q*. Generally speaking, theologians argue for four different approaches to the millennium. The titles derive from how the return of Jesus relates to the millennium: his return is either before (pre-) or after (post-) the millennium.

- **Historic Premillennialism.** Christ's return immediately precedes the thousand-year reign. Afterward, another round of apocalyptic events would occur. While following the narrative of Revelation, this has the complication of two judgments, one before and another after the millennium.
- **Postmillennialism.** Christ's return will come after the thousand-year cycle. The millennium will start sometime in the course of history, and it will be marked by peace, conversions, the decline of war, and the Christianizing of intuitions and governments. It will climax in Jesus's return. This position struggles with the apocalyptic imagery of the tribulations associated with Christ's return.
- **Amillennialism.** Similar to postmillennialism, Christ's return will come after the one thousand years but this will not be a time of peace. The millennium does not (hence the prefix *a-*) point to a literal earthly kingdom in the future but refers to the church's already / not yet experience of the kingdom of God now.
- **Dispensational Premillennialism.** This approach follows the same basic timeline of historic premillennialism, but it includes a rapture of the church (see below) distinct from Christ's return to rule. It is grounded in a distinctive interpretive model that separates Israel from the church. First articulated in the 1830s, this approach holds that the literal promises to the Jews in the Old Testament will be fulfilled in the millennial kingdom, not in the church age (the current age). Early dispensationalists

were adamant that Israel and the church were unrelated, whereas contemporary dispensationalists significantly amended the approach to recognize connections between various covenants in the Bible.

Historically, amillennialism has been the most prominent position in the church, though dispensational premillennialism has become very popular in the last few decades, particularly in many **low church** traditions. Which view is best? How does the millennium (Rev 20) relate to the eternal (universal) restoration described in the rest of the Bible?

The Rapture

The term *rapture* refers to believers (still living) being "caught up" to meet the Lord in the air when he returns at his *parousia* (1 Thess 4:17). Historically, the church viewed this event as occurring at the establishment of Christ's reign on earth. They viewed it according to the arrival of a great king in the ancient world. If a great king came to your city, the people would walk out to meet the king as a sign of honor and accompany him back to the city. Seen in this light Christians are called up to accompany Christ to the creation he is reclaiming. A recent but now very popular view is that the rapture is a separate event from Christ's second coming. According to dispensational premillennialism (popularized in the *Left Behind* novels), at the rapture Christ will gather all Christians with him *in the air* and then return later to the earth (at the end of the tribulation) to establish his thousand-year reign. How should we view the rapture in regards to Christ's second coming? How does a theology of the rapture relate to the kingdom of God and the call to cruciformity?

Rewards and Punishment

Participation in salvation is free and by grace alone, but the Bible speaks regularly of believers receiving rewards and unbelievers receiving punishments. Older Christian traditions allow a hierarchy of blessing and judgment in the afterlife, meaning that there are levels of blessing and punishment. Think, for example, of Dante's *Divine Comedy*: those who are closer to God in heaven have greater beatitude, and those who are worse sinners face greater suffering. Protestants, however, tend to think in binary terms—you are either in heaven or hell without any differentiation once you get there. The nature of rewards, however, leads to an expectation of differentiation. Why talk of rewards at all if the experience is all the same?

Consider these passages on rewards: Matthew 5:11–12; 6:1–6, 16–20; 16:27; 1 Corinthians 3:11–15. Likewise consider passages that speak of differing levels of sin and punishment: Matthew 11:20–24; John 19:11. What is the relationship between freely receiving salvation by grace through faith and receiving rewards by God's grace? How should we understand the distinction between levels of rewards and punishments?

Competing Eschatologies: Utopian and Dystopian

Narratives that compete for our understanding about the goal and purpose of life abound. These competing eschatologies, like any vision statement, draw people in. Here are a few utopian models that have been offered over the past couple of centuries:

- **Secular Progress.** Enlightenment voices sensed that liberty and reason would bring prosperity. Some rejected the idea of God but retained the sense that the future held promise. Science, reason, and access to education virtually assured civilized people that progress was inevitable. Yet anger raged against institutions or ideas that stood in the way of progress. Without a robust idea of God, politics appears to be a life-and-death struggle since opposing political opponents put the future at risk.[11]
- **Marxism.** In this narrative, the emergence of private property (a fall) unleashes selfish greed. After suffering under ever more repressive economic systems, the world will move into an ideal and enduring state of communism. The utopian vision never seems to materialize: while perhaps at odds with some of Marx's ideas, communist nations ruled by totalitarian regimes have killed several times more people than Nazism did.
- **Eternal Reoccurrence.** Nietzsche affirmed a version of ancient Greek history without a happy life-affirming end. He envisioned life as a steady unrelenting return to the same. Life is not going anywhere. It does not have an ending or resolution that makes sense of the previous chapters. Nietzsche reminds us of the radical contribution that Christianity makes to our sense of history.

In distinction to these false utopian visions, a flood of dystopian books and films abound. These all imagine a future where hopes for an ideal place and time are long forgotten. A brutal and beastly scenario evolves, and hope or even survival seem in question. Irony abounds; the entities once trusted to make things better have proved inhuman. The heroes have to survive apocalyptic ordeals by street smarts, courage, and brutality.

Why do dystopian narratives so vastly outnumber utopian ones? Do people watch these as cautionary tales ("I should have voted and recycled")? Are these dystopian pictures just political cartoons for our current age, showing us the heroic virtues necessary to make life worthwhile? How do these relate to the Christian apocalyptic visions?

Social Eschatologies

While many approach eschatology as individualists, other models open up questions: How does the kingdom of God relate to social issues like justice, economics, and the community? When Western students share their favorite verses they typically recall

---

11. See George Weigel, *The Cube and the Cathedral: Europe, America, and Politics without God* (New York: Basic, 2005), 29–34, 49–53.

verses that celebrate God's mercy to forgive us as individuals. To the surprise of Western students, students suffering from oppression may well recite key verses that picture graphic justice being poured out on evil oppressors. For many undergoing oppression, God's victory must include punishment of the oppressors. Consider, for example, the imprecatory prayers in the Psalms.

Moving in a similar communal direction, a perspective called liberation theology arose in the last century. It is primarily identified with believers in Central and South America who suffer political and economic repression and who see a merely personal version of salvation as inadequate. In light of God's steady concern for the poor and oppressed, they believe the church must actively engage the struggle for social justice. Evangelicals fear that some versions of liberation theology ignore the kingdom's call for spiritual transformation, whereas liberation theologians fear the semi-Gnostic version of some evangelicals, who ignore the social focus of Jesus's ministry.

This social and economic interest is also represented in prosperity theology (i.e., prosperity gospel), though with a different emphasis. Numerous low church groups teach that God not only sustains believers but promises wealth for the truly faithful. Reflecting a Deuteronomistic perspective, this approach often represents an overrealized eschatology. Prosperity theology is often associated with those struggling economically: poor Christians don't have money but may not embrace faith unless they are assured money. The pursuit of the "American dream" is often a secularized version of a prosperity gospel: those in wealthy circumstance have money but may not embrace the gospel unless they are permitted to keep it. The love of money can corrupt people of any circumstance.

How might you embrace a balanced view of the kingdom that does not privatize religion but also does not reduce it to economic terms?

Further Issues

- **Intermediate State.** What happens to believers when they die? How should we understand God's work of progressive sanctification and its relationship to the idea of purgatory, paradise, or soul sleep?
- **Ghosts.** Can restless spirits or ghosts of the dead haunt us? Historically, theologians have attributed spiritual activity to demons, not wandering souls. However, many attempt to communicate with the dead through mediums, a practice forbidden in the Bible.
- **Nature of Final Punishment.** Is hell a place of eternal conscious torment or a description of the destruction of existence as in annihilationism?
- **Transhumanism/Posthumanism.** As we explored in the chapter on humanity, there is a movement called transhumanism, or posthumanism, seeking to move humans beyond their current physical limitations through technological integration. How should Christians engage this (secular?) eschatological vision for humanity in light of biblical values?

- **Reincarnation.** In Eastern religions reincarnation is seen as the problem from which one should seek salvation, but Westerners who are attracted to reincarnation often see it as a chance at a redo. Orthodox Christians have always rejected the idea because of the hope of personal identity in resurrection. Is reincarnation a problem or a solution?
- **Cremation.** Historically Christians have avoided cremation, not because burned bodies couldn't be resurrected but because burial gave witness to the importance of bodily resurrection. Now more cremations happen than burials, but should Christians maintain their historical practice?
- **Losing Your Salvation?** As we explored in the chapter on salvation, Christians debate the possibility of losing your salvation. How does the reality of present faith shape and influence the reality of eschatological salvation in the future?
- **Postmortem Conversion.** In the popular book *The Great Divorce*, C. S. Lewis offers fictional narratives of those who still encounter the call to salvation after death while on a trip to heaven. While postmortem conversions are not reported in the Bible, Lewis's account raises interesting questions about whether people could or, in the story's case, would convert.

PRACTICING THE FAITH

Eschatological living (this side of Christ's return) demands living with the both/and reality of the overlapping ages, as we fully pursue the kingdom of God while also rejecting the kingdom of Satan.

Pursuing the Kingdom

If the kingdom of God has really begun through the work of Christ and the Spirit, then the most eschatological thing we can do is to live in that kingdom reality now rather than simply waiting for Christ's return. This supernatural existence takes eyes of faith and prayers to see God's work. Wherever we see the Spirit at work to bring life, we know the kingdom is already there. We seek the kingdom reality of life in the midst of death: wrongs forgiven, illnesses healed, broken relationships restored, communities transformed, addictions broken, enemies loved, the dead raised, outsiders accepted. The church often pursues some of these things but can be surprised when they occur rather than living lives suffused with the supernatural. In simple terms, the kingdom is expressed most clearly wherever the fruit and the gifts of the Spirit are operative. How might you look beyond natural limits or pessimism to pursue this kingdom way of life?

Prayer: Eschatological and Apocalyptic

The Lord's Prayer (Matt 6:9–13) is a central model for Christian prayer that is inherently eschatological. Jesus teaches us to pray by calling for the new age of God to come or, at the least, to let some of the future God has for us to come upon us now. "Your kingdom come, your will be done on earth as it is in heaven." We also see the apocalyptic tenor when we pray "deliver us from the evil one." Whatever we need, desire, and wish for finds its grounding and fullness in God's future for creation. Will you commit to eschatological and apocalyptic kingdom prayers?

Where Is Your Hope? Politics and the Eschatology of the Secular Age

Growing up, I (BCB) was unfortunately in a few disputes over points of doctrine. While these kinds of arguments were not good, these days I rarely see anyone get heated over doctrinal disputes. Politics are another matter entirely. People regularly get in serious and near violent exchanges about their political views. The relative vigor toward politics reveals where most people's (even most Christians') eschatological hope lies. In this secular age, our culture has lost a sense of **transcendence**, the reality of the coming fullness of Christ's kingdom.[12] As a result, one's hope and therefore one's energy is put into mastering the immanent frame, which is the world running autonomously through its current power structures. In this way, politics has become the new religion of the secular age, with politicians as the priests and the news media as prophets. Rather than seeking power according to this world's standards, according to the kingdom of Satan, the New Testament calls the people of God to live as strangers and aliens (Heb 11:13–16; 1 Pet 2:11; cf. John 15:18–19; 17:16; Phil 3:20). Rather than seeking the way of politics and the path of power over others, the way of discipleship is to love your enemies like Christ did. It is the way of cruciformity, where we suffer for those who are different than us rather than seeking to defeat them: Mark 8:27–9:1; 9:30–37; 10:32–45. As you follow Christ in serving others, how can you engage this world and seek its welfare without being drawn into its struggle for power?

Cruciformity—The Path of Martyrdom

The call to follow Christ in suffering is perhaps the hardest challenge in the Christian faith. It comes from the exhortation to obey God and love our neighbor, whether friend or enemy. Just as Jesus's submission to crucifixion was seen as foolish (1 Cor 1:18–25), the path of nonviolent love is equally foolish to those who seek to assert their rights and power over others. The cruciform path is the path of martyrdom. Inspired by the Cambrai Homily (an early Irish sermon), some have used different colors to describe the various paths of martyrdom.[13] There are red martyrs, or blood martyrs, who gave up their lives for the sake of their faith. There are brown martyrs, Christians who gave up wealth and success to seek a life of prayer as monks and nuns in the Egyptian dessert. There were also green martyrs, who instead of seeking the life of solitude sought to follow monastic

---

12. See, e.g., James K. A. Smith, *How (Not) to Be Secular: Reading Charles Taylor* (Grand Rapids: Eerdmans, 2014).

13. Cf. Thomas Cahill, *How the Irish Saved Civilization: The Untold Story of Ireland's Heroic Role from the Fall of Rome to the Rise of Medieval Europe* (New York: Anchor, 1995), 151–95.

vows in communities of faith. Lastly, there are white martyrs, who have taken up the challenge to be evangelists and missionaries to those that have not yet responded to the kingdom message. These are but a few examples of the different ways that we can follow Christ in his death and resurrection. How might you better follow Christ sacrificially for the sake of the kingdom? How might your hope for the coming kingdom motivate you to sacrifice your life, your goods, your rights now for the sake of others?

Investing in a Losing Bet?

Many in the modern world struggle to have any strong eschatology since they are so invested in making it in the here and now. Others that have a stronger eschatology at times struggle to invest in the authentic flourishing of this world; some, for example, do not care for the environment since this world is passing away when Christ returns. One might hear, "Just focus on the spiritual because investing in the mundane is like polishing the brass on the Titanic." Jesus's ministry shows that the spiritual and earthly go together. That is why he spent so much time healing people. Grabbing hold of this idea means that we have to let go of the quasi-Gnostic hope to escape this world. Experiencing the fullness of God's life takes encountering a new vision for this world based on the narrative of Scripture (from creation to new creation). It includes seeing God's vision for things like work, community, justice, creativity, and generosity. As you take this journey, we highly encourage the video series *For the Life of the World: Letters to the Exiles.*[14]

Pursuit of Holiness

If pursuing holiness was ever culturally acceptable, it surely is not in vogue now, outside or even inside the church. To most, holiness is associated with being judgmental or just plain weird. The problem is that holiness is one of the key virtues of an eschatological life. To catch a glimpse of the thrust of the whole New Testament, take a moment to read through two letters where eschatological perspectives are evident: 1 Thessalonians and 1 Peter. Believers are called to stand firm in their faith and pursue God in holiness even amid opposition. Holiness is living in wholeness, rightly connected with God, oneself, the community, and our place. We pursue the fullness of life that God holds out for us, recognizing that suffering is part of discipleship. In seeking God's greatest glory through obedience, believers receive the greatest blessing, but this depends on having a vision that eschatological values matter more than the goods of the current age. How might you pursue the life of holiness more fully?

Further Issues

- **The Spirit and the Cross.** Often Spirit-people are considered "enthusiasts," looking to experience the fullness of life now. While the presence of the Spirit

---

14. See *For the Life of the World: Letters to the Exiles*, video series, Acton Institute, www.letterstotheexiles.com.

is a sign of the already present kingdom of God, a Spirit-driven life also makes sense of the "not yet" of the kingdom, the time of suffering while God's people await Christ's return. In 1 Corinthians 1–3, Paul argues that Spirit-people will live out the foolishness of the cross and follow Christ in the path of suffering and service.

- **Evangelism.** With the distinct destinies held out by the Bible for believers and unbelievers, all believers are called to participate in evangelism to help as many people as possible experience God's blessings. Evangelism includes sharing the truths of the kingdom of God, but also includes praying for miraculous experiences. Most of the healings in Jesus's ministry were for those not yet his disciples.

- **Sabbath.** While keeping Sabbath is not a command repeated in the New Testament, its principle is inherently eschatological. It links the purpose of creation to the hope of restoration and is grounded in trust that we do not have to constantly work because God provides. How might you pursue a regular Sabbath as an eschatological commitment?

- **Generosity.** The desire to pursue wealth for personal gain reflects a value system driven by this immanent age. In distinction, a life marked by generosity to others reflects eschatological values with higher goals than just success and comfort in this life. As with other aspects of the faith, obedience brings its own reward: research has demonstrated that those who are most generous are also happier people. How might you pursue a more limited lifestyle so that you can be radically generous?

- **Communion.** In a larger discussion of the Lord's Supper, Paul describes the early Christian practice in 1 Corinthians 11:23–26 and declares, "Whenever you eat this bread and drink this cup, you proclaim the Lord's death until he comes" (v. 26). The practice of communion is eschatological: recognizing the inauguration of the kingdom in Christ's first advent as we look forward to his second advent.

- **Prayers of Lament.** In lament prayers, someone cries out to God in the midst of suffering. These prayers recognize both the reality of suffering and the hope of God's act of restoration and vindication. The fact that they are the most frequent type of prayers in Psalms means there are many models for this eschatological prayer. Consider starting with Psalms 3–5; 22; 42–44; 73–74; 142.

Eschatology is much more than speculative ideas about how the world will end. Rather, a biblical eschatology connects believers to the full scope of the Bible's narrative of salvation. It thus becomes one of the most practical doctrines, establishing the grounds for an ethic of obedience, sacrifice, and holiness. Believers have the opportunity to live in the kingdom of God now inaugurated through Christ and the Spirit, and we wait in confident expectation for Christ's return to establish his kingdom fully.

CLOSING PRAYER

The following has been adapted from John Wesley's Annual Covenant Renewal Service:

> Heavenly Father,
> Let me live eschatologically.
> Let me be your servant, under your command.
> I will no longer be my own.
> I will give up myself to your will in all things.
> Lord, make me what you will.
> I put myself fully into your hands:
> put me to doing, put me to suffering,
> let me be employed for you, or laid aside for you,
> let me be full, let me be empty,
> let me have all things, let me have nothing.
> I freely and with a willing heart give it all to your pleasure and disposal.
> Amen.[15]

15. "Covenant Renewal Service," *The United Methodist Book of Worship* (1992), United Methodist Publishing House, www.umcdiscipleship.org/resources/covenant-renewal-service.

CHAPTER 12

Conclusion

I s theology relevant? That question provoked this book. Though none have been so blunt, I (BCB) get the feeling a few of my students think of it more like this: "Orthodoxy, who cares?" At its best, many think orthodox doctrine is just a collection of abstract facts without connection to a biblical faith or the pragmatics of daily life. At its worst, orthodoxy could be seen as oppressive, hindering authentic individuality and freedom of conscience. The goal of this book was to show that theology does not reflect a dry, dead faith but engagement with the living God in a dynamic world. Approaching theology from its biblical, historical, and practical perspectives, we have argued that it grows out of the singular Story of God's loving interaction with the world through creation, fall, and renewed creation. As we come to the end of this book, we want to articulate more specifically how this Story encounters life today. We will first explore the context for us encountering the Story and then how we live out that Story.

RECAPPING THE STORY: CULTURE MEETS THE STORY OF GOD

Our Cultural Context

Since the time of Constantine, Christianity has played a dominant role in the social and cultural identity of the West. With significant shifts over the last five hundred years, the church's influence has begun to wane due to factors from within and from without. While we think this loss of presumption that weds Christianity to empire is helpful for the church, it also creates challenges. Philosopher Charles Taylor has recently explored the issues that shape our contemporary "secular age" in the modern West.[1]

---

1. Charles Taylor, *A Secular Age* (Cambridge, MA: Belknap, 2007). For an assessment and interaction, see James K. A. Smith, *How (Not) to Be Secular: Reading Charles Taylor* (Grand Rapids: Eerdmans, 2014).

As time progresses, Westerners have sensed that faith in God's activity and existence seem to grow less plausible, and this loss of confidence is described as disenchantment. With this growing **secularization**, atheism has advanced, and faith has been pushed into the private sphere of one's life.

Taylor argues that this version of secularity challenging faith is not the only influence on Western society. The rise of religious **pluralism** presents another version of secularity. It is not so much that the West has lost its religious impulse; rather, that religious impulse is now distributed among numerous world religions as well as more syncretistic varieties that include horoscopes, crystals, and so on.[2] When there is one dominant (religious) perspective, social pressure reinforces that perspective, but pluralism dilutes. Our greater engagement with a plurality of worldviews means that those who continue to hold religious commitments tend to hold them less vigorously because they are not buttressed by the community at large. This fragmentation creates a more fragile faith. Thus secularity entails faith being not only removed but also less vigorous.

This is the culture in which we find ourselves. Part of this shift over the past five hundred years was an optimism that we would move beyond religious divisions and find a new common ground within a secularized public square devoid of those fights. Rather than a narrative influenced by faith, secular narratives, like that of the American dream, now drive most Westerners, even those in the church. However, the cultural optimism coming out of **modernity** proved false. The political and cultural battles that were associated with religion were replaced with secular variations, as the wars of the twentieth century made evident. The cultural optimism of modernity has given way to a cultural pessimism of **postmodernity**. This skepticism is evident in the large number of dystopian novels and movies that characterize our age. We thought we were moving beyond social and personal problems, yet they haunt us ever still—crime, racism, poverty, economic disparity, nationalism, human trafficking, war. What place does Christian theology have in this pluralistic environment shaped by such skepticism and social disturbance?

This question is not new. In fact, it is the same type of question we addressed when discussing the apocalyptic literature of the Old and New Testament.[3] These writers also sat at the crossroads of cultural optimism and pessimism. The Deuteronomistic perspective in the Mosaic **covenant** argues that good people would prosper and bad people suffer. The eschatologically minded prophets and apostles acknowledged the opposite was often true: the righteous suffer and the wicked prosper. Life is not so mechanistic as to run by a simple algorithm. During the time of the prophets, God's people fell subject to foreign powers and were even exiled to live among foreign nations. Is theology relevant in a world that seems to run so backward? Yes, the apocalyptic prophets say, but you

2. People of our (the authors') generation engaged world religions in college as an experiment in thought, discovering the beliefs of peoples in faraway places. Today, you are much more likely to engage world religions and alternative forms of Christianity at the lunch table in public school or at work.

3. See ch. 11.

have to understand the difficult events in light of a larger Story. Thus these prophets narrate current and future events in light of God's providential action. Thus the larger Story, God's larger Story, enables the people of God to understand their circumstances.

Likewise, the people of God today must recapture that same apocalyptic vision to make sense of our challenging world. You might remember that we started the book by noting how the Story of God as Father, Son, and Holy Spirit sets the foundation for and shapes the nature of Christian doctrine. Similarly, we argued that this Story is also shaped eschatologically. Though it is a loaded theological term, **eschatology** points primarily to God patiently accomplishing his Story in the world: you cannot understand the beginning and middle without understanding the ending. Therefore, **Trinity** and eschatology, the main character and the plot, are central to Christian theology in this broken world. Before we consider how this Story shapes our engagement with the world, we should reconsider its key elements first.

The Story of God

When someone mentions *theology*, you might think first of the various "-ologies": **soteriology**, **ecclesiology**, **pneumatology**. But engaging *theo*-logy means first and foremost engaging *Theos* (God). Since we encounter God as Trinity, Trinity is not just one doctrine of theology but the lens to understand all the other doctrines.[4] We have approached theology in this book from three primary perspectives—biblical, historical, and practical. Each of these three lenses has its focus on the Story of God.

Biblical

The Story of the Bible is a narrative of creation and covenant. God creates the world, and he covenants with his people to bring restoration, undoing the sinful gone-wrong-ness of creation. He created the world for flourishing, and his covenantal restoration allows the world to embody the flourishing that he intended. This salvation history plays out through the Abrahamic, Mosaic, Davidic, and new covenants. The New Testament spells out the culmination in the new covenant through the **Messiah** and the Spirit as the **kingdom of God**. This is no simple and easy progression of history; rather, the kingdom breaks in eschatologically: the Messiah dies on the cross and is raised from the dead; the Spirit empowers the fight against the kingdom of Satan. God's kingdom is both here now and will be fully established when Christ returns. As we recognize one God working together to fulfill his intentions as Father, Son, and Holy Spirit, we see how the biblical story is the Story of God.

Historical

While systematic theology has a semichronological ordering that coheres with the biblical narrative (as you see in the progression of the chapters in this book), it is

---

4. This argument is wonderfully made by Fred Sanders, *The Deep Things of God: How the Trinity Changes Everything*, 2nd ed. (Wheaton, IL: Crossway, 2019).

important to note that dividing things up to treat the doctrines distinctly can create artificial separations. In contrast, the Nicene Creed treats theology according to the narrative of the Bible.[5] Rather than a disparate set of "-ologies," the creed narrates the act of one God as Father, Son, and Spirit from creation to new creation. Thus the Trinity is not just one doctrine of theology, but the foundation on which all other doctrines stand.

THE TRINITY AND THE DOCTRINES

We encounter God as Trinity throughout Christian theology, and Trinity shapes the most fundamental way that we understand and engage each aspect of theology:

- **Revelation:** Christ is the central **revelation** of God, and the **inspiration** of the Holy Spirit is what makes Scripture God's Word.
- **God and World:** We recognize God's **immanence** and **transcendence** when we see Father as Creator and covenant maker, the Son as incarnate Savior, and the Spirit as God's empowering presence in church.
- **Humanity:** Humans are created in the **image of God** and transformed into the image of Christ through the presence of the Holy Spirit.
- **Salvation:** The Father sends the Son to die and rise to achieve salvation and sends the Holy Spirit to apply salvation to a gone-wrong world.
- **Church:** The church is God's people and Christ's body; they are made one in the Spirit.
- **Eschatology:** The kingdom of God is begun by the first advent of Christ and the presence of the Spirit, and it is consummated by Christ's second advent at his return.

Therefore, the doctrine of *Theos* (God) as Trinity is absolutely fundamental for *theo*-logy.

Practical

This one Story in its biblical and historical frame is not just an abstract set of ideas; rather, it is the narrative that makes sense of our particular stories. We are living out the subplots that play out within God's larger narrative. Due to the pervasiveness of sin and demonic powers in the world, our stories are often marked by senseless evil and violence. In that way, our stories are not so different than those in the Bible who experienced evil. God addressed them through prophets and apocalyptic visions in order to give his divine perspective. Without the wider eschatological point of view about God's advancing

---

5. One key aspect underrepresented in the Creed is the story of Israel.

kingdom, we would conceive movements in history or even our own story as meaningless. Likewise, we would consider God as capricious. Understanding God's eschatological action in the world does not make evil less evil,[6] but it does recast evil in light of God's act to bring justice and peace to the world in Christ and through the Spirit. The Christian faith is, therefore, about participating in the life of God eschatologically, experiencing Christ's cruciform life in the brokenness of this age as we look forward to the fullness of the kingdom in the age to come.

This Story, therefore, is the common narrative shared by all orthodox Christian traditions—Protestant, Roman Catholic, and Eastern Orthodox. In this way, the Nicene Creed, which reflects the fundamental biblical story, serves as the basis for ecumenical unity since Christians share in one common faith. C. S. Lewis described the common affirmation of this one Story as "mere Christianity," a recognition we achieve when we focus on the essentials rather than the nonessentials (which are still very important).[7] Importantly, there are no "mere Christians" because we always live within particular traditions and within particular cultures. Yet Christians still unite around the common Story as a Trinitarian faith, even if we view that faith from our own vantage points. Having captured this general sense of the Story, we are still left with the question: How do we live it out in our own lives?

LIVING THE STORY: THE STORY OF GOD MEETS CULTURE

Engaging theology means engaging *Theos* (God), that is, participating in the life of God by participating in the Story of God. We have rehearsed the continuity of the biblical, historical, and practical aspects of the Story of God, but simply noting the centrality of this Story does not magically make it appear in our lives. To participate in the Story, we must learn not only (1) to attend properly to the various elements of theology in light of the Story but also (2) to consider how our own story fits within God's wider narrative. We will address those two aspects in turn.

Engaging the Story of God

Gaining the standpoint of the centrality of the Story of God is like climbing a mountain; it gives you perspective on everything else around. Throughout the book, we have attempted to highlight the interconnection of the particular doctrines of Christian theology within the larger Story, but we have the opportunity to plot these doctrines from our renewed vision. Thus we spell out here how this understanding of the whole shapes the parts.

---

6. God is not the cause of evil. To affirm his providence does not entail that we should view evil in our lives as good because it is simply part of his plan. One of the most fundamental aspects of Christianity is that evil is bad, and so we need salvation from it.

7. C. S. Lewis, *Mere Christianity* (New York: HarperOne, 2015 [1952]).

The Creed and History

While some view theology as focused on hairsplitting and abstract philosophical principles, we remember that the creed (like the earlier **rule of faith** upon which it depends)
focuses 90 percent on the narrative of God and only 10 percent on the philosophy of
God. The philosophy is only there to help you understand the Story rightly. If you only
engage the Trinity via metaphysical ideas of oneness and threeness, as through the terms
ousia (nature) and *hypostasis* (subsistence/person), you have missed the importance of
the creed. Its focus is encountering God as a person who acts, and this tripersonal God
engages the world as Father, Son, and Spirit. The emphasis is the Father who is Creator,
the Son who is Savior, and the Spirit who is Completer. The fact that they share one
nature (*homoousion*) is necessary to tell the Story rightly: they do this together, not as
three Gods.[8] The Story (or the **economic Trinity**) is the focus of the creed, just as it is
the focus of the biblical narrative.

This view of God's activity in the world reshapes our view of history. It was com-
monplace among ancient conceptions of history to see life as a churning cosmic cycle,
always coming and going, creating and destroying, living and dying. Eastern religions
often conceive of history as cyclical, with little or no discernable progression, and in many
modern secular narratives, dystopian visions feature little hope of advancement as we
cyclically suffer under oppressive regimes or cultural struggles. By contrast Christians
think the human family moves through time. By revealing himself in time, God gives
history a sense of story. God has had a purpose and destiny for the world from the very
beginning. He did not create begrudgingly or mistakenly, and creation reveals God's
deep-rooted disposition to share, care, and love. For Christians, life in the world has
potential that is developed eschatologically, bringing creation to its fitting end.

Trinity and Incarnation

The mysterious teachings of the Trinity and the **incarnation** are the heart of the
faith. It is a heavy irony that so little is understood or said about the Trinity today when
almost everything Christians do rests upon the Trinity. The teaching of the Trinity keeps
us from mistakenly surrendering the unity of God's being and nature (as one) or the
distinctiveness of Father, Son, and Spirit (as three). More positively, the Trinity provides
the insight into God needed to make sense of the grand Story of the Bible. Make no
mistakes, Trinitarian language and **liturgy** is rooted in the Bible (Matt 28:19–20; John
1:1–3; 17:1–5; Eph 2:18). But we are drawn to Trinity because when we think in terms
of Trinity we can grasp the big picture, the overarching teaching of faith (Doctrine).

A crucial part of the deliberation of Trinity calls for Christians to articulate the
mystery of the Son becoming incarnate. The incarnation keeps us from mistakenly

---

8. Even though for sake of simplicity the creed assigns particular roles, one central corollary to the fact that all
three persons of the Trinity share one nature is that they also share one will and one activity. Thus they are always
mutually engaged in all work together.

surrendering the Son's solidarity with and identity as God (fully God) or surrendering the Son's solidarity with and identity as a genuine human person (fully human). His story reveals the mystery of God's great love; God did not send someone else to do his dirty work. Jesus challenges the pervasive idea that lesser, weak persons serve greater persons. Jesus teaches that true greatness is measured by how many you serve, not how many serve you (Mark 10:43–45). The Son defers to and serves the Father not out of weakness but out of love, shared vison, and mission. Following this divine way of relating, this changes how we see and relate to other people. Trinity and incarnation are not, therefore, just abstract principles.

Revelation and the Bible

At his core, the triune God desires to commune, reveal, and love, as we see revealed in Jesus. Additionally, the Bible is a great storehouse of God's words and deeds, founded on the reality of inspiration. God does not inspire texts by insulating them from the influence of human authors; rather, he communicates his message in and through human authors in their vocabularies, style, and contexts. This approach may seem odd, but it is in step with a Son who is truly human and truly God.

Reading Scripture faithfully requires a humble patience that knows that God reveals himself in and through history. We cannot understand one element of the story without considering the whole. For example, we do not arrive at Scripture's teaching on divorce by selecting any saying at random. God spoke a word to Moses that was gracefully accommodating to rebellious listeners. Jesus forbids using this word as an excuse for ignoring the grand vision for marriage in the unfolding Story of God (Deut 24:1–4; Matt 19:3–10). Just as we cannot understand the narrative of Scripture as if it is a collection of disconnected factoids, we cannot understand the life of discipleship as disconnected from the narrative of Scripture. Trusting the Bible is not so much placing the information extracted from the Bible into our perspective; trusting the Bible is locating our life into the larger Story of God. We do this by immersing ourselves and dwelling in the biblical text. More than just extracting information, believers occupy this sacred story with wonder and exuberance and come to see themselves as recipients and participants. When we are immersed in the Scriptures, the Spirit can transform as well as inform us. The Trinity makes sense of these extraordinary convictions about and experience of the Bible.

Church

We believe the Son gathered a community to himself, and this community receives the Spirit. This people who follow the Son in the sustaining power of the Spirit have been called by the Father to be his people. The followers of the Son awaken to an awareness and disposition within us that we hold the status of a genuine son or daughter; this new disposition is fashioned in us by the Spirit poured out by the Father (Rom 8:15). This gathered people worship and serve God. Their mission includes reaching the world since

God will gather a people for himself, including persons from all the peoples of the world. Despite these gathered people bearing the gone-wrong-ness and injustice of the world, we still declare them to be the Body of Christ. This makes sense if God was incarnated in the broken world.

To engage theology well you must understand these elements of the story in light of the larger Story so that the parts always come back to the center, which is our engagement with God. This movement from the whole to the parts, from *Theos* to the doctrines of theology, reflects God's loving and creative engagement with the world. Thus to engage God means that we naturally should engage others, namely, our culture.

Engaging Culture

Mountain climbing is great for getting a perspective on the rest of the world, but we don't live on mountaintops. Unfortunately, many academic works on theology reinforce the mentality that theology only works on a pristine mountaintop because they only treat the head (and heart) aspect rather than the hands—that is, what you think (and believe) instead of what you do. However, practices are essential to theology. Like a worldview, everyone has a theology, and that theology is played out in their daily practices. In fact, we know much more about what someone believes by what they do than by what ideas they say they affirm.[9] Since there is a coherent and central Story that undergirds biblical and historical theology, the goal for Christians is to let that Story guide your theology and practice in the world rather than letting competing narratives shape your practice. Engaging theology is not just about learning new ideas, but engaging in the practice of theology, that is, participating in the life of God through the Story of God.

Engaging the Life of God

We believe Christian pilgrims share, or participate, in the fellowship of God. Focusing on foundational Christian ideas is necessary, but it is not enough. Christianity bears a personal and relational dimension that centers on learning to know and trust God. Rather than learning facts, engaging theology is more like learning to speak a language. This type of learning demands rituals, practices, mentors, apprenticeship, and community. The purpose of all that work is to relate to others, but you cannot get there without personal practice and effort. Like speaking a language, theology is a venture with instructions and exhortations. With a lot of practice, one gets the knack of it, grows in confidence and competence, and slowly it becomes a natural part of your existence.

The relaxed approach to Christianity taken by many means that other narratives, like the one they ingest through hours of media daily, sets the narrative of their lives. Discipline and study are uncommon. Formal catechism, Bible reading, and efforts to conform our

---

9. It is for this reason that Charles Taylor uses the term *social imaginary* instead of worldview: life embodied in communal realities (social) reflects your thinking (imaginary). Charles Taylor, *A Secular Age* (Cambridge: Belknap Press, 2007), 171–76.

lives to Christ are relics of the past for many believers. But if you want to embody the narrative, you must know it. As a starting point, we encourage two key practices: reading the whole Bible and memorizing the Nicene Creed. These are like learning the grammar of the language. However, to have engaged conversations, you have to go beyond grammar and practice the faith. Many who face the challenges of the changing world are adrift from their Christian moorings. Worldview camps and apologetics, which attempt to address this deficit, are signs of panic or dread. As valuable as such efforts are, they are no substitute for the ongoing tasks of learning and practicing faith in a local church community. Community can strengthen a faith made fragile by contemporary pluralism because in communities theology changes from a set of ideas to an embodied reality as you experience the life of God through the community of God.

Engaging a Global Church

One's local community is essential to a true engagement with theology, but we also need the wider church. We live out faith in our respective traditions, but we also commend a mere Christianity that allows us to partner with those of common faith, who hold to the Nicene Creed. Without ceasing to be Protestant (and in our case baptistic/charismatic), affirming the faith of Roman Catholic and Eastern Orthodox traditions allows us to be strengthened as we unite in a common cause for the kingdom of God. This does not mean that we ignore differences; many (even serious ones) remain. But we need one another, particularly in a pluralistic world. The depth and variety of traditions represented in the body of Christ gives strength when we stand together and learn from one another.

We draw strength not only from diverse confessional communities but also from the global expression of Christ's body. We live in a new, global age of the church. While the life of the church is at times dormant or in decline in the West, explosive growth has occurred in the Christian family around the globe. There are sometimes theological concerns about aspects of these new movements, but we would be foolish to ignore the exponential movement of the Spirit among these communities. Rather than seeing ourselves as those with resources to send to others, we need to see one another as partners in mutual exchange. Their living faith as evidenced by the work of the Spirit surely has much to teach the West where our light is dimming culturally. As we form a sense of communion and family with Christians from around the world, we will better practice the eschatological Story of God. We already see evidence of that communion dawning; the most recent podcast sermon my (RLH) friend passed along came from Uganda, not Houston or Dallas. We encourage you to undertake a new journey with an awareness of brothers and sisters from Africa, South America, Asia, and India. As we focus on this global and catholic nature of our faith, Christians will be less focused on the drive toward nationalistic division and racism. Our common allegiance to Christ through the experience of the Spirit is our common ground, and our futures are tied together.

Engaging a Pluralistic Culture

Appeals to unity with the global church might be seen as an attempt to regain the cultural dominance enjoyed by the church in the West since Constantine. With the rise of secularity—in its atheistic or its pluralistic forms—many Christians perceive this as a loss, particularly a loss of cultural power. Some have unfortunately scrambled to retain power by fighting battles with cultural and political weapons rather than spiritual ones. Rather than seeking cultural dominance, we see the eschatological Story of God as embodied through faithful and sacrificial presence. This is both modeled by Christ and is consistently proclaimed by the Old and New Testament apocalyptic voices. Martyrdom, not political power, expands the kingdom. Sacrifice, not violence, embodies the kingdom. Unfortunately, many Christians embody the false gospel narrative of redemptive violence from the average superhero movie instead of the narrative of Christ when they engage the world culturally and politically. As a result, Christians are cast in the role of the suppressor who enacts exploitation, not justice.

The church, rather than a nation-state or an ethnic heritage, should form our identity as citizens of the kingdom. As resident aliens, Christian allegiance lies elsewhere.[10] We live as exiles in a foreign country, not because this physical world is a bodily imprisonment but because the ruler of this world is Satan, and we are waiting on God to redeem it. What does it look like to live as resident aliens in exile? In Jeremiah 29, Jeremiah gives a letter to the exiles who are living in Babylon. Many are familiar with a particular verse in this chapter: "'For I know the plans I have for you,' declares the LORD, 'plans to prosper you and not to harm you, plans to give you hope and a future'" (v. 11). This is a true message of hope, but it only makes sense in context of the command to settle there and "seek the peace and prosperity of the city to which I have carried you into exile. Pray to the LORD for it, because if it prospers, you too will prosper" (v. 7). Living in exile demands an eschatological vision: a commitment to flourishing here and now while also maintaining a wider hope. This future expectation allows believers to sacrifice present goods rather than trying to hoard them. There are a variety of ways that Christians might practice this,[11] and we encourage believers to become disciples of the cross rather than of the sword.

Let's consider how we might practice evangelism in light of this alternative stance toward culture and power. When we (the authors) were growing up, evangelism often embodied a confrontational mode with direct questions like this: "Do you know where you would go if you died right now?" This was paired with an ordered presentation of the gospel (e.g., the "Four Spiritual Laws" or the "Romans Road"). There is a time and place for questions and presentations, but they can set an oppositional tone. Might we consider other ways modeled by Jesus? In our chapter on Christology, we noted how

---

10. Stanley Hauerwas and William H. Willimon, *Resident Aliens* (Nashville: Abingdon, 1989).

11. James Davison Hunter, *To Change the World: The Irony, Tragedy, and Possibility of Christianity in the Late Modern World* (Oxford: Oxford University, 2010).

his ministry of preaching, teaching, and healing embodied the kingdom. Jesus engaged unbelievers with conversation, but more often he began by healing them. Indeed, most of the healing miracles in the Bible were for those not yet in the community of faith. To follow his model, consider coming alongside someone and asking, "How can I pray for you?" Then, through prayers for healing (both physical and spiritual), the gospel, which has been demonstrated in action, provides the impetus for further explanation.[12] Instead of being seen as against them, you are seen as standing with them. We encourage you to seek the welfare of your community by praying kingdom prayers and living out a kingdom reality. That method of humbly embodying the kingdom is the kind of faithful presence Jesus models.

The ministry of Jesus shows that theology is more than a set of ideas. It is a lived reality of the kingdom of God where people have the opportunity to participate in the life of God. Engaging theology is more than engaging a set of ideas; it is an ongoing encounter with the living God. We encourage you to walk with one another on this journey together.

WHERE DO YOU GO FROM HERE?

As an introductory textbook, we have only scratched the surface with all the issues we have addressed. With the wide and varied voices in the church, we do not lack for resources to take the conversation further. Indeed, there are so many options that it may be difficult to know where to start. We recommend these resources to help you in the next stage of your journey:

Bartholomew, Craig G., and Michael W. Goheen. *The Drama of Scripture: Finding Our Place in the Biblical Story.* 2nd ed. Grand Rapids: Baker Academic, 2014. This volume explores how the various and distinct parts of the Bible contribute to one coherent narrative.

Bird, Michael F. *Evangelical Theology.* Grand Rapids: Zondervan, 2013. There are many good one-volume systematic theologies, but Bird's represents a similar vision as ours with his distinct biblical engagement and interest in setting theology in an eschatological frame.

For the Life of the World: Letters to the Exiles. Video series. Acton Institute. 2015. www .letterstotheexiles.com. This creative and engaging series of videos situates the Christian engagement with the world in light of God's economy and his purpose for creation.

Foster, Richard J. *Streams of Living Water: Essential Practices from the Six Great Traditions of the Christian Faith.* San Francisco: HarperSanFrancisco, 1998. Focusing on

---

12. John Wimber and Kevin Springer, *Power Evangelism* (Bloomington: Choosen, 2009 [1986]).

distinct traditions throughout Christian history, Foster demonstrates the embodied nature of the Christian spirituality expressed by these traditions as drawn from the Bible.

The Popular Patristics Series published by St. Vladimir's Seminary Press. This series of short and accessible translations of patristic texts gives a window into the world of patristic theology, where deep theology is also met with a concern to practice the faith.

Sanders, Fred. *The Deep Things of God: How the Trinity Changes Everything*. 2nd ed. Wheaton, IL: Crossway, 2019. This fine text helps extend the conversation around the importance of the Trinity in our theology and practice.

Shelley, Bruce L. *Church History in Plain Language*. Edited by R. L. Hatchett. 4th ed. Nashville: Thomas Nelson, 2013. This accessible volume introduces readers to the scope of church history.

Smith, James K. A. *How (Not) to Be Secular: Reading Charles Taylor*. Grand Rapids: Eerdmans, 2014. In this short volume, Smith expertly participates in a conversation about the state of the postmodern world and how Christians should navigate our place in it. Beyond this volume, we commend his library of works for helping the church embody faith.

Tennent, Timothy. *Theology in the Context of World Christianity: How the Global Church Is Influencing the Way We Think about and Discuss Theology*. Grand Rapids: Zondervan, 2007. This volume helps readers understand theology in the global context of world Christianity.

Glossary

Agency, Competitive and Noncompetitive: Agency refers to the ability to act; an agent acts and exercises authority. With competitive agency, the ability to act or cause an outcome is distinguished from the agency of others, such that responsibility is distributed. With noncompetitive agency, the operation of the agents is on different levels.

Amillennialism: The view that the thousand-year reign (millennium) of Revelation 20:2–3 is not a future earthly kingdom before the eternal state; rather, it is the present rule of Christ manifested in the church.

Analogy: A comparison between ideas that involves both a similarity and dissimilarity. Analogies are distinct from univocal statements (where words are used with precisely the same meaning) and equivocal statements (where words are used with completely different meanings).

Anthropology: The study of things pertaining to humans/humanity. It is derived from *anthropos* (Gk), meaning man/human.

Apocrypha: A collection of Jewish texts which were (generally) written between the Old Testament and the New Testament and which are combined with a Greek translation of the Old Testament to form the Septuagint. With their inclusion in the Septuagint, these were considered authoritative by patristic Christians and therefore accepted by Roman Catholic and Eastern Orthodox Christians as canonical, but they are rejected by Protestants as Scripture because they were not part of the Hebrew canon. They are called "deuterocanonical" ("second canon") by some.

Apophatic Theology: An approach to theology that works from the perspective that God is infinite and mysterious. Accordingly, affirmations about God are therefore limited since they derive from a finite perspective. See Cataphatic Theology.

Arminianism: The outlook of Jacobus Arminius who argued God elects or chooses people on the basis of his foreknowledge of their faith decisions. See Election.

Aseity: The concept that God is "from himself" because he is not derived from or dependent upon any other being or principle.

Atonement: The doctrine of what the Christ event accomplished in his incarnation, death, and resurrection. It is derived from "at-one-ment" and describes that which unites humanity to God (makes them "at one").

Byzantine Era: This time period runs roughly from AD 500 to 1500, and geographically it pertains to the area of Central/Eastern Europe under the control of the Byzantine Empire and to the (primarily) Greek-speaking church.

Canon: A collection of authoritative writings, or scriptures. The Christian canon is the Bible. All Christian traditions accept the thirty-nine books of the Old Testament and the twenty-seven books of the New Testament. In distinction to Protestant traditions, Roman Catholics and Eastern Orthodox Christians (following the ancient Christian use of the Septuagint) accept additional ancient Jewish texts called the Apocrypha, or Deuterocanonical texts, written between the Old Testament and the New Testament. See Apocrypha; Septuagint.

Cataphatic Theology: An approach to theology that works from the perspective that God is knowable. Accordingly, humanity can make direct and substantive claims about God. See Apophatic Theology.

Cessationism: The view that the miraculous spiritual gifts (like tongue speaking, prophecy, and healing) stopped after the time of the (initial) apostles and the formation of the Scriptures.

Christology: The study of things pertaining to Jesus Christ, the second member of the Trinity. Derived from *christos* (Gk), meaning anointed one (messiah).

Church: A term used for local congregations, the universal church comprised of all believers, or a particular faith community, such as the Roman Catholic Church. See Ecclesiology.

Cosmogony: A theory or account of the origin of the world.

Cosmology: A view of the world that envisions its overall makeup and function as an ordered whole.

Covenant: A binding agreement or treaty that governs a relationship. Biblically, these are initiated by God with his people.

Creed: A statement of faith. It is derived from *credo* (Lat), meaning "I believe."

Cruciformity: The spirituality shaped by embodying Christ's death through suffering and sacrifice for God and others, such that believers bear the form of the crucifixion.

Deism: The view that God remains disengaged from the world after creating it. It arose with seventeenth and eighteenth century thinkers who gave preference to reason over revelation, but it can be more popularly applied to views regarding a detached and disinterested God, such as the clockmaker God.

Dualism: The belief that there are two kinds of realities, usually material stuff and spiritual stuff, which exist in distinction from one another.

Ecclesiology: The study of things pertaining to the church. Derived from *ekklesia* (Gk), meaning church.

Economia: God's plan played out in history. See *Theologia*.

Economic Trinity: The approach to or revelation of the Trinity which arises from God's acts in history as described by narrative descriptions rooted in the Scriptures. See Immanent Trinity.

Ecumenical: An approach to theology that concerns the unity of the whole church, particularly as different traditions work together. It is derived from *oikoumene* (Gk), meaning the (whole) "inhabited world."

Election: The act of God choosing peoples or persons for a variety of purposes, particularly with regard to salvation.

Epistemology: The study of knowledge, particularly what things can be known and how it they can be known.

Eschatology: The study of last things or the end times. It is derived from *eschatos* (Gk), meaning the end.

Eucharist: The liturgical practice of taking bread and wine as a symbol or sacrament of Christ's body and blood. It is derived from *eucharistia* (Gk), meaning thanksgiving, due to the thanksgiving prayers offered to bless a meal. Other terms for this meal include Communion, the Lord's Supper, and the Table.

Exegesis: The process and practice of interpreting a text. This is often contrasted with eisegesis (reading meanings into the text).

Existentialism: A philosophical approach which stresses that life is not defined by fixed essences (or nature) but by the individual's exercise of freedom as their manner of existing.

Filioque **("and the Son"):** A Latin term meaning "and the Son" appended to the phrase in the Nicene Creed that the Holy Spirit "proceeds from the Father." The addition by the Western church helped precipitate the Great Schism (1054) between the Eastern and Western church.

Fruit of the Spirit: The virtues and dispositions formed by the Holy Spirit's transforming presence in the life of a follower of Jesus. Galatians 5:22–23 gives the classic listing.

General Revelation: The knowledge God reveals to all—through material creation, human experience, and conscience—and perhaps God's direction of history. See also Special Revelation.

Gnosticism: An umbrella term referring to an approach to theology rejected by the early church because Gnostic thinkers viewed (1) the material creation and history as inherently evil, (2) salvation as a deliverance from the evil physical world, (3) Jesus as unconnected to his Jewish environment and theology, and (4) the idea of God's restoration of the world (and resurrection) as misguided. By analogy this term is applied to contemporary dualistic approaches to theology.

Hamartiology: The study of sin and its consequences. It is derived from *harmartia* (Gk), meaning "sin," or "missing the mark."

Hermeneutics: The study of issues related to interpretation, such as theological (e.g., inspiration, revelation, and canon), philosophical (e.g., the nature and function of language), and cultural matters (e.g., assessing historical and cultural conditioning).

High Church: A categorization of churches which are typically characterized by (1) more formal worship patterns and (2) more hierarchy in leadership. Regarding worship patterns, they often use a lectionary and a worship manual, and they are often described as "liturgical." Regarding leadership, they recognize (denominational) authority outside of the local church in the form of bishops (an episcopal form of government). Most common examples: Roman Catholic, Eastern Orthodox, Anglican/Episcopal, and Lutheran. See Low Church.

Holy Love: A description of God's engagement with the world that emphasizes the mysterious reality that the great, holy, and upright God of all the world is also the God who encounters us in the loving mission to reclaim the world.

Homoousion: The term from the Nicene Creed which affirms that Jesus is of the same nature (*homo* + *ousia*) with the Father in distinction to subordinationist positions. See *Ousia*; Subordinationism.

Human Flourishing: A modern expression concerning human well-being in terms of realizing one's holistic potential.

Hyperdeterminism: A view of providence generally understood to move beyond a general determinism (which believes that the course of history is divinely foreordained) to one in which God is the author of evil and human responsibility is nullified.

Hypostasis: A term employed theologically to refer to the threeness of God as distinct persons; there are three *hypostases* in the Godhead who share one *ousia* (nature). The Greek term means crudely "that which underlies something" or "subsistence." See *Ousia*.

Image of God (*Imago Dei*): The concept that humanity is made with a likeness to God as his image. The nature of that likeness is interpreted differently among various traditions. Most Christians believe that the image still persists in humans in some deficient state after sin.

Immanence: The nearness or proximity of someone to something. In the context of creation, it refers to God's sustaining presence in the world. See Transcendence; Pantheism.

Immanent Trinity: The approach or understanding of the Trinity that focuses on the inner relationship of the persons of the triune God as they have existed eternally. The focus is on the Father as unbegotten, the Son as begotten of the Father, and the Spirit as proceeding from the Father. See Economic Trinity.

Incarnation: The teaching that the divine Son took on a human nature for the purpose of reuniting God to humanity.

Inspiration: The process by which the Holy Spirit guides human authors to communicate God's message to others, such that these human words are also called the Word of God.

Intermediate State: The condition persons experience between their death and their judgment before God at the second coming of Christ.

Jansenism: A Roman Catholic perspective which follows the teaching of Cornelius Jansen who promoted Augustine's ideas of irresistible grace and a necessary special grace to enable obedience.

Kingdom of God: A phrase portraying the rule or reign of God. Jesus taught that he inaugurated the rule of God in his acts of power and preaching. The end of time is anticipated as the full arrival, victory, and completion of his kingdom.

Lectionary: A book or listing that contains a collection of Scripture readings appointed for worship on a given day or occasion. Typically, there are four readings for each Sunday: Old Testament, a psalm, New Testament letter, and a gospel. The lectionary readings reflect the church calendar that celebrates different seasons/events in the life of the church (e.g., Lent/Easter; Advent/Christmas; Pentecost; etc.).

Liturgy: This is the order of worship used in an official church service (e.g., Sunday mornings). All church traditions have a liturgy because they all follow some regular form of worship, but "high church" traditions are often described as "liturgical."

Low Church: A categorization of churches which are typically characterized by (1) less formal worship patterns and (2) less hierarchy in leadership. Regarding worship patterns, they do not use a lectionary or a worship manual; rather, the service focuses on singing and preaching. Regarding leadership, they usually do not recognize any (denominational) authority outside of the local church. That is, they follow a "congregational" form of government. Most common examples: Baptists, Bible churches, nondenominational churches, and Pentecostal/charismatic churches like the Church of God in Christ, Assembly of God, and Pentecostal. See High Church.

Manichaeism: A dualistic religious tradition popular in the ancient Mediterranean which asserted that there are two indestructible material principles of good and evil. The term is used loosely at times for any dualism between good and evil. See Gnosticism.

Medieval Era (aka Middle Ages): This time period runs roughly from AD 500 to 1500, and geographically it pertains primarily to western Europe and the Latin-speaking church under the authority of the Pope.

Messiah/Christ: The role of a person who is marked out for special service to God, especially kings but also priests and prophets. The terms *messiah* (Heb) and *christos* (Gk) both mean "anointed one." The title belongs supremely to Jesus and suggests his unique kingly identity.

Metanarrative: A larger story or plot which explains and gives meaning to subplots or smaller stories.

Metaphor: A description and understanding of things by means of comparison with something else. See Analogy.

Middle Ages: See Medieval Era.

Modalism: A Trinitarian heresy rejected by the church, which denies that God eternally exists as three distinct persons. Rather, God is one person and was only acting or revealing himself in the successive modes of Father, Son, and Spirit. The real God remains hidden and only appeared as Father, then as Son, and later as the Spirit.

Modernism/Enlightenment: A philosophical and cultural movement primarily in Europe and North America, dating specifically to AD 1650–1800 though its influence runs strongly until the advent of postmodernism in the mid-1900s. It is characterized by an eminent trust in reason (particularly expressed by the scientific method) and by a distrust of authority, whether political (monarchs) or religious tradition.

Monergism: A view that focuses on divine agency as the sole determinative factor in human salvation. It is derived from two Greek words: *mono* (one) + *ergon* (work). See Synergism.

Monotheism: The belief that there is only one God.

Open Theism: A view that the course of the future and God's interaction with it are not fixed because the future only exists as a possibility and not a settled fact foreknown by God.

Ordinance: A view of the key liturgical practices of baptism and the Lord's Supper, and occasionally foot washing, that focuses on their purpose to help believers remember the grace already achieved by Christ. The name derives from these acts being explicitly ordained by Jesus. This view is an alternative to the sacraments. See Sacrament.

Original Sin: The effects of Adam's sin on the entire human family.

Orthodox vs. orthodox: "Orthodox" with a capital O is shorthand for the Eastern Orthodox church or theology. With a lower-case O, "orthodox" refers to Christian theology that is within the boundary of historical Christian affirmation and belief. Teachings contrary to what is "orthodox" are considered heterodox or heretical.

Ousia: A Greek metaphysical term for nature (or essence, substance). It became the key term to describe the unity or oneness in the Trinity, since the Father, Son, and Spirit have one *ousia* but three persons (*hypostases*). See *Hypostasis*.

Panentheism: A belief system which posits that the divine exists and interpenetrates every part of nature while timelessly extends beyond it. Thus, God and the material universe are interrelated but not identical.

Pantheism: A belief system which views God and the material universe as identical (or synonymous).

Patristic Era: This time period runs roughly from AD 100 to 500. It derives from *pater* (Gk/Lat), meaning father, and it describes the time of the fathers and mothers of the church.

Pelagianism: A view of human agency named after the patristic monk Pelagius which holds that humans can turn to God without the enabling grace of God. It was condemned as heretical because it underestimates the disabling effects of sin upon humans.

Penal Substitution: The atonement model that Christ took the penalty belonging to the sinner upon himself as a substitute. See Atonement.

Pentecostalism: A worldwide movement beginning in the early 1900s that emphasizes the distinct outpouring of the Holy Spirit on believers like that of Pentecost (Acts 2). The term can refer to specifically Pentecostal denominations or to charismatic renewal in general, but what unites these wider movements is the manifestation of miraculous gifts of the Spirit like speaking in tongues, prophecy, and healing.

Pluralism: The environment (or awareness) of multiple contrary and contending religions or worldviews.

Pneumatology: The study of the Holy Spirit, the third person of the Trinity. It is derived from *pneuma* (Gk), meaning Spirit, wind, breath. A related and older term for the Holy Spirit is Holy Ghost.

Polytheism: The belief that there are many gods.

Postmodernism: A philosophical and cultural movement which runs from the early 1900s to present. It is largely a reaction to the optimism of modernity related to scientific or objective efforts to explain reality. Rather than a focus on universal truths, postmodernism values the perspective of individuals and particular communities. See also Pluralism; Relativism.

Premillennialism: The view that the return of Christ will occur before the thousand-year reign (millennium) of Revelation 20:2, in which he will establish an earthly kingdom distinct from the eternal state. Historic premillennialism saw the one thousand years as a transitional period between the end of history and the onset of the eternal state. Dispensational premillennialism emphasizes the millennium as a fulfillment of God's literal promises to Israel, in distinction from the church.

Proclamation: A term used for preaching, a public declaring of the gospel message or an explanation and exhortation concerning a biblical text.

Protology: The study of first things or beginnings and, as pertains to theology, related to creation. It is derived from *protos* (Gk), meaning first.

Reformed vs. reformed: "Reformed" with a capital *R* most often refers to theology following in the Calvinistic (or monergistic) tradition, such as, Presbyterian theology and the Westminster Confession. It is often used in distinction to Arminian traditions. With a lower case *r*, "reformed" is a much broader term referring to all Protestant denominations, that is, those of the Reformation.

Relativism: The perspective that all judgments such as true or false, good and bad are without external standard. Judgments are instead rooted in some individual or social convention.

Resurrection: God's act to raise the dead by giving them immortal, bodily life. Jesus was bodily raised from the dead, and Christians will likewise be raised at Christ's return.

Revelation: God's act of making himself known in the world. See General Revelation; Special Revelation.

Rule of Faith: A short, mostly narrative summary of essential Christian teaching, which is particularly associated with the early church and which forms the basis of the Nicene Creed.

Sacrament: A view of the key liturgical practices that focuses on both the remembrance of the grace achieved by Christ and the communication of that grace to the one who partakes in the practice. These outward signs embody a spiritual grace. This view is held by Roman Catholics, the Eastern Orthodox, and some Protestants. See Ordinance.

Scripture: An inspired and therefore authoritative writing. The term is used interchangeably with the Bible. See Canon; Inspiration.

Secular/Secularism: The idea that faith perspectives are being marginalized from society, either by being removed altogether or by fragmenting the vigor with which faith perspectives are held. This movement has been strongly influenced by rationalism and pluralism. See Pluralism.

Septuagint (LXX): A collection of authoritative Jewish texts in Greek that includes the Greek translation of the *Tanakh* as well as other Jewish writings now known as the Apocrypha. The abbreviation LXX is the Roman numeral for seventy and is based on the tradition that seventy (or seventy-two) Jewish translators translated the Hebrew Pentateuch into Greek. See *Tanakh*.

Soteriology: The study of salvation. It is derived from *soteria* (Gk), meaning salvation.

Sources of Theology: These are what theologians draw upon to know God and therefore develop theology. This primarily includes Scripture, tradition, reason, and experience, which are sometimes called the Wesleyan Quadrilateral.

Special Revelation: What God reveals through his distinctive work in history to restore creation, supremely in his Son become human as well as his communication through prophets and apostles. See General Revelation.

Spiritual Gifts: The enabling to perform a special task or service helpful in the church's ministry and mission. These gifts are appointed and given by the Holy Spirit.

Subordinationism: An approach to the relationship between the Father, Son, and Spirit that distinguishes the Father as a supreme and perfect God from the Son and the Spirit as lesser divine beings. See *Homoousion*.

Synergism: A view that focuses on the cooperation of human and divine agency in human salvation on the basis of the saving work of Jesus. It is derived from the Greek term: *syn* (with/together) + *ergon* (work). Since this view maintains a priority of divine grace as necessary, it should not be confused with Pelagianism. See Monergism; Pelagianism.

Talmud: A collection of foundational texts from Rabbinic Judaism which includes the earlier Mishnah as well as providing additional commentary and interpretation. There are two forms: the Palestinian Talmud is earlier and shorter than the more authoritative Babylonian version.

Tanakh: The name of the Hebrew Bible, which also corresponds to the Christian (Protestant) Old Testament. The term is an abbreviation standing for the first letter of its three parts: the *Torah* (Instruction), *Nevi'im* (Prophets), and *Ketuvim* (Writings).

Theism: The belief in a god. Christian theism holds that God engages the world but is distinct from it. See Pantheism; Panentheism.

Theodicy: In a technical sense, it is the modern effort to argue that the concept of God is justified in the face of evil. Popularly the term can refer to many efforts to understand or cope with evil.

Theologia: Our theologizing and contemplation about God and his work in the world. See *Economia*.

Theological Interpretation of Scripture: An approach to reading Scripture as a theological document from an unapologetic theological point of view. Theological reading need not impose a foreign set of ideas or forbid historical studies. It affirms the Scriptures find their more complete meaning when read as part of the larger theological inquiry (learning about God and his purpose).

Theology: The study of things pertaining to God, but it is usually more broadly applied to the study of Christian teaching or doctrine. Derived from *theos* (Gk), meaning God. "Theology Proper" refers specifically to God the Father in distinction to God the Spirit and God the Son.

Theosis: A model of salvation that emphasizes how believers become like God by sharing in divine attributes like immortality and holiness, while still acknowledging the distinctive nature and identity of God. Theosis (Gk) is equivalent to deification (Lat).

Torah: The Hebrew word meaning "law" or "instruction." It also refers to the first five books of the Bible, known as the Pentateuch.

Total Depravity: The notion that every dimension of the human person and all creation are compromised and injured by the effects of sin.

Transcendence: This term communicates the uniqueness, grandeur, and distinctiveness of God. In the modern era it typically is pictured as God being remote. See Immanence; Deism.

Trinity: The doctrine that one God eternally exists as three persons—Father, Son, and Holy Spirit—and each of the three persons fully and equally share one divine nature. As the primary affirmation of the Nicene Creed, this doctrine is the most fundamental aspect of Christianity, and it serves to distinguish Christianity from all other faiths.

Typology: An interpretative method which discerns a shared pattern, connection, or correspondence (occasionally a contrast) between two stories (regarding persons, events, and institutions). It derives from *typos* (Gk), meaning pattern or archetype. The first story (the type) anticipates a second story (the antitype) which completes the meaning of the first story.

Index